Latin Hitchcock

HOW **ALMODÓVAR, AMENÁBAR, DE LA IGLESIA, DEL TORO** AND **CAMPANELLA** BECAME NOTORIOUS

D1557383

Dona M. Kercher

To Melanie —

One of my fondest & happiest
colleagues & friend

Best wishes —

Dona

April 2015

WALLFLOWER PRESS
LONDON & NEW YORK

A Wallflower Press Book
Published by
Columbia University Press
Publishers Since 1893
New York • Chichester, West Sussex
cup.columbia.edu

Cover image:
On the set of *Broken Embraces* (2009)
photograph by Emililo Pereda © Universal International Pictures / The Kobal Collection

A complete CIP record is available from the Library of Congress

ISBN 978-0-231-17208-0 (cloth : alk. paper)
ISBN 978-0-231-17209-7 (pbk. : alk. paper)
ISBN 978-0-231-85073-5 (e-book)

Columbia University Press books are printed on permanent
and durable acid-free paper.
This book is printed on paper with recycled content.
Printed in the United States of America

c 10 9 8 7 6 5 4 3 2 1
p 10 9 8 7 6 5 4 3 2 1

CONTENTS

ACKNOWLEDGEMENTS

I am drawn to think of the early scene in *Vertigo* when Madeleine goes for a drive with Scottie out to the California coast and visits the redwood forest. She points to the rings in a cross-section of a huge redwood trunk on display and asks if she has lived before, or not. Trying to fix in time all the layers that have made up this book, the product of about two decades, and all the encounters that have marked it, as well as the personal vicissitudes, is as difficult and at times troubling as Madeleine's memory of history implies. It is hard to connect each ring to a specific event or path suggested in the romantic mystery of a book's creation. Any omissions here are entirely due to my own uncertain perceptions, and not to the lack of significance of any contribution.

Without the encouragement of Marvin D'Lugo and Marsha Kinder, whose joint seminar on Spanish Film at Clark University set me on a journey to interpret film as film, I would never have begun to teach or publish on cinema. Marvin has been a steadfast mentor. I remain ever grateful for his counsel and encouragement. At that initial seminar I also met Kathleen Vernon, Susan Martin-Márquez and Nancy Membrez, friends and models in the field of Hispanic cinemas from whom I continue to learn.

My academic life has likewise been immeasurably enriched by exchanges that have occurred during conferences, the multiple cycles of Cine-Lit in Portland, Oregon, the many panels at SCS, then SCMS, as well as LASA, not to mention more recently, Facebook. For their inspiration and support, I want to thank Guy Wood, Jaume Martí-Olivella, Malcolm Compitello, Robert Lang, Catherine Benamou, Tamara Falicov, Jeff Middents, João Vieira, Gilberto Blasini, Yeidy Rivero, Nuría Triana Toribio, Verena Berger, Deborah Shaw and Rielle Navitski.

During regular trips to Madrid, I have felt at home, and well guided, at the Spanish Film Archives. From its generations of dedicated archivists and scholars I would like to thank Dolores Devesa, Alicia Potes, Javier Herrero, Miguel Valle Inclán and Margarita Lobo. To the Ocho y Medio Bookstore, and its owners María Silveyro and the late Jesús Robles, who was already talking of translating this book when it was in its early stages, I owe a great debt for their cinematographic publications and selections, as well as for their advice and unforgettable welcome. In Spain I would also like to thank Manuel Gutiérrez Aragón, with whom interviews became an ongoing conversation, the organisers of the San Sebastián Film Festival for granting me cultural credentials, and my Basque 'family' in Bilbao and Donostia for sharing their lives with me.

In the US I have benefited from the guidance of, and papers provided by, Jenny Romero of the USC Warner Archives, as well as from the assistance from librarians at the Widener Library, and at the University of Massachusetts Amherst. My home institution, Assumption College, has supported me through sabbaticals and Faculty Development grants for research. At Assumption I owe a special debt of gratitude to Tom Begley, who sadly passed away in 2014, for commenting on the early chapters of this book, as well as for sharing his joy in and immense knowledge of Spain and its cultural history with me over the years. For putting his faith in my project and supporting it through major pauses, I must thank Yoram Allon, Commissioning Editor at Wallflower Press.

To Elliot and Alisha, my son and daughter, whose intellects never cease to amaze me, I will always remember and cherish our times on research trips together in Madrid, Sevilla, Buenos Aires, Bogotá and Hitchcock's San Francisco. Finally, to my husband Norman, mi Alma, who – like Hitchcock's Alma – is the unsung but true judge and editor, who has inspired and supported me always, all my love.

Introduction

Alfred Hitchcock is arguably the most influential director of the twentieth century, or of the first century of film history. Significantly, the reach of his work has long been international. As befits a canonical artist, the Hitchcock bibliography, in print and in other media, is prodigious. There are more than a few lifetimes worth of criticism written on his works, certainly enough to give one pause before setting off to write more. The essential, hefty biographical tomes of Donald Spoto, *The Dark Side of Genius: The Life of Alfred Hitchcock* (1999), disavowed by the Hitchcock clan, and Patrick McGilligan, *Alfred Hitchcock: A Life in Darkness and Light* (2003), more favoured by them, are locked in a virtual duel. Two recent bio-pics, focusing on Hitchcock's interactions with women, show not only the enduring fascination for all things Hitchcock but also the staying power of Spoto and McGilligan's diametrically opposed views of him. *The Girl* (2012), a TV film based on Spoto's book, depicts Hitchcock's treatment of Tippi Hedren during the filming of *The Birds* (1963) as abuse, whereas *Hitchcock* (2012), lovingly foregrounds his working relationship with wife Alma Reville during the filming of *Psycho* (1960). Moreover, new critical books in English, such as Jerome Silbergeld's *Hitchcock with a Chinese Face: Cinematic Doubles, Oedipal Triangles, and China's Moral Voice* (2004), *Hitchcock and His Rivals* (2005) and *After Hitchcock: Influence, Imitation, and Intertextuality* (2006) continue to explore his enduring impact on filmmakers. Yet works in English until now regularly exclude filmmakers from Spain or Latin America, with the rare exception of two anthologised essays on individual Almodóvar films by Ernesto Acevedo-Muñoz.[1] Even Spanish-language publications from Spain or Latin America – such as Guillermo del Toro's *Alfred Hitchcock* (1990) or José Luis Castro de Paz's *Alfred Hitchcock* (2000) – notably lack any discussion of the influence of Hitchcock on films in Spanish. My aim in this volume is not to dress Alfred Hitchcock up in a *charro* hat or a *traje de luces*, though Mr. Hitchcock was certainly known to have enjoyed donning costumes and playing pranks, but to acknowledge, query and interpret the reception of Hitchcock in the Spanish-speaking world. To do so is to begin to understand important intersections of global and local cultures, and to trace these in terms of two languages, Spanish and English, which are on the ascendancy worldwide.

In the 1990s young Spanish directors, such as Álex de la Iglesia, Julio Medem and Alejandro Amenábar, began to produce '*cine de terror*', thrillers or suspense films. These films looked new and different and were immensely popular at the box office, a rarity for Spanish films in Spain. As a woman I saw this genre of films more often associated with young adolescent males as an obligation. Anticipating a transmigrated *Scream* (1996) franchise, I was not a happy camper going to see *Día de la bestia* (*Day of the Beast*, 1995) in Madrid the first time. Over the years I had company in my initial lack of enthusiasm. These Spanish thrillers were looked down upon by some filmmakers of the earlier generation. When I interviewed Manuel Gutiérrez Aragón, one of the major filmmakers of the period of the transition to democracy (1975–1982), he spoke of the new '*cine de terror*' as technically brilliant, but devoid of ideas.[2] My own attitude changed when I began first to look carefully at the aesthetics of these films, and second, to think in terms of a more general cultural landscape, about how these films interfaced with local and global referents. These thoughts became persistent as I taught film analysis through Amenábar's popular *Tesis* (*Thesis*, 1996) in my classes, and published on humour and politics in Álex de la Iglesia's *Muertos de risa* (*Dying of Laughter*, 1998). When I chatted on the bus from the Spanish film archives about *Rear Window* (1954) with Spanish film students who had never heard of Laura Mulvey, just how differently Hitchcock has been received in Spanish film criticism became clear. This book traces where my classroom and mass transit experiences, and my subsequent archival research, have taken me.

While I had always thought of and taught the tradition of a particular satirical black humour, common both to Spanish film of the 1950s and to much of Buñuel, the humour, which was so important to the '*cine de terror*' in the 1990s, was often quite different. Moreover, these were not just art house films in Spain. Thinking about the '*cine de terror*', I kept coming back to a Hitchcock paradigm: comic thrillers, immense box office success and international reach. The time period of the '*cine de terror*' also coincided with the Hitchcock centenary in 1999. Spanish film journals, such as *Dirigido*, published major retrospectives. Yet none of these retrospectives dealt in depth with the impact that Hitchcock had, or was having, in film in Spanish. They were aimed at helping a Spanish audience interpret a world in English. As a publishing strategy, the approach was logical as young Spaniards, now Europeans, and Latin Americans too, were looking at a global economy and a media culture dominated by English.

It has often been observed that Hitchcock was not perceived as a great director, as a true artist, until François Truffaut conducted his extensive interviews in the fall of 1962 and proclaimed Hitchcock great. His book, *Alfred Hitchcock: A Definitive Study* (1967), based on these conversations is now a classic. The American filmmaker Peter Bogdanovich, who also interviewed Hitchcock around the same time as Truffaut and who likewise published a book, *The Cinema of Alfred Hitchcock* (1963), lauding his achievements, also played a part in the re-valuation of Hitchcock. It may be slightly simplistic, but not untrue, that before Truffaut and Bogdanovich, Hitchcock's body of work was critically overlooked and considered pure entertainment. What is interesting about the exchanges with Truffaut and other *Cahiers du cinéma* writers is that they were aimed at a transnational audience, published in French and then translated into English. Indeed criticism of Hitchcock's work is multilingual, but English is its *lingua franca*, yet there are significant bibliographical gaps in how much of this material finds its way into English translation.

When I began to look at the interviews with Hitchcock that had been published in English – Truffaut's in translation, of course, but also the collection by Sidney Gottlieb, *Hitchcock on Hitchcock: Selected Writings and Interviews* (1995) – I found translations of interviews from several European languages, but nothing that had originally been in Spanish appeared in these collections. Not that Hitchcock had not been to Spain or Latin America; he had twice won the Silver Shell at the San Sébastián Film Festival, which only began giving international prizes in 1955, for *Vertigo* (1958) and *North by Northwest* (1959). Each time he dutifully attended the festival, met the press and received the award in person. In the broadest terms then, it became clear to me that whereas Spain and Latin America have been marginal to a concept of global film, which Hitchcock epitomised, his work has been crucial to the development of film with global aspirations from those cultures. The purpose of this book, therefore, is to explore this cultural terrain initially suggested by my work with Spanish cinema of the 1990s.

Although Hitchcock made only three, or stretching it five, films with a Spanish or Latin American location, a great majority of his career total of 53 films – not just *Spellbound* (1945) which could immediately be identified as 'Spanish' due to Dalí's dream sequence in it – were shown in Spain and Latin America. Almost always dubbed into Spanish, they became an integral part of Spanish and Latin American culture. In light of the work of Benedict Anderson, especially *Imagined Communities: Reflections on the Origins and Spread of Nationalism* (1983), we can speak of a 'Latin Hitchcock'. By this denomination, I mean to highlight the place of Hitchcock's films and his legendary career in the cultural imaginary of Spain and Latin America. Close analyses of the films will show how five Spanish and Latin American directors borrowed significantly from Hitchcock, to the extent that we can say they largely learned their craft through these borrowings and patterned their careers in the hope of achieving his international success, which they did.

A word needs to be said about the choice of the word 'Latin' in the title to include both Spain and Latin America. Since I deal with filmmakers whose first language is Spanish and who sometimes cross over to make films in English focusing on a common language, 'Hitchcock in Spanish' would not do. Nor would 'Spanish Hitchcock', using the modifier to designate heritage, because it would exclude Latin Americans, whose proud heritage is as often indigenous or *mestizo* as Spanish. On the other hand, Spaniards generally do not call themselves Latin, and certainly not Hispanic either. Not all their languages, notably Basque, have Latin roots; moreover the Roman era was a long time ago.[3] Nowadays it is acceptable, and relatively common, to call them European. Only within the United States is Latin, the English translation of the Spanish 'latino', a category that includes people from Spain and Latin America. It is a term for a cultural rather than racial or ethnic umbrella. This represents the imperfect context and perspective from which I write. In the current charged US political climate that fractures into ideological camps over immigration and demographic shifts, 'Latin Hitchcock' stands as a provocation to recognise a common cultural imaginary not only for Spain and Latin America but for the US as well.

Although I began this project to understand a localised phenomenon in Spain in the 1990s, as I proceeded my interest sharpened to focus on a limited generational cadre of filmmakers in whose work references to Hitchcock repeatedly surfaced. I limited the selection to those who had completed a major body of work and hence established a career profile that I could compare to Hitchcock's trajectory. I closely analysed the films of these directors tracing the presence of Hitchcock's motifs and aesthetics in them, and explored how and when these filmmakers reached for a global market, and/or crossed over to making films in English.

At the same time as I studied the careers of these filmmakers in terms of negotiating their authorship in local and global terms, I also began to think analogously about how Hitchcock was first received in Spain and Latin America to provide a historical framework for the contemporary directors whom I was calling 'Latin Hitchcocks'. I wanted to know when Hitchcock was perceived to have crossed over or become more global, and whether the initial reaction to his films in the Spanish-speaking world was in any way unique. Since existing Hitchcock criticism, or historical studies of Spanish or Latin American cinema in general, did not provide answers to my questions about reception I began to explore the archives, first in Spain and also in the US. Finding premiere dates, an essential precursor to locating and reading newspaper reviews, however, was difficult for Spain, but unbelievably discouraging for Latin America. Many a

librarian and archivist whom I contacted, all of notable good will, were as sty-
mied as I was in this seemingly basic search to establish a timetable of Hitchcock
openings for any major Spanish-speaking city in Latin America. Because I was
developing chapters on contemporary Mexican and Argentinean filmmakers
I looked most intensively for the records for Mexico City and Buenos Aires.
Finally, since I was able to find more complete sources for Mexico City than
for any other capital, I chose it for my case study. The decision to include two
reception chapters and research limitations impacted the eventual structure of
the book, which is divided into two parts corresponding to Spain and Latin
America. Each part opens with a historical overture to a city. For Spain there is
a case study of the initial reception of Hitchcock in primarily Madrid, but also
with references to San Sebastián and Barcelona. This case study also includes a
more general discussion about what a Spanish or Latin American location meant
for Hitchcock. Thematic auteur studies follow on Almodóvar, De la Iglesia and
Amenábar, which are organised chronologically according to when they began
their careers. The second part of the book on Latin America opens with a case
study of Mexico City, followed by studies of Del Toro and Campanella. The
resulting structure is a two-pronged attack – representing archival research and
interpretative analysis – to the topic of Hitchcock in Spain and Latin America.
This framework allows the reader to appreciate historical and aesthetic connections as well as to review Hitchcock's own career in an original context. I have
tried to strike a balance that allows for a depth of critical interpretation in each
chapter.

Although I hope the reader will also take pleasure in making new connections
as a result of this study, some may see gaps between how the chapters fit together
as defects rather than possibilities. For Paolo Antonio Paranaguá, a great critic
of Latin American cinema, nationally identified auteurs are a particular bane of
existence, which he calls 'deslindes' (demarcations) of a problem. In *Tradición
y modernidad en el cine de América Latina* (Tradition and Modernity in Latin
American Cinema) he notes in exasperation: 'Reductionism is only applied to
peripheral or dependent cinemas, which are subordinated or marginalized in
the same dominant historiography: no one would have the gall to reduce French
cinema to Renoir or Godard' (2003: 15).[4] While I by no means see Del Toro and
Campanella as the only possible representatives, respectively, of Mexican or
Argentinean cinema, and certainly not of Latin America as a whole, it is worth
noting, as Paranaguá himself observes shortly after the above comment, that
the debate about depth versus breadth is culturally charged, and generation-
ally inflected: 'While the old encyclopaedic ambition looks for ways to renovate
through the convergence of collective work and the plurality of focuses, popularisation seems to narrow the horizon instead of broadening it' (ibid.). While by

Paranaguá's standards my study may seem reductionist, my approach, however, is informed by and aspires to a US/UK tradition of cinema scholarship that is on the whole more thematic and often auteur driven and which differs starkly from many more encyclopaedic critical works that have come out of Spain.[5]

As my 'Latin Hitchcock' project took shape, I developed three main theses. I offer them now to the reader as a guide to the general outline of my argument:

Thesis One: *The reception of Hitchcock in the Spanish-speaking world has been largely ignored in world film history and criticism.* 'Latin Hitchcock' has certainly been overshadowed by 'French Hitchcock' because of Truffaut, but it has also been ignored in the numerous books on the international reception of Hitchcock.

Thesis Two: *Because he represented a model of a localised director moving successfully onto a broader international stage, Hitchcock was crucial to the individual development of major Latin and Spanish directors.* His influence, which exceeded Buñuel's, is an important factor in the rise of Spanish national cinema from the period of the transition to democracy up to the present day. Increased interest in Hitchcock is, moreover, directly tied to the rise of film studies in Spanish and Mexican universities.

Thesis Three: *The reception of Hitchcock in the Spanish-speaking world has been different.* Not only is his cinematic style repeatedly alluded to in major recent films, in great specificity, but also *his humour is appreciated and plays an important role in Latin suspense films.*

Although I began to think about 'Latin Hitchcock' because of the Spanish 1990s *'cine de terror'*, the more I worked on the project the greater variety I found in the Hitchcockian influence. Whereas Hitchcock is known as 'the master of suspense', anyone who has seriously studied his work knows that this is a promotional tag and that his generic range was in fact huge. As I delved into the work of specific Spanish and Latin American filmmakers, it became clear I was looking at serious students of Hitchcock, or at least, as Almodóvar and De la Iglesia refer to themselves (echoing Picasso's dictum – 'good artists borrow; great artists steal'), talented 'robbers'. Surprisingly, since Almodóvar is not even remotely associated with the *'cine de terror'*, the key to noting this range of allusions is precisely the generically hybrid films of Pedro Almodóvar. Although this study did not begin with Almodóvar, the interpretation of his films and career from the perspective of Hitchcock is in many senses the fulcrum of this book. After an overview, chapter one, entitled 'First Loves, First Cuts: The Initial

Response to Hitchcock's Films in Spain', about the commentary on Hitchcock's films in the decades of their release in Spain, chapter two, 'Pedro Almodóvar's Criminal Side: Plot, Humour and Cinematic Style', will address both the intense referencing of Hitchcock's films in Almodóvar's and the impact of Hitchcock as a global model for Almodóvar's career.

Almodóvar has served as the metaphorical godfather to a number of the other filmmakers discussed here through his production company El Deseo. He gave Álex de la Iglesia his start when El Deseo produced the latter's first film *Acción mutante* (*Mutant Action*, 1993). Likewise, El Deseo stepped in to help redefine and produce Guillermo del Toro's *El espinazo del diablo* (*The Devil's Backbone*, 2001) when that project was floundering in Mexico. It is not too far-fetched to argue that an intellectual, or visceral, kinship based in Hitchcock drew Pedro Almodóvar and his brother Agustín to the work of these other filmmakers. Chapter three, 'Drawing on a Darker Humour, Cultural Icons and Mass Media: Álex de la Iglesia's Journey from Outer Space to the Spanish Academy', and chapter six, 'Guillermo del Toro's Continuing Education: Adapting Hitchcock's Moral and Visual Sensibilities to the World of Horror', explore the work of these two directors in the light of Hitchcock and may lead us to posit a Latin school of Hitchcock. Schooling is the operative term here, for all three directors – Almodóvar, De la Iglesia and Del Toro – learned their craft studying Hitchcock. The Mexican Del Toro went further. He was a film studies professor in Guadalajara and wrote a book on Hitchcock before he made his own feature film debut.

To enrich our reading of Del Toro's undertakings, Chapter Five, 'Latin American Openings: The Reception History for Mexico City', traces an enthusiastic and nationally inflected welcome for those films there. On the one hand, how Hitchcock's movies were marketed to highlight melodrama, rather than crime or mystery, circles back to themes of humour and melodramatic hybridisation, seen earlier in the Almodóvar chapter, but on the other hand, it also locates them within the specific context of the Golden Age of Mexican cinema. Emphasising the impact of a national narrative on film reception this chapter details some surprising revelations regarding how Hitchcock's movies became part of a major historical event, Trotsky's arrival in Mexico City, as well as how they fit into the narrative of the county's economic development and progress, especially through the expansion of movie houses and airline travel.

Like Del Toro in Mexico, Alejandro Amenábar was intimately, and conflictingly, involved with a film school in Spain. He depicted the film school experience in his debut film *Thesis*. Many say he revenged himself on the professor who failed him. Internationally Amenábar's career has evolved as a rival to that of Almodóvar. In 2005 they battled for critical acclaim with *Mala educación* (*Bad*

Education, 2004) opening the Cannes Film Festival and *Mar adentro* (*The Sea Inside*, 2004) winning the Best Foreign Language Film Academy Award. The operative term here is opposition, for early on in his career Amenábar cagily disparaged Hitchcock's exalted place in cinema history. Yet chapter four, 'Against Hitchcock: Alejandro Amenábar's Meteoric Career', will show how Amenábar, too, has drawn on Hitchcock's work for inspiration.

The book's seventh and final chapter, 'Understanding Osmosis: Hitchcock in Argentina Through the Eyes of Juan José Campanella', returns to an exploration of the role of suspense and the thriller genre in Latin American cinema. Seeing Campanella's Academy Award-winning film *El secreto de sus ojos* (*The Secret in Their Eyes*, 2009) as I did at the 2009 San Sebastián Film Festival was a revelation for many, myself included, who had dismissed his films, to put it unkindly, as melodramatic pap. Yet seeing that film and intervening at the press conference – the title of the chapter refers to Campanella's response to one of my questions, that Hitchcock influenced him 'by osmosis' – sent me to research his career trajectory and to study the considerable impact of Hitchcock on his films. Campanella left Argentina to attend film school in the US at New York University and subsequently to direct for TV. His US training complicated the critical reception in Argentina when he returned to filmmaking there. How Campanella melded film cultures and genres, especially with an appreciation of humour, will be the focus of this final auteur study.

***

In *Diferentes, desiguales y desconectados: mapas de la interculturidad* (Different, Unequal and Disconnected: Maps of Interculturality, 2004) Nestor García Canclini called for a re-examination of intercultural communication. He differed from anthropologists who attempt to assume completely the internal point of view of the elected culture because he argued instead for studying the interactions between cultures. Further, he defines the cultural not as the collection of characteristics that differentiate one society from another, but as, quoting in part Arjun Appadurai, a 'system of relationships that identifies "differences, contrasts and comparisons"' (2004: 21). García Canclini argues that to rethink what culture is also necessitates a new method of study:

> Instead of comparing cultures that would operate like pre-existing and compact systems, with the inertias that populism celebrates and ethnographic good will admires for their resistance, one tries to pay attention to the mixes and misunderstandings that link the groups. In order to understand each group one has to describe how it appropriates and reinterprets other peoples' material and symbolic products: the musical and soccer related fu-

sions, the television programmes that circulate according to heterogeneous cultural styles, the Christmas decorations and the Early American furniture made in the Asiatic Southeast (2004: 21).

García Canclini calls for a shift in emphasis that 'leads to conceiving the politics of difference as something more than the need to resist' (ibid.) and moves beyond 'the indiscriminate exultation of fragmentation and nomadism' (2004: 22) which has characterised postmodern theory. In the penultimate chapter of his book, Latin American cinema serves as a model for his theory of intercultural communication, for it is the ideal terrain on which to critique the aesthetic and economic effects of deregulation and the opening of borders.

García Canclini cites studies from various Latin American countries that show 'the convergence of the tastes of audiences and the styles of US cinema' (2004: 200), namely a preference for action genres (thriller, adventure and spy films). He concludes: 'In sum, US cinema succeeds in imposing its global hegemony by combining the politics of aesthetic and cultural development, which thereby take advantage in a more clever way than those of other producers of the trends in media consumption through policies of authoritarian control of the markets that are destined to convert demographic majorities into cultural minorities' (ibid.). García Canclini finds in the movies 'divergence in the ways of conceiving *social multiculturality* within the US and, on the other hand, politics of *rejection of diversity in cultural industries*, as much within the nation as in its control of international markets' (2004: 201; emphasis in original). Overall he laments that the speed of change in the culture industry 'reduces the variety of information and the historic density of cultures with respect to matters of public interest' (ibid.). Moreover he cautions that 'it is also disturbing that it is in the more diffuse zones of cultural and political formation, such as the movies, music and television, the promises of global interconnection, once and for all, are diluted into monolinguism or the dissemination of isolated pieces of a few cultures' (ibid.).

At various junctures, the career trajectories of the five major Spanish and Latin American directors studied in this book illustrate the contraction of diversity under the aggressive policies of free market globalisation. Del Toro's long and ultimately unsuccessful search to find Mexican funding to make *The Devil's Backbone*, a film set during the Mexican Revolution, is a prime example. We will note many others in this book. Yet at the same time the work of these Hispanic filmmakers, from cultures of majorities but operating globally as minorities, as termed by García Canclini, is a very rich terrain of contemporary intercultural communication which begs to be explored in order to understand both the evolution of global culture and its current state today. It is time that their work be evaluated not just in light of national film histories, as resisting hegemonic Hollywood, but also in the context of the global standards to which they aspire. These filmmakers adapted the work of Hitchcock to be recognised, to become auteurs themselves, and thereby to survive economically from their positions of inequality in the global market. Yet, most especially, they looked to Hitchcock to speak in the emerging fusion language of their own Latin cultures.

At the end of *Diferentes, desiguales y desconectados*, García Canclini himself returns to Hitchcock. He confesses in a personal and generational remark that because of Marxist prejudices against the commercial he never paid any attention to Hitchcock, until he was 'discovered' by Truffaut. Through Truffaut on Hitchcock, however, he found that the relationships between commercial cinema and auteurship were more complex than had been proclaimed in Marxist criticism. He uses this confession to argue that 'the world would be much more comprehensible, habitable and even enjoyable, if the arts and ideas that transnational companies broadcast, even within the US, were to take into account what isn't written in English and is filmed far from Hollywood' (2004: 205). I hope by quoting from film criticism in Spanish in this book, and by interpreting lesser known as well as the well distributed foreign standards of major Latin filmmakers, to contribute to expand the horizons, and maybe the enjoyment, of an English-speaking audience.

NOTES

1   'Melo-Thriller: Hitchcock, Genre and Nationalism in Pedro Almodóvar's *Women on the Verge of a Nervous Breakdown*,' in David Boyd and R. Barton Palmer (eds) (2006) *After Hitchcock: Influence, Imitation, and Intertextuality*. Austin: University of Texas Press, 173–94, and 'The Body and Spain: Pedro Almodóvar's *All About My Mother*,' in Julie F. Codell (ed.) (2006) *Genre, Gender, Race and World Cinema*. Malden, MA: Wiley-Blackwell, 38–55.

2   'Looking for Don Quijote's Own Shadow: An Interview with Manuel Gutiérrez Aragón about His Film *El caballero Don Quijote* (2002),' *Arizona Journal of Hispanic Cultural Studies*, 6 (2002), 138–9.

3   The invention of a 'Latin race' can be traced back to mid-nineteenth-century France when intellectuals and political leaders promulgated the idea that part of the Americas had a linguistic affinity with the Romance cultures.

4   Unless otherwise noted all translations are mine.

5   In Spain serious, highly influential film critics have published comprehensive histories of Spanish cinema, including: Román Gubern (1995, 2005 fifth edition) *Historia del cine español*; J. M. Caparrós Lera (1999) *Historia crítica del cine español*; Carlos H. Heredero (1999) *20 nuevos directores del cine español*; and Miguel Angel Barroso and Fernando Gil-Delgado (2002) *Cine español en Cien películas*. Also *Diccionario del cine español* (1998), published under the direction of José Luis Borau, fits into this category of comprehensive research coming out of Spain. Most resemble telephone books, to evoke a metaphor for those of us who remember that soon passé and ubiquitous guide. On the other hand, in

the US serious film critics have published more thematically organised books, such as Marsha Kinder's *Blood Cinema* (1993) and *Refiguring Spain* (2002) or Kathleen Vernon and Barbara Morris (eds) (1995) *Post-Franco, Postmodern*. In the UK, John Hopewell's *Out of the Past* (1989, revised), although reasonably comprehensive in its listings, also organises material thematically, as did Barry Jordan and Rikki Morgan-Tamousunas volume, *Contemporary Spanish Cinema* (1998). Peter William Evans' anthology *Spanish Cinema: The Auteurist Tradition* (1999) is a prime example of limited extensive studies. To use one example from Latin America, the critical approaches to Mexican cinema are more mixed: two standard works are comprehensive – Emilio García Riera (1998) *Breve historia del cine mexicano, Primer Siglo (1897–1997)* and Rafael Aviña (2004) *Una mirada insólita: Temas y géneros del cine mexicano*. The latter is also thematic since it deals with individual film genres. *Mexican Cinema* (1995), the important anthology originally written in French and edited by Paulo Antonio Paranguá, is also a hybrid, as is John King (1990) *Magical Reels: A History of Cinema in Latin America*.

PART I
SPAIN

First Loves, First Cuts:
The Initial Response to Hitchcock's Films in Spain

I. INTRODUCTION

Were Hitchcock's films greeted with enthusiasm when they were first seen in Spain and Latin America? Was he an instant sensation? Well, no. Hitchcock's relationship to the Spanish-speaking world evolved over the course of the six decades of his long career; his visits to Spain bracketed two important stages of that career. In the early 1920s when he was first setting out he scouted Spanish locations for the silent film *The Spanish Jade* for Famous Players-Lasky. Later in the 1950s at the height of his creative output he launched *Vertigo* and *North by Northwest* in San Sebastián, site of the premier film festival of the Spanish-speaking world.[1] There in August 1958 the press compared Hitchcock to Santa Claus. Despite his almost universal name recognition, the reception history of Hitchcock's films is neither well studied nor uniform worldwide. The sequence and circumstances under which his films opened in Spain reveal significant differences from the conditions of their releases elsewhere in the world. For instance, certain films – *Lifeboat* (1944) and *Psycho* (1960) – were substantially cut in Spain. Others – *Rebecca* (1940) and *Spellbound* (1945) – immediately impacted on cultural politics and served as rallying cries for a new type of cinematic aesthetics. The 'Latin Hitchcocks' of the 1980s and 1990s, who are the subject of subsequent chapters, arose from this specific historical and cultural terrain. We will explore whether, and if so how, humour, aesthetic innovation and a moral tone reflective of Hitchcock's Catholic background – elements that became fundamental to these post-Franco directors – factored into the initial public response in Spain.

To survey the reception of all of Hitchcock's 53 films and TV programmes in Spain and Latin America is a topic worthy of one or more doctoral dissertations, or at least a book-length guide similar to Jane E. Sloan's *Alfred Hitchcock: The Definitive Filmography* (1993). A comprehensive answer lies beyond the scope of this chapter. Hence, as a first step to narrowing our focus, we will examine the range of Spanish or Latin American locations or motifs in his films. Whenever Hitchcock represented the Latin world throughout his career he laid the foundation for a unique dialogue with the viewing public. In effect the selection of a Latin location privileged the film's reception history for that area. As a second step, in order to highlight and analyse the impressions Hitchcock's films first created, we will turn to Spain as a case study, since all the directors subsequently studied in this book have at very least intervened in the Spanish market at one time, if not worked out of that country as their primary base of operations. This approach, moreover, will allow for an overview of important sources for reception studies in Spain for the period of Hitchcock's active career.

II. LATIN LOCATION, LOCATION[2]

Alfred Hitchcock did work in Spain in his early years when he was getting into the film business and climbing the ladder at the British Famous Players-Lasky studio from errand boy, then significantly to art director, then director. As Patrick McGilligan notes in his biography *Alfred Hitchcock: A Life in Darkness and Light*, Hitchcock's third project as an art director was the silent film *The Spanish Jade* (directed by John S. Robertson) in 1921 – Hitch was then 22 – for which 'cast and crew traveled to Spain'. McGilligan comments that 'overseas travel became routine in the Islington years' (2003: 51). More important than the location, however, is Hitchcock's career path, as McGilligan argues: 'In all of film history only a small percentage of directors have come from the ranks of production design. This foothold gave Hitchcock a distinct advantage when thinking in pictures. From the start, the "right look" – for people and places – was integral to his vision' (ibid.).

He knew, for example, when in 1956 he took on the project to adapt and modernise the French novel *D'entre les morts* for *Vertigo*, that San Francisco was the perfect location. He thought the city, which he had loved since he first came to California, sufficiently European in character. Part of this European background was its Spanish heritage. The picturesque Mission Dolores was chosen as a location from the earliest stages of the project. The climatic scenes of the film would take place in the most Spanish of sites, Mission San Juan Bautista, south of San Francisco. McGilligan, incidentally, confuses the two Spanish missions in his biography of Hitchcock, saying 'Hitchcock had picked the Mission Dolores for its picturesque quality, even though the church didn't have a bell tower' (2003: 541). Dolores includes a more baroque church that indeed has a bell tower.[3] According to Dan Aulier in *Vertigo: The Making of a Hitchcock Classic* (1998), Hitchcock's longtime Director of Photography Robert Burks did not want a site that was 'too obviously pretty' and Hitchcock himself 'wanted a location that looked abandoned' (1998: 64). Since this mission's church no longer had a bell tower when it was chosen, an enormous set, the largest single expense in the film's budget, was created at the studio. Hence, for *Vertigo* 'Spanish' meant an austere site of history, religion and judgement. In an interview in July 1958, published in Spanish translation in *El cine británico de Alfred Hitchcock* (The British Films of Alfred Hitchcock, 1974), Carlos Fernández Cuenca, the Director of that year's San Sebastián Film Festival in which *Vertigo* was entered, asked Hitchcock whether he had been concerned with religious problems or themes in any films other than *I Confess* (1951) and *The Wrong Man* (1957). Hitchcock immediately recalled that he and Burks in fact had counted Catholic churches in fifteen of his films. Hitchcock called their presence, including that in *Vertigo*, 'un fruto claro del subconsciente, un deseo de amparar los conflictos humanos bajo la sombra de los símbolos de la religión' ('an obvious product of the subconscious, a desire to shelter human conflicts under the shadow of symbols of religion') (1974: 36). Furthermore Hitchcock added: 'No hago cine concreta y deliberadamente católico, pero me parece que nadie dudará de que mis películas están hechas por un católico' ('I don't make Catholic cinema concretely and deliberately, but it seems to me that no one will doubt that my movies are made by a Catholic') (ibid.).

Hitchcock was almost forced to address the Spanish Civil War when he was making *Foreign Correspondent* (1940), but he never quite had to. In the film a green American press correspondent is sent to Europe to cover the war in August 1939. The producer Walter Wanger believed film could 'change the course of human events' (Spoto 1999: 222), calling motion pictures, in his own words, 'almost as important as the State Department' (ibid.). Hence, Wanger's vision for *Foreign Correspondent* was both idealistic and highly topical. He insisted on rewrites to incorporate the most up-to-date information on the war, including at one stage references to the Spanish Civil War, but events followed in fast succession so that the specific war references with which the film ends are to the bombing of London, not Guernica. Overall Hitchcock tried to avoid politics in his films, officially at least because it was bad box office. In the case of *Foreign Correspondent* he merely humoured his producer, did not do the suggested retakes and kept the film as general as he could. As *Foreign Correspondent* turned out to be 'not a piece of anti-Nazi, anti-war propaganda', as Wanger had hoped, but 'a picaresque story, a romantic melodrama with considerable comic tone' (Spoto 1999: 227), it has stood the test of time better for it. The Spanish may have prevailed in this gesture to the origins of the picaresque. Donald Spoto describes the shift to the generic well: 'The finished film (except for the last minute) has about as much to do with the politics of the war as Tosca has to do with Napoleon's campaign in Italy: the historical setting provides a distant background for a personal story of adventure, love and betrayal' (1999: 230).

Although *Notorious* (1946) was filmed almost entirely on studio sets in Los Angeles, with the notable exception of the projection shots of Rio de Janeiro taken from an aeroplane, it spans the Americas in its Latin locations. This sweep to crisscross the globe was integral to Hitchcock's new business plan. Hitchcock conceived the film as the first project of his dream company 'Transatlantic Pictures', named to suggest the collaboration between Europe and America. According to McGilligan, the story of Transatlantic Pictures is 'a chapter in Hitchcock's life [that] has been inadequately reported, and misunderstood' (2003: 365). He emphasises that the 'prescient' choice of locales – Miami and South America – for *Notorious* was entirely Hitchcock's decision, one that aimed to attract a global audience with important world issues. Hitch at that time, moreover, was genuinely concerned about world security, including the future of Nazis and Nazi sympathisers. At the end of 1944 he had pitched a short film called *Watchtower over Tomorrow* about threats to peace to the State Department. Its imaginative scenario 'alarmed US officials'.[4] Some precedent already existed for Hitchcock thinking Latin when it came to complex war scenarios. His first Latin character had been 'the Mexican', an Armenian professional assassin who tries to pass as a Mexican general, in *Secret Agent* (1936), a World War I spy film.[5]

This political and economic back story shows how far *Notorious* moved away from the original New York City locale of the serial called 'The Song of the Dragon' upon which the film was based. Nonetheless although the new Latin locations implied a link to real international intrigue and current events, if not futuristic predictions, the drama that unfolded in Hitchcock's film, in Miami and Rio, recalled time-worn Latin stereotypes of wild parties and ill-gotten wealth.

Notorious opens at a courtroom in Miami. A distraught Alicia Huberman (Ingrid Bergman) witnesses the reading of the final guilty verdict at her father's trial, then rushes out. Later at a party in her apartment she drowns her sorrows in booze and establishes her image as a Miami party girl. Her sparkly beach stripe shirt and bare midriff, which Devlin (Cary Grant) later humorously covers with a scarf when they leave for a drive, enhance the look. The Latin theme of the party is further underscored when a footloose yachtsman, played by the real life intelligence agent Charles Mendl, tries to get her to sail with him to Cuba. Shortly after the farewell party she leaves town to fly down to Rio as an undercover spy

A humorous rebuke to her Miami party girl image: Devlin minimally covers Alicia's bare midriff with a scarf before they go out for a drive in *Notorious*.

on the trail of the film's MacGuffin, uranium stored in a wine bottle, owned by the fascist-in-exile, Alexander Sebastian (Claude Rains), she is sent to seduce. The party scene at Sebastian's mansion in Rio today ranks as one of Hitchcock's most famous sequences for his invention of a massive crane shot that sweeps down to show Alicia's hand holding a key. In subsequent chapters on their careers we will explore the effect these Latin party scenes in *Notorious* had on Guillermo del Toro's *Cronos* (1993) and on Juan José Campanella's *Love Walked In* (1997).

Nonetheless, the reception of *Notorious* has more often foregrounded *mise-en-scène* in all its aspects – set and wardrobe especially – than cinematographic innovation, or even narrative. At the opening of *Encadenados* (*Notorious*) in Madrid in 1948, for example, Donald, the reviewer for the newspaper *ABC*, did not think much of the film's emotional impact, writing 'that plot is poorly realised in the sets and situations that they provoke. Despite the intensity that they want to convey, they don't manage to excite' (1 October 1948: 15). Indeed he found the effect of the dialogue rather comic – 'what the characters say causes unexpected effects that become comical' (1948: 16). However, the film's glamour, the essence of the party scene, did impress him: 'On the other hand one could say that Hitchcock has limited himself this time to achieving a vivid series of fashion plates, for the most part worthy of appearing in a luxurious high-end magazine whose pages show exquisite feminine clothes for every hour of the day and homes and mansions of the rich' (ibid.). To convey the essence of Ingrid Bergman's image, the illustrator even included her her suit and fedora hat in the caricature that accompanied Donald's review. That image contrasted vividly with the Bergman caricature the same artist did for *Spellbound* the previous year that shows her ample wavy hair and come-hither expression.

Precisely because they represented fashion plates, the iconic images of their times, as Donald noted, Hitchcock's films enjoy a prominent place today in Madrid's new Museo del Traje (Costume Museum), which opened in 2004. In the galleries, which are organised by decades, large video screens play film clips of several Hitchcock films, which include one featuring Bergman in *Notorious*. Another film of love and betrayal like *Notorious*, *Topaz* (1969), based on Leon Uris's novel of the same title, is the only other Hitchcock film with a Latin American location. Focused on espionage during the Cuban missile crisis, *Topaz* shares a distinctly political scenario with some of his other films, such as *Notorious* and *Torn Curtain* (1961). The Cuban scenes, which McGilligan considers 'among the best in the film' (2003: 689), are both the most tragic and the most visually inspiring. I will discuss the impact *Topaz* had on Almodóvar's *Flor de mi secreto* (*Flower of My Secret*, 1995) in the chapter 'Pedro Almodóvar's Criminal Side'.

Conceivably Hitchcock's most direct contact with a Spanish location was his difficult, and ultimately unhappy, collaboration with Salvador Dalí's imagination for the dream sequence of *Spellbound*. In fact the Spanish government officially recognised the Spanish connection to this film when King Juan Carlos and Queen Sofía opened the exhibition of the original backdrop paintings Dalí made for the sequence in the Dalí Theater-Museum in Figueres, Spain. In 2004, in anticipation of the 2005 Dalí centenary, the main image of the San Sebastián Film Festival, was a backdrop of huge eyes reminiscent of Dalí's *Spellbound* sequence. Significantly, on its main poster San Sebastián chose to feature a photo of Hitchcock touting his career total of 53 films to mark its own 53rd edition in 2005.

Although Hitchcock made only three films (*Notorious*, *Vertigo*, *Topaz*), or stretching it five (with *Foreign Correspondent* and *Spellbound*), with a Spanish or Latin American location, a great majority of his career total of 53 films were shown in Spain and Latin America. In Spain they were almost always dubbed into Spanish. On the other hand, in Latin America they were more frequently shown with Spanish subtitles in their initial release. Chapter five, 'Latin American Openings: The Reception History of Hitchcock's Films for Mexico City', will address the transition from subtitling to dubbing as we explore in detail how Hitchcock's films were first received in Mexico. Either way, dubbed or subtitled, Hitchcock's films became an integral part of the Spanish and Latin American culture and what we have termed in light of the cultural imaginary of the region, Latin Hitchcock.

III. HITCHCOCK IN SPANISH ONLY: A VIEW FROM THE ARCHIVES OF RELEASE DATES AND DUBBING

In order to construct a history of the reception of Hitchcock's films in Spain it is necessary to know if and when each of his films debuted there. This information is not easily found. The traces of Hitchcock's silent period, or even of his early British sound films in contemporaneous Spanish newspapers, for example, are faint and infrequent. One important source from that period for some of this information, especially from the 1930s onwards, is Carlos Fernández Cuenca's card catalogue of individual films that had Madrid openings. As Head of the National Department of Cinematography, Fernández Cuenca (1904–1977) founded the Spanish National Film Archives, where this catalogue is stored, and served as the Archives' first Director from 1953 to 1970. Fernández Cuenca was a key cultural authority, even a political kingpin, for his times. He was a member of Movimiento and SEU, as well as head of the Sindicato Nacional del Espectáculo (National Entertainment Union). He was Director of the Escuela Oficial de Cine (Official Cinema School) and of the San Sebastián Film Festival. He served on the juries of the Venice Film Festival in 1954 and 1958. Besides six film books, stories and screenplays, he regularly wrote for the magazines *La Época*, *La Voz*, *El Nacional* and *Marca*. He was film critic for the newspaper *Ya* and editor of the journal *Primer Plano*.

The last book Fernández Cuenca wrote was a small tome, *El cine británico de Alfred Hitchcock* which culminated a career of watching Hitchcock in Spain. He even appended a previously unpublished personal interview he had with Hitchcock in San Sebastián in 1958. For him Spanish critics lagged behind their American and French counterparts in Hitchcock criticism. Coming from the pen of someone who always meticulously noted where and when a film debuted – finally, he was a librarian – the details of reception history frame Fernández Cuenca's text. They were integral to his very being as a critic. For instance, he explains that a retrospective of American films at the French Cinémathèque in 1956 inspired the French reassessment of Hitchcock's place in world cinema. With customary detail Fernández Cuenca even tells the reader the times of the multiple daily sessions of the extended series that left French spectators 'day after day sacrificing their dinner hour' (1974: 13). He concludes the introduction to *El cine británico...* again referring to Hitchcock's reception history:

> He who has written it knows almost all the films in question: at their precise hour he saw the ones which were shown in our country and he wrote about the majority of them in various Madrid newspapers; he has been able to screen others in London and in Paris, thanks to the generosity of the British Film Institute and the French Cinémathèque, taking pertinent notes during those screenings which I am now revising. It has seemed useful to me to point out in each case the criticism that the movies merited from contemporaneous critics, from those afterwards, and from Alfred Hitchcock himself. (1974: 14)

Fernández Cuenca writes about himself in the third person with Biblical certainty. Given his pledge to tell the whole Truth, the gaps in his appended Hitchcock filmography about screenings in Spain for certain early Hitchcock films leave in doubt whether all these films were even shown there. Unlike other Spanish authors of books on Hitchcock, who aimed at a global audience, and a universal interpretation of Hitchcock's films such as Diego Montes in *La huella de Vértigo* (The Trace of Vertigo, 2004), an analysis that references art history, Fernández Cuenca had a keen sense of interpreting essentially for a national audience and acknowledging the particular Spanish reception of Hitchcock.

Most distinctively Fernández Cuenca explains, after quoting Truffaut on the subject, what the English word 'suspense' means in Spanish. As befits some-one educated in philology, who would expect the same background from his audience, he first evokes classical rhetorical analysis:

> The good technique of 'suspense', the way that Hitchcock uses it, consists in that that feeling is conveyed from the characters who feel it to the spectators. In classical treatises of eloquence one speaks of 'attentional suspension' as a device that by drawing out paragraphs and even elongating the syllables of each word creates anticipation in the audience given the absolute certainty that they must wait. In rhetoric there is a figure called 'suspension' that consists in postponing, in order to heighten the interest of the listener or the reader, the statement of the concept that a sentence is heading towards or which will wrap it up when it is said or written. 'Suspense' in Spanish has the meanings of 'surprised' or 'perplexed'; this last one can fittingly describe the effect that certain Hitchcock scenes have on our mind. But any Anglo-Saxon dictionary will tell us that the most exact equivalents of the word 'suspense' are 'uncertainty' and 'anxiety'. (1974: 11–12)

Fernández Cuenca explains for his Spanish audience that the word 'suspense', used to refer to the 'master of suspense', really doesn't have an exact translation in Spanish. Ads and reviews of Hitchcock repeatedly used the English, most often in quotes.

The following chart is based on Fernández Cuenca's data, a composite of his catalogue notes and the filmography in *El cine británico de Alfred Hitchcock*. It compares the opening date of Hitchcock's films in Madrid, and the running time of the Spanish dubbed copy, to the information about the original release of each film as noted in Sloan's *Alfred Hitchcock: The Definitive Filmography*.

Hitchcock's films were presented in Spanish. The intertitles of his silent films were translated. As Spanish law mandated from the 1930s onwards, all of Hitchcock's sound films – that is, beginning with *La muchacha de Londres*

Spanish Title	English Title	Madrid 'Estreno' (Opening)	Original Release Date	Spanish Running Time	Original Running Time
De mujer a mujer	Woman to Woman	18 Nov. 1927	1923	2,274 metres	
Champagne	Champagne	22 April 1929	August 1928	2,434 metres	104 min.
El enemigo de las rubias	The Lodger	1 March 1930	Sept. 1926	2,336 metres	100 min.
El Ring	The Ring	21 July 1930	Oct. 1927	2,553 metres	110 min.
La muchacha de Londres	Blackmail	5 March 1931	June 1929	85 min.	80 min.
Valses de Viena	Waltzes from Vienna	15 July 1935	1933	80 min.	80 min.
El hombre que sabía demasiado	The Man Who Knew Too Much	18 Nov. 1935	Dec. 1934	84 min.	85 min.
Treinta y nueve escalones	The Thirty-Nine Steps	6 Jan. 1936	Sept. 1935	81 min.	81 min.
Agente secreto	Secret Agent	27 Nov. 1939	Jan. 1936	83 min.	83 min.
Posada Jamaica	Jamaica Inn	24 Feb. 1941	May 1939	99 min.	100 min.
Alarma en el expreso	The Lady Vanishes	9 March 1942	Oct. 1938	97 min.	97 min.
Rebeca	Rebecca	10 Dec. 1942	March 1940	130 min.	130 min.
Matrimonio original	Mr. and Mrs. Smith	17 Sept. 1943	Jan. 1941	95 min.	95 min.
Sospecha	Suspicion	10 Dec. 1943	Sept. 1941	99 min.	100 min.
Inocencia y juventud	Young and Innocent	10 July 1944	Nov. 1937	80 min.	80 min.
Sombra de una duda	Shadow of a Doubt	29 Jan. 1945	Jan. 1943	108 min.	108 min.
Sabotaje	Saboteur	27 Dec. 1945	April 1942	108 min.	109 min.
Recuerda	Spellbound	30 Sept. 1946	Oct. 1945	111 min.	110 min.
Naúfragos	Lifeboat	1 July 1947	Jan. 1944	76 min.	96 min.
Ventana indiscreta	Rear Window	3 Oct. 1955	July 1954	112 min.	112 min.
De entre los muertos	Vertigo	29 June 1959	May 1958		
Psicosis	Psycho	2 April 1961	June 1960	103 min.	110 min.

(*Blackmail*, 1931), were dubbed into Spanish for their initial exhibition. 'Versión doblada' is almost always noted on Fernández Cuenca's index cards although he does not make these notations in his book. The dubbing process alone explains the delay of approximately a year from the film's initial release to its opening in Madrid. By the 1960s the gap was down to about six months. Though the table based on Fernández Cuenca's data only represents 22 of Hitchcock's 53 films, it does show that his films were shown with great regularity in Spain. All of the above films opened at major movie theatres in Madrid, most often at the Palacio de la Música, but also at the Avenida, Roxy B, Gran Vía, Lope de Vega, Carlos III and Callao. The British films opened most often at the Avenida and later at the Palacio de la Música, but also at the Princesa, Ideal, Palacio de la Prensa, Figaro and Cinema Palace. Comparing the original running times in the chart based on Cuenca's catalog shows that *Lifeboat* and *Psycho* were cut or censored substantially for their Spanish showings.

As Virginia Higginbotham notes in *Spanish Film Under Franco*, American movies flooded Spanish screens even before the Spanish Civil War, and 'the Hollywood star system literally outshone the home product, so that Spaniards deserted their national cinema in droves' (1998: 4). According to Higginbotham, American incursion into Spanish cinema 'reached alarming proportions in the 1950s' (ibid.). In 1941 a law was passed, reaffirming the policy already in effect since the early 1930s, that made it illegal to show foreign films unless they were dubbed into Spanish. Foreign films, including Hitchcock's, entered into the ideological equation of supporting the dictatorship in a particularly pernicious fashion. Spanish producers were granted import and dubbing licenses for the more lucrative foreign films, depending on how well the native films they produced passed the Spanish censors. Higginbotham notes that an undercover trade of import licenses was rampant in the 1950s. Part of the attraction of Hollywood films for Spanish audiences was that even though they went through the dubbing process, which significantly delayed their release, foreign films were censored less than the native product. Even when the absolute requirement to dub foreign films was lifted on 31 December 1947, the practice continued because, as Higgenbotham observes, 'dubbing, now a small industry within Spanish cinema, had become expected by the Spanish public' (1998: 9). In an extensive interview in the film magazine *Fotogramas* in 1946, the Spanish director Florián Rey came out vigorously against dubbing. He insisted that it gave American films, like Hitchcock's, an unfair commercial advantage that they would not have had if Spanish moviegoers had to read subtitles. Responding to the interviewer's query 'And does dubbing damage our production so much?', Rey states:

> Naturally; we contribute the only value, our language, so that they compete with us, who are and will be technically inferior. Without dubbing, the public would be wanting to hear Spanish. And as long as foreign films speak in Spanish, our cinema will be stunted. (15 December 1946: n.p.)

The film journal *Triunfo* questioned the practice of dubbing more from aesthetic rather than commercial grounds. In 1961 *Triunfo* prominently featured letters from readers who wrote in favor of V.O. or 'versión original'. E.R.T. from Madrid asserted that its absence was a sign of Spain's provinciality when compared to other European countries: 'I can't understand why Madrid, having the importance that it has as a great city, doesn't have any movie theatre dedicated to the exhibition of movies in their original version' (5 January 1961: 1) Another reader, J. M. Hernández Lucas, rails against the absence even of original titles: 'Could it be possible for the foreign films that are screened to show the original title next to the Spanish title? A lot of confusion will be avoided this way for those of us that see foreign films and also some "impostors" operating a bait and switch (offering movies that "seem" important and really are unbearable "rip-offs")' (4 May 1961: 1). The advent of V.O. theatres in Spain, which arose as art-house phenomena, and hence not the logical exhibition space for a Hitchcock film, comes after the release of Hitchcock's last film in 1976. With the important exception of the San Sebastián Film Festival, Hitchcock's films debuted in Spain dubbed into Spanish. Most received wide commercial distribution.

IV. HITCHCOCK FOR THE TRADE: ASSESSING VIABILITY AND RATINGS BEGINNING IN THE 1950S

Another principal source that documents the reception in Spain of Hitchcock's films post-1950 – that is, at the height of his commercial success – is *Cine asesor*, or 'Movie Assessor', a trade journal for movie theatres. By monitoring the reception of each film at its Madrid opening, the journal projected the box office potential of the film. It also suggested promotional blurbs for press ads and for theatre marquees as the film opened in the rest of the country. Each entry in *Cine asesor* includes the Madrid opening date, the theatre's name, the running time of the Spanish print of the film and the approved rating code. Entries also give brief quotes from five or six Madrid newspapers, a paragraph synopsis of each film, and most interestingly a paragraph assessment of the film's quality and earning potential. Most, but not all, of Hitchcock's films after 1954 were reviewed in *Cine asesor*. Through *Cine asesor* we know for example that for *Psicosis (Psycho)* theatre owners were encouraged to imitate Hitchcock's innovative marketing campaign, used in the US: 'The "extra" publicity, which ought to be done, will include as an advertising slogan the prohibition against entering the movie theatre once the movie has begun, in addition to Hitchcock's request that no one reveal the ending' (1961: 2432). *Psycho* more than any other Hitchcock film consolidated his reputation as the master of suspense in Spain.

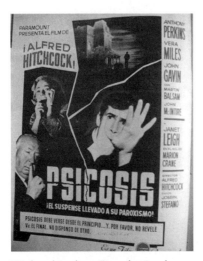

Hitchcock's admonitions for *Psycho* were prominent in Spanish ads.

Cine asesor only obliquely acknowledges the existence of censorship which, as we shall see shortly, was significant in the case of *Psycho*; usually it listed running time as 'Tiempo de proyección sin cortes' ('Running time without cuts') and included the official rating for each film. Nonetheless, a comparison of the times in *Cine asesor* and those listed in Sloan's filmography shows that of the eight films reviewed in *Cine Asesor* only two – *The Birds* (1963) and *Frenzy* (1972) – did not have their running time shortened for Spanish release. These cuts were the marks of the censors. Even after these cuts most of Hitchcock's films that *Cine asesor* reviewed, which are listed in the table below, received a rating classification of 'Rosa' (3) – that is, for a public 18-years-old or above. *Dial M for Murder* (1954) and *Torn Curtain* (1967) received a rating of 'Rosa (3) – Provisional,' for a public years 16-years-old or above. The rating for *Frenzy* was put at 'Rosa (3)', but a possible further restriction of 'Rosa (4)' was suggested.

The following table is derived from the entries in *Cine Asesor*:

Spanish Title	Original Title	Madrid Opening	Original Release	Spanish Running Time	Original Running Time	Entry No. & Rating
Crimen perfecto	Dial M for Murder	23 Dec. 1954	April 1954	102 min.	123 min.	836 Rosa (3)-Prov.
La ventana indiscreta	Rear Window	3 Oct. 1955	July 1954	108 min.	112 min.	1036 Rosa (3)
Psicosis	Psycho	2 April 1961	June 1960	103 min.	110 min.	2432 Rosa (3)
Los pájaros	The Birds	7 Oct. 1963	March 1963	120 min.	120 min.	285–63 Rosa (3)
Marnie, la ladrona	Marnie	22 Oct. 1964	June 1964	111 min.	120 min.	260–64 Rosa (3)
Cortina rasgada	Torn Curtain	13 April 1967	July 1966	92 min.	120 min	98–67 Rosa (3)-Prov.
Topaz	Topaz	30 Nov. 1970	Dec. 1969	122 min.	126 min.	298–70 Rosa (3)
Frenesí	Frenzy	21 Dec. 1972	May 1972	115 min.	115 min.	318–72 Rosa (3), can be 4

The entry in *Cine asesor* for *Crimen perfecto* (*Dial M for Murder*), the first Hitchcock film reviewed by the trade journal, gives a sense of what Spanish distributors thought of a Hitchcock film in the 1950s and hence how a Hitchcock film was initially presented to the Spanish public:

> The director of this film has a well-earned reputation in the crime genre, and combine that with the fact that the general plot of this work is well known, already staged theatrically in several Spanish locations, to complete the appropriate advertising. Made in good 'Warner Colour', this feature film isn't boring in spite of the fact that it happens almost completely in an interior space – the apartment of the protagonist couple. Given the masterful direction and the magnificent acting, interest grows as the climactic scenes near, fulfilling the wishes of the audience in the triumph of justice, a good solution for the emotional 'suspense' of the plot. We project that, due to its qualities and interest, this film will get the public's approval, being able to bring in a GOOD RETURN at the box office at any locale at which it is shown. For audiences more interested in action films it could turn in a MEDIUM profit due to the fact that it takes place almost totally in one location and with excessive dialogue. It can be programmed for regular weekends in any locale. (*Cine Asesor* IV: 836)

This commentary on *Dial M for Murder* reveals more about the sophisticated cultural scene into which Hitchcock entered than about the film itself. His public was an affluent crowd that went to the theatre and the movies, and read *ABC*. Most Madrid newspaper critics excerpted here wrote about the differences bet-ween play and film since the play upon which the film is based had already made it to the Spanish stage when the film opened. *ABC*'s judgement represents a majority opinion, albeit phrased in a circumlocution: 'we can't say that what we are offered is photographed theatre' (ibid.). *Marca*'s unimpressed reviewer dissents from the others, writing: 'Detective plot without mystery but with surprises, written for the theatre and transplanted to the movies without changes' (ibid.).

Although there are gaps in *Cine asesor* – some Hitchcock films of his later productive period were not reviewed – the documentation for the openings of his films of the 1950s until his death is the most extensive, however localised, overview of their initial reception in Spain. If this approach comes to the topic *in medias res*, it describes a mutually reinforcing relationship. *Cine asesor* appears on the scene because the movie market, in which Hitchcock's films participated, showed tremendous growth in Spain in the 1950s. We should also look back upon what preceded this peak period.

V. FIRST STEPS, MANY FEWER THAN *THIRTY-NINE STEPS*

Although current books in Spanish that survey the whole of Hitchcock's career, such as Guillermo Balmori's edited critical anthology *El universo de Alfred
Hitchcock* (The Universe of Alfred Hitchcock, 2007), look upon his British period, both of silent films and later talkies, as predicting the narratives, themes
and aesthetics of his later career, it is hard to make the argument that in their
initial showings in Spain any of the characteristics for which 'British Hitchcock'
was eventually celebrated radically stood out in the cultural landscape. These
movies were judged by different criteria then or barely at all. The initial reception record of this period in Madrid or Barcelona, as can be discerned in reviews
in the major metropolitan newspapers, is a matter of minimal, though positive
paragraphs. The first mention of one of his films to be shown in Madrid, his co-
directorial silent film debut *De mujer a mujer* (*Woman to Woman*, 1923), was
praised more for the elegance of the Princesa movie theatre and the beauty of the
actress Betty Compton. The film received 'sincere laudatory comments' afterwards from the spectators. When *Champagne* (1928) debuted as the second film
of a double bill at the Palacio de la Prensa on 23 April 1929, the *ABC* reviewer
lauded British comedies in general, calling the film 'a magnificent cinematographic comedy, British brand, that completes the programme of this theatre
and that has achieved outright and definitive success, like all of those of this
brand that have been shown this season' (1929: 45). *Champagne* is also the first
film for which Fernández Cuenca serves as an original source since he attended
the premiere. Throughout *El cine británico de Alfred Hitchcock* Fernández
Cuenca rails against 'the youth of the *Positif* group' and their disparagement
of Hitchcock's British films in that journal after the 1956 Cinematheque series.
He uses his recollections as eyewitness to the first screenings in Madrid to set
the record straight. It puts him, however, in the difficult position of defending
Champagne, one of Hitchcock's minor works:

> Peter Nobel considers it one of the most disappointing works of Hitchcock
> and the director himself would recognise later, according to what he told
> Truffaut that 'it is probably the lowest ebb in my output'. The members
> of the *Positif* group come to the conclusion that the first and last frame
> of the film, 'of a Hitchcockian virtuosity, are ridiculous'. Absolute false-
> hood, because there is nothing ridiculous in *Champagne*. I remember its
> premiere in Madrid very well and that we all enjoyed ourselves a lot with
> this comedy, which is quite pointless and doesn't go into any depth about
> anything it comes up with, made somewhat in the American style, but with
> a perfect and refined technique, with an abundance of photographic effects

like double images, deformations and fast motion. It wasn't a great movie, not even a good movie; perhaps we Madrid fans wouldn't have paid much attention to it had we not had absolute proof of Hitchcock's merits, but we did feel deceived although not annoyed. (1974: 39–40)

Fernández Cuenca is claiming that his Madrid chums already intuited Hitchcock's merit in 1929. Certainly he became a fan early on. However, more research is needed on how a more general public opinion was shaped regarding his British films that today we view as more significant, such as *El enemigo de las rubias* (*The Lodger, a Story of the London Fog*, 1926) or Hitchcock's first talkie, *La muchacha de Londres* (*Blackmail*). Since as Fernández Cuenca notes the process of dubbing did not exist at the advent of sound film, *Blackmail* may have been the only Hitchcock film to have debuted in Spain in its original version with Spanish subtitles. Curiously Fernández Cuenca notes its running time as five minutes longer than the time Sloan gives for the American version.

A search of the Spanish titles of the films in *ABC* and *La Vanguardia* yields no other paragraph-long reviews, and no mention of Hitchcock in the 1930s until *Valses de Viena* (*Waltzes from Vienna*, 1933), which is also the first Hitchcock film that Fernández Cuenca records in his card catalogue as opening in 1935. The review of this period film in *ABC* is brief and bland. To extend the dance metaphor, this represents an insecure, and hence supremely tentative, first step since speaking of *Waltzes from Vienna*, a bio-pic of Strauss father and son, Hitchcock despaired to Truffaut: 'It had no relation to my usual work. In fact, at this time my reputation wasn't very good, but luckily I was unaware of this. Nothing to do with conceit; it was merely an inner conviction that I was a filmmaker. I don't remember ever saying to myself, "You're finished; your career is at its lowest ebb." And yet outwardly, to other people, I believed it was' (Truffaut 1984: 85). Fernández Cuenca, who had more opportunities to see Hitchcock films than most people, for instance travelling to London in 1931 to see *The Skin Game* (1931), which never opened in Spain, writes of his contemporaneous impression of *Waltzes from Vienna*: 'We critics who already felt admiration for the powerful personality of Alfred Hitchcock felt disappointed when faced with a routine work that didn't contain even the minimum spark of that personality' (1974: 59).

By 1935, when *El hombre que sabía demasiado* (*The Man Who Knew Too Much*, 1934) debuted in Madrid, there was no doubt that Hitchcock was viewed positively as an auteur in Spain. Fernández Cuenca not only saw it shortly upon opening but immediately went back to see it again:

I keep a vivid memory of this movie: I saw it in the afternoon session of the Madrid Avenida theater and was left so taken in and even bewildered that before writing my review I went back to see it again in the evening session in order to appreciate, now free of the sorcery of its disturbing accelerating action, the strictly cinematographic qualities of the story. And I came to the conclusion that it was an extraordinary film. (1974: 64–5)

Fernández Cuenca in particular praised the use of projection slides in the Albert Hall sequence for giving the effect of an immobilised backdrop of engaged spectators. For him, moreover, *The Man Who Knew Too Much* inaugurated 'a new genre: the spy melodrama with strong intrigue and many elements of suspense' (1974: 64). Much later he mocked the 'absurd opinions' of *Positif* group critics who found the film 'incredibly poorly constructed' (1974: 65). He remained a passionate defender of the *The Man Who Knew Too Much* throughout his career, perhaps even more so as the years went by because in San Sebastián in 1958 he asked Hitchcock himself if he preferred his British original or his Hollywood remake. Always cognisant of his audience, Hitchcock obliged and answered without missing a beat, 'La primera, claro, porque es la más locamente imaginativa' ('The first one, of course, because it is the most crazily imaginative') (ibid.). Since this interview was never published it is worth pausing for a moment in our chronological presentation of Hitchcock's initial Spanish reception to note for posterity what else Hitchcock said to Fernández Cuenca in 1958 about the two versions and what shifting to make films for a US audience meant:[6]

Hubo que sustituir la fantasía por el sentimentalismo, que en América es fundamental. No olvide usted que es femenino el ochenta por ciento del público que en los Estados Unidos va al cine. Esto obliga a aceptar compromisos que a veces no son buenos. (We had to replace fantasy with sentimentality, which is fundamental in America. Don't forget that eighty per cent of the public that goes to the movies in the US is female. That forces one to make compromises that sometimes aren't good.) (1974: 65)

For Hitchcock, then, his crossover to Hollywood meant adjusting to a primarily female audience and becoming more melodramatic. Since this shift in tone and genre had a major impact in how Hitchcock's crossover was received in Mexico, we will come back to this topic again in chapter five.

To return to our chronological survey of the Spanish reception, *Treinta y nueve escalones* (*The Thirty-Nine Steps*, 1935) received a substantial review in *ABC* when it opened in Madrid on 8 January 1936. Importantly in praising the film the reviewer Alfredo Miralles points to the balance between humour and intrigue:

Alfred Hitchcock has chosen to base this movie on Jack Buchan's novella entitled *The Thirty-Nine Steps*, not for its more or less crime theme, but since it is one of so many stories whose plot offers a good director, like him, the chance to produce a good, interesting film, more interesting still since there is intrigue in it besides the main event. And thus, he has begun making it *his film*, treating it to first-rate refined comedy, encrusting its scenes with great expressive force, which is as much comic as dramatic; employing an excellent photographer and some magnificient natural locations – the desolate and wild mountains of Scotland – that add to the events a very fitting atmosphere for the adventures of spies, counterspies and counter-counterspies whose impenetrable schemes were the original object of attraction for the author. (8 January 1935: 49; emphasis in original)

For Miralles, Hitchcock's incorporation of both comedy and drama is one of the signatory characteristics and great positives of his filmmaking. As a first impression of Hitchcock, moreover, we may say that at least one influential Spaniard appreciated his humour especially when taken against the backdrop of scenarios of desolation and intrigue.

Miralles perceived defects in *The Thirty-Nine Steps*, too. Although he argued against interpreting the film realistically, he critiqued its plot for 'the popular method of hastening towards the climax through channels lacking in originality' (ibid.). Nonetheless, the film kept Miralles thinking long after it ended, for as he concluded his review, 'after all in a mystery film it can't surprise us that certain things remain enveloped in the shadows of the inexplicable' (ibid.). It is not hard to imagine that the world of spies and counterspies, or 'the shadows of the inexplicable' that Miralles saw in *The Thirty-Nine Steps*, resonated with the uncertainties of the Civil War that shrouded the country.

To recall, Madrid was under siege from November 1936 to March 1939. Although the Battle for Madrid spared the movie theatres concentrated along the Gran Vía from serious damage, Hitchcock's British films made during those years – *Inocencia y juventud* (*Young and Innocent*, 1937), *Alarma en el expreso* (*The Lady Vanishes*, 1938), *Posada Jamaica* (*Jamaica Inn*, 1939) – opened in Spain after the Civil War. *The Lady Vanishes*, which opened at the end of 1941 in Madrid and Barcelona, received the most notice of his British films after *The Thirty-Nine Steps*. The ad from *La Vanguardia* (20 Dec. 20, 1941: 4) shows how aesthetics and entertainment, as well as Hollywood prizes, were used to launch the film with the Catalan public.

To complete our listing of Madrid openings of Hitchcock's films, and fill in the dates for the films not recorded either by Fernández Cuenca or in *Cine Asesor*, we turn to the opening day reviews in *ABC*, the principal newspaper

Ad for *The Lady
Vanishes* from
La Vanguardia.

of Madrid and the national paper of record until the launching of *El País* after
Franco's death. Ideologically opposed to the dictatorship due to its monarchist
stance, *ABC* was well respected by the intellectual elite for its cultural criticism.
The caricatures of the female and male protagonists of Hitchcock's films that
accompany many of these reviews, upon which I will comment intermittently
throughout this chapter, indicate how significant these films and their stars were
for the Spanish readership of the times since only a select few cultural events, let
alone films, were illustrated on any given day by the paper's signature artist.

Spanish Title	Original Title	Review Date in *ABC* (Madrid)	Original Release	Madrid Theatre(s)
Treinta y nueve escalones	The Thirty-Nine Steps	8 Jan. 1936	Sept. 1935	Figaro
Enviado especial	Foreign Correspondent	1 Dec. 1944	August 1940	Palacio de la Música
Encadenados	Notorious	1 Oct. 1948	July 1946	Coliseum
La soga	Rope	18 Nov. 1951	August 1948	(Not listed)
Atormentada	Under Capricorn	4 Nov. 1952	Sept. 1949	Palacio de la Música
Yo confieso	I Confess	26 Feb. 1954	Feb. 1953	Avenida
Atrapa a un ladrón	To Catch a Thief	18 Nov. 1958	July 1955	Lope de Vega
Falso culpable	The Wrong Man	17 June 1959	Dec. 1956	Carlos III, Roxy B
Con la muerte en los talones	North by Northwest	29 Dec. 1959	July 1959	Palacio de la Prensa, Carlos III, Roxy B
El hombre que sabía demasiado	The Man Who Knew Too Much	26 July 1960	May 1956	Palacio de la Prensa, Roxy B
Pero...¿Quién mató a Harry?	The Trouble with Harry	15 Nov. 1960	Oct. 1955	Popeya, Palace, Gayarre
Pánico en la escena	Stage Fright	9 May 1961, Sevilla; 12 July 1961, Barcelona	Feb. 1950	

El caso Paradine	The Paradine Case	7 July 1967	Dec. 1947	Palacio de la Prensa, Bilbao, Progreso, Velazquez
La trama	Family Plot	14 Oct. 1976	March 1976	Amaya
Blackmail, Murder, Number Seventeen, Rich and Strange		V. O., 10 Dec. 1981		Alexandra
La mujer solitaria	Sabotage	V.O., 4 August 1983		Capitol

VI. WHAT ESCAPED CENSORSHIP AND WHAT DID NOT: *LIFEBOAT* AND *PSYCHO*

Although both Fernández Cuenca and *Cine asesor* are incomplete in noting which Hitchcock films played in Spain and when – cards for *The Thirty-Nine Steps* or for *The Birds* are missing in Fernández Cuenca's catalog, and *Cine asesor* has nothing on *To Catch a Thief* (1954) or *Family Plot* (1976) – the record of all films that were reviewed in contemporaneous Spanish newspapers, taking together the perspective of a film scholar and that of an industry specialist, shows which Hitchcock films were judged noteworthy in their times.

The charts above from *Cine Asesor* and Fernández Cuenca point to which Hitchcock films were cut, and even on that they do not always agree, and they do not tell us what was removed when the film was first shown. Spanish Film Archives do not contain prints of foreign films. To ascertain what was actually cut is, regrettably, beyond the scope of this project.[7]

Although this chapter concentrates on what happened in Madrid, it bears noting that under Franco the pattern and policies that were set in Madrid, especially as concerned film censorship, were hegemonic. How censorship was subsequently even further exercised throughout the country, however, was extremely arbitrary. In 1963 José María García Escudero, head of Dirección General de Cinematografía y Teatro, codified Spanish censorship and spelled out the list of prohibited topics – 'those favoring divorce, abortion, euthanasia, and birth control and those appearing to justify adultery, prostitution, and illicit sexual behavior' (Higginbotham 1998: 12). Though not explicitly noted on this 1963 list, the prohibition of nudity and of any satirical depiction of the military were constants of film censorship from the 1930s until after Franco's death.[8] Before 1963 censorship had been much more arbitrary. Film research is only now beginning to note, if not unravel, its effects. One key document is the recent collection of articles from the journal *Secuencias*, edited by Laura Gómez Vaquero and Daniel Sánchez Salas, *El espíritu del caos: Representación y recepción de las imágenes durante el Franquismo* (The Spirit of Chaos: Representation and Reception of Images During Franco's Era, 2009). In his article in this volume 'El espíritu del caos: Irregularidades en la censura cinematográfica durante la inmediata postguerra' ('The Spirit of Chaos: Irregularities in Cinematographic Censorship during the Immediate Post War Period') Josep Estivill studies the correspondence in 1940 with Metro Goldwyn Mayer Ibérica. He quotes from a letter of an MGM representative to the Under Secretary for Press and Propaganda in the Government Ministry in which the former complains with exasperation of the impossible situation for movie distributors if 'the campaigns by the press, certain organisations like Catholic Action and certain provincial authorities continue to be tolerated as they have been up to now' (2009: 83–4). Though Hitchcock was not produced or distributed by MGM at the time, but rather by Selznick and Universal, or Warner Bros., this statement provides a list of shared woes of the most bothersome, if not effective sources of censorship in Spain for American movies. Estivill notes that what was actually shown outside of Madrid in the provinces differed because each movie theatre went its own way in doctoring the print shown. Estivill's laments demonstrate how little we know about what was actually screened: 'We also don't know exactly what relationship was forged between the censor and some of the most emblematic films of the period, such as *The Great Dictator* (Charles Chaplin, 1940), *Citizen Kane* (Orson Welles, 1940) or *Battleship Potemkin* (Sergei Eisenstein, 1925)' (2009: 63). Simply put, much remains to be learned about whether Hitchcock's films were censored or not, and if so, how.

Lifeboat provides one case in which we know for certain that Hitchcock's film was censored. According to Fernández Cuenca's catalog it was severely cut by ten minutes from its original running time. I have not been able to see the censored version for a comparison, but I surmise that the presentation in the film of the suicide of Mrs. Iggley after realising her baby was dead was one likely cut. Still, when *Lifeboat* opened in 1947 in Barcelona, H. Saenz Guerrero, writing in *La Vanguardia*, called the film 'one of the most significant movies that we have seen in recent times' (15 January 1947: 2). On the same page of *La Vanguardia* as this laudatory review there was an ad for *Casablanca*, so Saenz Guerrero's estimation was high praise indeed in 1947. *Lifeboat*'s *topos* of isolation could well have spoken to the particular condition of Spain as a country cut off from Europe and the rejuvenating stimulus of the Marshall Plan. Yet the contemporary newspaper reviews in *ABC* and *La Vanguardia*, which praised the film highly, spoke of the clash of universal values rather than of an allegory of Spanish marginalisation. Luis Mariano González González, in his book on historical films under Franco, *Fascismo, Kitsch y el cine histórico en*

España (1931–36) (Fascism, Kitsch and Historical Movies in Spain (1931–36), 2009), notes that the official film policy in fact encouraged films that depicted Spaniards as courageous underdogs, as a way of rallying public opinion against international sanctions of the Franco regime, such as its exclusion from the League of Nations. To turn to a contemporaneous voice, in 1947 the regular columnist Floristán of *Fotogramas* in an article entitled 'Alfredo Hitchcock y Ricardo Wagner' ('Alfred Hitchcock and Richard Wagner') does present an interpretation of *Lifeboat* which addresses marginalisation:

> Why a Wagnerian melody for a black man's flute? This music is associated with the German in a situation in which he is every one's enemy. We can't believe that Hitchcock picked this music at random. He must have had his reasons. The black man, racially excluded from that community of white men, is the one who is best situated above the fray. He finishes the prayer that another has begun; he and the German sing Schubert's 'Wild Rose' together. The boat, wracked with anxiety, slips away over the silent ocean, and a black man plays the marvelous Wagnerian melody that speaks of immutable beauties and of a world of poetry and dreams that knows nothing of cruelty. Afterwards, much later, when in a fit of anger everyone throws themselves onto the enemy, he watches the horizon. It seems as if he is asking himself: What kind of men could there be to come to save us? (15 February 1947: n.p.)

Floristán's analysis, which links musical appreciation to racial politics, privileges the position of the black man in *Lifeboat*. The query 'Who may be coming for us next?' appears to justify a climate of fear and reaffirm a stance of isolation. The black man's non-intervention indeed may signal nostalgia for Germanic ideology, a position that would have been entirely consistent with the Franco regime.

Overall, as far as we know today, the censorship of Hitchcock's films in Spain through extreme excision was infrequent. It was nothing compared to that endured by the greats of European art cinema like Ingmar Bergman whose films were not only cut but also reorganised like jigsaw puzzles to present an ideological argument directly opposite to the original version's. No Hitchcock film was ever banned like Rossellini's or Buñuel's. For this reason Hitchcock's witty evasions of the US movie code, including his depictions of homosexuals, reached a Spanish audience, too. Even in the high-minded review of *Lifeboat* quoted above Hitchcock's humour was also noted.

A recent book by Alberto Gil, *La censura cinematográfica en España* (The Cinematographic Censorship in Spain, 2009) illuminates the breadth of censorship of Hollywood films in Spain. He addresses censorship in Spain of films of all nationalities in terms of three thematic blocks: love and sex, morality and religion, and politics and society. Gil confirms that although Hitchcock had laboured long for the *Psycho* shower scene to pass US movie censors, the implied depiction of nudity even when carefully framed, did not pass muster in Spain. Nonetheless *Cine asesor* expected the film to be profitable for exhibitors: 'GOOD YIELD that will reach VERY GOOD among fans of the genre: "With all its horrors and artifices it is one of those films that are viewed with bated breath and that cause an impact of hallucinatory "suspense" until you get to the surprising ending"'. (1961: 2432). The cuts to *Psycho* did not affect either the film's popularity in its initial runs or its iconic status, which is seen in the repeated reference to *Psycho* in reviews of subsequent Hitchcock films. *Psycho* became the single most important reference point in defining Hitchcock's artistry in the Spanish-speaking world.

VII. TRANSFORMATIONAL MOMENTS: *REBECCA* AND *SPELLBOUND*

Although *Vertigo* represents the cinephile's Hitchcock, *Psycho* brings forth the *Jeopardy* answer (always in the form of a question) 'What is a Hitchcock film?' in most parts of the world. How then is the reception of Hitchcock culturally unique to Spain? *Rebecca* and *Spellbound* provide two keys to understanding these divergences. For one, *Rebecca* is immensely important as it represents a transnational moment on multiple fronts. It was Hitchcock's first Hollywood film, and thus constitutes his crossover moment from British to American, and a huge leap for him in production values. Likewise it inaugurated the first Berlinale, thus heralding the era of European film festivals and delineating a place for some Hollywood films in them as well. In fact, Hitchcock reentered Europe with a film that relied on an essentially British ambience. *Rebecca* represents a new hybridisation that was closely studied in Spain. For another, *Spellbound*, or *Recuerda* (literally 'Remember') as it was known in Spain, is significant for the collaboration of Dalí whose minor intervention had a long-term impact. Psychoanalytical complexity, especially when represented as a dream sequence, became recognised as a key element in Hitchcock's films.

One of the legendary ironies of Hitchcock's career, which is often evoked to show how true greatness is ignored during the time in which the artist lived and worked, is that Hitchcock was nominated five times for an Academy Award as Best Director but never received this accolade. He won the Best Picture Academy Award only once, for *Rebecca*; and Selznick symbolically snatched that honour away in Hollywood because Selznick, not Hitchcock dominated the news for his feat of producing the winning Best Picture two years in a row, first with *Gone with the Wind* (1939), then with *Rebecca*. These statistics are often evoked to console someone who has lost out on a prize. Martin Scorsese became sick of hearing it at Academy Award time.[9] There is some truth to the lesson of Hitchcock's history of disappointing award results and we need to keep it in mind as we survey the initial reaction to his films in Spain. Curiously, though not everyone got the facts right, Hitchcock's move to Hollywood was widely celebrated at the time. In 1944 a large ad in *La Vanguardia* for the opening of *Inocencia y juventud* (*Young and Innocent*, 1937), touts this British period Hitchcock, considered today one of his minor works as 'El film que le valió el salto de Inglaterra a Hollywood' ('The film that made possible his jump from England to Hollywood') (2 July 1944).

The advertiser knew that the jump to Hollywood was a big deal that could sell films. Hitchcock's crossover moment – which *Rebecca*, not *Young and Innocent*, represents – set the pattern. It received a slew of Academy Award nominations in all categories, won for Best Cinematography and Best Picture, but not for Best Director. Hitchcock pleased the public, but not those who voted for prizes. This provided the evidence that defined him as a commercial director, but not a great artist, the paradigm that Truffaut later deflated. The reception history of *Rebecca* in Spain, however, has come to symbolise the complex significance of spectatorship in Spanish political and cultural history that goes beyond merely tagging Hitchcock as commercial or tallying prize lists.

Marsha Kinder in the chapter, 'Micro- and Macro-Regionalism in Catalan Cinema, European Coproductions, and Global Television' in *Blood Cinema* interprets the case of the Catalan filmmaker Lorenzo Llobet Gracia and his film *Vida en sombras* (*Life in Shadows*, 1946–7) to illustrate how the film's celebration of Hollywood style, and most particularly that of Hitchcock in *Rebecca*, fits into a dynamic of regional resistance. Kinder writes: 'During the Francoist era, any difference in verbal or filmic language in Catalan cinema carried subversive implications, even when the plot seemed more personal than political' (1993: 394). She further observes that Catalan cinema subverted Castilian dominance 'by exposing it as marginal (and regional) within the international

Ad for *Young and Innocent* from *La Vanguardia* touts Hitchcock's jump to Hollywood.

context, thereby allying itself with other dominant cultural centers, like Paris or Hollywood' (1993: 395).

To provide some background, *Life in Shadows* tells the story of a filmmaker and movie-lover called Carlos Durán, who was literally born in a movie theatre. He becomes a documentary filmmaker. While filming the action at the outbreak of the Spanish Civil War, he witnesses the death of his wife by a stray bullet. He blames himself for her death and subsequently quits his film career. Yet watching the scene in *Rebecca* in which Max de Winter (Laurence Olivier) and his second wife (Joan Fontaine) themselves watch home movies of their honeymoon together, Durán becomes inspired to make movies again.

The particular sequence from *Rebecca* that allows the character Durán to resume making films has been interpreted as homage to Hitchcock's own home life in which Alma and he happily bantered over movies. This slice of life, however, is a part of the film that had no connection to Du Maurier's novel. Hitchcock chafed at Selznick's insistence that he keep closely to the book in his adaptation. McGilligan calls Mr. de Winter's line in the home movie sequence ('Oh look, there's the one where I left the camera running on the tripod, remember?') 'far and away the purest Hitchcock moment in *Rebecca*' (2003: 243). Significantly, the moment Llobet Gracia selected for inspiration was that rare sign of humour in *Rebecca*, which Hitchcock himself told Truffaut was his most humourless film. Kinder describes the adapted scene in *Life in Shadows*:

> After watching the scene from *Rebecca* in which Joan Fontaine and Laurence Olivier are looking at home movies from their own happier past, Durán (who physically resembles the young Olivier) returns to his room to watch home movies of himself and his dead wife. This act of double spectatorship enables him to find a way out of his own entrapment. Gradually, the close-ups of him as spectator replace his screen image in the home movie. He is able to suture himself into the imaginary scene from the past and as an empowered spectator to actively draw a blessing from the ambiguous image and words of his dead wife. Like the scene in John Ford's *Young Mr. Lincoln* (1936) in which the hero consults his dead love about whether to study the law, Durán uses the recorded words of his dead wife ('What do you want me to say?') to authorize his own desire to resume his pursuit of cinema. (1993: 410)

Although Llobet Gracia does not maintain the light-hearted tone of Hitchcock's original scenario, still it is important to note that Hitchcock inspired Spanish filmmakers, and that these same filmmakers recognised and adapted Hitchcock's originality and humour.

For the filmmaker Llobet Gracia seeing *Rebecca* after the end of the Spanish Civil War, in which his father had fought on the Republican side and died, was a life-changing experience. Just as in the film the character Durán overcomes his grief over his wife's death through watching *Rebecca*, in his own life Llobet Gracia resumed filmmaking, perhaps putting aside his grief over the death of his father in the war, through a similar act of spectatorship of Hitchcock's film. Because *Life in Shadows* realistically depicted the Spanish Civil War on screen, and moreover sympathised with the Republican side, the film was heavily censored and virtually unknown for decades. Even after Franco's death there were only occasional screenings in film clubs in the 1970s until the Spanish Filmoteca or Film Archives reconstructed the film in the 1980s. Even then it was only seen at limited festival screenings and is still known mostly through the writings of critics such as Marsha Kinder and John Hopewell. Nonetheless *Rebecca* has come to represent a gesture of opposition or liberation in Spanish cultural history. Kinder argues that emulating Hollywood, and *Rebecca* in particular, had the positive effect of stimulating not just Llobet Gracia, but the whole Catalan film industry as a micro-regional force in opposition to the xenophobic national policies, which emanated from the centre, Madrid. Above all she finds *Life in Shadows* to be 'a model for how to use a personal romantic/sexual discourse to talk about political topics that were otherwise suppressed' (1993: 409).

Llobet Gracia's exceptional case of spectatorship is only one sign of the localised significance of *Rebecca* in Spanish cultural history. Hitchcock's melodrama touched a nerve in Spain as no other Hitchcock film had before. It became an ideological flashpoint from the moment it opened. A comparison of the reviews of the major newspapers of Barcelona and Madrid shows the strong impact that *Rebecca*, which was shown uncensored, had throughout the country. Reviewers sparred in hyperbolic language that bordered on Biblical exegesis as much as film criticism. To begin on the political right, on the premiere of *Rebecca* in Madrid the *ABC* film critic Rodenas came close to invoking Old Testament wrath upon Hitchcock for the moral turpitude of the character of Rebecca and for the tacit acceptance of suicide that the film's conclusion implied:

> The title of this movie, that recalls the name of that woman who was the wife of the patriarch Isaac, doesn't have anything to do with the protagonist. Rebecca is a phantasmal shadow, a being that lived the life of a libertine, perhaps to gain notoriety and at the same time stir up the hate and scorn of her husband, a nobody Mr. Winter, who still has issues of considerable magnitude to settle against his – seriously scatterbrained – wife.
>
> It's important to recognise, in spite of the award that this 'film' received from the Academy of Motion Picture Arts and Sciences of North America,

that the subject matter isn't decent because the tacit agreement between husband and wife to carry out her suicide goes against our sensibility, against our criterion as Christians, and seems inconceivable and monstruous to us. (16 December 1942: 16)

Continuing his review, Rodenas begrudgingly mentions the film's Academy Award and then is forced to acknowledge the masterful hand of Hitchcock as auteur despite the film's subject matter. Hitchcock, as he had in *Lifeboat*, implicitly condoned suicide, which was a moral taboo. Although the immorality of it all – accessible to those with 'sick' imaginations – sticks in his caw, Rodenas still has to admit the film is superlative on all other accounts.

We have set forth our due judgement on the merits of Daphne du Marier's story, which actually is crude, excessively strong, based on feverish morbose lucubrations of its author. Now then: the production is admirable, because in a matter such as this, so accessible to sick imaginations, there is no more fitting technical display, nor more beauty, nor more artistic sensibility than that which Alfred Hitchock [sic] has used in making 'Rebecca'. In this regard all the praise seems sparing, poor to us. The atmosphere is captured with impeccable subtlety. The echo of the voice in the garden and abandoned castle is of a great symbolic force, and the moment of the fire is impeccably done. Everything else about 'Rebecca', including the most insignificant details, which are the enchantment of the movie, show the marks of a masterful hand, who is the one who has given emotionality and liveliness to a matter accessible to any troubled mind. (ibid.)

After having noted the appropriate Christian reaction to *Rebecca* – that is, first to condemn the acceptance of suicide in the film – Rodenas has to admit, twice, that the film is 'impeccable' even in the smallest details. But one can almost hear him cringe and not be able to articulate the unspeakable – that is, that this film gave life to 'a matter accessible to any troubled mind'. These circumlocutions show that Rodenas did not miss the full range of Hitchcock's sexual representations in Rebecca, including Mrs. Danvers' lesbian attraction to her former mistress. *Rebecca*'s full import as a lesson in the representation of gender in Spain, though significant from its first showing, remained unspoken for many decades. Only recently Boris Izaguirre cogently analysed this significant aspect of Hitchcock's *Rebecca* in his book *El armario secreto de Hitchcock* (*The Secret Closet of Hitchcock*, 2005).

On the political left, the reviewer in *La Vanguardia* of the Barcelona opening of the film, a few weeks later than the Madrid opening, also chooses Biblical language, as had Rodenas, but the *La Vanguardia* reviewer writes of miracles, to gush about *Rebecca*.

> There is something in the movies that is irreplaceable because definitively it is its basic force – that is to say, it is everything: technique. But technique put in service, subordinated at every moment to something even less irreplaceable: the immanent talent of its own filmmaker. These two sides, technique and talent, can work – excuse us the hyperbole – miracles. There it is giving credence to our assertion, one of the best movies that in these times American cinema has offered us is: 'Rebecca'.
>
> 'Rebecca', which 'United Artists' has produced and Alfred Hitchcock has directed, is purely what has been noted: a prodigy, a miracle of the technique of a cinematographer in absolute maturity and above all, of an acute and intelligent vision put into service for this technique. And it is that it was truly difficult, very difficult to translate a vulgar and in certain moments melodramatic novel, as is the work of Daphne du Maurier, into a very beautiful symphony of rigorously cinematographic images.
>
> It was also difficult to manage time and time again for the camera to be positioned in the exact, just, precise angle, such that in a lesson of good cinematic practice, there would be captured on film everything that needed to be shown and nothing more than what needed to be shown. (9 January 1943: 7)

The reviewer, F. G. S., then expounds at length about the acting and concludes his report seconding the judgement of the Academy Award bestowers: 'But overall we find that first prize for acting, very just, very legitimate, so deservingly awarded to the protagonists of "Rebecca" in Hollywood' (ibid.). Although the reviewer got it wrong, since no actor or actress won an Academy Award for *Rebecca*, his enthusiasm for the film, which did win Best Picture in 1940, is unbridled. He expresses none of the moral reservations of the *ABC* reviewer and praises Hitchcock for dealing so masterfully with the 'vulgar' material that he had to work with from Du Maurier's novel. The *Vanguardia* review confirms the overwhelmingly positive reception that Hitchcock through *Rebecca* had as an artistically liberating force in Catalan film culture, if not among the Spanish left in general.

Hitchcock's other transformational film also involved Catalonia through its native son Salvador Dalí. In a different take on the macro/micro regional politics then we saw with Llobet Gracia's *Life in Shadows*, Dalí's collaboration in *Spellbound* marked it on a more macro or national scale as the most Spanish of Hitchcock's films. The role that Dalí played in the film's conception would be repeatedly evoked in Spain whenever a special Hitchcock event was staged in that country. Today, because much of what Dalí created for *Spellbound* was never used in the film or ended up on the cutting room floor, the general impression is that the Hitchcock/Dalí collaboration was not just rocky, but unsuccessful. Although years later Hitchcock did describe Dalí as 'really a kook' in an interview for the BBC (quoted in McGilligan 2003: 364), a blunt assessment that many nonetheless share, that judgement does not diminish Hitchcock's appreciation of Dalí's artistic vision, or specifically of his painting. The attention paid to Dalí globally has not waned over the years. As Sara Cochran states in the catalogue for the exhibition *Dalí and Film*, a transnational venture between the Tate, MoMA and the Fundación Dalí, Hitchcock not only requested Dalí's participation in the design for the dream sequence but also had a clear concept of how he, too, would innovate in filming Dalí's product to 'give his sequence a sharper focus than the rest of the film – almost ironic ultra realism' (2007: 178). In a later TV interview, quoted by Cochran, Hitchcock explained his vision:

> I requested Dalí. Selznick, the producer, had the impression that I wanted Dalí for the publicity value. That wasn't it at all. What I was after was … the vividness of dreams … [A]ll Dalí's work is very solid and very sharp, with very long perspectives and black shadows. Actually I wanted the dream sequence[s] to be shot on the back lot, not in the studio at all. I wanted them shot in bright sunshine. So the cameraman would be forced to do what we call stop it out and get a very hard image. This was again the avoidance of the cliché. All dreams in the movies are blurred. It isn't true. Dalí was the best man for me to do the dreams because that is what dreams should be. (2007: 178)

Closer to the truth is that Hitchcock and Dalí 'got on well' but that the transformation of some of Dalí's designs onto the Hollywood set never worked out. One vignette intended to have ornate pianos suspended over immobilised dancers: Cochran says Selznick 'decided to make miniature pianos and suspend them from the ceiling' (2007: 181); McGilligan claims 'Hitchcock substituted miniature pianos dangling over the heads of live dwarfs' (2003: 362). Whether the cost-cutting design came from Selznick or Hitchcock himself, when Dalí and Hitchcock viewed the filming together in August 1944 they concurred that, in Dalí's words, 'one saw, simply, that they were dwarfs' (Cochran 2007: 181) and that the segment had to go.

Much of the lore around the most extensive vignette for *Spellbound* that went unused, the ballroom sequence in which Ingrid Bergman was to become immobilised into a classical statue, focuses on how Dalí's vision actually fulfilled Hitchcock's own sexual fantasies of capturing the unassailable Nordic star.

Indeed Hitchcock and Dalí were kindred spirits and Dalí praised Hitchcock as 'one of the rare personages I have met lately who has some mystery' (McGilligan 2003: 361). Their collaboration on *Spellbound* transcended what was used in the film. What hit the cutting room floor of what Dalí drew or painted has not been lost but has become legendary. Its cultural history was rewritten many times over in Spain and elsewhere. To evoke Benedict Anderson's concept from *Imagined Communities* (1991), the Dalí/Hitchcock collaboration forms part of the 'imaginary museum' of Hitchcock in Spain. It was widely reported that King Juan Carlos and Queen Sofía opened the exhibition of the Dalí *Spellbound* backdrops at the Museu-Fundación Dalí in Figueres in 2004. Even if a Spaniard has never seen *Spellbound* or seen Dalí's work, he or she has general knowledge of this part of Spanish cultural history. The Dalí museum is the second most popular tourist destination in Spain, second only to the Prado in Madrid.

Although Hitchcock sought out Dalí for reasons beyond the latter's publicity value, an idea onto which Selznick immediately grasped, that there was a lot of mileage to be gained by the association with Dalí particularly in Spain, is undeniable. It went beyond the publicity for *Recuerda* (*Spellbound*). Dalí was called upon again for the launching of *Vertigo* in Spain, even though he could claim no direct credit for film's artistic conception as he had received for *Spellbound*. The recent exhibition and book, edited by Matthew Gale, *Dalí and Film* lists *Vertigo* in 'A Cinematic Cronology of Dalí 1941–1989' (2007: 160–1) as one of the most important films Dalí saw in the late 1950s. It is not surprising that at least in Spain Dalí would make an appearance to support the film, for *Vertigo*'s nightmare sequence recalls the stylised fall in *Spellbound*'s dream sequence.

In 1959 Dalí appeared as a judge in Barcelona for a *Vertigo* doubles lookalike contest. As reported on for the film magazine *Triunfo*, seen in the photo below, two Kim Novaks were chosen from a paltry field of five contestants, one blonde and one brunette.[10] Although this doubling alludes to the film's narrative, the staging of the contest in this way also suggests a particularly Spanish reception to the film, given that more Spanish women are brunettes than blondes. One of the now forgotten marketing strategies Hollywood, particularly Paramount, used to launch a film in the 1950s was to stage a glamorous lookalike contest based on the female stars of the film. As reported in an article entitled 'Cientos de "Sabrinas" compiten con Audrey Hepburn' ('Hundreds of "Sabrinas" compete with Audrey Hepburn') in *Fotogramas* (1955 II: 22), to launch *Sabrina* Paramount held simultaneous Audrey Hepburn lookalike contests in Madrid and Barcelona. Hundreds of hopefuls turned out in both cities. Contestants were judged by means of interviews and fashion parades. The grand prize-winners appeared on stage on the night of the film's opening in their respective cities and later were given a paid trip to Paris. Pilar Rubio, the Madrid 'Sabrina',

Kim Novak

The field of candidates (top) shown for the Kim Novak lookalike contest in Barcelona from *Triunfo*. Salvador Dalí, lookalike contest judge, shown with the two winners, one blonde, one brunette from *Triunfo*.

a clerk in a perfume shop with dreams of stardom, explained in *Fotogramas* that she would have liked to be in films 'because selling perfumes ends up being somewhat monotonous' (ibid.). Although today the internet teems with mainly comic lookalike contests, drag queens imitate Hollywood idols in clubs, and Gael García Bernal channels Sara Montiel in *La mala educación* (*Bad Education*), in the 1950s lookalike contests were serious, mainstream publicity stalwarts. They represented one way that local Spanish markets adapted Hollywood's images.

Rivalries played out in these publicity stunts as well as in Spanish cinema and fan magazines. Audrey Hepburn faced off against Grace Kelly, then Kim Novak, for popularity among fans. Audrey came out a clear winner in the 1950s, a phenomenon that continues in Spain to the present day, though perhaps for other reasons than in the 1950s.[11] In Hitchcock's lifetime Hepburn frustrated Hitchcock's plans more than once. *The Nun's Story* (Fred Zinneman, 1959), in which she starred, beat out *North by Northwest* for the Golden Shell in San Sebastián, although Eva Marie Saint's kiss with Cary Grant was the talk of the press throughout the country. The festival report in *Triunfo* made it clear that her prolonged kisses in that film would never pass the Spanish censors. Today Hitchcock is thought of in terms of suspense and terror, and as we will see as a model for that trend in the 1980s and 1990s in Spain, but at the moment of these film's openings, under Franco, it was often the sex, and especially the forbidden sexual innuendos, that captured the news and pushed the boundaries. As McGilligan notes, in *North by Northwest* Hitchcock crossed Code officials in the US with Eva's suggestive line, 'I never make love on an empty stomach' uttered in the dining car sequence. Hitchcock did not eliminate the line from the shooting, but over-dubbed it as 'I never discuss love on an empty stomach' (2003: 573). There was wit and humour to this foreplay, and to how Hitchcock presented sex on screen.

The Spanish public got it. The history of film festivals, especially that of the San Sebastián, helps us understand how that happened.

VIII. HITCHCOCK LIGHTS UP THE FESTIVAL CIRCUIT: *VERTIGO* AND *NORTH BY NORTHWEST* AT SAN SEBASTIÁN IN 1958 AND 1959

Since Hitchcock excelled at promotion, it should come as no surprise that he recognised early on the importance of film festivals, such as the Berlinale, for the success of his films and for his overall reputation. In addition, the old world European cities that were the sites for the major film festivals were like second homes for Hitchcock, the epicurean traveler. The opening sequence at the St. Moritz resort in the 1934 version of *The Man Who Knew Too Much* reflected Hitchcock's own choice of winter vacation venues. Significantly Hitchcock brought *Vertigo* to the third annual San Sebastián Film Festival. Although we generally speak of British and American Hitchcock, Hitchcock was more than British. Having apprenticed in Germany with Fritz Lang in Berlin, he was a European filmmaker. This formative period has recently been commemorated in an exhibition, 'Casting a Shadow: Alfred Hitchcock and His Workshop', which focuses on the impact of this period on his cinematic style.[12] It is still impressive to remember that Hitchcock spoke German and French. For example, in 1972 he did video interviews in French for *Frenzy* in Cannes. Few in Hollywood to-day can claim his command of languages.[13] But he did not speak Spanish. The fifty-hour interview, the most famous of his bilingual meetings and one that resulted in Truffaut's book, however, was conducted with Helen Scott serving as interpreter. Truffaut spoke in French, and Hitch in English. As readers, we perceive the book as as a dialogue between monolinguals whereas in reality it represents a bilingual experience.

Where Hitchcock travelled is one guide to gauging the significance or relative impact of the first screening of his films. When he competed at the major film festivals in Europe, the Spanish press covered these events. Along with *Rebecca*, *Stage Fright*, *Psycho* and *Torn Curtain* were also shown in Berlin. At Cannes he competed with three films – *Notorious* (1946) at the first festival, *I Confess* (1953) and *The Man Who Knew Too Much* (1956). He later presented *The Birds* (1963) and *Frenzy* (1972) in Cannes, but out of competition. In 1955 he brought *To Catch a Thief* to the Venice Film Festival. In San Sebastián he entered the main competition with *Vertigo* and *North by Northwest*. Very early on Hitchcock, or his Hollywood production team, seemed to grasp the importance of the new phenomenon of film festivals in marketing a film successfully, not only in the country of the given festival but also through the multiplying repercussions of press reviews worldwide.

Two films – *Vertigo* and *North by Northwest* – are especially associated with Spain because Hitchcock entered them in competition at the San Sebastián Film Festival in 1958 and 1959 respectively. San Sebastián is particularly significant since it is the oldest and most important film festival in the Spanish-speaking world. Spanish pride was much in evidence at those sixth and seventh editions, as San Sebastián struggled to place itself on par with Cannes, Venice and Berlin. *Film Ideal* put it bluntly in its headline 'Las dos películas españolas debieron "quedarse en casa"' ('The two Spanish movies should "stay home"') while affirming 'the news of greatest importance: San Sebastián won recognition for Spain at last as a top calibre Film Festival' (September 1958: 7). Hitchcock's personal appearances each time at the screenings and press conferences added to the reputation of the festival. However, each time he won not first, but second prize, the Silver Shell. *Vertigo* even had to share the Silver Shell with the Italian film *I soliti ignoti* (*Big Deal on Madonna Street*, 1958). Fernández Cuenca, the Director of the Spanish Film Archives, agreed with this assessment of *Vertigo* calling the Salomonic decision of the Jury 'una lección de ecuanimidad y seriedad' ('a lesson in impartiality and seriousness') (*Blanco y Negro*, 9 August 1958). The Grand Prize winner was a Polish comedy *Ewa chce spac* (*Eve Wants to Sleep*, 1958). Throughout Spain newspapers and magazines of all kinds reported on Hitchcock's triumphs and disappointments. *Film Ideal* revealed its attitude toward *Vertigo* in a short piece entitled 'Menos Mal' ('It Could Be Worse') that ends quoting Hitchcock on Kim Novak: 'Kim no estropea la historia.' ('Kim doesn't mess up the story') (23 September 1958: 3). José María Latiegui's more complete assessment later in the same issue, nonetheless, was even more backhanded. Acknowledging San Sebastián as the gastronomic capital that it has always been, he uses a dining metaphor:

> 'Vertigo', the most anticipated film on the programme, because of the name of its director and its actors, only managed to disappoint us. Naturally one can't find faults in Hitchcock's filmmaking, perfect in its very imperfection; but it fails in the 'tridimensional' story – crime, love, psychological – that far from coming together, diverges and disperses. 'Suspense' exists, but so extenuated that it ceases to be. Someone said after the screening that it was like inviting ten people to a dinner for two, stretching it out in multiple courses: the result is ending up hungry. (23 September 1958: 8)

In sum, *Vertigo* received only a lukewarm initial reception in San Sebastián; it could even be called a flop if it were not for the popularity of James Stewart, who was also called on to share the Actor's Prize with Kirk Douglas for *The*

Vikings (1958). Nonetheless, Hitchcock himself was an enormous hit. His humour and sharp wit charmed the press at the festival. Guillermo Bolin breezily makes Hitchcock into Santa Claus in his overview of San Sebastián in *Blanco y negro* (*Black and White*):

> On the other hand, Hitchcock, the genial director, came, flying from Hollywood, passing over the North Pole, to attend the screening of 'Vertigo', which although awarded the Silver Shell, has been reviewed less enthusiastically than the press conference which was celebrated the day before its premiere. And, truly, he said some interesting and substantial things. One of them was that in making movies he was always thinking about the spectator and his reactions. A simple formula, almost Columbus' egg, but of absolutely sure effects. (9 August 1958: 63–4)

Bolin likely uses the Santa Claus analogy to make yet another comment on Hitchcock's weight. Yet if one looks at the substance of his remarks, he builds up the universal mantra of Hitchcock – that is, Hitchcock in a nutshell, or as 'Columbus' egg' for the Spanish-speaking world: think in terms of the audience and their reactions.

In 1958 San Sebastián showed *Vertigo* subtitled in its original version. When it finally opened in its dubbed version across Spain, *Vertigo* was officially called *De entre los muertos* after the title of the Du Maurier novel. Donald, the *ABC* film critic, preferred *Vértigo*, lamenting that for once when an American title made sense in Spanish, dubbers still went for something else. His review in *ABC* at the film's opening in Madrid a year after having been shown in San Sebastián, though not entirely positive, is much more appreciative of Hitchcock's talents than were earlier assessments:

> In the movie one notices the hand of a master, a man who can be called, now rightly so, a magician for keeping the soul of the spectators on a string and for playing a game with them that thrills them as much as it entertains the one who is making the moves: stalking the unexpected, the surprising.
>
> It is important to note that in the film we also find the atmosphere controlled and within the unexpected, each type given his just measure, his exact psychological dimensions.
>
> And nonetheless – we wrote about it in our last commentary and we reiterate it now – this movie does not achieve the force and quality of direction of the other ones of the admired master in the art of intrigue and suspense. The first part develops slowly and the ending 'strikes' one as a contrived solution reached after a laborious search. (30 June 1959: 63)

In *ABC*, headliner films always received an accompanying line illustration, drawn by the resident artist Joal Ude. Though Jimmy Stewart is almost unrecognisable in his Vertigo caricature, the treatment shows the high status of the film for the Spanish market despite the critiques of its plot. The film, moreover, would stay associated with Spain in the public's imagination due to its Dalíesque dream sequence.

In 1959, shortly after *Vertigo* opened across Spain, Hitchcock returned to the San Sebastián Film Festival to try again, this time with *North by Northwest*, titled in Spanish *Con la muerte en los talones*, roughly 'with death on your heels'. The film was infinitely better received than *Vertigo* had been. The regular festival reviewer in *Triunfo* gushed that the film was 'bomba-rebomba' ('the bomb, the double bomb) as well as 'pure cinema', the epithet used to praise the French New Wave. All predictions were for it to receive the grand prize, the Golden Shell. When *The Nun's Story* won Gold and *North by Northwest* won Silver, critics wrote that it was Hitchcock's usual unjust fate in award ceremonies. Nonetheless, because *North by Northwest* had played San Sebastián, this classic action film gained enduring notoriety in Spain. This time the film's glamorous cast received more attention than Hitchcock did in the press.

Significantly at San Sebastián *North by Northwest* was shown uncut in V.O., 'versión original' – that is, in English with Spanish subtitles. It would be another six months until *Con la muerte en los talones*, the dubbed and censored version, came out in the rest of the country. But the news of Eva Marie Saint's kisses in *North by Northwest* coincided with the general opening in Spain of Hitchcock's earlier films, specifically *La ventana indiscreta* (*Rear Window*). In this way the Hitchcock blondes – Eva Marie Saint and Grace Kelly – merged into one image of desire.

Issues of *Triunfo* (1955), an important Spanish film journal of the period, show how this played out in a piece entitled 'Grace: Se quitó los guantes blancos' ('Grace: She took off her white gloves'). Grace Kelly was not yet the restrained princess of Monaco at that time, but rather another star whose love life sold magazines. She is shown in slacks suggestively from low angle with a leg up on a sideboard, as the caption reads: 'Grace, in an absolutely informal pose, but not one that makes her lose that dignity which is the key to the difference between her and the common canon of stars.'

One cannot underestimate the enduring importance of the magazine *Hola* and glossies like it to Spanish popular culture. Even if people did not go to the movies, they flipped through *Hola*'s celebrity and royal photos. Accordingly, the ending of *Rear Window* when Grace Kelly puts down Jeff's (James Stewart) adventure book and picks up her fashion magazine after he dozes off resonated with Spanish culture, and I would argue with the reception of Hitchcock's films initially, to embrace Hitchcock's films for Hollywood glamour, style, gossip and witty sexual innuendo, as much as, if not more than for adventure.

IX. THE RIGHT MAN IN *THE WRONG MAN*: HITCHCOCK WITHIN THE CATHOLIC MORAL FRAMEWORK

On 15 December 1964 *Film Ideal*, a major film weekly, put a suntanned image of a pensive and formidable Hitchcock on a film set on its cover with the text, 'Again the round face of Alfred Joseph Hitchcock presides over this second issue dedicated to his greater glory and comprehension' as it published a major retrospective of his work in two issues. Hitchcock was virtually enshrined as a god. The language, 'to his

An informal Grace Kelly from *Triunfo* (1955)

greater glory', was ecclesiastic. The lead article by Félix Martialay, who founded *Film Ideal* in 1956, entitled 'Alienación: Verdad y aparencia' ('Alienation: Truth and Appearance') analyses Hitchcock's work in a Catholic framework. The captions to the film stills that illustrate the piece and clue the reader into Martialay's tridentine approach are almost laughable as film criticism: *Psycho* 'conciencia' ('conscience'), *The Birds* 'confesión' ('confession'), and *North by Northwest* 'milagro' ('miracle'). No one writes about these films in such terms today. Yet in 1964 when *Marnie* was released, close on the heels of *The Birds*, an enormous commercial success in Spain, the moral positioning of Hitchcock's films within Catholicism presented a concern. Martialay writes:

> Non-Catholics, they say, invented conversations with the psychiatrist. Hitchcock, immersed in an evidently decristianised world, frequently plays a double game. Psychiatry and sacramental confession form the body of the catharsis. But in Hitchcock confession, even without being sacramental, takes on a similar value. Only the character that confesses the truth to another – or to the audience – sets himself free; because confession is an encounter with oneself, an encounter with Grace, through sincerity and recognition of guilt. Only confession restores the character's unity, infusing life into the death of the alienated being. (1964: 829)

It is not that these kinds of comments were not part of the discussion of Hitchcock in other parts of the world, too. However, as we define what the tenor of the initial public reception to Hitchcock was in Spain we should recognise the strong imprint of Catholic ideology in his reception there. The vast majority of his films opened under Franco.

Comments on Hitchcock's politics or religion, particularly on his having been raised Catholic, is not something we would generally expect to find in newspaper reviews. However, as noted in *ABC* his film *Falso Culpable* (*The Wrong Man*) was screened in the inaugural session of the IV International Week of Religious Cinema in Valladolid. Cecil B. de Mille's *Ten Commandments* (1956) was the closing film. The announcement in *ABC* of the festival, full of official titles, read as follows: 'With the assistance of local authorities, representatives of national and foreign cinema and more than two hundred participants that during this week will engage in conversations about Catholic cinema, the IV International Week of Religious Cinema, organised by the Provincial Delegation of Information and Tourism in collaboration with the Catholic Office of Motion Pictures and the National Ecclesiastical Delegation of Cinema, was inaugurated this afternoon in the Palace of the Holy Cross' (7 April 1959: 59). In Valladolid, historically one of the most conservative regions in Spain, Hitchcock's work was accepted, and promoted not just as religious, but as Catholic.

Another Hitchcock film that was singled out for moral interpretation was, as one would expect from the title, *Yo confieso* (*I Confess*). Interestingly, although Donald, the regular *ABC* reviewer who had first seen the film at Cannes, found the film worthy of Hitchcock's autheurial reputation, he thought the story overall was a little bleak and heavy going:

> I pointed out at the time that the characteristic style of Hitchcock was present in his effort and that the film reflected the anguish of the story, centred on the secret of confession kept by a priest, on whom a criminal casts suspicions about having committed the murder that he confessed to him. The atmosphere at every moment is dense, and the situations sombre, in keeping with the plot and its tone.
>
> Hitchcock is, naturally, the great director as always, but the book that he is dealing with, the adaptation that the images translate, is what, to my judgment, is a little tedious. (26 February 1954: 30)

X. DELAYED OPENINGS, CULTURAL CONVERGENCES

Hitchcock's work was constantly reexamined, reframed, each time another one of his films debuted. Hitchcock's most notable trips to Spain were made in conjunction with the promotional tours associated with film festivals. When *Vertigo* debuted in San Sebastián, *Rear Window* re-opened for another run in

Madrid. This was a common strategy for Paramount that had produced and was marketing both films. *Rear Window* had debuted in 1955 at the same time as one of the most significant Spanish films of the Franco period, Juan Antonio Bardem's *Muerte de un ciclista* (*Death of a Cyclist*, 1955). *Fotogramas* featured parallel, competing reviews of the two films. The photos which illustrated the reviews suggest a dialogue, too, in how they position Lucia Bosé, the protagonist of *Death of a Cyclist*, on the phone, and Hitchcock with head turned in her direction, speaking.

Although in the film Bosé is only troubled by what she hears on the phone – that is, either that someone knows that she abandoned the scene of a fatal accident, or that she is having an affair – *Fotogramas* depicts her smiling. Indeed Jaime Lucas's review of her film, 'La estética funcional de "Muerte de un ciclista"' ('The functional aesthetics of "Death of a Cyclist"') is not only far more laudatory than Luis Gomez Mesa's of *Rear Window*, 'Alfred Hitchcock, maestro del sensacionalismo' ('Alfred Hitchcock, master of sensationalism'), but also implies that Bardem, 'the most interesting and transcendental filmmaker of our cinema', has won the duel because of superior artistry and more profound themes. This really presents an unfair comparison between two cinematographic masterpieces with lasting impacts in world cinema. However, because *Rear Window* is used in this context to elevate national cinema against the perennial hits of

Layout in *Fotogramas* suggesting a dialogue between *Death of a Cyclist* and *Rear Window*.

Hollywood, Gomez Mesa is forced to criticise Hitchcock in *Rear Window*, and moreover throughout his career beginning with his British period, to which Gomez Mesa first refers, for a lack of content, for being 'sensationalist':

> And this melodramatic, 'Gran-Guignolesque' play of shocking the nerves of spectators – those who are easily excitable and impressionable and some who are not – to the point of exaggeration, has allowed him to rely primordially on technique in such a way, with such exceptional expertise, that he is allowed all sorts of conventionalisms and childish acts that are not accepted from others. This is a privilege that is uniquely conceded to those of recognised mastery in their specialty, and the other title that Alfred Hitchcock, 'the man who knows too much technique', has earned is this one: 'master of sensationalism'. (30 September 1955: 23)

Gomez Mesa expresses a good deal of disdain towards the easily excitable fans of Hitchcock's technical prowess, too. Although he finally admits *Rear Window* is well crafted, or at least supremely watchable – 'No pierde en ningún instante su cardinal nota de interés' ('It doesn't lose its fundamental attraction at any moment') – somehow one gets the feeling Gomez Mesa isn't someone who would admit to enjoying 'puerilidades' ('childish acts') like spying on Miss Torso's dance. It is important to remember that *Rear Window* was known by its Spanish title *La ventana indiscreta*, the indiscreet window, which already implied a moral judgement towards exhibitionism and voyeurism. *La ventana indiscreta* continues to circulate today as the title of a Spanish TV gossip show on La Sexta.[14] Even though the negative critique of Hitchcock as sensationalist is not uncommon, taking the ingenuity and joy out of the experience of *Rear Window* seems more than a little harsh. This perspective is part and parcel of the criticism of Hitchcock as 'commercial'. What is important here is to see specifically how Hitchcock's films were received in the specific cultural landscape, as opposed to a national melodrama such as *Death of a Cyclist*.

As discussed earlier, Hitchcock visited the San Sebastián Film Festival twice, however he also stopped in Spain on promotional tours for other films, for example in 1956 after *The Man Who Knew Too Much* had played Cannes. Commenting on Hitchcock's visit to Madrid, the *ABC* cultural critic first lists the Hitchcock films he considers most important – *The Thirty-nine Steps*, *Secret Agent*, *Jamaica Inn*, *Rebecca*, *Suspicion*, *The Shadow of a Doubt*, *Lifeboat*, *I Confess*, *Rear Window* – then observes that Hitchcock was unjustly denied the Cannes prize for best director, concluding: 'But Alfred Hitchcock is above however many prizes and distinctions they could award him' (27 June 1956: 52). When *The Man Who Knew Too Much* finally opened in Madrid three years after Hitchcock's stopover, Donald, writing in *ABC* and altogether a much greater Hitchcock fan than Gomez Mesa, praised 'the effects of surprise' and 'the mastery in its development' (26 July 1960).

With these lists and retrospectives the different facets of Hitchcock as *auteur* came into clearer view. Again and again Hitchcock was perceived as a stylist. This is seen, for instance, in a review of *The Birds* in *La Vanguardia*. The reviewer complains that the film disappointed him because it did not have the suspense and surprise he expected, or even a satisfactory resolution to the plot, but begrudgingly he lauds the film's artistic style as characteristic of Hitchcock. Newspapers reported on the huge crowds, lines around the block for the opening, the very image of Hitchcock as a commercial success.

The following chart, a composite of the previous ones in the chapter, shows that 41 of Hitchcock's 53 films were screened in Spain during his lifetime. It allows a better overall view of the delayed releases, sequencing, and the overlapping of theatrical showings of Hitchcock's films in Spain.

Spanish Title	Original Title	Spanish Release	Original Release
De mujer a mujer	*Woman to Woman*	Nov. 1927	1923
Champagne	*Champagne*	April 1929	August 1928
El enemigo de las rubias	*The Lodger*	March 1930	Sept. 1926
El Ring	*The Ring*	July 1930	Oct. 1927
La muchacha de Londres	*Blackmail*	March 1931	June 1929
Valses de Viena	*Waltzes from Vienna*	July 1935	1933
El hombre que sabía demasiado	*The Man Who Knew Too Much*	Nov. 1935	Dec. 1934
Treinta y nueve escalones	*The Thirty Nine Steps*	Jan. 1936	Sept. 1935
Agente secreto	*Secret Agent*	Nov. 1939	Jan. 1936
Posada Jamaica	*Jamaica Inn*	Feb. 1941	May 1939
Alarma en el expreso	*The Lady Vanishes*	March 1942	Oct. 1938
Rebeca	*Rebecca*	Dec. 1942	March 1940
Matrimonio especial	*Mr. and Mrs. Smith*	Sept. 1943	Jan. 1941
Sospecha	*Suspicion*	Dec. 1943	March 1940

Inocencia y juventud	Young and Innocent	July 1944	Nov. 1937
Enviado especial	Foreign Correspondent	Dec. 1944	August 1940
Sombra de una duda	Shadow of a Doubt	Jan. 1945	Jan. 1943
Sabotaje	Saboteur	Dec. 1945	April 1942
Recuerda	Spellbound	Sept. 1946	Oct. 1945
Naúfragos	Lifeboat	July 1947	Jan. 1944
Encadenados	Notorious	Oct. 1948	July 1946
La soga	Rope	Nov. 1951	August 1948
Atormentada	Under Capricorn	Nov. 1952	Sept. 1949
Yo confieso	I Confess	Feb. 1954	Feb. 1953
Crimen perfecto	Dial M for Murder	Dec. 1954	April 1954
Ventana indiscreta	Rear Window	Oct. 1955	July 1954
Atrapa a un ladrón	To Catch a Thief	Nov. 1958	July 1955
Falso culpable	The Wrong Man	June 1959	Dec. 1956
De entre los muertos	Vertigo	June 1959	May 1958
Con la muerte en los talones	North by Northwest	Dec. 1959	July 1959
El hombre que sabía demasiado	The Man Who Knew Too Much	July 1960	May 1956
Pero...¿Quién mató a Harry?	The Trouble with Harry	Nov. 1960	Oct. 1955
Psicosis	Psycho	April 1961	June 1960
Pánico en la escena	Stage Fright	June 1961	Feb. 1950
Los pájaros	The Birds	Oct. 1963	March 1963
Marnie, la ladrona	Marnie	Oct. 1964	June 1964
Cortina rasgada	Torn Curtain	April 1967	July 1966
El caso Paradine	The Paradine Case	July 1967	Dec. 1947
Topaz	Topaz	Nov. 1970	Dec. 1969
Frenesí	Frenzy	Dec. 1972	May 1972

La trama	Family Plot	Oct. 1976	March 1976
Blackmail, Murder, Number Seventeen, Rich and Strange		V. O., 10 Dec. 1981	
La mujer solitaria	Sabotage	V.O., 4 August 1983	

As can be seen from the chart, not all of Hitchcock's films were picked up immediately for distribution in Spain. In several cases their openings were timed to piggyback on the success of other Hitchcock films. *¿Pero... Quién mató a Harry?* (*The Trouble with Harry*, 1960), one of Hitchcock's few ensemble pictures as we can see from from how the *ABC* illustrator represented four cast members rather than the customary pair, was released shortly after *Psycho*. Donald in *ABC* remarked not only on the delay and the correct Hitchcock chronology but also observed 'la película conserva su fragancia del primer día' ('The movie kept its fragrance of the first day'). This 'fragrance', or original freshness, consisted overwhelmingly of humour, as Donald wrote: 'From what he presents in this film we would compare Hitchcock to an exceptional juggler who might combine the skill of his amazing ability with a no less amazingly developed sense of humour' (15 November 1960: 70).

Donald celebrated the tone of the film: 'And all the film, in spite of the dead body, which is ever-present for the characters as much as for the audience, if not materially at every moment then certainly in spirit, is optimistic, happy, full of humorous and funny features' (ibid.). Donald praised *Atrapa a un ladrón* (*To Catch a Thief*), another film delayed in Spain, later in Hitchcock's career for the same sense of humour:

> *To Catch a Thief* was shown in the 'Mostra' of Venice in 1955. Hitchcock, the magician of suspense, who always likes to mix it with humour, even in passages that could seem amongst the more dramatic ones of his endeavors, had rather increased the doses of humour in that movie, which now has opened here in the Lope de Vega cinema. In fact this unequalled filmmaker plays with jokes and intrigue and revels in portraying characters whose conventionality, when it's there, we forget about since they seem so convincing. (18 November 1958: 60)

Likewise the remake of *The Man Who Knew Too Much*, which Donald praised highly for 'mastery in its development' through 'an extremely skillful play of contrasts', opened with a considerable four-year delay from its first notice in

Cannes. Most of these delays were lamented but had little to do with the film's subject matter. The exception, however, was *La soga* (*Rope*, 1948), Hitchcock's first film in colour, which only opened decades after it did in the US, as noted by César Santos Fontela in '"*La soga*", más allá del alarde técnico' ('"*Rope*," beyond the technical display') (*Blanco y Negro*, 1 August 1999: 41). The film's innovative aesthetics were less of a commercial concern than its representation of homosexuality.

Not every film kept its freshness after a considerable delay. According to Félix Martialay writing in *Film Ideal* this was the case for *Pánico en la escena* (*Stage Fright*, 1950). It opened in June 1961, right after *Psycho* did in Madrid in April of that year, but eleven years after the film's US release. Martialay uses the opportunity to review the salient characteristics of successful Hitchcock films:

> Another Hitchcock on Spanish screens. A Hitchcock with nothing less than eleven years of delay. And you can really tell it. Because the fat little English director has sufficiently evolved to have perfected his tricks to the maximum, as happens in 'Psycho'. In this movie, 'Stage Fright', you see this too much. The whole film is a big trick, in which, to my judgement, those drops of humour, which console the spectator when his leg is pulled, are missing. There certainly isn't so much of that here and the trick used stands out. Then it's the spectator who goes wrong on his own, effectively helped through the double subjective/objective role of the camera. (1961: 29)

First for Martialay, a good Hitchcock film has humour, and second, suspense, which in *Stage Fright* 'está muy tamizado, muy difumado' ('is very filtered out, very toned down') in a revelation made too obvious by the shift between subjective and objective camera shots. The third characteristic of good Hitchcock is psychologically complicated, yet believable characters:

> The eleven-year gap from other Hitchcock films is evident in the absence of human beings, of persons, with a psychology that, deviant or not, is always within the range of human types. Also missing is that normal man on whom abnormal, but believable circumstances accumulate. A great deal of the best Hitchcock is missing. (Ibid.)

Fourth, 'good' Hitchcock has a wrong man plot, and fifth, Maritalay adds, a quirky Hitchcockian mother, the only 'good' element *Stage Fright* does have, for 'the character of Eva's mother, for example, is a delicious type "made in" Hitchcock' (ibid.). Likewise, Martialay does grant, six, the presence of excellent narrative structure:

> In formal values Hitchcock has not varied in the most minimal manner.
> It has the same descriptive freshness and narrative flow that we have been
> seeing in his recent creations. Also the dialogues have his ironic stamp. The
> rest, nothing. Trash. (Ibid.)

What Martialay dismisses as 'vulgaridad' (trash) or 'bad' Hitchcock is best explained by his conclusion to the review:

> The movie runs and finds its end in its entertainment. With forays more
> or less into crudeness, centered on the character of Charlotte/Marlene, the
> major subject of them. The inconsistency of the characters makes the actors
> take on a conventional air, of amusement about their job. And they ably
> fulfill their puppet roles with which the director is playing. Only Marlene
> takes it seriously, and that is just what it seems that Hitchcock intended.
> (Ibid.)

It would be a good wager to say that Marlene Dietrich's sultry stage number
'I'm the Laziest Girl in Town', which she sings slipping on and off a divan,
probably kept the film out of Spanish movie theatres for those eleven odd
years. It actually kept Marlene Dietrich on the world stage, however, as it
became the signature number of her stage show for the rest of her career. This
naughty number, which provocatively slides in its implications from 'lazy'
to 'loose woman' or prostitute, cannot have pleased the censors. Martialay
is indeed right to criticise *Stage Fright*. Hitchcock himself found plenty in it
to criticise to Truffaut – he used a flashback that was a lie, the actors when
playing aside Dietrich were too insecure, and especially the villain is not vil-
lainous or dangerous enough. As Hitchcock expounds: 'The great weakness
of the picture is that it breaks an unwritten law: The more successful the
villain, the more successful the picture. That's a cardinal rule, and in this picture the villain was a flop!' (Truffaut 1984: 191). In his review of Hitchcock's
'flop' Martialay gave a good overview of what the Spanish public came to
expect from Hitchcock. Still he never tries to explain the reasons for the elev-
en-year delay. Perhaps it was due to the assessment that the film had weak
characterisation, or more likely, one morally deficient, erotically charged
character. Interestingly a Latin stereotype is at play in her characterisation in
Stage Fright. Charlotte (Dietrich) in the dressing room after her steamy stage
show lets Jonathan, her husband's killer, who is covering up any complicity of
Charlotte in the murder, know he is only a passing fancy to her, that theirs is
not a long-term relationship, by suggesting he flee to South America where she
may join him 'for a week or two'.

X. ANOTHER CONVERGENCE: HITCHCOCK PRESENTS TELEVISION

Finally one cannot underestimate the importance of Hitchcock on television from the late 1950s onwards as that medium began to make inroads in Spanish households as a rival to the movies for entertainment. Hitchcock's show, *Alfred Hitchcock Presents*, had as big an impact in Spain as it did in the US. In general the impact of American television series and movies was magnified in Spain because the national production was so paltry in comparison. Norberto Alcover's edited anthology *La cultura española durante el franquismo* (Spanish Culture During Franco's Era, 1977) lists imported television series and foreign films as the first two major categories of programming on Spanish television during the years of the dictatorship. Though it concentrates on the American context, a book by the Spanish Hitchcock scholar José Luis Castro de la Paz, *El surgimiento del telefilme: Los años cincuenta y la crisis de Hollywood: Alfred Hitchcock y la televisión* (The Rise of the Television Program: The Fifties and the Crisis in Hollywood: Alfred Hitchcock and Television, 1999) studies all of Hitchcock's TV episodes. Hitchcock's physical image and his dry wit in introducing each episode of the TV programme were ubiquitous and well known. This was also the style of some of the most well known trailers to Hitchcock's films, which were also shown in Spanish movie theatres, namely the house tour for *Psycho* and the pitch for a holiday abroad for *North by Northwest*. Moreover, many viewers first saw Hitchcock's films on TV. *La cultura española durante el franquismo*, one of the first and most important books to evaluate the cultural landscape in Spain under Franco from the perspective of the post-Franco era, lauds how television elevated the artistic sensibilities of the Spanish public through its film programming, and the nasal-voiced film critiques of Alfonso Sánchez Martínez:[15]

> Thanks to Spanish television one saw movies in this country and one learned, something in itself, to appreciate quality. Cinephiles owe a lot to the polyps and stutterings of Alfonso Sánchez. To the auteur and actor cycles, *Cine-Forum* on Channel Two and the pleasing surprises that popped up suddenly among the four thousand movies that TVE programmed in its history, the country owes the distinction of a general improvement in artistic sensibility, which is a good way to make culture. (Alcover 1977: 217)

Hitchcock himself said that he filmed most of certain movies, *Dial M for Murder* and *Psycho* for example, just like TV programmes, with the notable exception of some sequences. Although *Alfred Hitchcock Presents* was shown on the second Spanish channel rather than on the main State number one, it still was a regular feature on television under Franco. This did not diminish its acceptance, or that of television in general. At the time even *Film Ideal*, which as its title indicates aspired to represent an ideal world, looked on television as supporting Catholic values. First quoting Pious XII, José María García Escudero argues against those who might find television dangerous. He supports television spectatorship as the healthy, moral alternative to the movies: 'On the other hand, television is viewed at home, in half-light, surrounded by family, or in a bar or café, and its most basic technique impedes the characteristic alienation of the movies' (1961: 18). We will comment on the influences of Hitchcock's television series on Almodóvar and on De la Iglesia in those respective chapters of this book.

XI. GROUNDWORK AND GAPS

Hitchcock came to be seen as a magician, or even a god, of filmmaking in Spain. The more he symbolised American life and modern aesthetics – with colour film, television or rapid cutting – the more popular his work became. This upward trajectory began with his crossover film *Rebecca*. The film was embraced as new aesthetics in Barcelona, as a representation of the region's oppositional stance to the dictatorship's cultural conservatism. Because Hitchcock's films could be taken lightly, due to the balance of humour and suave glamour within the structure of suspense and intrigue, they most often passed censors and entertained the masses. Although the spy stories could have been interpreted as metaphors for real life wartime or post-war situations, the allegory could also be ignored. Likewise psychoanalytical dilemmas could be, and were, reframed in terms of hegemonic Catholic morality. Inconvenient representations of nudity in *Psycho* and suicide in *Lifeboat* were cut; still the impact of *Psycho* was strong and long lasting. Its aesthetics were cutting edge and its production values attainable. Although some representations of homosexuality were kept from distribution, as in the case of *Rope* (whose plot never constituted especially gripping film anyhow), other representations of sexuality either passed the filters of the censors, as with *Rebecca*, or as with *North by Northwest* became known by reputation in the reviews from film festivals where the original versions were screened. As we have emphasised, at the height of his career Hitchcock premiered *Vertigo* and *North by Northwest* in Spain, and the former film engaged with the surrealist groundwork of Dalí and Buñuel. Even though the Spanish public was not impressed at first showing, in line with the film's initial tepid reception in most countries, it has come to embrace its native son's work.[16] The chase movie *North by Northwest*, however, was an immediate hit, mostly because of its scenes of healthy sexuality, in the famous train sequence, among others. Reviewing the 50th anniversary DVD edition and remastering of the film for the *New*

York Times, Charles Taylor calls *North by Northwest* paradoxically the 'most American of Hitchcock's American films' as well as 'the most British of his American films' because of 'Hitchcock's affectionate and absurd vision of the bigness of his adopted country' (1 November 2009). The monumental scale of the New World, a European version of America, loomed as an unassailable challenge to future 'Latin Hitchcocks'. These were the elements of the reception of Hitchcock in Spain in its secondary, dubbed release. The films fit into the moral framework of the times, but suggestively produced a yearning for something else, if only the glamour and the glitz.

The gaps or omissions in the reception history in this chapter may well prove more significant than what I have detailed here. Questions remain, for instance, regarding how much and when British Hitchcock was shown in Spain. Concentrating on Spain, then Madrid, then even the reviews in one newspaper, *ABC*, brings only a small part of the Hitchcock reception history into sharper focus against an ideologically charged milieu. Hindsight reveals bloopers, such as dismissing *Vertigo* as second rate, or calling *Young and Innocent* Hitchcock's first American film, as well as hegemonic limitations. Hitchcock retrospectives in Spain have corrected many of these errors. Nonetheless in laying the groundwork for our study of Latin Hitchcocks, we have seen how in Spain humour, moral tone and aesthetic innovation figured in the initial response to his films, but also how that fascination for fashion and sexual innuendo stood out again and again. The survey of some contemporary sources and the resulting charts chronicle the magnitude of the reception history of Hitchcock in Spain. Similar surveys and charts do not yet exist for Latin American capitals. Time limits my own ability, though not my desire, to explore the details of the reception history for all major Latin American capital cities, where in most cases Hitchcock was shown in the original language at the film's first release. In chapter five we will explore this history for Mexico City; other cities remain areas, among many others, for further research.

NOTES

1   Hitchcock also visited Spain as a tourist in June 1956. His presence in Madrid was noted with a brief biography in *ABC* that ends commenting on his lack of festival prizes: 'This year he presented his second version of *The Man Who Knew Too Much* at the Cannes International Film Festival, with which he ought to have won the prize for best director, which was given to the director of the Russian movie *Othello*. But Alfred Hitchcock is above however many prizes and awards they could give him' (27 June 1956: 52).
     Perhaps this positive note encouraged Hitchcock to return to Spain to present his films in competition there.

2   In the US real estate agents say that in evaluating a property it all comes down to 'location, location'.

3   See the photo captioned 'Hitchcock sizes up San Francisco's Mission Dolores' in Dan Aulier (1998) *Vertigo: The Making of a Hitchcock Classic*. New York: St. Martin's Press, xvii.

4   See Sidney Gottlieb (1997) 'The Unknown Hitchcock: *Watchtower over Tomorrow*,' *Hitchcock Annual (1996–97)*. Based on his own research into the Edward R. Stettinius papers, McGilligan expands on Gottlieb's findings about the fate of this film: 'Although some published sources indicate that Hitchcock may eventually have shot a couple of scenes for the short film, ultimately titled *Watchtower over Tomorrow*, John Cromwell was credited as director. Whether it was ever shown publicly is uncertain. As with his war work for England, this quasi-Hitchcock film for the US State Department not only bucked conventional politics, but went unreported for years' (2003: 368–9). In short, Hitch's cinematographic language was not diplomatic enough; his ideas were 'too hard-hitting' (ibid.).

5   The idea for the Mexican came from Somerset Maugham's short stories 'The Hairless Mexican' and 'The Traitor' in his collection *Ashendon*, or *The British Agent*, upon which the movie is distantly based (see McGilligan 2003: 178).

6   In his book Fernández Cuenca publishes only his transcription in Spanish of Hitchcock's interview. There is no record of Hitchcock's actual words in English. To emphasise that the English words are mine, not Hitchcock's, I have included the Spanish in the text.

7   Future research would have to focus on other sources, such as the VHS and DVD copies of Hitchcock films, those of the dubbed copies, when available, and compare them with the original versions. US Hitchcock archives, as well as those of the US production companies, are possible research venues.

8   Some forbearance towards censorship in the years of decline before Franco's death in 1975 was symptomatic of 'la dictablanda' or soft dictatorship as the period was called. R. Moreno Alba's *Pepita Jiménez* and José Luis Borau's *Furtivos*, two movies that debuted in 1975 but were in production well before it, are emblematic of the era. Both showed bare breasts. *Diccionario del cine español* calls *Furtivos* (*Poachers*) 'the key film of the political effervescence that Spain was living while Francoism was agonising and the country was moving towards democracy' (Borau 1998: 381).

9   In his acceptance speech for the Best Director Academy Award for *The Departed* (2006) Scorsese quipped, 'Could you please double-check the envelope?', then referring to being pursued by the moniker of also-ran: 'I'm so moved. So many people over the years have been wishing this for me. Strangers – I go into doctors' offices, elevators, I go for an X-ray – they say, "You should win one"' (David M. Halbfinger and Sharon Waxman, '*The Departed* Wins Best Picture, Scorsese Best Director,' *New York Times*, 26 February 2007). Hitchcock, the other famously snubbed director, as documented in numerous online lists and blogs, was definitely on Scorsese's mind during this period. Most interestingly, he channelled Hitchcock in a humorous, Spanish context. He made *The Key to Reserva* (*La clave de la Reserva*, 2007), a Christmas short film commercial for Freixenet, the Spanish champagne company, as false documentary and satire of his Hitchcock cinephilia. On camera in the film Scorsese declares his premise, 'to preserve a Hitchcock film that was not made'. The commercial alludes to many of Hitchcock's films, including *The Man Who Knew Too Much*, *Notorious*, *Psycho* and *North by Northwest*. Before cutting to a shot of hundreds of perched blackbirds at the film's end Scorsese wryly says, 'I feel that Hitchcock is looking over my shoulder. I hope that he takes it in the right spirit.' Besides being shown on Spanish TV, *The Key to Reserva* was an enormous online hit globally. When asked at the film's Madrid launch if he felt publicity was art, he deflected the question by replying, 'After making movies for 37 years, I'm not even sure if what I make is art' (Pablo Guimón, 'De las malas calles a Freixenet,' *El País*, 27 November 2007; translation mine).

10   'Kim Novak por partida doble: Un concurso presidido por Salvador Dalí, que alegró la noche barcelonesa de San Juan' ('Kim Novak through double entry: A contest presided over by Salvador Dalí, which brightened up Barcelona's St. John's Night'), *Triunfo* 698, 2 July 1959: 23.

11   Almodóvar remade Penelope Cruz in the image of Hepburn for *Los abrazos rotos* (*Broken Embraces*, 2009).

12   See William Cook, 'The Master and Murnau,' *The Guardian*, 27 February 2009.

13   The Austrian actor Christoph Waltz, in saying he was 'über-happy' to accept the Best Actor Academy Award for his role as Colonel Hans Landa in *Inglourious Basterds* (2009), playfully emphasised his role as polyglot, an exception in English-dominant Hollywood. The remark also recalled the language code shifting in Tarantino's film that creates Hitchcockian suspense. In the opening scene Colonel Landa shifts between German, French and English as he interviews the farmer Perrier LaPadite. Landa changes to English to make LaPadite reveal (to Landa and the audience, but not to the helpless victims, called 'rats' in the film) that he is harboring a Jewish refugee family beneath the floorboards of the home. When the Nazi colonel changes again to gentile banter in French, he gestures to his soldiers where to shoot into the floor. *Inglourious Basterds* alludes to Hitchcock in many ways. Shosanna, the daughter who escapes this massacre, assumes another identity as a French owner of a cinema. In this role as a French woman owner of a cinema with a desire for revenge, she recalls Mrs. Verloc from Hitchcock's *Sabotage*.

14   'Telecinco ficha por sorpresa a la reportera de La Sexta Pilar Rubio' ('Channel Five accidentally catches Pilar Rubio, reporter for Channel Six'), *El mundo*, 13 Nov. 2009.

15   In 1959 Alfonso Sánchez Martínez (1911–1981), a popular journalist, film critic and Hitchcock fan, began a long career of reviewing foreign and national movies on TV shows, such as *Punto de vista, El Antena and Panorama de actualidad*, even as he continued writing reviews for major newspapers and film magazines. In 1972 he published *Iniciación al cine moderno* (Introduction to Modern Cinema). His distinctive nasal voice and perpetual cigarette in hand made him a frequent subject of comedic parodies in an era when it was illegal to satirise political figures. To hear Sánchez, listen to the RTVE archive http://www.rtve.es/alacarta/audios/archivo-sonoro/archivo-sonoro-alfonso-sanchez-13–02–10/694382/ (accessed 20 February 2014) or see José Luis Garcí's short documentary, *Alfonso Sánchez* (1980).

16   For the US reception history see Dan Aulier (1998) 'Premiere and Beyond', in *Vertigo: The Making of a Hitchcock Classic*, 162–87. Aulier describes the Latin-inflected scandal, which the Spaniards would term 'intrigue', that 'figured prominently' in press reports after *Vertigo*'s premiere in San Francisco. Kim Novak had accepted the gift of a Mercedes Benz from Lt. Gen. Rafael Trujillo, Jr., son of the leader/dictator of the Dominican Republic, whom she was dating; at that same moment Congress was debating increasing aid to the Dominican Republic (1998: 169).

CHAPTER TWO

Pedro Almodóvar's Criminal Side: Plot, Humour and Cinematic Style

I. INTRODUCTION: SELF-EDUCATION VIA HITCHCOCK

Much has been written about the impact of Hollywood classics on Pedro Almodóvar's corpus of works.[1] Almodóvar himself has responded to interview questions citing admiration for specific examples of 'Golden Age' Hollywood, to the extent that even he discusses choosing an aesthetic, 'la más *hollywoodiense* de todas' ('the most Hollywood-like of all'), for *Tacones Tejanos* (*High Heels*, 1991) (Strauss 1995: 131). An extensive interview by Lynn Hirschberg in the *New York Times Magazine*, which appeared before the screening of *La Mala educación* (*Bad Education*) at the New York Film Festival, exemplifies the placing of Almodóvar in world film history. Hitchcock is not first on the list, nor the first name out of his mouth, yet Stephen Holden of the *New York Times* and many Spanish critics noted the presence of Hitchcock in *Bad Education*. V. A. Musetto's observation in the *NY Post* – 'From the Hitchcockian opening credits to the final frame, Almodóvar has Hitch on his mind' – served as one of the major advertising blurbs for the film (*New York Times*, 11 December 2004). It is time, then, to look back at how signs of Hitchcock have been present throughout Almodóvar's *oeuvre*, as we will see that Hitchcock was Almodóvar's primary textbook and industrial model. Even after the global success of *Mujeres al borde de un ataque de nervios* (*Women on the Verge of a Nervous Breakdown*, 1988) established him as a major filmmaker, Almodóvar continued to study and learn from Hitchcock's films.

It is important to remember that among contemporary Spanish directors Almodóvar is not a product of film school, or even of a fine arts education (as was Bigas Luna of the previous generation), but self-taught. He learned his craft experimenting with a Super-8 camera and watching movies. Hitchcock's films have been easily accessible on subtitled videos in Spain for a long time, and his reputation as an innovator, among the first to incorporate sound in *Blackmail* and to experiment with it as a stylistic element in that very first sound film, makes his work an undeniable reference point for learning the craft of filmmaking. Moreover, Hitchcock is one of the few financially successful masters with a long career to study. In *Alfred Hitchcock: A Life in Darkness and Light* Patrick McGilligan attempts to redress a more monstrous view of Hitch put forward by Donald Spoto in his earlier *Alfred Hitchcock: The Dark Side of Genius*. McGilligan stresses Hitchcock's success in the industry to reach this new balance concluding: 'Hitchcock was not only the ultimate film director; he also mastered the pitfalls and politics of studio filmmaking that dogged him both in England and in America, and emerged as the industry's consummate professional' (2003: 747).

These factors argue for Hitchcock's work being an essential reference point in Almodóvar's autodidactic cinematic education. In fact the title of Frédéric Strauss's collection of interviews, *Almodóvar: Un cine visceral* (Almodóvar: A visceral cinema), comes from Almodóvar's comment on his eclecticism in his movies due to his self-education: 'El ecleticismo en mis películas es algo como visceral que probablemente tiene que ver con el hecho de que yo no tengo una educación académica, no he aprendido cine en la escuela, lo que me da una especie de indisciplina y libertad' (1995: 39); ('Their eclectism is natural, instinctive. No doubt because I never had an adademic education, because I never went to film school, I've always remained undisciplined and free') (Strauss 2006: 25).[2] In the Strauss interviews Almodóvar mentions Hitchcock only cursorily when he discusses his early discovery of film classics. He cites *Vertigo* as the 'mother of many movies' in the session on *¿Qué he hecho yo para merecer esto!* (*What Have I Done to Deserve This?*, 1984) (1995: 61). Yet Hitchcock's name pops up at key moments of that text, from *Laberinto de pasiones* (*Labyrinth of Passion*, 1982) onwards. Almodóvar explains that when he came to Madrid he spent three years in the 1960s and early 1970s reading about film and screening films in the Filmoteca.[3] During this period he first saw John Ford's films, among other Hollywood classics, and Hitchcock's work and criticism of it is well represented in the Spanish film archives.

When Strauss, addressing the attention to spatial design in *Kika* (1993), suggests that Hitchcock is one of Almodóvar's favorite directors, Almodóvar's reply gives a historical perspective to his reception of Hitchcock:

Yes. And I forgot to mention him! His work is visually the richest in the history of cinema. I discovered Hitchcock when he started shooting in colour.

I was an adolescent at the time and simply considered him an entertaining director.[4] [...] Later, when I went back to see his films a second or third time, I started to understand the enormous genius operating behind each one of his images. Aesthetically, he's one of the greatest innovators. All the visual elements in his work are artfully and deliberately thought out by the director. (Strauss 1995: 143, 160)

Just as Almodóvar corrects himself to recover his self-education through Hitchcock, we too will explore how Hitchcock's aesthetics resurface throughout Almodóvar's career. This is more than a passing relationship. What is most intriguing is how it appears to have been marginalised, or repressed.

II. ALMODÓVAR'S GUILT COMPLEX: FROM *SPELLBOUND* TO *LABYRINTH OF PASSION*

The impact of Hitchcock on Almodóvar is profound and far-reaching. Hitchcock is a reference point from Almodóvar's earliest forays into film, in his cult movies depicting the *Movida*. When Strauss asks him to discuss the role of the psychoanalyst in *Labyrinth of Passion*, Almodóvar replies at length that Hitchcock's flashbacks to childhood were his reference point for his own parody of psychoanalytic explanations. It is worth looking at this exchange between Strauss and Almodóvar in detail. Almodóvar's self-construction via Strauss, his preferred chronicler, follows the interview model famously developed in the Truffaut-Hitchcock interviews. In bilingual sessions, Truffaut, who was Hitchcock's professional equal, prompted Hitchcock to assess his career trajectory in terms of aesthetics, industrial strategies and world film history. For publication the interviews were organized chronologically according to the release date of the first film mentioned in the chapter. By following this model, Strauss, as a non-Spanish or 'foreign' expert, positions Almodóvar for transnational recognition as a serious artist just as Truffaut had for Hitchcock. Strauss prompts:

One of the funniest characters in *Labyrinth of Passion* is the psychoanalyst. She has nothing to say about the psychology of the characters she sees. She comes across as a purely comedic character. One feels you liked her for herself and not for one moment do you take her seriously. (2006: 25)

Almodóvar responds:

Yes, my use both of the character and psychoanalysis is strictly parodic. I wanted to do something which, in fact, I still haven't dared do: to make

65

a parody of all those films – Hitchcock's included, which I like very much – where an elaborate flashback to the character's childhood attempts to explain the inexplicable. The two main characters of *Labyrinth of Passion* often speak of their nymphomania and I decided that they should do so to a psychoanalyst in order to show that this type of behavior has no explanation. That's my opinion, in any case. For certain scenes I used music by Béla Bartók very similar to Bernard Hermann's scores for Hitchcock. The flashbacks to childhood are some of my favorite parts of the film. (Ibid.)

We know from Hitchcock's own comments that he as well was none too fond of psychoanalysis (Peck's character calls it 'a lot of hooey' in *Spellbound*), telling Truffaut that *Spellbound* was 'another manhunt wrapped up in pseudo-psychoanalysis' and that he also railed against superfluous explication in film, preferring to create character through a layering of details. So we cannot look at Almodóvar as an accurate film historian in this passage. However, what is evident here is his deference to Hitchcock in his own development as a filmmaker, and his choice of Bartók to evoke the classic Hitchcock score at a critical juncture of *Labyrinth of Passion*. This is a conflation of several Hitchcock references, for his most famous representation of a female psychoanalyst is Dr. Constance Sedgwick, played by Ingrid Bergman, in *Spellbound*, whose score is by Academy Award-winner Miklós Rózsa. Hermann did not come on board as a composer for Hitchcock until the 1950s with *The Trouble with Harry*. Almodóvar may refer to Hermann's most famous score to *Psycho* or the thematic cueing of suspense in Rózsa's score to *Spellbound*. Significantly, the primacy of music for childhood flashbacks reappears in Almodóvar's films. Perhaps the strongest instance is the breathtaking 'Moon River' sequence in *Bad Education*.[5] Certainly in 2004 Almodóvar no longer dares to present the childhood flashback as a parody anymore. From a wiser, more compassionate perspective, childhood traumas are too deeply felt to be subject to this treatment. However, the coupling of strong music with these sequences has its origin in Almodóvar's appreciation of Hitchcock's style.

Almodóvar is being rather devious in his mention of Hitchcock in regard to *Labryrinth of Passion*, for the Hitchcockian inspiration is profound, and not only in the psychoanalyst sequence. It is embedded in the picture's title. In *Spellbound*, in the sixth sequence, late one evening, Dr. Sedgwick pulls a book from the asylum's library shelves. Its title is shown in close up – *Labyrinth of the Guilt Complex*. She uses the book, ostensibly written by the new asylum director, being impersonated by the false Dr. Edwardes (Gregory Peck), as a subterfuge to visit him in his room. At that moment she does not know he is an imposter. The book's autograph will be the key through which she finds him out.

The obnoxious Pittsburgh traveler tells Dr. Sedgwick (Ingrid Bergman) he knows she's a wife trying to find her husband in order to make up in *Spellbound*.

Their dialogue, at first about the book, turns into a confession of love, which then is masterfully punctuated by shots of a long corridor of a series of doors being opened. These shots represent a subjective reality of the couple. The leitmotif of psychoanalysis – opening doors – began the movie's intertitles. The more interesting analysis/interpretation in *Spellbound* is not retrospective then, but rather very present, in the passions of love, which is precisely Almodóvar's take on Hitchcock. *Spellbound* is a 'labyrinth of the passions', especially Sedgwick's passion for Ballantyne which overwhelms her 'reason' as psychoanalyst.

Further, in *Labyrinth of Passion* Almodóvar selects another important aspect of Hitchcock's *Spellbound* to parody, namely the psychoanalyst in the movie itself. Hitchcock in fact engages in a similar bit of mocking humor in the sequence entitled 'Pittsburgh in Manhattan'. Sedgwick is trying to track down Ballantyne who has fled to a Manhattan hotel because he was about to be unmasked as an imposter. When an obnoxious traveller from Pittsburgh approaches Sedgwick on the sofa of the hotel lobby, the house detective intervenes and throws him out. Both the Pittsburgh lout and the detective try to 'read her'. The detective congratulates himself for identifying her as a schoolteacher following her husband to make up after a tiff. He calls himself a psychologist, but of course gets everything wrong. Sedgwick plays along, to the pleasure of the audience, and gets the information she wants, the number of Ballantyne's hotel room. It is a classic Hitchcock moment, and a surprisingly feminist one as well, where the audience shares a joke with the female character. Indeed this sequence portrays a classic Hitchcock theme that domestic fiction not only passes as, but also is preferred to truth. Significantly Hitchcock's cameo also takes place in this same sequence.

At first glance Almodóvar's response to Strauss' citing Hitchcock in the discussion of *Labyrinth of Passion* seemed out of place from my original recollection of the film which centered on Almodóvar's 'cameo' – his crossdressing performance with call and response interaction that has given *Labyrinth* an extended life as a kind of Spanish version of *The Rocky Horror Picture Show* (1975) that emphasises audience participation in its kitsch world. Hitchcock's films are not an obvious referent, even in parody. However the inspiration of Hitchcock's films, especially of *Spellbound*, is pervasive in *Labyrinth of Passion*'s plot elements and leitmotifs. This does not detract from the recognition of Almodóvar's originality, or an appreciation of the incredible cultural chasm between the US in the 1950s and Spain in the early 1980s. Almodóvar not only takes on a female psychoanalyst, Susana (Orfelia Angélica), to echo Bergman's role, but he plays with Sedgwick's's most salient character trait in *Spellbound*, her initial frigidity. He inverts this by oversexing the female psychoanalyst, and further attributes the problematic Sedgwick frigidity to Sexilia's (Cecilia Roth) father, a doctor who specialises in artificial insemination to compensate for his own lack of libido.

Spellbound abounds in father figures in all the doctors: one, the murder victim, Edwardes; two, the old head doctor of Green Manors, who turns out to be Edwardes' murderer, whom critics have suggested was Hitchcock's private representation of, and hence revenge on, his psychoanalysis-obsessed producer David O. Selznick; three, Sedgwick's own first analyst, Dr. Bruhlo; and finally, the amnesiac John Ballantyne (Peck) whom Sedgwick first meets when he poses as Edwardes, the new head of the asylum. Hitchcock commented to Truffaut that he found *Spellbound* 'very confusing' (McGilligan 2003: 379). For Hitchcock, the guilt spread over *Spellbound* is of a dearth of testosterone that causes murder, even Ballantyne's 'accidental' childhood killing of his brother. For Almodóvar, the problem is displaced primarily onto the female characters, especially Sexilia, who is doubled/impersonated by the cleaner's daughter, just as Ballantyne doubled for Edwardes. Moreover, as Ballantyne cures Sedgwick of her lack of passion, so, too, the cleaner's daughter cures Sexilia's father of his. The similarities in plot are most interesting when seen combined with the repetition of motifs.

Sexilia seeks analysis due to photophobia; Ballantyne reveals his repressed guilt in trances provoked by whiteness. *Labyrinth of Passion* develops this parallel in the sequence in Tarfaya Salevi's (Helga Liné) hotel room as it builds towards Sexilia's flashback, the scene cited by the director in the above interview. In the dénouement Riza Niro (Imanol Arias) has just lost his virginity having sex with Tarfaya when Sexilia bursts into Riza's room to see her. Sexilia slumps onto a stool against the wall at her realisation of the incest.

The film cuts to a medium shot of Tarfaya's menacing face directing a mirror's beam of light toward Sexilia as the reflection of light whites out the frame. A reaction shot shows Sexilia with the light beam on her face vowing never to love again. Violin music, similar to the thematic strains associated with

Toraya's mirror beam used as a weapon in *Labyrinth of Passion*.

Sexilia with the light beam on her face in *Labyrinth of Passion*.

Sedgwick and Ballantyne in *Spellbound*, accompany Sexilia's next appearance, in a travelling shot as she runs to her psychoanalyst's office.

Eventually Sexilia's love for Riza will cure her of her photophobia, which is in turn a symptom of her nymphomania, just as Sedgwick's love cures Ballantyne of his whiteness trauma and guilt complex. In one of the more famous scenes of *Spellbound*, Ballantyne goes catatonic over the white light off the tracks in the winter snow streaming in the window of Dr. Bruhlo's office.

John Valentine (Gregory Peck) is transfixed by the blinding white light seen from the window in *Spellbound*.

In *Labyrinth of Passion*'s
flashback, Sexilia lies
buried in the sand, eyes
covered, as Toraya and
Riza move behind the
bushes to make out.

Sedgwick has identified 'white' as a clue to his illnes; the couple head off
to a ski resort to probe the repressed truth further. In *Labyrinth of Passion*
Almodóvar inverts the northern light world into a southern coastal beach sun.
At the psychoanalyst's office, Susana opens the curtains so that strong sun-
light falls on Sexilia who is seated against a white wall. The film flashes back
to Sexilia's childhood, where as a young girl she walks on a blindingly bright
beach. Ballantyne's brief childhood flashback reveals he killed his brother when
he slid down a banister and pushed the brother into impaling himself on an
iron fence. Sexilia's flashback is longer in duration and more elaborate; in the
flashback sequence Tarfaya pulls Riza away to make out with him behind the
bushes as Sexilia remains buried in the sand up to her armpits with her hands
covering her eyes.

In revenge Sexilia agrees to be 'la mujer de todos' ('the woman/wife of everyone') and in a game of house she engages with all the remaining adolescent
boys. The young Sexilia is only shown with her bathing suit strap unfastened.
Labryinth of Passion suggests but does not show adolescent sex, incestuous or
otherwise, but this taboo gives force to the film. In a sense, following Hitchcock's
paradigm allows Almodóvar to find and define cultural boundaries.

In the film's conclusion, Sexilia flees with Riza to Contadora Island in
Panama, the place of exile of the real Shah of Iran in 1979. In retrospect the
political context in *Labyrinth of Passion* of Islamic terrorists is prescient, especially given the early twenty-first century's global preoccupation with Islamic
militants. Likewise, at the moment of release of *Women on the Verge*, Candela's
problems with Shiites only sounded like some funny alliterative words uttered
by a fruitcake personality, whereas after the Iraq War (2003–2011), Shiites
and Sunnis are now commonly recognised distinct groups. There are very few
movies, and even fewer comedies of this period, that make so many political
references, and this for Almodóvar who was considered famously apolitical at
the time. In integrating a political backdrop, but not making political films, he

again follows Hitchcock. To recall, Hitchcock said, 'Politics is bad box office anywhere' (McGilligan 2003: 539). There are more minor details in common, such as the policeman in *Labyrinth of Passion* who draws glasses on a magazine cover of Riza when they are seeking him, just as the policeman in *Spellbound* draws glasses on a photo of Sedgwick when she is sought.

The final scene of *Labyrinth of Passion* strongly alludes to Hitchcock. He ends *North by Northwest* with a high-angle shot of a train whizzing into a tunnel; the protagonists' voices are heard making love inside their train car. Hitchcock has said explicitly in interviews that the tunnel scene meant sexual intercourse (Truffaut 1984: 150). He was proud of skirting the censors with the tunnel scene, which is considered audacious for his time. Almodóvar ends *Labyrinth of Passion* with a prolonged take of an airplane rising, a clear phallic image. In voiceover Sexilia comments to Riza on their exceptional climax: 'Darling, you're the first man I've screwed in mid-air.' For as explicit as Almodóvar is in depicting transgressive sex – gay, communal, and incestuous – throughout *Labyrinth of Passion*, it is curious that he returns to a heterosexual couple at the happy ending. The sequence acknowledges his Hitchcockian 'guilt complex'; further, he embeds Hitchcock's well-known ending in his own as if it were a purloined letter, or a book in plain sight that is the clue to the mystery in *Spellbound*.

III. CASTING AND CLOSE-UPS IN *DARK HABITS* AND *STAGE FRIGHT*

Entre tinieblas (*Dark Habits*, 1983) is the Almodóvar film most overtly concerned with Catholicism due to its setting in a convent. Yet it epitomises more secular, industrial preoccupations for it represents the first of several struggles for control with producers. As Almodóvar recounts to Strauss, *Dark Habits* was not only 'a producer's movie' (Strauss 1995: 45), but one made, on spec, to showcase and woo Cristiana S. Pascual, the wife of his financial backer, Hervé Hachuel, after Pascual had threatened to leave him. Meeting Hachuel, he immediately understood the unwritten rule that Pascual, though only an aspiring actress, had to be the star of the script that Hachuel was shopping for.[6] Almodóvar dutifully wrote *Dark Habits* as a star vehicle for Pascual, casting her as Yolanda, the actress who takes refuge in the convent.

The history of Hollywood is littered with stories of battles between directors and producers over casting and other elements of creative control. Few are more legendary, prolonged, or well documented than David O. Selznick's dictatorship over Hitchcock.[7] It is worthwhile to compare how Hitchcock handled casting, especially that imposed on him by his producer for *Stage Fright* (1950), and how Almodóvar dealt with a similar dilemma, or opportunity, for *Dark Habits*. Both films depict the world of the theatre. Most significantly, Marlene

Dietrich was the source of inspiration for both films. In the conception of *Stage Fright* Selznick made it clear to Hitchcock, his director under contract, that he wanted the picture to star Jane Wyman, also under contract to Selznick. *Stage Fright* was already a star vehicle at this point, for it was written with Dietrich in mind. Coincidentally this caused numerous rewrites of the script's ending because it was argued that a leading lady like Dietrich could be the prime murder suspect, but the audience would never accept her as the actual murderer. The solution was for her character's lover to confess to the murder.

Stage Fright marks Hitchcock's sole collaboration with Dietrich. Almodóvar said that Dietrich, especially the theatrical Dietrich of *Der blaue Engel* (*The Blue Angel*, 1930), was his prime reference for Pascual's part when he wrote *Dark Habits* (Strauss 1995: 46). The problem for Hitchcock was not really Dietrich, for he handled her masterfully and convinced her to choose for one of her contract-mandated musical numbers 'The Laziest Girl in Town', a Cole Porter song that became her signature piece. Hitchcock's more vexing problem was Wyman because he did not think her appropriate for the part of the ingénue who goes undercover as a maid/dresser to Dietrich. He insisted that the ingénue dress in a homely fashion for most of the film, which went against Wyman's desire, to literally shine in her wardrobe. Wyman was a star in Selznick's stable, but it was tough, if not impossible, for any other star to shine opposite the diva Dietrich. When Hitchcock gave in to Wyman and Selznick, and dressed her up in a glitzy garden party frock, the effect in *Stage Fright* was discordant. Hitchcock has Dietrich comment sarcastically on the transformation: 'Whatever happened to that peculiar girl?'

In a sense Cristina Pascual was Almodóvar's Wyman because *Dark Habits* had in its cast more established stars such as Julieta Serrano in the part of the Mother Superior. Almodóvar has said about his career: '*Dark Habits* is when I begin to realise what cinematographic language is' (Strauss 1995: 48). Finally,

Dietrich and a pouting Wyman in the dressing room in *Stage Fright*.

Julieta Serrano in close-up, transfixed by love in *Dark Habits*.

his producer now provided him with enough resources with which to experiment. Furthermore, one of the most important steps in his learning process was to discover the force of the close-up, the use of which is generally considered the *sine qua non* of the contractual definition of a star. He discovered in *Dark Habits* that Serrano could hold a close-up, could express deep emotions via the shot, whereas Pascual's role was not working out. In a sense, the veteran stage actress Serrano, like Dietrich from Wyman, stole not just a scene, but the whole movie from Pascual. The plot changed because of Almodóvar's experimentation with close-ups. Significantly when Yolanda performs her raunchy stage number, Serrano steals the spotlight with her soulful close-up reaction shot that shows she has fallen in love with Yolanda.

The reaction is later magnified in Yolanda's dressing room as Serrano, like a modern day St. Veronica, contemplates the cloth with Yolanda's image on it from the removal of her make-up. In comparison, we can recall Hitchcock's masterful lighting of Dietrich, as she always demanded, in *Stage Fright* especially in the climatic section when the detective is holding her in custody in the

Marlene Dietrich telling the detective her story of unrequited dog love in *Stage Fright*.

Extreme close-up of
Marlene Dietrich closing
a scene in *Stage Fright*.

theatre. Charlotte (Dietrich) has just come under suspicion for the murder, but
her demeanour shows her unperturbed. She is seated in a dark backstage area in
front of a curtain facing the camera with a tall detective standing next to her. A
beam of light falls over her. The mood is sombre.

She makes innocuous, but symbolic conversation to fill the time, telling the
detective she once had a dog. When it did not love her, or respond to her absolute
love, she had it killed. The spotlight and her intense facial expression communicate soulfulness, worldliness. No matter what, she is in control just as she
controls her final close-up, which closes the scene.

Dietrich/Charlotte's soulful domination, as she spins a tale of unrequited
love, is similar to how the melancholy Serrano/Mother Superior controls the
screen and eventually the narrative of *Dark Habits*, as Yolanda abandons her.
Almodóvar calls the resolution to the love story 'the most dramatic part of the
story, which almost comes as a slap to the spectator because it is not a nice ending, but it is the most honest solution that occurs to me' (Strauss 1995: 56).

Stage Fright is a movie of significant close-ups, not only of Dietrich. In
the amended conclusion, which takes place ostensibly below stage, Charlotte's
lover takes Wyman captive and reveals that he, not Charlotte, indeed killed
Charlotte's husband. Both Wyman and the murderer are portrayed in extreme
close-ups that show her distress and his madness. Wyman is effective here, in
the true locale of the 'stage fright', the theatre, when she does not have to share
the scene with Dietrich.

Looking at Almodóvar and Hitchcock together in this generally unexpected
comparison shows a similar production history, a common blending of musical
and theatrical numbers in balancing the films' designated castings, and a masterful use of the close-up in both cases. It shows, moreover, how in both cases
the need for close-ups altered the film's narrative.

IV. THE DOMESTIC CRIME SCENE ENLIVENED BY WALLPAPER: 'LAMB TO THE SLAUGHTER' AND *WHAT HAVE I DONE TO DESERVE THIS?*

Many Spanish critics have long been highly critical of Almodóvar's films. They criticise particularly what they see as the incoherence of his scripts.[8] On the other hand, French and American critics have interpreted, and pardoned, the excesses, or incoherencies, within the generic parameters of melodrama.[9] Frédéric Strauss, in the introduction to *Pedro Almodóvar: un cine visceral*, points to scriptwriting as both the definitive characteristic of the director's work, as well as its primary defect: 'Such meanderings are the weakness which make up the strength of Almodóvar's films; incapable of giving his scripts a rigid structure, of curtailing his imagination, his limitless inventiveness, he allows each story, each character, major or minor, to live to the full; in other words, sometimes anarchically' (Strauss 2006: xii).

However, interpreting Almodóvar via Hitchcock, and particularly through the lens of Hitchcock's generic preferences, of individualistic strands of suspense and comedy, can give us a different, and perhaps better appreciation of Almodóvar's development as a filmmaker as it brings other elements into focus that have not yet been looked at together. Looking at Almodóvar through Hitchcock foregrounds Almodóvar's detective side, or the crime story, in the narrative structure of his films. This is true for *What Have I Done to Deserve This?*, *Women on the Verge of a Nervous Breakdown*, *High Heels*, *Kika*, *Flor de mi secreto* (*Flower of My Secret*, 1995), *Carne trémula* (*Live Flesh*, 1997), *Todo sobre mi madre* (*All About My Mother*, 1999), *Hable con ella* (*Talk to Her*, 2002), *Bad Education*, *Volver* (2006), *Broken Embraces* and *La piel que habito* (*The Skin I Live In*, 2011).[10] *What Have I Done to Deserve This?*, *Women on the Verge* and *Bad Education*, which span his career, offer salient cases of this detective side or crime story. Almodóvar's turn to the crime story coincides with what I am terming his commercial career – that is, the beginning of significant international distribution. This career really begins with *What Have I Done to Deserve This?* in 1984. This film was the first to receive distribution in France, three years after its Spanish release. Attention to Hitchcock in this film served as a bridge to commercial success on an international scale.

In *What Have I Done to Deserve This?* we find the first elaborate Hitchcockian structure to Almodóvar's narratives. The film is basically a crime story, a detective story with a murder in it. The harried Gloria, who works as a cleaning lady, kills her cab-driver husband Antonio with a ham bone. The plot is in fact a rip-off of one of Hitchcock's most well known TV stories from *Alfred Hitchcock Presents*, namely 'Lamb to the Slaughter', which Hitchcock directed in 1957. It starred Barbara Bel Geddes, who played Midge in *Vertigo*, and was made immediately following that masterpiece. Patrick McGilligan describes the episode: '"Lamb to the Slaughter," based on a short story by Roald Dahl (who also wrote the teleplay), was about a devoted wife, spurned by her louse of a husband, who clubs him to death with a frozen leg of lamb. As detectives scour her house for clues to the crime, the lamb cooks delectably, ultimately becoming their supper' (2003: 556). Almodóvar changed the meat course to ham; he also has the detectives accepting a cup of the broth from the incriminating stew rather than sitting down to a full meal. He waits until *Women on the Verge of a Nervous Breakdown* to invite detectives to sit down and partake of a suspicious potion made by a female lead, in this case the gazpacho with sleeping pills. In both 'Lamb to the Slaughter' and *What Have I Done to Deserve This?* the murderesses escape punishment, but are left isolated in their houses.

The final sequence of 'Lamb to the Slaughter' shows the detectives and their team feasting on the lamb/murder weapon at her dining table. The camera moves back to reveal the doorway and Bel Geddes in the other room. Then the film cuts to Bel Geddes who sits alone rigidly upright on a straight-backed chair against a wall of the living room. She absurdly maintains a conversation with the detectives from the other room that emphasises the sense of a purloined letter. When one detective comments while reaching for more meat that the murder weapon must still be 'right under our very noses', the film shows her wicked, but at the same time idiotic, smile.

Her expression tells the viewer she has gotten away with the murder. She is portrayed against large print graphic wallpaper, a decorative motif that dominates Almodóvar's *mise-en-scène* throughout *What Have I Done to Deserve This?* as well. The reincorporation of the wallpaper shows Almodóvar's attitude toward cinematic influences. Speaking on *What Have I Done to Deserve This?*, a film in which grandmother and grandson watch *Splendor in the Grass* (1961)

Mrs. Maloney's (Barbara Bel Geddes) smile in 'Lamb to the Slaughter.'

The sorcerer's brush
on the wallpaper in
*What Have I Done
to Deserve This?*

at the cinema together, Almodóvar emphasised that any borrowing should not be reverential but rather undertake significant 'active' revisions that become markers of his own authorship:

> Cinema is always present in my films, but I'm not the kind of cinephile di-
> rector who quotes other directors. Certain films play an active part in my
> scripts. When I insert an extract from a film, it isn't a homage but outright
> theft, and becomes an active presence rather than a homage, which is al-
> ways something passive. (Strauss 2006: 45)

This call to action is taken literally in *What Have I Done to Deserve This?*. The wallpaper, which is a featured element of the *mise-en-scène* of Hitchcock's tele-play from the scenario of the murder to the Cheshire smile of Mrs. Maloney at its end, assumes an even more prominent role in *What Have I Done to Deserve This?* such that it becomes Disney-inspired – 'active'.

After Gloria has killed her husband, she hesitantly agrees to watch the psychic redheaded child Vanessa for Vanessa's mother Juani, who despises her daughter. Symbolically turning over a new leaf, Gloria is about to repaper the kitchen. She finds out that Vanessa 'has magical powers' when the child repa-pers the kitchen telepathically. The wallpaper brush moves over the walls like Mickey's mops when he plays the sorcerer's apprentice in Disney's *Fantasia* (1940). Gloria's smile, shown against a backdrop of the vintage wallpaper, rec-reates Mrs. Maloney's sense of satisfaction at the end of 'Lamb to the Slaughter'. The viewer sympathises with the female leads through reaction shots, which symbolise their freedom in the domestic realm.

These magical special effects demonstrate Almodóvar's desire to assert his own humorous tone and demonstrate mastery of the original cinematic mate-rial. The use of special effects, which are rare in Almodóvar's films and Spanish cinema of the 1980s, underscores the claim to originality at the same time as it appeals to mass culture.

The representation of forgery in *What Have I Done to Deserve This?* serves to characterise the cab-driver husband Antonio. As he proudly hands his passenger a book of Hitler's letters he has forged, he tells him of his love for a German singer he met while a *Gastarbeiter*. This scene characterises Antonio both as a Fascist sympathiser and as a two-timer, which gives him a similar profile to the policeman husband Patrick Maloney in 'Lamb to the Slaughter'. Never taking off his policeman's blue coat while he downs a whiskey neat, Patrick tells his wife bluntly that he is seeing another woman and wants a divorce. Through the forgery leitmotif Almodóvar silently acknowledges his debt to Hitchcock's plot of 'Lamb to the Slaughter'. It is one of a series of the staging of scenes of simulation that runs throughout Almodóvar's work; yet the postmodernist interpretation also serves to reinforce the interpretation of the forgery leitmotif as an allusion to the stealing of Hitchcock's plot of 'Lamb to the Slaughter' as the basis for *What Have I Done to Deserve This?*. Just as Antonio is proud of passing his talent for forgery to his son, Almodóvar proudly cites other classic American films to displace his 'theft'.

This theft is further obscured by references to other plots. When the illiterate grandmother begs her son to compose a letter back to her village, she asks him to imitate Grace Kelly's style; a glamour shot of Kelly is inserted. Grace Kelly, one of the classic Hitchcock blondes, became a star through her work with Hitchcock, beginning with *Dial M for Murder* (1954). In this film the husband (Ray Milland) tries to frame his wife Margot (Kelly) for a murder he himself staged. He incriminates her by planting one of her love letters in the coat of Swann, whom she kills when he attempts to strangle her. A head-shot poster of Paul Newman, star of one of Hitchcock's later films *Torn Curtain* (1966), also appears on the wall of Gloria's son's bedroom. These allusions are meant to divert our attention from the primary 'robbery' of 'Lamb to the Slaughter' to a more general appreciation of cinematic history and Hitchcock's place in it.

Both directors approached filming tragicomedy through similar techniques. Although *Dark Habits* included crane shots, which Almodóvar says in interviews give the angle of God, their use in *What Have I Done to Deserve This?* is even more effective and communicates a social commentary, as did a similar use of this shot in the blackmail sequence of *Dial M for Murder*. The debonair husband Tony Wendice strides back and forth in the apartment to demonstrate how the dishevelled, penurious Swann should enact the murder of Tony's wife before paying him off.[11] In *What Have I Done to Deserve This?* the high-angle shots – that transgress the possible boundaries of the claustrophobically small, familiar apartment – effectively convey the oppression of Gloria by her husband Antonio. An example of the use of the high-angle shot occurs in the 'Bien paga'o'

('Well paid') sequence in which Antonio forces Gloria to have sex in order to get bus money out of him to get to her job. The film intercuts and gives a musical soundtrack to the exploitation, with Almodóvar himself playing an officer in the zarzuela sequence of the song on the TV program, which the grandmother is watching in the other room. These transitions between sequences, whose effect is to thematically comment on Gloria and Antonio's marriage, mark one of the most brilliant moments of the film.

Almodóvar found his narrative stride in *What Have I Done to Deserve This?* through the hybrid mix of the kind of melodramatic crime story that gave Hitchcock his renown.[12] How profound is the forgery, or as Almodóvar prefers to call his reworking of other films, 'the robbery'? Was the early scene of sex in the martial arts academy shower room an allusion to Hitchcock, in this case, *Psycho*? What is clear is that *What Have I Done to Deserve This?* 'steals' Hitchcock's teleplay narrative, which is substantially reworked in the recurring motif of the ham bone/chicken leg/club/curling iron. All of these items are obvious phallic symbols, as was the leg of lamb Mrs. Maloney took out of the freezer, as were the 'recurring motifs (including the phallic implications of certain household objects)' (McGilligan 2003: 472) in *Dial M for Murder*. Their humourous effect is broad, domestically oriented, and analogous in Hitchcock and Almodóvar. The basic story of both *What Have I Done to Deserve This?* and 'Lamb to the Slaughter' is of revenge on the caveman.

Yet the ironic humour of situations remains part of the plot as the movie ends by coming full circle. Back on her job as a cleaning woman at the martial arts studio, and working out her frustrations with heavy chops of the weapon sticks there, she again encounters the policeman she had sex with in the film's opening shower scene. When she confesses that she killed her husband with a ham bone, he rejects this story and waits for her to invent another version. He chooses to believe she is only distraught. Hitchcock played with similar narrative ironies often that tweaked our sense of the plausible, and reminded us playfully that we are watching cinema. The milkman in *Foreign Correspondent* (1940) would not accept that spies could pursue the dashing protagonist John Jones, who was pleading for help wearing a disguise. Jones had to quickly weave another fiction to get the milkman's cooperation. The milkman was only ready to believe the story of a domestic affair – that is, that Jones was trying to avoid a jealous husband. Just like the detectives of 'Lamb to the Slaughter' the investigator in *What Have I Done to Deserve This?* overlooks the obvious, wilder possibilities, and underestimates the protagonists. In both Hitchcock and Almodóvar the rejection of the protagonists' confessions shows that patriarchal society is not yet ready to accept the changed role of women.[13] These films, however, position the viewer to recognise the process that set that change in motion.

V. LOOKING THROUGH OBJECTS AND ALMODÓVAR'S 'MACGUFFIN': FROM *DIAL M FOR MURDER, STRANGERS ON A TRAIN, REAR WINDOW,* AND *THE THIRTY-NINE STEPS* TO *WOMEN ON THE VERGE OF A NERVOUS BREAKDOWN*

We cannot underestimate both Almodóvar's desire to make it as an international director and the effect that the two films that preceded *Women on the Verge of a Nervous Breakdown* in distribution – *Matador* (1986) and *La ley del deseo* (*Law of Desire*, 1987) – had on his reputation as a director. True or not, those two films pigeonholed him as a director for a gay audience, and even more crudely, as a director of kinky sex. Almodóvar was almost given a dare to make a PG-13 film for the sake of his career. Also, as Paul Julian Smith notes, by achieving foreign popularity he could make credible his claim within Spain 'to represent post-Franco Spain to the outside world' (1994: 102). Once again Hitchcock, who fought the censors valiantly over the years to put sex, double entendres and taboo subjects on screen, with abundant humour and enormous success, was the perfect model. Hitchcock managed to entertain without offending the public. While incest is suggested, infidelity abounds, the protagonist will have a baby out of wedlock and female orgasm is depicted, Almodóvar's next film, *Women on the Verge of a Nervous Breakdown*, was received as 'pure theatre'. Since clothes are kept on, film censors judged the film totally inoffensive. Almodóvar slyly winks at (his self-)censorship in one of the final sequences. As Pepa (Carmen Maura) walks by the fully-clothed Carlos (Antonio Banderas) and Candela (María Barranco) making out on her sofa, Pepa pulls a towel up over Candela's cleavage. The towel is so small that the gesture only serves to mock facile rating standards.

While the story of *Women on the Verge of a Nervous Breakdown* speaks more to American screwball comedies – a genre Hitchcock only tried once, successfully, too, in *Mr. and Mrs. Smith* (1941) with Carole Lombard – both the overall balance in tone that melds comedy and drama/crime story, and especially the construction of certain shots and sequences that evokes 'pure cinema', show a deep appreciation of Hitchcock. Almodóvar planned the shots of *Women on the Verge of a Nervous Breakdown* in storyboards, which represented a change in his practice. Hitchcock was known for such careful storyboarding that the legend goes that he was bored when he came to the actual filming.

Although Cocteau's short story *La voix humaine* (*The Human Voice*, 1930) served as the inspiration for the film, the key object of modern life at the centre of the film's story – the telephone – sent Almodóvar thinking of Hitchcock again. In commenting to Frédéric Strauss on the importance of objects, particularly the answering machine, in *Women on the Verge of a Nervous Breakdown*,

Object lesson: the giant tea-cup in *Notorious*.

Almodóvar refers to Hitchcock's special effect used to give an object prominence in the frame in relation to action in deep focus.

Almodóvar gives the example of a cup. To recall, in *Notorious*, Alicia (Ingrid Bergman) is drugged with a spiked cup of tea, but the true, repressed referent here are the large telephones Hitchcock used for *Dial M for Murder*, for the filming and for the marketing. The giant phone later became part of the publicity campaign for the film, just as Almodóvar used a giant shoe for his opening night publicity parade for *High Heels*. Almodóvar explains his technical challenge in *Women on the Verge of a Nervous Breakdown*:

> The machine in the film doesn't really have the presence I wanted it to have. This made it difficult to compose shots where the machine was in the foreground and Pepa behind. When Hitchcock wanted a teacup in the foreground with characters in the back, he had a giant teacup made. You think it's the lens which enlarges the object whereas in fact it's a trick. (Strauss 2006: 81)

The most notable, famous sequence with a prominent telephone in *Dial M for Murder* occurs when Margot gets up in the middle of the night to answer a call from her husband who is plotting her murder. The shot is filmed from the supposed vantage point of the hired strangler, whom the viewer has seen hide behind the room's curtains. Suspense and sympathy are built in the viewer as Margot crosses the living room, in her innocent and sexy white negligee backlit with the light from her bedroom, to answer the phone and is immediately attacked. Margot, however, withstands the onslaught and kills the intruder with her sewing scissors. The phone is a protagonist in the sequence as it both initiates the sequence of events and represents the husband on the other end of the line who has plotted the killing.

We should recall here as well that Almodóvar worked as an administrator at Telefónica, the Spanish national telephone company, during his early years of cinematic self-education. The Salón de Actos (auditorium) of Telefónica headquarters in Madrid also was the site for film screenings with actors and directors present. Even though Peter W. Evans in his BFI monograph on *Women on the Verge of a Nervous Breakdown* dismisses the importance to the film of Almodóvar's telephone company years, as a 'wish to take a parting shot at his former employers' (1996: 13), Almodóvar's attitude towards this experience has been more positive. He looks back on these years through the lens of a developing class consciousness: 'I learned a great deal about the Spanish middle class which I could never have learned otherwise. This discovery is reflected in my films. Until then, all I knew about was the rural lower class' (Strauss 1995: 21).

In 1996 Telefónica itself published a book *Teléfonos de cine* (*Movie Telephones*) by the critics Mariano Cebrián Herreros, Agustín García Matilla and Eduardo Rodríguez Merchán. The authors devote substantial attention to the films of Hitchcock and Almodóvar. They analyse the significance of the phone booth in *The Birds*, *North by Northwest*, *Psycho*, as well as in *Dial M for Murder*, comparing it especially to *¡Átame!* (*Tie Me Up, Tie Me Down*, 1990) and *Women on the Verge of a Nervous Breakdown*. At very least this 'industrially' generated text, a luxurious volume, confirms a general, continued and important appreciation of Hitchcock's work in Spain. It is worth looking at how the authors describe and interpret the sequence that Almodóvar referred to in the Strauss interview as his technical challenge, akin to Hitchcock's:

The shot plan of the woman-machine encounter, the aberrant insert shots that give those machines this dualistic atmosphere, are underscored, if it could be even possibly more, by the Saturnian red of Pepa's telephone. There exists a kind of dialectic or personal dialogue between Pepa and the answering machine; there is a moment of anthropormorphisation of the object. In fact, when the protagonist listens to the messages, she replies to the voice as if Fernando Guillén really were in front of her. There is an analogous scene that takes this relationship of dependence with the answering machine to its climax: in one of her trips home Almodóvar shows her with her eyes glued to the answering machine that appears foreshortened. As always, Pepa walks toward the table and the director moves the camera in until the machine appears in extreme close-up while she presses the button. But Almodóvar goes further: the answering machine, as if it were another character, looks back at the protagonist from its insides. A surprising subjective camera shot from the interior of the answering machine creates

Pepa's (Carmen Maura) eyes through the reels of the answering machine in *Women on the Verge of a Nervous Breakdown*.

a disturbing image in which the orifices of the recording tapes align with Pepa's bulging eyes. (1996: 55)

It is particularly in this looking through objects where Almodóvar's *Women on the Verge of a Nervous Breakdown* seems inspired by Hitchcock's exceptional camerawork. The objects themselves represent a modern consciousness that distances and deceives in their superficial function to establish communication. Hence, not only is the telephone and its subsidiary apparati (the answering machine, the phone booth, the microphones connected to them) the leitmotif of the film, as seen in the shot of Pepa's eyes, but looking at and through objects is its complex and transgressive *modus operandi*. The loudspeakers connected to the telephone being left on by the dubbing studio receptionist symbolise *Women on the Verge of a Nervous Breakdown*'s melodrama. All intimate details are broadcast to the public even as we look through the supposedly private space of the phone booth.

Besides the telephone sequence and leitmotif, there are other sequences of the film that allude to Hitchcock and carry through their common perspective of looking through objects and drawing attention to the cinematic apparatus as well. In an early sequence when Pepa is dubbing her voice for that of Joan Crawford in a scene from *Johnny Guitar* (1954) for which Ivan has already

The fainted Pepa through her eyeglasses on the floor in *Women on the Verge of a Nervous Breakdown*.

recorded the Sterling Hayden role, she faints and falls backwards. The final image is shot at floor level and shows her glasses in the foreground with Pepa in deep focus.

This dramatic conclusion to the sequence alludes to Hitchcock's stunning visual effects in the strangulation sequence in *Strangers on a Train* (1951). To recall, two strangers, Bruno and Guy, meet on a train. Bruno suggests exchanging murders. He will kill Guy's wife; then Guy should kill Bruno's father. Bruno lures Guy's wife Miriam to a deserted island at a carnival. As Bruno strangles her, her glasses fall off and we see her falling down in the reflection of these glasses. Hitchcock used a giant concave mirror to achieve the floating shot of the fainting. He then double printed it on the image of a pair of giant glasses. Almodóvar stages his adaptation of Hitchcock as a rerun or dubbing of an old movie in a darkened room, like the carnival's island at night.

In his article, 'Melo-Thriller: Hitchcock, Genre and Nationalism in Pedro Almodóvar's *Women on the Verge of a Nervous Breakdown*', Enrique Acevedo-Muñoz states: 'The shot of Pepa on the floor is a direct citation of Miriam's death in *Strangers on a Train*' (2006: 181). In comparing the respective sequences Acevedo-Muñoz makes two points: first, 'formally, Almodóvar's shot is different from Hitchcock's since we see Pepa not reflected, but *through* the glasses, so it appears as mediation rather than a cinematic reflection'; and second, since the dubbing director, whom Acevedo-Muñoz considers a stand-in for Almodóvar, rescues Pepa, 'the perversion of Bruno's (and Hitchcock's) action is here neutralized' (ibid.). While Acevedo-Muñoz correctly appreciates the importance of the formal characteristics of this shot, when placed in the larger context of Almodóvar's cinematic language of filming through objects, also seen in *What Have I Done to Deserve This?*, his interpretation of Hitchcock's shot as 'cinematic reflection' is too literal and limiting. In the elaborate construction of the glasses shot Hitchcock 'mediated' the cinematic experience of the viewer as well. Although Pepa does not die as Marion did (although the carnival spectators when they find her body first yell 'she's fainted'), Pepa does have, in Acevedo-Muñoz's words, 'her first hysterical crisis over a Hitchockian moment'. To me Hitchcock's 'perversion' – that is, the ability of cinema to affect the spectator – is very much exploited and left intact, rather than 'neutralised' in Almodóvar's appropriation.

Almodóvar amplifies Hitchcock's 'perversion', or focus on cinematic effects, when he integrates *Rear Window* into *Women on the Verge of a Nervous Breakdown*. When Pepa leaves her apartment at night for the street in her frantic search for Ivan, she stakes him out at his ex's apartment building. She calmly sits down on bench across the street where she gazes at a varied tableau of actors and actions framed in the windows of the apartment building above

Miss Torso's dance to 'Fancy Free' in *Rear Window*.

The sexy dancer that Pepa spies in the first window in *Women on the Verge of a Nervous Breakdown*.

her. The first point of view character Pepa the voyeur sees is a clear allusion to *Rear Window*'s Miss Torso, a buxom lady entertaining the viewer with her sexy dance to 'Fancy Free' in her underwear. In a second apartment she sees a young man crying into a handkerchief. The third window she trains her view on reveals the protagonist of the crime yet to be committed. Carlos, Ivan's son, argues with his crazy mother Lucía (Julieta Serrano), who will later attempt to murder her ex.[14]

Almodóvar stages 'La ventana indiscreta' – literally, 'the indiscreet window' as *Rear Window* is known in Spanish-speaking countries – with a Madrid location shoot, rather than with a single elaborate studio set, as Hitchcock famously did. Nothing is hidden in a back courtyard, but rather every character crosses the imaginary boundary of the private space of a dwelling, whose Beaux-Arts style is decidedly more opulent than Hitchcock's Greenwich Village backyard set, to impinge on the public space of the street. With huge windows swung open to the night, Almodóvar's 'Miss Torso' 1988 dances in the golden glow of a chandelier's illumination. Significantly both the weeping man and the angry Lucía are not depicted within the confines of the window frames at all, but rather he poses on his sumptuous balcony as she paces on and off hers.

Hitchcock told Truffaut that *Rear Window* appealed to him for the technical challenge of 'doing a purely cinematic film' to show how the art of montage shapes a narrative (Truffaut 1984: 215). He gives the example of using the same reaction shot of Stewart smiling which could be read as 'kindly' if a little dog being lowered in a basket had been shown, or as 'dirty' if the film had cut from a 'half-naked girl exercising' (1984: 216). Likewise Almodóvar's series of vignettes – exhibitionist, tearful and angry – always cut away for Pepa's reactions, slight changes in facial expressions which we interpret as accepting, empathetic and upset because they are set up by the minimalist visual scenes which immediately proceed them. There is one exception to the alternating montage: the film cuts from Pepa to Marissa (Rossy de Palma), Carlos's fiancée, sitting in a car waiting for him and peering at her via the rear-view mirror before it sweeps up to Lucía arguing with Iván above. Although in the subsequent confrontation with Pepa at the telephone booth Marissa expresses disapproval of 'the slut' who dances every night, her comment reaffirms that she did not turn away but watched the exhibitionist scene. In his more public *mise-en-scène* Almodóvar reaffirms and expands on Hitchcock's point that 'We're all voyeurs to some extent, if only when we see an intimate film' (Truffaut 1984: 216).

Although the dominant tone of *Women on the Verge of a Nervous Breakdown* is comic, moments of suspense, and not just in the climatic chase sequences, give the film its balance and drive. These changes in tone are signalled by a change in the soundtrack's theme, and with cuts to low-angle shots of Pepa's shoes pacing across her living room floor or on the stairs to and from her apartment. Hitchcock was notorious for shots of lower legs in motion. Both *The Thirty-Nine Steps* and *Strangers on a Train*, two of the most significant films of his British era, begin with low-angle shots of primarily men's shoes walking. These shots characterise the well-heeled and convey a generic marker to establish a sense of action. Almodóvar achieves similar effects with these low-angle shots in a feminine register. They create tension for the crime story, mark Pepa's social class and emphasise her active sexuality. Later Almodóvar repeats his generic marker when he ends *High Heels* with a shot through the basement apartment window of high heels passing by.

Of all of Almodóvar's crime stories, *Women on the Verge of a Nervous Breakdown* is structured most like Hitchcock's films because of its use of a MacGuffin. In Hitchcock's films a MacGuffin is a storytelling device that motivates the plot, but which is in itself inconsequential. A prime example is the secret society called 'The Thirty-Nine Steps' which Mr. Memory elucidates at the conclusion of the eponymous film. In *North by Northwest* the MacGuffin, a Precolombian statue, or 'pot' as Roger Thornhill (Cary Grant) jokes, that contains microfilm, even evokes Hispanic culture. The use of a MacGuffin was often taken to indicate the apolitical nature of Hitchcock films because they were absurd or 'deliberately beside the point' by the time they were clarified (McGilligan 2003: 159). As McGillian writes in a section of his biography devoted to MacGuffins, 'Although Hitchcock shied away from taking political stands himself, his circle was thoroughly socialist and antifascist, even including Communists like Montagu' (2003: 158). In *Women on the Verge of a Nervous Breakdown*, Candela functions within the narrative as the bearer of the news of the MacGuffin. Almodóvar's own mother, who reads a fake news broadcast describing a terrorist threat, further inscribes the film's MacGuffin. The threat of Shiite terrorists kidnapping a flight to Stockholm sets up the final chase and dénouement of the film; it gives shape to the narrative like a Hitchcock spy picture. Yet in 1988 Shiite terrorism was not a great political force on the minds of most Spaniards.[15] Although any inscription of terrorism within Spanish film of the time may perhaps be interpreted as a veiled reference to Basque terrorism, the absurdity and comic effect of Candela pronouncing 'shiitas' in her Andalusian accent argues more strongly for an apolitical stand.

Women on the Verge of a Nervous Breakdown alludes to more Hitchcock films than any other of Almodóvar's films. Peter W. Evans, who notes the musical allusion to *Psycho* in the airport pursuit scene, the reference to *Strangers on a Train* in Pepa's fainting fit, and Pepa's voyeurist evening as evoking *Rear Window*, finds 'these three direct allusions to Hitchcock in the film, all ultimately related to a shared interest in male anxieties about powerful women, and especially powerful mothers' (2005: 15). Yet Evans misplaces the emphasis in his comments on Hitchcock. The mother role, especially that of Lucía's mother, is of only minimal significance to *Women on the Verge of a Nervous Breakdown*, although the film indeed concerns 'anxieties about powerful women'. Finally *Dial M for Murder*, the Hitchcock allusion that Evans overlooks, affords the best insights for a comparative interpretation. In that film Grace Kelly, like Carmen Maura in *Women on the Verge of a Nervous Breakdown*, is dressed in vibrant red as she entertains her American lover in front of her husband. Both women are threatening, but oh so attractive, in their liberated sexuality, both on and off the screen. The actresses, and their respective characters, ultimately prevail in these respective films, which are truly star vehicles. Finally it is not similarities in plot, or psychological stance as Evans has it, but the 'pure cinema' technique of the *Dial M for Murder* telephone shot which *Women on the Verge of a Nervous Breakdown* shares with Hitchcock's films. Almodóvar looks through the representative objects of the middle class, connects with that class and triumphs at the box office with a high international standard of production values.

Hitchcockian tenets of filmmaking, such as storyboarding and the use of the MacGuffin, which Almodóvar newly employs in *Women on the Verge of a Nervous Breakdown*, helped him fashion his authorial brand. Like Hitchcock, Almodóvar understood the role of exceptional marketing in its creation. As

Paul Julian Smith notes, the publicity campaign for *Women on the Verge of a Nervous Breakdown* in which Almodóvar posed in shots with the cast as had Hitchcock before him, was an 'attempt to theatricalise the publicity on a much wider scale than had hitherto been attempted' (1994: 102). To reinforce the connection between the two auteurs Juan Gatti, Almodóvar's preferred publicity photographer, who began doing posters for Almodóvar's films with *Women on the Verge of a Nervous Breakdown*, specifically mimicked Hitchcock's iconic publicity shots in his series of portraits of Almodóvar that continue to be widely exhibited (see Almodóvar et al. 2006).

VI. BONDAGE BETWEEN NEW STARS: *THE THIRTY-NINE STEPS* AND *TIE ME UP! TIE ME DOWN!*

Women on the Verge of a Nervous Breakdown marked a definitive break between Almodóvar and his muse/actress Carmen Maura. They made a public display of their split by entering the Shrine Auditorium separately at the 1989 Academy Awards for which *Women on the Verge of a Nervous Breakdown* was nominated for Best Foreign Film, but did not win (see Basterra 1989). His next project had to feature a new female lead. Almodóvar speaks of the difficulty he had in retraining Victoria Abril to his method: 'Victoria was ready to explode and scream, but she was also extremely modest and loath to express the simplest emotions both as an actress and as a woman' (Strauss 2006: 93). While there are no quotes from Almodóvar indicating he thought of Hitchcock when he conceived of *Tie Me Up! Tie Me Down!* (1990), it is plausible that the well-known story of how Hitchcock used bondage to manipulate his actors in *The Thirty-Nine Steps* may have coloured his relationship with his new lead. It certainly resonated plotwise.[16] According to McGilligan, in order to break down the 'icy, forbidding' (2003: 173) persona of the actress Madeleine Carroll, Hitchcock deliberately did not introduce her to her co-lead Robert Donat before the first day of shooting of *The Thirty-Nine Steps*. Then immediately after they shook hands, he handcuffed them together, did a few takes, then left them handcuffed together. McGilligan praises Hitchcock's technique with actors: 'Adopting an attitude toward his actors that the story took toward their characters: it was a Hitchcock strategy rarely expounded upon; perhaps it was subconscious, but it was effective' (2003: 174). While Almodóvar did not emulate Hitchcock's attitude to his actors, the anecdote highlights the sadistic actions of the character Ricki (Antonio Banderas) and recalls the blend of suspense and romance in *The Thirty-Nine Steps*. Like the fugitive Richard Hannay (Robert Donat) in that film, who bursts in on women in his flight, Ricki bursts in on Marina (Victoria Abril) in her apartment; the ensuing bondage is read as love by Ricki and sadism by Marina. This contradictory reading doubles the kitchen conversations between the crofter's wife (Peggy Ashcroft) and Hannay in which a touching but dark kinship between her unhappy married state and his criminal profile emerges. Although the wife recognises him as a fugitive, she helps him escape again. In close-up we see her face as her husband begins to beat her upon discovering Hannay gone. This sequence doubles the overarching story.

In *The Thirty-Nine Steps* Hannay is pursued by foreign spies who think he has secret information. He bursts into the train compartment of Pamela (Madeleine Carroll) and kisses her to disguise his flight. Pamela later denounces him to the police, who refuse to believe Hannay's story of foreign intrigue. The bad guys manage to kidnap Hannay and Pamela from the police station and handcuff the two together so they will not escape. They jump out of the car and wander across the countryside handcuffed until Pamela manages to squeeze her hand out while they are hiding as a married couple at an inn. Though physically liberated from her bonds, she falls progressively more in love with Hannay. The film ends with a close-up shot of their linked hands.

Like *Tie Me Up! Tie Me Down!*, *The Thirty-Nine Steps* is notable for its sensitive treatment of a woman in an unhappy marriage, and for its unconventional courtship, which features bondage. Many audiences objected to the almost sadistic actions of Ricki in *Tie Me Up! Tie Me Down!* Neither bondage nor forced sex was understood as metaphorically philosophising marriage, as Hitchcock's handcuffs were in *The Thirty-Nine Steps*. Almodóvar bitterly recalls the film's reception and defends this symbolic interpretation:

> *Tie Me Up! Tie Me Down!* is almost a romantic fairy tale, but many people attacked it because they took it for precisely the kind of sadomasochist movie it isn't. A lot of people went to see it in the States with pre-conceived ideas and expected God knows what. (Strauss 2006: 100)

Perhaps Almodóvar expected to repeat the reception of Hitchcock's classic, also about marriage, which was embedded in the unconventional treatment of the topic of the film.

VII. LONG TAKES AND MULTIPLE CONFESSIONS: THE OTHER SHOE DROPS FROM *MARNIE* TO *HIGH HEELS*

When Almodóvar completed *High Heels* in 1991 he had a number of films in the pipeline at different stages. He was enjoying the financial security and independence of his own production company, away from studio pressures. Nonetheless *High Heels* takes the spectator into the realm of Hitchcock Hollywood, less for their shared star discourse, than for other aspects of their cinematic style and narrative constructs. As a constant source of inspiration, Hitchcock's own self-imposed cinematic challenges, notably the long take, become Almodóvar's own obsessions.

One well-known experiment of Hitchcock's was the long take he planned for *The Paradine Case* (1947). According to McGilligan, 'Keane (Gregory Peck) and Sir Simon Flaquer (Charles Coburn) walk toward the camera as they enter Lincoln's Inn, part of the venerable fourteenth-century law complex. The two are seen entering the building, closing the door, walking up the stairs, turning the corner, heading along a landing into an office, and then continuing into the office, all in a single cut' (2003: 395). Selznick, to whom Hitchcock was under contract, was dead set against the long take and deleted Hitchcock's favorite effect from the film. Although *The Paradine Case* 'was in the books as a permanent loser' (2003: 396) – except in Mexico where it played well as *Agonía de amor* as we shall see in chapter five – Hitchcock persisted in his fascination with uninterrupted long takes at this stage in his career. Shortly thereafter when freed from his contract with Selznick, with his own production company Transatlantic Pictures, and now filming at the Warner Bros. studio, Hitchcock indeed realised his ambition and filmed his next project *Rope* (1948), based on Patrick Hamilton's play *Rope's End*, in sequential long takes of almost ten minutes in duration. The takes were so long he had to incorporate black shots of people's backs when he had to change reels. According to McGilligan, this technique would 'yield side benefits in both costs and publicity' (2003: 400). Today critics consider *Rope*, the story of a murder planned for sport, one of Hitchcock's most daring pictures not as much for his 'gimmick' of sequential long takes, as the scriptwriter Arthur Laurents calls it, as for how it represents the homosexual relationship at the core of its narrative, and how he escaped the censors to do it.[17]

Although it is not a sequence of motions as was the ill-fated take from *The Paradine Case*, in *High Heels* Almodóvar has Rebeca (Victoria Abril) describing Ingmar Bergman's film, *Autumn Sonata* (1978), as a poignant analogy for the relationship between her mother and herself, in one long take set in an empty courtroom. Almodóvar recognised that this long take represented the film's tipping point: 'Before shooting it, I told Victoria the monologue could kill the film' (Strauss 2006: 107). However, this closely coached sequence so held the technical crew in rapt fascination during its production performance that Almodóvar took the show on the road, so to speak, and had Abril perform the uninterrupted sequence at the film's Paris opening to market the picture.

In his interviews Almodóvar does not specifically mention Hitchcock's long takes in regard to *High Heels*. Obviously many long monologues are found in other master directors' films, and certainly in Bergman's. Rather, achieving a long take, and marketing it, was part of an industrial decision, and marked a certain stage in, and parallel between, Almodóvar and Hitchcock's careers. Furthermore, as Almodóvar tells Strauss, he sees Hitchcock as the model for the multiple confessions of in *High Heels*' narrative:

> [Rebeca] confesses three times in the film and each time she's truthful and sincere. The three confessions are complementary and give us an ambiguous impression. It was a huge risk, first of all because as a woman's confession it had to be done in close-up. Watching an actress do a monologue confessing the same thing three times could have been rather boring. But Victoria managed to perform three different confessions, all very moving and different. From the start, this way of handling the story had the advantage of being less obvious, less classic and more difficult to achieve than the wrong man theme, having a false and a real killer. Hitchcock is the one who's done it best. Throughout Rebeca is both guilty and falsely accused, but the difference is that she's always accusing herself, which gives the impression of a superhuman control to the confession. (Strauss 1995: 118)

Which of the many confessions in Hitchcock films does Almodóvar refer to? To the confession of Mrs. Paradine (Alida Valli) on the witness stand? To Hitchcock's first talkie *Blackmail* (1929) in which the protagonist Alice (Anny Ondra) tries to confess repeatedly to her beau Frank (John Longden), a Scotland Yard detective, that she murdered the painter Crewe (Cyril Ritchard) to thwart rape? After another suspect for the murder falls to his death in a chase, *Blackmail* ends with Alice attempting to confess at the police station. Her confession is thwarted by Frank. As the enamoured couple jauntily exit the station together, she is a free woman because of his protection. The situation of *High Heels* resembles *Blackmail* since in both films a representative of the law is sexually involved with a female who has committed homicide. In *High Heels* Judge Domínguez/Letal (Miguel Bosé) impregnates Rebeca and then tries to marry her. Or is the allusion to *Rebecca*, as signalled by the names of both mother and daughter in *High Heels*? In *Rebecca* information is progressively divulged; one of the most masterly revelations occurs in the extensive sequence in the boathouse where the husband Maxim deWinter (Laurence Olivier) confesses to his second wife (Joan Fontaine) his role in his first wife Rebecca's death. The naming of the female protagonists Becky and Rebeca certainly directs us to Hitchcock.

Yet the strongest allusion is to the melodramatic mother/daughter tensions of *Marnie* (1964) for the two films share significant plot elements and leitmotifs. Marnie (Tippi Hedren), like Rebeca, feels rejected by her mother and is obsessed

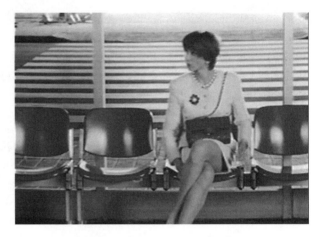

Rebeca (Victoria Abril) tugs at the hem of her Chanel skirt while she waits for her mother to arrive at the airport in *High Heels*.

with recovering her mother's love. In the final climatic sequence the mother, Bernice Edgar (Louise Latham), reveals to Marnie and her husband Mark Rutland (Sean Connery) the reason for distancing herself from her daughter. The mother falsely confessed to the murder of a sailor, one of Mrs. Edgar's 'johns'. But it was Marnie who actually killed the sailor because she believed the man was hurting her mother. Parts of the crucial scene are depicted in flashback.

High Heels makes many subtle allusions to *Marnie*'s *mise-en-scène* from the beginning of the film onwards. Rebeca, who like Marnie, a master of disguise, is characterised by her 1960s wardrobe, wears a stunning white suit Chanel with a red purse. As she sits waiting for her mother's arrival in the airport lounge, Rebeca squirms in the seat and tugs at the hem of the short skirt to pull it down. In the frontal shot the gesture emphasises her legs. What generally is a passing nod to good breeding and modesty is nonetheless the same gesture that Marnie makes when she waits to be interviewed by Mark Rutland for a job as his secretary in an early scene of the film.

In *Marnie* it is precisely Mark's rememberance of having seen an attractive girl do the same skirt pull in the office of Mr. Strutt (Martin Gabel), a business

Marnie's (Tippi Hedren) skirt tug hints at her identity as a thief in *Marnie*.

client of Rutland's, that leads Mark to hire Marnie in order to find out what makes her lie and steal, and not coincidentally, bed her in the process. Strutt, who never asked for references because he was blinded by Marnie's charms, has just been robbed by the elusive secretary when Marnie comes to apply for the job at Rutland's.

High Heels repeats the same fetishistic leitmotifs of purses and shoes found in *Marnie*. In both films their presence is exaggerated and a source of ironic humour. Marnie hides all her loot from safe robbing in her large handbags. The film repeats and ends with the children's rhyme, 'call for the doctor, call for the nurse, call for the lady with the alligator purse'. In *High Heels* Rebeca always carries a padded Chanel bag, contrasting with the colour of her suit, even to her mother's deathbed. She takes the gun with which she killed her husband out of her purse and has her mother handle it. The fingerprints will bolster the mother's false confession and save Rebeca. As to shoes in the two films, in a famous sequence from *Marnie*, celebrated for how it allows the viewer to participate in suspense and to know more than the characters, Marnie robs Mark's safe after-hours. To avoid being heard by the cleaning lady, who is revealed as the camera pulls back to show both Marnie and the woman, Marnie takes off her high heels and puts them in the pockets of her coat. At a moment of tense silence in the soundtrack, we see in close-up insert shots how gradually one shoe slips out and clunks on the floor. However, the cleaning lady does not react nor turn around. The next sequence with a co-worker reveals that the cleaning lady is in fact deaf. Is it purely a coincidence that *High Heels* ends with Rebeca's monologue about the *sound* of high heels representing her mother's love for her? The quest for affirmation from her mother motivated Marnie to steal.

On the one hand, the kind of Hitchcockian confession Almodóvar elaborates on – 'that Rebeca confessed to her crime from the very beginning but no one believed her' (Strauss 1995: 118) – returns us to the many scenes of rejected or overlooked admissions in Hitchcock films, which we have already discussed, such as the milkman refusing to believe that Johnny Jones was being pursued by assassins in *Foreign Correspondent*, or even Mary Maloney's smile of confession to her husband's murder in 'Lamb to the Slaughter'. On the other, it should also return us to consider that in *High Heels'* confession Almodóvar claims to have improved on Hitchcock's 'wrong man' theme whose epitome was *I Confess* (1951) about a priest wrongly accused of murder. The film closely respected Church rites in its language, had a theologian as a consultant, and received the full backing of the Catholic Church upon release. To this day it appears on the list of approved films of many religious groups, and even film scholars, such as Bill Krohn proclaim its ending, the final dying words – 'Father forgive me' – of Otto Keller (O. E. Hasse) the murderer to Father Logan (Montgomery Clift), 'liturgically and thematically right (tranference of guilt healed by confession)' (McGilligan 2003: 462). Precisely the presence of confession emphasises a kinship in the common Catholic backgrounds of Almodóvar and Hitchcock. Hitchcock in particular had fans in the priesthood, had his California vineyards farmed by seminarians, and was a major donor to Catholic charities. Not to be too virtuous about it, as McGilligan tells it, 'Priests intrigued him; he found it amusing when the ones he met confessed their enjoyment for his sexiest, most violent films' (2003: 440). Yet Hitchcock had a gruelling time trying to make *I Confess*, and the project was almost canceled several times. In the film, the priest is the Hitchcockian archetype of the wrong man – that is, he is falsely accused of murder. Yet he must respect the sanctity of the confessional and not reveal the true murderer who has confessed his sin. One controversial sticking point, which was expurged from the film, was that Hitchcock wanted the priest to have an illegitimate child. Moreover, the film was always conceived of as an anti-capital punishment manifesto. To give this poignancy, Hitchcock originally wanted the 'wrong man' priest to hang, but this gruesome ending was vetoed. Both politics and religion made the film a hot potato for Hollywood studios in the 1950s. So ironically, given the era's conservatism, while Hitchcock was negotiating what he could or could not include in *I Confess*, he quickly made *Strangers on a Train*, with its 'criss-cross' murders and 'criss-cross' sexuality, with full and enthusiastic studio backing of Warner Bros. *I Confess* was a film that did notably better at the box office in Spain and in Europe than in the US.

Just as in *Marnie*, in which the last confession is that of the mother Bernice Edgars, likewise the last confession in *High Heels* is of the mother, Becky del Páramo (Marisa Paredes). Interestingly, Becky's confession is a religious one conducted by a Catholic priest. The scene is a throwback to Hitchcock's time and specifically to *I Confess*, for the priest acknowledges changes in the Church's rites and asks Becky to confess using the words of her childhood with whose language she is more comfortable. In Spain of the 1990s the presence of a Catholic rite at the film's conclusion, with realistic, doctrinally appropriate dialogue but a newfound humanistic intent – Becky finally only confesses, 'I repent for unhappiness' – reassured the audience. Overall it struck a balance in the film, particularly for an ascendant, increasingly Europeanised, middle class in Spain, which felt comfortable going out to Villarosa to see a female impersonator, or the movies to see both Miguel Bosé and Bibi Anderson impersonating the film star Sara Montiel, but still felt the need to invoke its Catholic heritage. Hitchcock found a similar balance, both socially and politically liberating while still rooted in tradition, for his worldwide audiences between his two contemporaneous films *I Confess* and *Strangers on a Train*.

High Heels can also be interpreted as an even more personal reconciliation, for Almodóvar has said that the final scene, reverential in tone, of Becky dying in her old apartment decorated in a Mexican style of her youth, recreates for him his own father's death around 1983. The family helped his father, who was critically ill with cancer like Becky, return to his old village home, to the house of his father's sister, to die in the bed in which he was born. Almodóvar's description of his father's final days is quite moving:

> In my movies I never talk about fathers, but about mothers, like the one played by Marisa Paredes in *High Heels*, but that case is one of the few memories I have of my father. My father died of cancer about twelve years ago. My family was living in Extremadura. When he was in his last dying stages my father told my mother to take him to the village where he was born. He was gravely ill at that moment. So they returned to our village, where we were born, and since we no longer have a house there, they set him up in the house of his sister, which had been their parents' house. It was the family home, where he had been born and lived. And then his sister had the good sense to put him in the same room where he had been born and in the same bed, in his grandmother's room. He was in bad shape when he arrived, in great pain, and it's incredible how death waited until he arrived at the place where he had begun his life. From the moment he arrived, he lasted about ten hours, his pains disappeared, and he died in the same bed where he was born. These memories are embedded in that part of Marisa's life in *High Heels*, and curiously I've never spoken about that scene. It happens very fast in the movie, I don't emphasise it, but it contains all that. (Strauss 1995: 68)

In this recounting of *High Heels*, Almodóvar reveals his own repressed emotions about his father's death, and comes closer to a distant father, just as Marnie reconciled with her mother. Almodóvar returns to the theme of familial reconciliation in *Volver*.

It is not necessary to know about Almodóvar's relationship to his father to interpret *High Heels* any more than it is necessary to know about Hitchcock's alleged impotence or advances on Tippi Hedren, who played Marnie – some of the most contested elements of Hitchcock's biography – in order to interpret *Marnie*. Yet these biographical details already participate forcefully in the cultural discourse. Almodóvar recites them, and judges himself in comparison to Hitchcock in these terms, while never divorcing his comments from an appreciation of what appears on screen:

> Hitchcock used the scenes of his films as a way of approaching his actresses. Sometimes his difficult relationship with women enriched his female characters and inspired the most memorable scenes of his films, even if they also

end up giving a rather negative image of the man. I don't have such a complicated relationship with women; mine is much more generous and above board. Hitchcock's talent was so enormous I'd prefer not to judge the man; probably in that regard he was a SOB. (Strauss 2006: 144)

The popular legends of these directors revolve around their respective representations of women in all their complexity.

VIII. DOMESTIC DETAILS AND THE REPRESENTATION OF RAPE AND SEXUAL VIOLENCE: *KIKA, PSYCHO, TORN CURTAIN, REAR WINDOW, MARNIE* AND *FRENZY*

Hitchcock has been a key referent for Almodóvar in constructing his scripts. Speaking of *Kika*, he says that its four chapters are each signalled by a change in music. The final chapter is cued by an intentional reference to *Psycho*:

This block begins when Rossy de Palma walks off alone in the street. I use the music Bernard Hermann composed for *Psycho*, music that will bind together the discovery of the hidden crime through an extract on the TV of Losey's *The Prowler*, and Andrea's entire nocturnal search through the videotape. Of all cinema composers, I consider Hermann to be the best manipulator of an audience. Even if only film buffs understand this, I allude through the music to another story of a man obsessed by his mother, just like Ramón is in *Kika*. It's an amusing parallel. When Ramón enters the Casa Youkalli to speak to Nicholas, he seems unhinged. The house smells of a dead woman. Of course, the body of the woman played by Bibi is lying dead in the house. But Ramón believes he can smell the perfume of his mother whose suicide he never accepted. That's where I use the theme of Kurt Weill's 'Youkalli'. (Strauss 2006: 113–4)

This is not the only time Almodóvar cites Hitchcock as inspiration for *Kika*'s effects. Discussing precisely the place in *Kika* of a domestic urge – to be 'a practical woman' – to manipulate the tone of the film, Almodóvar brings in his knowledge of the kitchen murder sequence of *Torn Curtain*, which is celebrated for its intensity and length, to bear on his idea for the prolonged rape of Kika. His comments are so germaine to our discussion that they deserve to be looked at in entirety.

In the film as it stands, Kika starts by resisting Paul, but the second he puts the knife to her throat she turns into a practical woman and tries to persuade him he has a lot of problems she can solve. This doesn't indicate any pleasure on her part, because she's passive; but it shows her enormous optimism. It demonstrates the strength women can call on in difficult, liminal, situations. For me it's like the triumph of matriarchy. Two women, Kika and Juana, one violated and the other gagged, negotiate with the rapist in order to find a solution. I wanted to show this because it's a feminine trait I admire a great deal. It's also what makes the scene funny. If I'd written only the first half of the rape scene it would have stayed merely violent. Yet since Paul Brazzo is on top of Kika for hours, the situation has time to develop. The rape becomes irrelevant; a thirteen-stone man is on top of her and after a while she has the urge to put the house in order, to pee, to blow her nose. What's important is that she's immobilized in spite of having a lot to do and all kinds of domestic worries.

Humour always arises out of everyday life. Besides, you can only prolong any situation by playing it out naturally; that's what makes things funny. In cinema, you normally use ellipses a lot, but if you dare to take a conventional situation that's generally narrated in a brief time and make it longer instead, it ends up being surprising. For example, in Hitchcock's *Torn Curtain*, there's a moment in which someone kills someone else, but Hitchcock decides to show how difficult – how slow and exasperating – it is to kill somebody, and the crime becomes something entirely different. (Strauss 1995: 148–9)

Hitchcock repeatedly got the viewer's attention with the humour of everyday life at critical moments in his films. For instance, in *Rope* as Rupert (Jimmy Stewart) leaves the party given by his former students, who are hiding the murder of a contemporary school chum, the maid hands him his hat which is bizarrely too small for his head. The plausible circumstance of getting the wrong hat at checkout is both a sight joke and a catalyst for Rupert to act as a detective, for he then deduces from the monogram that it is the murder victim's hat left behind in the closet. What we see clearly in the above citation is that Almodóvar not only gets the humour of inserting elements of daily life into film, as did Hitchcock, but also he interprets Hitchcock's work in a humourous direction when he cites Hitchcock's film *Torn Curtain* in his own. Overall these are essential points in the reception of Hitchcock in Spain and Latin America.

The importance of using domestic details for comic effect in an intense situation is major strategy of *Tie Me Up! Tie Me Down!*, too. As Almodóvar notes:

I think it's something many people have experienced: recognizing the sound of one's partner arriving, saying 'it's me' before you even see them. It's always an emotional moment. The situation becomes comic in the film. Ricky announces his arrival so as to calm Marina when it's precisely his arrival which terrifies her. He fixes the tap, he does the things any man would do for his girlfriend. These little things become much more significant within the situation the film describes. (Strauss 2006: 99)

The Strauss interview with Almodóvar on *Kika* turns more and more towards Hitchcock. It is as if in the artificial world of *Kika* that he sees himself as a mature director of Hitchcock's stature. Strauss probes, 'Were you thinking about *Rear Window* when you were making *Kika*?', and Almodóvar aquiesces:

Yes, the backdrops in *Kika* have the same significance. They're a painting that represents the city. Whenever one shoots in a studio, one's main aesthetic reference is Hitchcock. This applies to everything and to every filmmaker. But I haven't yet reached the extremes Hitchcock did in *Marnie*, where there's an entire fake port with boats next to Tippi Hedren's house. (Strauss 1995: 160)

Representing rape is always, and should always be, controversial. Neither Hitchcock nor Almodóvar shunned the challenge. Numerous Almodóvar's films make rape integral to their respective narratives, especially *Tie Me Up! Tie Me Down!*, *Kika*, *Talk to Her*, *Bad Education* and *The Skin I Live In*. Hitchcock made resisting rape the motive for the homicide in *Murder!* (1930). *Marnie* posed a dual challenge to viewers and the censor board alike – whether the wedding night scene was to be interpreted as rape, and whether the repressed murder scene was to be interpreted as attempted child rape. Hitchcock fired Evan Hunter, his first scriptwriter on the project, because he questioned Hitchcock's intention to portray the honeymoon cruise confrontation as rape.[18] The second scriptwriter, Jay Presson Allen, followed Hitchcock's bidding, and asserted in her script for the sequence that 'fear and revulsion [are] manifest in her frozen face,' as quoted in William Rothman's *Must We Kill the Thing We Love?* (2014: 233). Rothman finds reason to suspend judgement over the 'alleged rape' in Marnie's 'frozen face' reaction shot, which Rothman interprets as 'a standoff between repulsion and attraction' (ibid.). *Frenzy*, Hitchcock's 'last dark testament' (McGilligan 2003: 714), contains the most lurid rape/strangling of all of his films through virtuoso montage. Hitchcock was considered ahead of his time in portraying a serial killer/sexual psychopath in *Frenzy*. Overall many of the murderous attacks on women in his films, so often committed with knives, from the British *The Thirty-Nine Steps* where the beautiful foreign spy gets a knife in her back and falls towards the protagonist's bed, to the American *Psycho*, though here yielded by a 'female-identified regressive' (Smith 1994: 112), can be viewed metaphorically as rapes as well. On the other hand, Almodóvar has portrayed sexual violence against both men and women. He has said that the ritual killing by hairpin in *Matador* is a sexual reversal (I would add, of violence against women): 'By contrast in *Matador*, Assumpta Serna has from the very beginning a very masculine role. She is the active partner in her relationships with men; she ends up penetrating and killing them with her hair pin, in a delibate imitation of a *torrero*' (Strauss 2006: 55).

Obliquely referring to the quandry of representing sexual violence on screen, Almodóvar has perhaps defensively termed *Matador* and *Kika* his most 'abstract' films. By this he means that they represent ideas, not characters or situations (Strauss 1995: 140). In the case of *Kika*, these ideas are moreover cinematographic concepts, as Almodóvar notes: 'The day of *Kika*'s premiere I felt more vertigo than ever because I felt I was pushing the envelope. It's a very personal work, full of purely cinematographic concepts, so I was afraid the audience wouldn't understand it (Strauss 1995: 142). We could add his later films *Talk to Her, Bad Education* and *The Skin I Live In* to the list of 'abstract' films. Analogously Hitchcock's 'abstract' films would be those of repressed memories: *Murder!, Spellbound, Vertigo* and *Marnie*.

The concept of voyeurism, which *Kika* probes in the foregrounding of the camera even in the costume design for Andrea Caracortada (Victoria Abril) and in the predominance of keyhole and iris shots, threads its way back to and through *Rear Window*. In Kika's story, framed within the film until she casts off Ramón's mother's ring and takes off with the stranded motorist, she is positioned as a mother figure, and as the object of Ramón's extreme scopophilic instinct. He insists on Polaroid photos of their sex, films Kika's rape, and is imaged in the frame, head down, nose prominent, as Dalí's 'The Great Masturbator' (1929). Almodóvar cites many of Hitchcock's characters and situations. The chest that flies down on a rope/pulley from Nicolás's upper-floor apartment, which we surmise contained the body of Susana (Bibi Anderson) whom he sadistically murdered, alludes to *Rope*. In that film the murder victim is placed in a chest kept in plain sight during a party. Ramón later discovers Susana's body in the bathtub of Casa Youkalli with the shower curtain prominent in the frame, a location even more evocative of Hitchcock and *Psycho*. Most characters in *Kika*, such as the masochistic lesbian maid (Rossy de Palma), are stylised abstractions. In this the film radically differs from Hitchcock's voyeurist masterpiece. Yet *Kika* takes as its point of departure the visual style of Hitchcock, and the psychoanalytical probing which his films suggest.

IX. TRAGIC LATIN FLOWERS AND A MOTHER'S VOICE:
FLOWER OF MY SECRET, *TOPAZ* AND *SHADOW OF A DOUBT*

After *Kika*, whose mixed reviews made critics and the public wonder what happened to their beloved, but now stereotypical, classic Almodóvarian comedy, Almodóvar looked backward in his career and in terms of Hollywood genres with *Flower of My Secret* (1997). The film is an ode to classic women's pictures, especially George Cukor's *Rich and Famous* (1981), but also Billy Wilder's *The Apartment* (1960), *Casablanca* (1942) and *Singin' in the Rain* (1952), among other films. Given the Hollywood films cited, and the general effect of pastiche, *Flower of My Secret* is rather removed in genre and spirit from most Hitchcock films. Yet some motifs we have already discussed as characteristic of Hitchcock are present in what Marvin D'Lugo has called the film's 'international style with culturally-specific narrative elements that highlighted Spain's gradual integration within a new European culture' (1997: 117). As in many of Hitchcock's works, the world of theatre frames the film and signals the artificiality of the filmic universe. *Flower of My Secret* brackets its story between an initial taped training session for doctors learning to present family members with the option of organ transplant, and the ending of a mother/son modern flamenco performance attended by the main characters. As in *Torn Curtain*'s climactic ballet performance, the lead dancers in *Flower of My Secret*, among them the amazing

Overhead shot of Blanca's (Manuela Vargas) extremely extended flamenco pose in a stage performance of a tragic love story in *Flower of My Secret*.

In *Flower of My Secret* Blanca falls backwards and drapes over the arms of Antonio (Joaquín Cortes) in a symbolic death.

Hitchcock's tragic flower in *Topaz*: The dying Juanita de Córdoba (Karin Dor) falls backwards onto the patterned floor like a flower opening after Rico Parra (John Vernon) shoots her in the back during their embrace.

Joaquín Cortes as Blanca's (Manuela Vargas) son, are also characters in the film's main story. The final stage performance of Leo's (Marisa Paredes) maid Blanca, dressed now in flowing blood red, a traditional flamenco colour, especially appropriate for the tragic love story told, emphasises the primary-coloured flowing and drape-like wardrobe of Leo throughout the film. The extreme overhead shot of Blanca and her swirling dress on stage as well as the climactic image of her backward fall recall the most celebrated shot of Hitchcock's only truly Latin-themed film, the spy thriller *Topaz* (1969), set in the world of the Cuban missile crisis.

Like *Flower of My Secret*, *Topaz*'s story has plenty of the elements of a *culebrón*, or serialized soap opera, among them a marriage on the rocks with a strategic expert husband more interested in getting away to the site of the current world conflict, in *Topaz*, to Cuba, in *Flower of My Secret*, to Brussels or Bosnia, than in dealing with his wife. To recall, *Topaz* marked another of the moments in Hitchcock's late career when he was trying to regain a former glory, this time, precisely after the disappointing showing of *Torn Curtain*. Almodóvar, perhaps following Hitchcock's path, likewise turned to the topics of entertaining, escapist narrative to recapture his audience with *Flower of My Secret*. In *Topaz* when the Cuban military official Rico Parra (John Vernon) discovers that Juanita de Córdoba (Karin Dor), his former lover and a widow of a revolutionary hero, a character inspired by Fidel's sister Juanita, is a double agent, he pulls her to his chest and proceeds to shoot her in the back, supposedly to save her from being tortured by others. An extreme overhead shot shows the dark Latin beauty Juanita lying on the floor, her long vibrant blue/purple dress pooled around her symbolising the blood flowing out of her. Hitchcock described the shot to interviewers as a flower opening:

> I had attached to her gown five strands of thread held by five men off-camera. At the moment she collapses, the men pulled up the threads and her robe splayed out like a flower that was opening up. That was for contrast.

Although it was a death scene, I wanted it to look very beautiful. (McGilligan 2003: 689)

Almodóvar has said he discovered Hitchcock when he was beginning to work with colour (Strauss 2006: 143). *Flower of My Secret* may in fact be Almodóvar's secret tribute to *Topaz*'s Latin palette, cinematography and general flower motif. In *Topaz* one of the American operatives in New York, a Caribbean black, such an unusual ethnic presence for Hitchcock's films, even runs a flower shop, where the spies exchange information in the cooler among the blooms.

Almodóvar worked on location for most of the interiors of *Flower of My Secret*. Doing so inspired his shots and distanced him from Hitchcock's preferred *modus operandi*, especially when dealing with romance. If we briefly compare Hitchcock's kisses to one of the most famous sequences of *Flower of My Secret*, the kiss between Leo and her husband Paco (Imanol Arias) in the vestibule of their apartment, in this shot the mirrored door fragments the images of husband and wife, foreshadowing their break-up. In a kiss in Hitchcock's films, such as the many kisses in *Notorious*, which so irritate the Mexican critic Francisco Sánchez Aguilar he calls them 'anti-cinematographic' (2004: 210), or even one depicting an unstable relationship, for instance in *Marnie*, at some point the camera, not the *décor*, is intrusive. One part of the sequence will always be in extreme close-up. However, another signature Hitchcock close-up is parodied in *Flower of My Secret*, the scream motif placed on a transitional cut. Examples in Hitchcock are the cut from the train's whistle to the woman's scream upon discovering Annabella Smith's (Lucie Mannheim) body in *The Thirty-Nine Steps*, and the cut to the shower scream in *Psycho*. *Flower of My Secret* cuts from the bedraggled Leo in her bathtub/shower, trying to shake off her suicide attempt, to an absurd 'Concurso de gritos', or scream contest, on the Spanish state-run television network. Moving from the more intimate contact of Leo's mother's voice, Almodóvar riffs on Hitchcock's 'internationalist' technique to recentre the film nationally on an old stand-by since Franco's time, the folkloric shows of RTVE.

Besides a certain visual bravado and theatricality, *Flower of My Secret* also repeats the domestic humour, which is a hallmark of Hitchcock, in the scenes with Chus Lampreave, who plays the part of Leo's mother. Almodóvar has said in his interview with Strauss that numerous segments of the dialogue in *Flower of My Secret* are inspired by the words and habits of his mother – the reciting of a poem about the *pueblo*, the remembrance of his birth, the discussion of an eye operation as splitting open a melon, and the citing of the proverb 'estar como vaca sin cencerro', literally 'to be like a cow without a bell', that is, to be disoriented or to not know what to do with oneself. *Flower of My*

Secret is the companion piece to the allusion to the father in *High Heels* in its nostalgic, personal tribute to his mother's world, even though she does not personally act in this film. Starting with her stilted reading of the TV news in *Women on the Verge of a Nervous Breakdown*, Almodóvar's mother appeared in several of Almodóvar's pictures before her death. Her presence, and often that of her other son Agustín as well, became almost like Hitchcock cameos.[19] Moreover, it should be recalled that it is Leo's mother's voice on her answering machine that brings Leo back from her suicidal stupor. Donald Spoto theorises that Hitchcock affectionately portrayed his own mother Emma, when she was close to her death, as the mother of the young Charlie (Teresa Wright) in *Shadow of a Doubt* (1942). Within the context of that picture she is the anchor of the smalltown values that are under threat. Overall Hitchcock's portrayal of Emma (Patricia Collinge) is much softer, and less frenetic than Leo's mother's in *Flower of My Secret*. For instance, her husband and daughter praise Emma for selflessly working all the time. Nonetheless, the two films both single out one common trait of their respective mothers for comic relief – their telephone behaviour. In *Flower of My Secret* mother/daughter (Chus Lampreave and Rossy de Palma), yell and fight over one telephone to get their side of the story to Leo. In an early sequence of *Shadow of a Doubt*, Emma's husband and children make fun of her for shouting into the telephone as she tries to take down a telegraph message. According to Spoto, it was a characteristic 'amusing behavior' of Emma Hitchcock (quoted in McGilligan 2003: 321). While noting the coincidence of the name Emma, and the scene in which Uncle Charlie (Joseph Cotten) presents the mother with a gift of paired portraits of their grandparents, Hitchcock's daughter, Pat Hitchcock O'Connell, in *Beyond Doubt*, the documentary accompanying the 2000 DVD rerelease of *Shadow of a Doubt*, categorically states that the character of Emma was 'nothing like her grandmother'.

X. SO MANY *FEMMES FATALES: LIVE FLESH* SPLICED BETWEEN BUÑUEL AND HITCHCOCK

Both *Kika* and *Carne trémula* (*Live Flesh*, 1997) were based on a mystery novel titled *Live Flesh* (1986) by the British writer Ruth Rendell. *Kika* treated material from the first chapter, and *Live Flesh* adapted the rest of Rendell's book. Among Almodóvar's works *Live Flesh* is distinctive for its noir genre and consistent tone.[20] After complaining of numerous narrative and stylistic deficiencies he finds in *Live Flesh*, Carlos F. Heredero in a review in *Dirigido* goes on to praise the film's 'notable step forward' due to its 'expressive coherence which allows one to excuse even some defects in character development or certain concessions in the reasons for their behaviour' (1997: 23). Despite the genre, 'passionate drama with touches of *thriller*' (1997: 22), the film recalls Hitchcock very little, if only in that the embedded film, Buñuel's *Ensayo de un crimen* (*The Criminal Life of Archibaldo de la Cruz*, 1955), which plays on the television during the early crime scene in *Live Flesh*, itself pays homage to Hitchcock's suspense films. Buñuel mocks psychoanalytical interpretation in *Ensayo de un crimen* precisely through his citation of two key motifs from Hitchcock films: the glass of milk from *Suspicion* (1941) and the razor from *Spellbound*. In *Suspicion* the poisoned glass of milk glows – a famous special effect – as the husband Johnnie (Cary Grant) carries it up the stairs to his rich wife Lina (Joan Fontaine). The glass of milk makes a reprise appearance in a pivotal sequence of *Spellbound*, often viewed as Hitchcock's debunking of psychoanalysis. In *Spellbound* while shaving, John Ballantyne (Gregory Peck) regresses and in his trance, holding his open razor, threatens Alex (Michael Chekhov), Constance's (Ingrid Bergman) psychoanalyst and master teacher, whose help in curing John through psychoanalysis he and Constance have come to seek. Alex gives John a glass of milk. The sequence finishes with a shot through the bottom of the glass as an image of milk, part of the film's white *leitmotif*, fills the screen. At that moment the viewer suspects that John kills the doctor with his razor, but it turns out that instead the doctor has drugged John with the milk. It is a clear case of Oedipal confrontation. In *Ensayo de un crimen* the protagonist obsessively drinks only milk, a fixation upon his childhood and his mother, when everyone else has cocktails. There are insert shots of his glass of milk. However, neither milk nor razors are in the sequences from *Ensayo de un crimen* that Almodóvar selects for *Live Flesh*. Both *Spellbound*, in the impersonation of Dr. Edwardes by John Ballantyne, and *Ensayo de un crimen*, especially in the fabrication of a mannequin of the model Patricia, deal with doubling at the core of their problematics. The meltdown of the wax mannequin, Buñuel's most famous shot in *Ensayo de un crimen*, because the effect was technically challenging and so expensive it could only be filmed once, is one of the signature sequences Almodóvar chooses for *Live Flesh*.

It is worth further exploring the nature of the doubles in these three directors' respective films. The femme fatale in *Live Flesh*, reprising Angela Molina's role from Buñuel's *Cet obscur objet du désir* (*That Obscure Object of Desire*, 1977), is, however, a dark Carmen, not a Hitchcock blonde, on the order of the doomed Madeleine/Judy/Kim Novak of *Vertigo*.[21] The sole (postmodern) blonde in *Live Flesh*, the Italian Elena (Francesca Neri) first appears in a frizzy blonde wig in her father's apartment, where the camera pans over huge paintings of erotic art, in particular Titian's 'Venus and the Organ Player'.[22] The contemplation of art in this sequence distantly recalls *Vertigo*. There Hitchcock's stylised eroticism and doubling is set in motion as Madeleine studies the portrait of her ancestor Carlotta in the early art museum scene.

As Marvin D'Lugo observes, 'Buñuel's film-within-Almodóvar's film emphasizes that *Live Flesh* is essentially a narrative about looking back and fits into the broader patterns of Spanish national cultural recovery though cinema and narrative of the 1990s' (2006: 97). Like *Dark Habits*, and later *Bad Education*, Almodóvar through Buñuel characterises the times and especially the protagonist Victor through irreverent placement of Catholic imagery. For instance, Victor holds a photograph of Elena's First Communion as he talks about having lost his virginity with her. The photograph almost protects him as she trains a gun on him to make him leave. Later Victor will often cite the Bible, which he studied along with Bulgarian in prison.

Live Flesh contains typical thriller or intrigue genre shots, such as the scream reaction shot of Elena, placed on a cut between sequences, as she hears the gun shots as Clara (Angela Molina) and Sancho (José Sancho) die in a murder/suicide in the film's dénouement. The cinematic style of Hitchcock is sutured into *Live Flesh* as is Buñuel's.

XI. DIVAS DON'T DRIVE: VEHICLE SHOTS, SUBJECTIVE CAMERAWORK AND ORCHESTRAL SCORES IN *ALL ABOUT MY MOTHER*

I met Almodóvar in March 2002 at a talk he was giving at the Círculo de Bellas Artes (Fine Arts Circle) in Madrid. This event was one in a series of directors speaking on cars in the movies. He was still bathing in the spotlight of having won the Best Foreign Film Academy Award, but was obviously processing, decompressing from his Hollywood triumph with his compatriots who saw his triumph as their own. Almodóvar was in top form entertaining, and genuinely relating to, the young, overwhelmingly Spanish audience. He spoke not only of the glitter of Hollywood, but humbly about his own shortcomings speaking English, which left many in the crowd nodding in agreement. He appreciated the irony of his participation in the series on cars because as he pointed out, he does not drive, though he owns a car. He told a funny story of hopping into the backseat of a stranger's car in his neighborhood that looked similar to his own, to the astonishment of the driver. The anecdote reminded the audience that divas do not drive, they are driven. Hitchcock never drove. He liked to be driven onto all sets to within steps of his director's chair. In *All About My Mother*, Manuela (Cecilia Roth) has an opportunity to get close to Huma Rojo (Marisa Paredes) one night after a performance when Huma gets stranded at the theatre because her lover Nina (Candela Pena) has left in a huff. The diva makes a point of saying she never learned to drive.

All About My Mother is generically nothing like a Hitchcock film. The story does recall at times the diva film, *Stage Fright*, discussed previously in regard to *Dark Habits*. In *All About My Mother*, Manuela, then later Agrado (Antonia San Juan), serve as personal assistants to the diva Huma Rojo in her dressing room. In *Stage Fright* Eve Gill (Jane Wyman) takes over the part from Charlotte's (Marlene Dietrich) real maid to serve as a dresser to Charlotte. In both films the female protagonist goes undercover. Eve Gill, a reporter, is searching for clues to a murder. Manuela, a nurse, is searching for rebirth, of herself and her dead son Esteban (Eloy Azorín), by going back to find Lola (Toni Cantó), Esteban's transvestite father. Yet to go much beyond these analogies not only forces the comparison, but shows how the representation of sex and gender has evolved since the 1950s. As with *Flower of My Secret*, the film whose transplant sequence inspired Almodóvar to continue the story with *All About My Mother*, the allusions are more generally to classic Hollywood, and especially *All About Eve* (1950). As with *Live Flesh* and Buñuel's *Ensayo de un crimen*, Hitchcock, whose *Stage Fright* with its perky Eve Gill preceeded *All About Eve*, is sutured into the film's narrative along with Joseph L. Mankiewicz's Academy Award-winning film.

As we have seen with other Almodóvar films, we can explore the continued emphasis on theatricality, and citations of famous Hitchcock shots, precisely from Hitchcock's *Concha de Plata* (Silver Shell) films of the late 1950s, namely the tunnel shot of *North by Northwest*, or the use of subjective camerawork, a prevalent technique in *Vertigo*. As discussed before, the closing tunnel shot of *North by Northwest* is considered a metaphor for sex. Almodóvar recalls Hitchcock's symbolism, but makes it his own in the tunnel motif of *All About My Mother*. After her son's death, Manuela travels from Madrid to Barcelona by high-speed train. At each stage in her mourning process, the tunnel *leitmotif* signifies re-birth, going back to relive the birth of Esteban by seeking Lola. Towards the end of the film when Manuela takes Rosa and Lola's baby Esteban with her to Madrid by train, the tunnel is first filmed from inside, from Manuela's point of view. Since Manuela now has a new adoptive son, the tunnel suggests a birth canal. The film then cuts to an overhead shot of trains going through two tunnels, stating it is two years later, as Manuela returns to Barcelona with the child Esteban, where she will attend the father's funeral, and find closure to her grieving for the first Esteban.

The first tunnel sequence, a subjective shot zooming into the tunnel, recalls the famous Hitchcock zoom techniques of *Vertigo*, which emphasise Scotty's mental distress. Subjective camerawork, resembling that shot, also structures the early sequence when a car hits Esteban. As often in Hitchcock's car sequences, for example as discussed and shown in Hitchcock's storyboards in the DVD documentary on the car sequence of *Family Plot* (1976), Hitchcock anchors the sequence with shots from inside the car. In *All About My Mother* we see Esteban's body break the windshield. The sequence here ends with even more powerful subjective camerawork. As in *The Wrong Man* jail cell shot of Manny (Henry Fonda), the camera moves erratically, in a random, yet circular motion, stressing Manuela's panic, and showing her point of view as she finds Esteban's body under the car.

Still, there are some other important parallels between Hitchcock and Almodóvar, in choices for the soundtrack, which are different than those already discussed and mark a change or break in *All About My Mother* with Almodóvar's previous films. Furthermore, these choices reaffirm the role of Hitchcock's soundtracks in his successful career formula. For Almodóvar, they represent a change in tone, which Almodóvar self-characterises as a mature voice (DVD interview, *All About My Mother*). Before *All About My Mother*, and after that film as well, the soundtracks of Almodóvar's films are distinguished by their vocal music. Music, and especially what we could call his songbook, played a huge role in Almodóvar's career to this point and after. As Kathleen Vernon points out, he became a 'cultural entrepreneur' in the global musical marketplace (2013: 386). Plaintive Latin American music, especially boleros – of Lola Beltrán, La Lupe, Trio Los Panchos, Chavela Vargas – sing the melodramatic messages of his films. The songs are so integral to the narrative that they must be subtitled for international distribution. Almodóvar has said, moreover, that he is rerighting a global injustice of Spain *vis-à-vis* Latin America with his popularisation of these classics songs:

> Spain is very unjust with other Spanish-speaking countries. It feels a sort of superiority far from solidarity. There was a lot of hypocrisy in the celebration of the quincentenary of the Discovery of America. I discover things in a sentimental way. It's gratifying to see how that works later on in the marketplace, because I think that it's reestablishing justice. (Strauss 1995: 126)

All About My Mother veers away from the vocal and asserts an internationalist tone with its primarily orchestral score, recorded by the City of Prague Symphony. Like Hitchcock, Almodóvar has worked with several different composers throughout his career: Bernardo Bonezzi for most of his early career in international distribution, from *What Have I Done to Deserve This?* to *Women on the Verge of a Nervous Breakdown*, then unhapppily (because Almodóvar felt the product was not original) with Ennio Morricone for *Tie Me Up! Tie Me Down!* and disappointingly with Ryuichi Sakamoto for *High Heels*. Almodóvar scrapped most of Sakamoto's score and substituted several vocals as well as existing instrumentals by Miles Davis and George Fenton. Almodóvar began to work with Alberto Iglesias on *Flower of My Secret* and *Live Flesh*, but really didn't give him full reign – that is, he did not move away from the presentation of the film through his incorporation of vocal music, until *All About My Mother*.[23]

Ironically a full orchestral score, even with its harmonica parts, is less intrusive, more subliminal, than the vocally dominant scores. As Jack Sullivan observes in *Hitchcock's Music* particularly referring to the recognition scene of *Vertigo*: 'A product of the silent era, Hitchcock distrusted words but came to trust music; it spoke a language deeper than dialogue, allowing the world of obsession and longing, his favorite subject to have its say' (2006: xix). This type of subliminal effect, through which the orchestral score seemlessly reinforces the melodrama, is perhaps best appreciated, and symbolised in its interplay, in one of the final sequences of *All About My Mother* when Manuela shows Esteban number three to Lola – Esteban number one – in a Barcelona café. The soundtrack features precisely a muted trumpet and the sequence dissolves out with a cropped image of the photograph of the lips of the dead son, Esteban number two. It is as if the Estebans were playing the trumpet.

XII. ATTRACTIVE CRIMINALS AND INVERSE SEQUENCING IN *TALK TO HER*

Both *All About My Mother* and *Talk to Her* begin and end in the theatre. Hitchcock pioneered this narrative structure in his early sound film *The Thirty-Nine Steps*, yet there are significant differences in the theatre pieces presented. In *The Thirty-Nine Steps* the spectacle is a variety show, most specifically the interactive segment with Mr. Memory, in which the audience calls out questions for him to recall the answers. The Mr. Memory segment is punctuated by some oddball questions although it has an overall serious undercurrent. In later Hitchcock the theatre of high culture, via orchestral scenes, frames *The Man Who Knows Too Much* (1956) from the initial close-up clash of cymbals to the climatic scene at the Royal Albert Hall. Almodóvar's theatre spectacles are decidedly high culture – Tennessee Williams' play *A Streetcar Named Desire* in *All About My Mother*, and Pina Bausch's modern ballet in *Talk to Her*. Nonetheless, the way the main characters are introduced in shots outward from the proscenium, as well as where the characters are seated in the theatre, is common to both Hitchcock and Almodóvar.

One prominent technique of Hitchcock's cinematic style – which he developed in his earliest silent films, consistently used throughout his career, and for which he is well known – was to begin a sequence with a close-up, and to pull the camera back gradually through the shots of the sequence to end the sequence revealing the full *mise-en scène*, in what conventionally would have been the view of an establishing shot. This sequencing was as often edited through cuts rather than in a continuous long take dolly shot. In a Hitchcock film this 'inverse' sequencing creates suspense and interest. Almodóvar uses a similar 'inverse' sequencing prominently and masterfully early in *Talk to Her* to introduce Benigno's (Javier Cámara) role as the nurse of Alicia (Leonor Watling) who is in a coma.

The sequence begins with an extreme close-up of Benigno's hands massaging Alicia's muscles. The inverse sequencing hides, or prevents the spectator from immediately identifying, both the gender of Benigno and the location where the massage is taking place. Withholding this information until the final shot of the sequence, which encompasses the room from the point of view of the end of Alicia's hospital bed, grants the information, or the surplus thereof, added importance. It brings a bit of a gasp to the viewer when she finally sees the male nurse Benigno and wonders if his soft physical appearance means he is gay, or if the erotically-charged massage of the beautiful Alicia that she first saw means he is heterosexual.

The comic dialogue between Dr. Roncero (Helio Pedregal), Alicia's father, a psychiatrist, and Benigno regarding the latter's sexual identification is both typically Almodóvarian and very much in the spirit of Hitchcock's comic relief in narrative as well, as already discussed in respect to *Foreign Correspondent* and *Spellbound*. We know the characters are fabricating stories, and then question the cultural beliefs that make infidelity, and homosexuality, both more plausible and more culturally acceptable.

Talk to Her, like *What Have I Done to Deserve This?*, is a crime story. It tells the story of Alicia's awakening from a coma through her sexual awakening, the prince's kiss of Sleeping Beauty, or in the eyes of current law, through her sexual violation. The actual representation of the penetration, through the inserted silent film, also restages significant comic sequences in *Kika*. The sympathetic yet compulsive talker Kika awakens the supposedly dead Ramón sexually in an early sequence by putting make-up on him, and in one of the concluding sequences by putting his phallic big toe in a light socket. In *Talk to Her* Benigno takes advantage of his patient in a coma and is summarily condemned to prison for it. One of the greatest difficulties to being a fan of Almodóvar, particularly for feminists, female or male, is that he often makes some criminals attractive characters. Moreover, their criminal actions, which our cultural norms sanction, are made not only palatable, but also seductively admirable in his films. This quandary became most prominent with *Tie Me Up! Tie Me Down!*[24] Although

Antonio Banderas carried over his undeniably seductive screen persona from *Law of Desire* to *Tie Me Up! Tie Me Down!*, his actions as Ricky in the latter film were criminal, as he lorded over a prolonged kidnapping of Marina Osorio (Victoria Abril). Gloria (Carmen Maura) was a murderer in *What Have I Done to Deserve This?*, but her oppressive milieu made the viewer sympathetically consider the crime close to domestic abuse. *Tie Me Up! Tie Me Down!* afforded no such rationalising escape.

The very existence of so many criminal tales in Almodóvar's opus argues at its most basic level for a strong appreciation of Hitchcock by Almodóvar. Yet how do Almodóvar's 'criminals' compare to Hitchcock's? The supplementary materials to the 2004 re-release of Hitchcock's Warner Bros. films note the common bond between Hitchcock and Patricia Highsmith, upon whose first book Hitchcock based *Strangers on a Train*. To recall, this film, one of Hitchcock's most highly praised, tells the story of Bruno (Robert Walker) and Guy (Farley Granger) who meet on a train. Bruno hatches the plan to crisscross murders to hide the motives for the crimes. Bruno then commits the first crime, murdering Guy's wife, and hounds Guy to follow through and murder Bruno's father in return. For Highsmith, the criminal was a Nietzchean *Übermensch*. Moreover, the reader was able to work through existential angst by relating to his plight. Likewise for Hitchcock, his Bruno was undeniably intelligent in launching the plot of *Strangers on a Train*. In Hitchcock's own favourite of his films, *Shadow of a Doubt*, the dapper but menacing Uncle Charlie (Joseph Cotton), perpetrator of the Merry Widow murders, is finally never absolutely condemned, but instead understood in his worldview in the final sequence between the young Charlie (Teresa Wright) and the detective (MacDonald Carey). Significantly, that sequence takes place on the margins, in the church vestibule at Uncle Charlie's funeral. Yet more than clever, which the criminals of Highsmith, Hitchcock and Almodóvar are (to kill with a ham bone, for example, and then to make soup with it), these criminals appeal to the viewer. As proof of the sympathetic persona of Bruno in *Strangers on a Train*, Peter Bogdanovich points to the famous sequence in when a child at the amusement park points a toy gun at Bruno, who in turn pops the child's balloon with his cigarette. Bogdanovich claims that the audience would not laugh at this sequence, which they reliably do, if the viewers did not consider Bruno a sympathetic character, all the while recognising his inherent malice (DVD Commentary, Final Release Version, Warner Bros. Entertainment, 2004: Disc 1). Hitchcock achieves this effect in the balloon sequence through point of view shots, first a high-angle shot looking down at the barrel of the child's gun, cutting then to an eye-level view of the balloon being popped. The viewer understands, yet cheerfully condones the action. Although innocent fun, the sequence foreshadows Bruno's future crime, strangling Miriam

(Laura Elliot) to death. The shot in *Strangers on a Train* of Miriam falling, seen in the reflection of her lens now on the ground, repeats the round motif of the balloon. On the surface clever, upper-class Bruno is miles apart from Gloria, Ricky or Benigno. Yet Benigno and Bruno share the same obsession, a total devotion to mother. They are paradigmatic sympathetic criminals.

XIII. CATHOLICISM IN ALMODÓVAR AND HITCHCOCK: *BAD EDUCATION* AND *I CONFESS*

Hitchcock was educated by the Jesuits, and Almodóvar in a Salesian boarding school. Religious, and particularly Catholic, imagery abounds in both directors' films. Its presence is, on the one hand, one of the clearest instances of autobiographical commentary in their films, and at the same time, one of the most interesting points of coincidence in their respective film histories through which to consider the particular reception of Hitchcock in Almodóvar, and later in Spanish-language film in general. How Catholic is the ideology of these films? How does the presence of Catholicism impact the reception of Hitchcock? I would argue, a lot. Probably the greatest difference in acceptance, translated in box office receipts, or in perception of box office receipts, comes in regard to Hitchcock's most Catholic films, namely *I Confess* and *The Wrong Man*, both of the mid-1950s. It is the *mise-en scène* of these films that makes them the most Catholic. *I Confess* tells the story of a Catholic priest in Quebec, Father Logan, wrongly accused of murder. Many scenes are set either in the church or in the rectory. *The Wrong Man* tells the true story of Christopher (Manny) Balestrero (Henry Fonda), who like Father Logan of *I Confess* is wrongly accused of murder, and abounds with Catholic symbolism. Balestrero keeps his rosary on him and prays with it during the trial. At a turning point in the narrative he stares at a picture of the Sacred Heart of Jesus on the wall of his house. A double exposure of his face and the city streets, on which the real robber will shortly be apprehended, follows this shot.

Taking the primacy of *mise-en scène*, Almodóvar's most Catholic films are *Dark Habits* and *Bad Education*. Neither of these films share the Neorealist style that Hitchcock was experimenting with in his dark, almost gloomy 'wrong man' films. We moreover cannot divorce Hitchcock's 'wrong man' films from the witch-hunt atmosphere of the McCarthy-era blacklisting. Yet the autobiographical is definitely conflated in these pairs of films. Almodóvar's responses to Strauss' questions on religion in *Dark Habits* show not an anti-clerical bent, or a desire for revenge, but a deeply felt humanistic appreciation of religion. Almodóvar describes how he uses an archetypical Catholic scenario, of communion for example, to convey amorous (here, lesbian) attraction between protagonists. Almodóvar's discusses *Dark Habits* in a confessional tone, as he recalls private masses with priests as a child:

> Let me tell you something I've never told anyone. Since this book is going to be published abroad it won't matter. I studied under Salesian priests; I don't hide it because I hate the Salesians. One of their duties is to say a great many masses a week. The grand public mass was held just once a week, but to fulfil their duty the priests also held solitary masses. So, by the time the nine o'clock public mass was held, they had already said at least two others, one at six, the other at seven, at dawn. Each priest needed an acolyte to say these masses. I remember this very well because I was often 'chosen'. Clearly, the priests chose the boy they found most appealing. This mass therefore became for the priest a secret, intimate, nocturnal act. (Strauss 2006: 36–7)

His comments above, including his actions as a choir boy, strongly presage *Bad Education*, especially the sequence in which the young Ignacio is presented as a birthday gift to the order's superior. He sings 'Jardinero' (Gardener) with special lyrics written by the other priests. Almodóvar specifically notes that much of *Dark Habits* is autobiographical: 'I'm talking about this now because for *Dark Habits* several things in my life with the priests inspired me. They're present but transformed in the film' (Strauss 1995: 51). On the other hand, in the DVD notes to *Bad Education*, Almodóvar calls the film's story 'very intimate' but not autobiographical. Furthermore he states he does not seek revenge on the Church through film, since he would not have waited more than twenty years to do so.

Hitchcock's demons on the other hand were the police and jail cells. Famously, one day in his childhood his father, through a policeman surrogate, briefly locked him up in a real jail cell as a punishment. This experience is the underlying inspiration for the sequence of Henry Fonda/Balestrero's psychological trauma in his cell in *The Wrong Man*, one of the film's most celebrated sequences for its camera work. Hitchcock reprises the representation of this trauma in the jail cell sequence of *Frenzy*, a late period 'wrong man' picture, through the use of an extreme overhead shot, which makes the jail cell appear like deep well. Interestingly, McGilligan calls *Frenzy* 'Hitchcock's most insidiously personal film, the Catholic director's final confession' (2003: 713).

XIV. WRITING AUTOBIOGRAPHIES OF DARK PASSIONS: *VERTIGO* AND *BAD EDUCATION*

Almodóvar classifies *Bad Education* generically as 'a film noir, or at least I like to think of it that way' (DVD notes, *El País*, 2004). The multiple themes of the film – blackmail, deception and doubling, sexual assault, murder and confession – are common to any number of Hitchcock pictures. Iglesias's orchestral score to *Bad Education*, moreover, cues multiple instances of suspense, in the style of Bernard Hermann. Yet it is finally the intricacy of the narrative, so rooted in autobiography, and exploring the dark side of human sexuality, which recalls Hitchcock's masterpiece *Vertigo*. Indeed Almodóvar hinted at the allusion to *Vertigo* in public forums, and never more strongly than when in France. As Lynn Hirschberg reported for the *New York Times Magazine*, 'in Cannes, after the *Bad Education* screening ended and the lights came up, the audience jumped to its feet, applauding madly. The crowd overwhelmed Almodóvar. Like a child at Christmas opening a dozen presents at once, he practically leapt from one well-wisher to another: "I have vertigo," Almodóvar said, half-joking' (5 September 2004: 38–9). *Bad Education* opened the Cannes Film Festival, the first time a Spanish film had that honour. As a clever effort to get audience members to spread the word about the film as a 'Vertigo' version while focusing their attention on the Almodóvar persona, the 'Vertigo' remark serves as promotional buzz, a talent for which Almodóvar shares with Hitchcock, and never more so than at a mature stage of his career.

Formally, *Bad Education* is a story within a story told in flashbacks, which are at the same time potential movie takes, as Enrique (Fele Martínez) the film director within the film would imagine the story filmed. Format changes signal the different periods. Ignacio's (Francisco Boira) short story 'La visita' ('The Visit') intersects with his 'real' life. To recall the intricate plot, Ignacio's insert story accuses Father Manolo (Daniel Giménez Cacho) of paedophilia. Juan/Angel's (Gael García Bernal) ending to the insert accuses Father Manolo and Father José (Francisco Maestre) of murdering Ignacio when Ignacio as the transvestite Zahara (Gael García Bernal) tried to blackmail them. The frame story, however, accuses Juan/Angel of inciting Manolo/Berenguer (Lluis Homar) to murder Ignacio. Further, Enrique is portrayed as using Juan, in yet another case of blackmail, for his own sexual satisfaction, and then usurping Juan's place as Berenguer's lover. In a sinister ending, Enrique controls, and most likely suppresses, the final public revelation of Ignacio's murderer. The film ends with documentary style 'what they did later' revelations for the major characters, Juan/Angel, Manolo/Berneguer, and Enrique. The final intertitle reads, 'Enrique Goded sigue haciendo cine con la misma pasión' ('Enrique Goded continues to make movies with the same passion'). The word 'pasión' is extracted from the script to fill the screen and then dissolves. This motif serves as a *leitmotif* and slogan for Almodóvar's cinematic style.

It is important to remember that the motif is written – it is an image of words, for with *Bad Education* Almodóvar affirms his mature filmic style and persona as a scriptwriter, even more than as cinematographer. As Paul Julian Smith notes in *Desire Unlimited*, Almodóvar's earliest texts are two unpublished short stories, now on file in typescript in the Biblioteca Nacional, Madrid, dated 1975: 'The Visit' and 'The Advertisement' (1994: 2). In some ways the complicated, but still tight, plot of *Bad Education* makes the viewer feel that a fully rendered visualisation of the narrative is missing. Or to interpret what is there instead of what is not, the working copy, the written script of *Bad Education* is incredibly present in the film. The format changes, for example, can almost be taken as paragraph indentations. Several sequences include shots of the typescript of 'The Visit'. Whereas *Law of Desire* simulated the visual, and *Women on the Verge of a Nervous Breakdown* the aural, *Bad Education* simulates the written. All are postmodern versions of passion. In independently developing this script, rewriting from his own earliest story, Almodóvar differs significantly from Hitchcock, who was much more collaborative in his working methods, but also hired according to the rules of the studio system. He went through several writers to adapt the Pierre Boileau and Thomas Narcejac novel *D'entre les morts* for *Vertigo*. Each script, nonetheless, was perfected through a process of daily brainstorming sessions with the main writer during which Hitchcock would endlessly retell the story. Significantly, *Bad Education* begins with a sequence in which Enrique Goded is suffering from writer's block in his meeting with his assistant Martín. Likewise *Vertigo*, now considered Hitchcock's most autobiographical film, begins with a discussion with Midge of Scottie's vertigo complex, which is keeping him from carrying out his job as detective. In *Bad Education* to break his impasse and find inspiration, Enrique cuts out a newspaper article about a dead motorcyclist. This reference also evokes Juan Antonio Bardem's *Muerte de un ciclista* (*Death of a Cyclist*, 1955), a glamorous Spanish noir classic about the personal and political immorality of the ruling class. In *Bad Education* the newsclipping is shown in an insert shot, just as an incriminating article 'Muerte de un ciclista' is shown at a suspenseful moment in that eponymous film. The effect is to self-reference the film's technique as well as the noir genre.

Almodóvar has only recently begun to publish his scripts as books. It is rather ironic that print, now considered old media, becomes one of his newest marketing directions. Its positive implications for the box office recall the earlier phenomenon of releasing soundtrack CDs before video/DVDs. Almodóvar's soundtracks have sold extremely well and support his brand image. On a broader cultural terrain, the publishing of his scripts reflects the parallel growth and development of the upscale Madrid bookstore 8½, which has taken on co-publishing cinema texts. Taken together these phenomena reinforce what Paul Julian Smith has observed, in *Contemporary Spanish Culture*, in light of Bourdieu's field theory. In this scheme Almodóvar has 'achieved cultural distinction to match his box office clout by reworking a form generally considered to be moribund: the "art movie", with its traditional qualities of formal perfection, thematic seriousness and social prestige" (2003: 4). Writing autobiography, in this case Esteban's last diaries, also figured prominently in *All About My Mother*. The act was memorably visualised in the 'under the glass table' shot of a fat pen writing. In *Bad Education* the vision of Ignacio writing on an old Olivetti in the 1980s is period correct, but it also underscores that the act of writing is labour intensive, it is hard work. Likewise, Zahara/Ignacio pens a long letter – in perfect, neat Spanish penmanship – to Enrique Serrano, which he leaves on the pillow next to Enrique's head. The letter reaffirms his love for Enrique, but in parting, Zahara passionately kisses the paper, not the face of his sleeping object of desire. Ignacio is Almodóvar's alter-ego. His tragic last words to Enrique Goded – 'Lo conseguí' – that he types, then collapses over the keys and dies, not only signify that Ignacio has succeeded in blackmailing Manolo/Berenguer, but that Almodóvar has achieved his own writing goals. In this murder scenario the impulse to write is thereby contextualised, not only as passion, a final love letter, but as a death impulse as well. Here very fundamentally, *Bad Education* and *Vertigo* intersect, for as has often been observed, the narrative arc of *Vertigo* – Scottie's path of obsessions that leads him to stand frozen on the precipice of the bell tower, a witness to Madeleine/Judy's fall – shows the inevitable connection between the erotic impulse and death.

The important act, the ultimate act of self-affirmation, in *Bad Education* is writing. Yet even though personal autobiography, this writing is destined for performance. For example, Father Manolo is credited with rewriting the words to the song the young Ignacio will sing for his birthday celebration, which is also his installation as Director of the school, a position of supreme power. Father Manolo envisions himself as 'El jardinero' of the school in the new words to the song. This revision resonates elsewhere in Hitchcock's filmography, too. In a coincidentally ironic but damning coincidence, the real murderer, who tries to frame Father Logan for the murder in Hitchcock's *I Confess*, works as the church gardener. *Bad Education* recalls *I Confess*, Hitchcock's most noir-ish film, in other ways as well, such as their expressionistic lighting to create extreme shadows.

Many critics worldwide have noted the presence of Hitchcock – especially *Vertigo* – in *Bad Education*. Roger Ebert is the most direct. He traces the Hitchcockian influence to the representation of gender in the plot:

> In *Bad Education*, [Almodóvar] uses straight and gay (and for that matter, transvestite and transsexual) as categories which the 'real' characters and the 'fictional' characters use as roles, disguises, strategies, deceptions

A virtual profile:
Zahara (Gael García
Bernal) looks like a
Hitchcock blonde
performing 'Quizás,
quizás, quizás' in
Bad Education.

or simply as a way to make a living. There's no doubt in my mind that
Almodóvar screened Hitchcock's *Vertigo* before making the movie and was
fascinated by the idea of a man asking a woman to pretend to be the woman
he loves, without knowing she actually is the woman he loves. When she's
not playing that woman, she's giving a performance – in his life, although it
works the other way around in hers. In Almodóvar's story, the Hitchcockian identity puzzle is even more labyrinthine, because the past depicted in
Ignacio's screenplay is not quite the past either Ignacio or Enrique remembers, and, for that matter, although Enrique loved Ignacio only 15 years
ago, he doesn't think Ignacio looks much like Ignacio anymore. 'Zahara',
the drag queen, begins to take on a separate identity of his/her own, and
then the guilty priest turns up with his own version of events. (http://www.
rogerebert.com/reviews/bad-education-2004)

The actor Gael García Bernal's performance as Zahara is a conundrum because
the sequence is bracketed as Enrique Goded's fantasy. He imagines the screenplay 'The Visit' which Juan/Angel has just given him. In giving Enrique the
manuscript, Juan tells him the first part of the story is true, but that he has
changed the second half. We may extrapolate then, too, that Ignacio wrote the
first half, but Juan/Angel rewrote the second. Hence, the image of the transvestite Zahara, who imitates Sara Montiel on stage, affords an especially complex
intersection of interpretations. While Zahara lip-synchs Sara Montiel's voice
on tape singing 'Quizás, quizás, quizás' ('Perhaps, Perhaps, Perhaps'), her costume, especially her blonde French twist wig, recalls not Sarita, who never wore
blonde wigs, but Scottie's double object of desire in *Vertigo* – Madeleine/Judy.
Further, the shots of Zahara's *soignée* performance emphasise profiles, which
figure prominently in *Vertigo*. Angel Comas describes the evocation of dualities
in Kim Novak's characterisation in *Vertigo*:

Novak carries off the character with a combination of carnality and mystery. Her presence borders on magic, especially in the first part, and her

eroticism surpasses that inspired by simple physical beauty. In order to differentiate the two stages of the protagonist, Hitchcock used her left profile when she is Madeleine and her right profile when she is Judy. (2002: 33)

Posing mostly in profile, Zahara's performance is Enrique Goded's successful projection. It alerts the viewer to his desire to recreate a feminised Ignacio. Critics of *Vertigo* note that Scottie in fact projects himself in the female doubles he makes over. To recall, Scottie begins the film wearing a corset for his rib injury. He wonders out loud to Midge, 'Do men wear corsets?' Recognising, confronting his erotic self, if not his feminisation, causes vertigo. Hence, Enrique will not accept Juan/Angel in the part of Zahara in the remake, not because Angel is a false copy, but because the repetition of Ignacio must be with the significant difference that he, Enrique Goded, is the feminised object of filmic desire, the blonde Madeleine/Judy of *Vertigo*, as played out in his memory. To recall, Enrique Goded wants to cast Angel as Enrique Serrano in 'The Visit'. Significantly, Almodóvar gives the spectator a particular reading of Hitchcock's *Vertigo* in *Bad Education*.

Likewise looking at *Vertigo* may shed light on how to interpret especially enigmatic images of *Bad Education*, namely the final shots of the pool sequence, a visually complex mating dance. Juan/Angel and Enrique arrive at the latter's house after a night at clubs. Enrique has just found out that Juan/Angel does not recognise Ignacio's old favorite Italian pop tune 'Verita', hence shedding doubt on whether Angel is merely posing as Ignacio. Enrique dives in the pool naked and tells Juan to follow. He dives over Enrique's head, but keeps on his briefs. Almodóvar's script is very specific about the kind of underwear (Ocean) for this sequence. Enrique gets out of the pool and after wrapping himself in a towel sits down on a lounge chair on the deck. Juan/Angel swims underwater over to the side of the pool directly in front of Enrique. In a striking frame the camera shows Juan/Angel holding his breath underwater obscured from Enrique's view, but with Enrique clearly waiting for him. This moment recalls Scottie's dive in *Vertigo*. Fully clothed he dives in to save Madeleine, so he thinks, from

Juan (Gael García Bernal) holds his breath underwater while Enrique waits for him poolside in *Bad Education*.

committing suicide by drowning under the Golden Gate Bridge. Through the dive he declares his love for her. Madeleine will later be shown naked, or as naked as the 1950s morality code allowed, in Scottie's bed. In *Vertigo* Scottie was aroused by her, but she was able to fake suicide, just as Juan/Angel held his breath in the water in *Bad Education*. Although the sequences in both films have complex implications, each of these erotic, watery sequences function to reveal a stage in the mind game that is the film. Viewing Juan's underwater breath control in the context of *Vertigo*'s suicide attempt makes us understand that the stakes of the impersonation game with Enrique have just increased. We can appreciate how the narratives unfold.

One of the most debated aspects of *Vertigo* is whether revealing to the viewer that Judy and Madeleine are the same person two thirds of the way through the film is effective or not. It is worth recalling that in *Vertigo*, Judy sits down in her hotel room to write a letter to Scottie, the text of which we hear in voiceover, telling him of her role as Madeleine's double. Although she tears the letter up, and goes on with her charade with Scottie, the audience knows of the duplicity at that point. In a famous controversy in the Spanish press the director Alejandro Amenábar used this example of an early reveal killing a suspense film when he was interviewed about his thriller *Thesis* to make light of Hitchcock's reputation. It is ironic, perhaps intentionally so, that Almodóvar cast Fele Martínez as Enrique in *Bad Education*, since Martínez launched his career in the role of Chema, the guy who gets the girl at the end of *Thesis*.[25] Almodóvar, however, sides more with Hitchcock than Amenábar in how he constructs suspense and controls information in *Bad Education*, for the viewer does know early on that Juan is not Ignacio. The only information withheld is that Enrique played along as if he did not know, although he did know all along. For *Vertigo*, Hitchcock said that the early reveal allowed him to turn the focus to the mental state of Scottie. Likewise, the dominant focus of *Bad Education* is Enrique's mind.

Visually, there are other significant allusions to *Vertigo*, again in some of the most memorable and innovative frames of the film. Perhaps the most striking frames of *Bad Education* depict the splitting apart of the young Ignacio's face as if a drop of blood from his forehead severed the image. These frames powerfully represent the consequences of the sexual assault by Father Manolo that Ignacio has just experienced. The motif of tearing is also repeated throughout the credit sequence. Its place in the narrative of the torn face, and how it represents subjective reality, recalls Scottie's dream sequence of *Vertigo* after the inquest. Both *Vertigo* and *Bad Education* exploit the graphic potential of film to represent a subjective state of victimisation. In *Vertigo* the headshot comes at a moment in the narrative of Scottie's maximum victimisation by Gavin Elster (Tom Helmore), and maximum confusion as to his own sanity in

The image of Ignacio's head, severed by a drop of blood, symbolises the sexual assault he has just experienced in *Bad Education*.

accepting his helplessness in Madeleine's (fake) suicide. Scottie's head appears in the centre of the frame of pulsating red.

Some critics have objected to the tonality of *Bad Education*, and the saturated palette of its *mise-en-scène*, questioning whether Almodóvar can successfully accomplish a film noir. James Berardinelli writes:

> Not exactly Humphrey Bogart. If there's one genre with which Almodóvar is incompatible, it's film noir. Known for his vivid, often garish use of colour, Almodóvar is not the kind of director who can work in the murky, desaturated realm that defines film noir. He tries with *Bad Education*, but the mismatch is apparent. The palette of hues is toned down, but not enough to generate the intense atmosphere that film noir requires. At the same time, the high energy that has defined Almodóvar's career is muted. (http://www.reelviews.net/php_review_template.php?identifier=1971)

Yet the tonality of *Bad Education* – the interiors of Enrique Goded's office decorated in primary colours, for example – recalls a similar intercalation of bright décor in *Vertigo*, for instance, in all the Midge scenes, both in her kitchen and studio. Although his role is much less important than was Midge's, Enrique's reliable helpmate Martín with his tropical shirts is very much her visual and sentimental analog in *Bad Education*. Hitchcock experimented with a red and green palette in his noir melodrama *Vertigo*. Nowhere does he create a more successful atmosphere through the use of colour than in the hotel kiss sequence in which the bedroom is bathed in strong green light through the curtain backdrop.

Hitchcock made his most despicable villains sympathetic in some way; Almodóvar has generally followed him in this. However in *Bad Education*, except for Paca or Ignacio's mother and aunt, all the male characters – and this is notably a film of male characters – are more darkly threatening than those in his other films. Incredibly, the most understandable, or even humanised, one of them is the despicable child molester, Father Manolo himself. *Bad Education* is a difficult Almodóvar film, not only because of the topic of child molestation, or gay sex, which together did dampen its popular reception in the US, but because almost none of the characters are attractive in terms of any conventional identification processes. The problem in *Bad Education* lies with Juan and especially with the uncomfortable fit between the actor Gael García Bernal and his role. There is little playfulness in Juan's interpretation of Zahara. The low camera angles, for example, emphasise Zahara's scandalous Sara Montiel/ Marilyn Monroe costume, but Juan/Gael's expressions do not work. The facial and hand expressions are stilted and ill-paced. There is not the voyeuristic pleasure to his performance that the 'real' Sara Montiel drag queen communicates later on. Also, Juan/Angel's face in the throes of gay sex expresses pure pain, not pleasure. The viewer comes to agree with Enrique Goded that Juan cannot play Zahara in the movie. Why? Because Juan is homophobic, and hence wanted to kill his brother. To defend himself as an actor working for a famous director, García Bernal has said that his inner transvestite is Mexican/Caribbean and not Spanish (see Hirschberg 2004). The film plays successfully with these Latin references in the one sequence when Juan, the object of Manolo/Berenguer's desire, a macho kid in Ignacio's home, does push-ups with a little waggle of his bum in the air to a Mexican folkloric TV program. This push-up sequence may allude to *Plata quemada* (*Burnt Money*, 2000), an important Argentinean movie by Marcelo Piñeyra based on Ricardo Piglia's novel, which deals with gay sex. By the end of the film, we almost feel sorry for Berenguer being taken in by Ignacio and Juan.

The haunting song 'Moon River' which Ignacio sings to Father Manolo's guitar accompaniment leads one back to *I Confess*. Both *I Confess* and *Bad Education* are disturbing journeys of passion. In *Bad Education* Father Manolo's attraction for the young Ignacio is gloriously suggested in the romantic sequence in which Ignacio sings 'Moon River'. The contrast is stark between the clarity of the young voice and the bright site of playfulness at the river with the priest's lust for Ignacio. Likewise in *I Confess*, Quebec City is approached by river on the ferry. In the score this vision is accompanied by a soprano melody. *I Confess* contains one of the most romantic, if not absolutely saccharine sequences in all of Hitchcock's works, told from the point of view of a woman. The film flashes back to the romantic tryst, a night of passion on an island, between Father Logan and Ruth Grandfort (Anne Baxter), when she was already married but he not yet a priest. They were discovered in the morning by the property owner Villette (Oliva Légaré), who finds out Ruth was married. The flashback is told from Ruth's point of view as she tries to exonerate Father Logan from an accusation of murdering Villette, who had been blackmailing her. Father Logan is revealed to be an ordinary man with a human heart, but Father Manolo is revealed to have a darker passion. Murray Pomerance writes of *I Confess*, 'Film posits a morality in which vision – and therefore performance – dominates' (2004: 172).

XV. GOING FORWARD, LOOKING BACK: REVISITED BY *VERTIGO* AND TRANSFORMED BY ART IN *THE SKIN I LIVE IN*

Two of Almodóvar's films post-*Bad Education* – *Volver* and *Broken Embraces* – nostalgically look back to specific earlier films in his career. *Volver* revisits *What Have I Done to Deserve This?*, and *Broken Embraces*, *Women on the Verge of a Nervous Breakdown*. Francisco A. Zurián perceives a revision of *Tie Me Up! Tie Me Down!* in *The Skin I Live In* (2013: 274). Within these retrospective gestures, Almodóvar continues to explore the crime film with narratives that leave the 'criminals' exonerated in the view of the audience. Since Hitchcockian allusions tend to occur in an early career stage for most directors, it is not surprising that Hitchcock can be a marginal source of inspiration compared to these films' manifest self-reflexivity, a trend which Marsha Kinder has consistently explored in her articles in *Film Quarterly* and in the anthology *Almodóvar: el cine como pasión* (2005).[26] Nonetheless Almodóvar cannot escape Hitchcock's shadow.

Volver significantly evokes *Psycho*'s motifs. Almodóvar picks scenes from *Psycho* that signal an end, as if he wanted to get rid of the master of suspense. When *Volver* returns to the story of *What Have I Done to Deserve This?*, to the story of a working-class mother who kills her husband to escape oppression, Raimunda's (Penelope Cruz) obsessive cleaning up after the murder not only recalls the day job of the working-class mother who kills her husband to escape oppression, but also Norman Bates' (Anthony Perkins) thoroughgoing bathroom duty after killing Marion (Janet Leigh). Likewise, when Raimunda watches the sinking of the freezer, which contains her husband's body, in the river, she stands metaphorically in the place of Norman Bates watching the sinking of the car with Marion's body in the trunk in *Psycho*'s swamp.

Through camera placement, Almodóvar weaves an intertextual history and pays off his debts. In a section of the author's commentary to *The Skin I Live In*'s script, titled 'Los invitados imprevistos' ('The Unexpected Guests'), Almodóvar says the film's opening shot was in homage to Buñuel's *Tristana* (1970):

Even Buñuel has his own citation, in the first image of the movie. It's an overview of the city of Toledo, which establishes the time and space of the narration. El Cigarral is located 4 kilometres from Toledo. To introduce the city I specified placing the camera in the same location that Buñuel had placed it in *Tristana* to give a general shot of the city. I tried to repeat that shot in homage to the master. (2012: 160)

Before crediting Buñuel, he emphasises his consistent, profound obsession with Hitchcock: 'Throughout the later stages of production unexpected guests have kept appearing, clear resonances related to the literature and films of the fantastic. It's impossible not to think of James Whale's *Frankenstein*, or Alfred Hitchcock's *Vertigo* and *Rebecca*' (ibid.). He returns to *Vertigo* later in his comments, where he sees the figure of the director imprinted:

> And, with respect to the master of suspense, it's very difficult to get away from the influence of Hitchcock, and specifically, of *Vertigo*. In *Broken Embraces* when the director Mateo Blanco directs Lena by whispering into her ear in the hair and make-up tests, he's creating a new woman for his own pleasure. For her to escape from her calamitous life and take refuge in a new woman, he proposes the role of Pina to her. *Vertigo* was already there – when James Stewart takes charge of the styling, the hair colour, the hairstyle, the clothes of Kim Novak, until he transforms her into the dead woman he loved so much. When I see Stewart rejecting suits in the dress salon, and the clerk telling him, 'I see the gentleman knows exactly what he wants,' I see myself with the actresses deciding and trying on the dresses that will help them become the 'other woman' for me. James Stewart represents the figure of the director. (2012: 160–1)

Although Almodóvar is speaking about *Broken Embraces*, the presence of *Vertigo*, and its obsessive transformations, is even stronger in the romantic

The Man Knows What He Wants: Scottie (James Stewart) selects clothes to dress Judy/Madeleine (Kim Novak) at Ramshoff's Department Store in *Vertigo*.

thriller, *The Skin I Live In*, whose primary sources were George Franju's horror film, *Les yeux sans visage* (*Eyes Without a Face*, 1959), and Thierry Jonquet's best selling novel, *Mygale* (1984).[27]

Through his experiments with artificial skin, Dr. Robert Ledgard (Antonio Banderas) transforms Vicente (Elena Anaya) into Vera, in the image of his wife Gal. Almodóvar writes, 'Over Vicente's face [Dr. Ledgard] has sculpted the face of his dead wife Gal (the distorted myth of *Vértigo* appears again)' (2012: 162). Gal had committed suicide by throwing herself out a window because her body, which had been burned in a fire, was so deformed she could not stand to see herself in a mirror. Both films, which are structured around doubling, have a pair of tragic falls from heights. In *Vertigo* Scottie sees the body of Madeleine, wife of Gavin Elster, thrown out of the window of the mission tower. Because Scottie can't intervene or insert control over this accident scene, since he can't overcome his vertigo to climb the tower, he stays trapped in his amorous obsession and search for the tragic Madeleine. *Vertigo* ends by repeating the mission scene when Judy falls to her death from the tower. Likewise in *The Skin I Live In* Norma, Gal and Robert Ledgard's daughter, repeats her mother's suicide when she throws herself out of the window. Norma can't overcome her psychological distress brought to a crisis state because of a rape.

Significantly *The Skin I Live In* reinterprets *Vertigo*'s obsessions and transformations through a feminist or LGBT critique of gender politics. Although in *Vertigo* Judy reluctantly allows herself to be transformed into Madeleine, in *The Skin I Live In* Dr. Ledgard transforms Vicente into Vera under great duress and control. At times Vera endures her captivity as a case of Stockholm syndrome. She eventually rebels and frees herself from Roberto by killing him. Before she shoots him, she tells him she had lied when she promised him she loved him. As we have already noted, works of art, respectively Carlotta's portrait, and Titian's Venus, mediate the males' obsessions in *Vertigo* and *The Skin I Live In*. The transgender perspective in the form of the film's critique of *Vertigo*, through which Vera becomes the active agent of her destiny, is also accomplished through the visual arts.

Although Vera has been transformed by Dr. Ledgard from a man, Vicente, into a woman, Vera, this bodily change does not affect his/her core identity. In the film Vera becomes fascinated by a TV program on Bourgeois' work, 'the sculptures with two sexes, the sackcloth heads, and the multiple dolls, some of which made with the cloth from the artist's own underwear' (Almodóvar 2012: 168). Vera consoles herself in captivity by contemplating and recreating Bourgeois' art. As Holland Cotter observed in the Bourgeois obituary in the *New York Times*, her sculptures, 'from first to last shared a set of repeated themes centered on the human body and its need for nurture and protection in

Art inspired by Louise Bourgeois: Vera (Elena Anaya) in the midst of her drawings and 'dressed' yoga balls in *The Skin I Live In*.

a frightening world' (2010). Vera fashions small clay sculptures and copies onto the wall drawings and phrases such as, 'Art is a symptom of health'. Almodóvar elaborates on her transformative activities: 'She also "dresses" some of the balls she uses to practice yoga with various pieces of cloth, from different items of clothing, all of this inspired by Louise Bourgeois and her own skin' (2012: 168). He notes that this takes her back to when, as Vicente, he made and dressed scarecrows for the windows of his mother's boutique. Besides appreciating the specific images that Vera peruses and remakes in the film as an art cure, for spectators of the film the mere inclusion of Bourgeois' work may have additional symbolic force that applies to a wider global discourse around gender. Bourgeois was known for her vocal defence of LGBT rights, and especially the freedom to marry, a cause she supported through the mass-market sale of prints of her work 'I Do'. She was also known for vertical twisting spiral sculptures, often staircases, such as those displayed in her 2000 Tate Modern installation, 'I Do, I Undo, I Redo'. The closing credit sequence to *The Skin I Live In* of abstract helices may be read as a combined homage to Bourgeois' art and Hitchcock and Saul Bass's spiral images that open *Vertigo*.

Vicente six years earlier dressing mannequins/ scarecrows for his mother's boutique in *The Skin I Live In*.

The final credit sequence of a helix in *The Skin I Live In*.

The obsession to transform the other through the selection of clothing, in which Almodóvar sees his role as a director, figures prominently in the aesthetics and narrative arc of *The Skin I Live In*. In the middle of the film, in the section 'Six years earlier', which deals principally with Norma's (Blanca Suárez) rape, we meet Vicente dressing a mannequin of a woman's clothing boutique, which is owned by his mother. Later Vicente tries to convince the clerk Cristina (Bárbara Lennie) to accept a gift of a flowered dress. Cristina, a lesbian, refuses the gift. The mere idea of trying it on and the sexual advances implicit in the gift upsets her. When after having killed Dr. Ledgard and his mother Marilia, Vera comes back to Vicente/Vera's own mother's store, and reconnects in a loving gaze with Cristina, it is precisely this earlier private conversation over the flowered dress that serves as the proof that reveals and confirms Vicente's submerged and unalterable identity. Almodóvar declares that *The Skin I Live In* is fundamentally a movie about identity: 'Although Vera has changed her skin, she hasn't lost her identity' (2011: 154). He even offers a synopsis of the movie via the dress:

Vera/Vicente returns to her/his mother's boutique to prove her/his identity by wearing the Dolce & Gabbana dress in *The Skin I Live In*.

It is the story of a very body-hugging, round-necked dress. The fabric is a print of light-coloured flowers, designed by Dolce & Gabbana. One day Vicente offers the dress to Cristina as a gift. He'd like to see how it fits her. Cristina turns him down. Vicente insists, emphasizing the item's details. Cristina answers, 'If you like it so much, you put it on.' Vicente disappears under strange circumstances and returns six years later to the same place in the store where he offered her the Dolce & Gabbana dress. But now he has it on, as a sign of identity so that Cristina will believe all he has to tell her. *The Skin I Live In* tells the unimaginable trials that Vicente has to suffer until he manages to return to his mother's boutique, wearing the Dolce & Gabbana dress on the body that has been imposed on him. (2011: 164–5)

While in Hitchcockian terms the dress is the picture's MacGuffin, it is also the motif through which Almodóvar asserts his role as a director. By naming the main character Vera, and representing her as a survivor of sexual torture, he not only calls attention to but also metaphorically 'redresses' the wrong done to Vera Miles. Hitchcock's treatment of Vera Miles, forbidding her to get pregnant because he wanted her to play Kim Novak's part in *Vertigo*, was an act that Almodóvar said he could not forgive (Strauss 2006: 144). Almodóvar's reinterpretation of *Vertigo* allows him to assert his own voice in contemporary gender politics.[28]

XVI. CONCLUSIONS: ECLIPSING BUÑUEL

In this chapter we have explored specific allusions to Hitchcock throughout Almodóvar's career. Indeed the depth and breadth of these instances, or 'robberies', lets us speak, in most conventional terms, of a strong, recurring influence. At other moments, in the case of *Dark Habits*, Hitchcock's career model, as well as his aesthetics in *Stage Fright*, served as a template and afforded an original perspective on the connections between them. How Almodóvar interpreted Hitchcock to build his career in his early stages has been perhaps the least explored, and at times the least acknowledged connection of all.[29]

What we have seen in these specific cases has been most often the serious side of the two directors' work. Exact parallels in terms of their sense of humour, the repetition of the same jokes, visual or verbal, are more difficult to construct, but no less important to underscore since it is in the continued presence of humour in crime narratives or suspense that Spanish or Latin Hitchcockian adaptations differ from their French or American counterparts.

Both directors have a fine appreciation of ensemble work. Their minor characters are genuinely memorable. Take Chus Lampreave, in almost any film, but for example as the mother-in-law in *What Have I Done to Deserve This?*; and compare her to Marion Lorne as Mrs. Anthony in *Strangers on a Train*. Both mothers are funny through different ways in their absurdities. Or consider the group social dynamics of the working class: compare the pair of girdle salesmen Richard Hannay encounters on the train in *The Thirty-Nine Steps* to the nurses on their lunch break in *Talk to Her*. How these workers interact is blunt and tone perfect in plausible dialogue, and yet incredibly funny as well. Both directors appreciate, and are finetuned to the place of, the domestic in creating identifiable comic effects, and in thereby really connecting with the audience. In *Murder!* the landlady chatters away with witnesses, while the crime scene is being examined right in her living room, about how to make a perfect cup of tea. Hitchcock uses this recipe to maximum humourous effect in *Frenzy*. The cheerful wife of Inspector Oxford (Vivien Marchant) lovingly recites her *nouvelle* recipes for 'soupe de poisson', quail and pig's foot, fancy meals which he tries to avoid eating and which make him long for meat and potatoes. All the while she intuitively dissects the case, cracking it literally as she does her breadstick, and points the inspector toward the real killer. McGilligan considers these scenes 'a transparent riff on Mr. and Mrs. Hitchcock' (2003: 702), who worked out their plots over mealtimes. During the filming of *Frenzy* Alma Hitchcock suffered a serious stroke, which preoccupied Hitchcock but only caused him to press on. Hence, the food interludes in *Frenzy* can also be considered an embedded love letter in the film, a motivation not unlike Pepa's in *Women on the Verge of a Nervous Breakdown*. Alma reportedly 'wept uncontrollably with pride' (McGilligan 2003: 712) when she finally saw *Frenzy* for the first time.

In *Frenzy* the food motif builds through many phases and even takes a Latin turn. The underling policeman is subjected to his boss's wife's too exotic and overly sour margarita, whose recipe she has carefully recited to him, as she always does to her husband. This final Latin twist to the joke may have been particularly suggestive to Almodóvar. A similar, domestic, extended joke is a crucial component of *Women on the Verge of a Nervous Breakdown*. Pepa (Carmen Maura) describes her recipe for gazpacho – which symbolises her love for Ivan (Fernando Guillén) – slowly and with maximum effect to the detectives, while she is waiting for the sleeping pills she has doped the mix with to kick in. Significantly, in *Frenzy* the wrong man Richard Blaney (Jon Finch) escapes from the prison hospital by getting the other patients to pool their sleeping pills. They drug the guard by putting their cache in his coffee. Even without delineating precise influences, we can say that Almodóvar's work shows a sense of humour not unlike Hitchcock's. The parallels, however, allow us to see how both Hitchcock, in his mocking of French cuisine and the Brits' preferences for stodgy cooking, and Almodóvar, in his ode to the Mediterranean gazpacho, play off national or local preferences for global effects.

It is significant that *Frenzy* marked Hitchcock's return to the UK, his first movie filmed outside of Hollywood in twenty years. Widely thought, erroneously, to be making his last film at the time, he was looking to recapture positive critical attention after *Marnie* and *Topaz* and match his earlier box office success. The movie begins acknowledging the shift in locale with postcard-style shots of London in a helicopter-ride view of the Thames and the Tower Bridge. In *Women on the Verge of a Nervous Breakdown*, whose very title recalls *Frenzy* in that it signifies the effects of the modern frenetic pace of life, Carlos (Antonio Banderas), Iván's son, holds up the postcards of Madrid's landmarks, the Cibeles fountain and the Puerta de Alcalá, written from his father to Pepa, which he discovers in Pepa's bedroom. Not only is Hitchcock a model for a good joke in the recipe recitations, but also how Hitchcock uses national references through broad, ironic tourism is likewise a pattern for true entertainment and resuscitated box office success. Almodóvar appreciated, and exploited both. The audience can share the nostalgia trip.

At the 2010 Cannes Film Festival Almodóvar gave a speech to introduce the film *Tristana* at a tribute to Buñuel. He began half tongue in cheek: 'I don't believe Buñuel would have found it amusing that I'm the one doing the presentation of *Tristana*. But since he's dead, I'll dare do it' (*ABC*, 16 May 2010: 69). Instead of introducing the film he proceeded to give what *El Mundo* called 'a homage from Pedro Almodóvar to Pedro Almodóvar', in which he spoke proudly, and at length, of the reputation he has acquired in France, his 'first market', and implied that his status now eclipsed Buñuel's (15 May 2010). The organisers, and *Tristana*'s star, Catherine Denueve who was present, were not pleased. Indeed as Almodóvar anticipated, Buñuel probably would not have taken the insult well either, yet an abbreviated version of the *El Mundo* headline is accurate – 'Almodóvar eclipsa a Buñuel' ('Almodóvar Eclipses Buñuel') (ibid.). Almodóvar may have shown poor manners, but for today's moviegoers, and from the point of view of world film criticism, if Spanish cinema is reduced to one name, it is Almodóvar and no longer Buñuel. His attention to Hitchcock, which at times, as in *Live Flesh*, has been mediated by allusions to Buñuel's work, has been a major factor in this generational shift away from Buñuel that has brought Almodóvar acclaim as the most important Spanish director of our times.

The presence of Hitchcock's films in Almodóvar's work spans both the breadth of Hitchcock's output, with notable emphasis on his British period in black and white as well as his later masterpieces for which he tends to be best known, and the breadth of Almodóvar's *ouevre*, from *Labryinth of Passion* to *The Skin I Live In*. Even if he has long ago ceased to be anyone's apprentice, his mature relationship to Hitchcock finds him mining the depths of the masterwork *Vertigo* in both *Bad Education* and *The Skin I Live In*. The intuitive modes of conduct that shaped his early films have now become both authorial strokes. While aspects associated with the creation of 'suspense' do not go unnoticed, as we have seen, his films show a far deeper appreciation of Hitchcock's cinematography and construction of narrative. Our comparative exploration has shed light furthermore on intriguing interplays in their sense of humour, representations of religion and gender, and interest in art and theatre.

NOTES

1   References to Almodóvar's Hollywood citations are virtually synonomous with his bibliography and encompass most critical approaches. These citations are seen as signs of postmodernity, as in Víctor Fuentes (1995) 'Almodóvar's Postmodern Cinema: A Work in Progress', in Kathleen M. Vernon and Barbara Morris (eds) *Post-Franco, Postmodern: The Films of Pedro Almodóvar*. Westport, CT: Greenwood Press, 155–70) or Peter William Evans (2005) 'Las citas fílmicas en las películas de Almodóvar', in Fran A. Zurián and Carmen Vázquez Varela (eds) *Almodóvar: el cine como pasión. Actas del Congreso Internacional 'Pedro Almodóvar'*, Cuenca, 26–29 Nov. 2003. Cuenca: Ediciones de la Universidad Castilla-La Mancha, 155–60. As Marvin D'Lugo notes, a Hollywood citation in Almodóvar's films from early on represents a recycling of pop culture that 'renders the audience complicit in its attacks on the culture of good taste' (2006: 19). The interpretation of Hollywood citations permeates genre studies, as Mark Allison remarks: 'One of the key features that mark out Almodóvar as an auteur is his consistent borrowing from genre movies, in particular his acknowledged debt to Hollywood melodrama', in 'Mimesis and Diegesis: Almodóvar and the Limits of Melodrama', in Brad Epps and Despina Kakoudaki (eds) (2009) *All About Almodóvar: A Passion for Cinema*. Minneapolis: University of Minnesota Press, 141. See also Allison's chapter 'Genre', in *A Spanish Labyrinth* (2001: 121–57).

2   Translations from the Almodóvar/Strauss interviews are noted by separate page reference with the name of the translator, Yves Baigneres, for the English edition. All other translations are mine.

3   See D'Lugo (2006: 13–15) on Almodóvar's early viewing practices from his move from Calzada de Calatrava to Cáceres to Madrid.

4   Baigneres' translation simplifies Almodóvar's words of admiration and commitment to studying Hitchcock. I have retranslated the last three lines to convey the original emphasis. Throughout this chapter when I have retranslated I cite Strauss 1995.

5   On music and childhood innocence in this scene see Vernon (2009: 60–3).

6   Almodóvar repeats this situation as fiction in *Los abrazos rotos* (*Broken Embraces*, 2009). For how Almodóvar bested the veteran filmmaker Carlos [sic] Berlanga in pitching their scripts to Hachuel, see Juan David Correa Ulloa (2005: 64–5). Correa Ulloa undoubtedly wants to refer to Luis García Berlanga, not Carlos Berlanga.

7   For more on this 'special relationship', see Leonard Leff (1999) *Hitchcock and Selznick: The Rich and Strange Collaboration of Alfred Hitchcock and David O. Selznick in Hollywood*. Berkeley: University of California Press.

8   While disagreeing with the harsh assessment epitomised by Sánchez-Biosca, Marvin D'Lugo puts this Spanish blindspot in historical context: 'The persistent failure of most Spanish commenators to appreciate the eccentricity of Almodóvar's storytelling strategies is, in essence, a refusal to see in his films the unique phenomenon of a popular cinematic

storyteller whose style is a composite of various strains that is also, ironically, highly original. In their directness, Almodóvar's films seem antithetical to the patterns of Spanish film production that had been lionized since the early 1970s as auteur cinema and *the* national cinema' (2006: 9).

9   On the French reception of Almodóvar see Jean-Claude Seguin (2013) 'Is there a French Almodóvar?,' in Marvin D'Lugo and Kathleen M. Vernon (eds) *A Companion to Pedro Almodóvar.* Chichester: Wiley-Blackwell. Seguin argues: 'Almodóvar's films thus will become known in France not because of any recognition of Spanish culture, but rather due to the cinephile parallels' (2013: 435).

10   By archiving key films of Hitchcock and Almodóvar under the rubric of 'the house' in her popular compendium *Escenarios del crimen* (Crime Scenes) Nuria Vidal, who published the first critical biography of Almodóvar in 1988, signaled a call, at least in Spain, to reassess Almodóvar and Hitchcock together to which our approach responds in more depth.

11   The critic Robert Schickel argues that making the devious husband so debonnaire was an 'indication of Hitchcock's distrust of the upper classes'. Special DVD Feature, 'Hitchcock and '*Dial M*', (2004) Warner Bros.

12   See, especially, Kathleen Vernon's reading of the film as postmodern melodrama, 'Melodrama Against Itself: Pedro Almodóvar's *What Have I Done to Deserve This?*', in Kathleen M. Vernon and Barbara Morris (eds) (1995) *Post-Franco, Postmodern: The Films of Pedro Almodóvar.* Westport, CT: Greenwood Press, 59–72.

13   Many critics have commented that *What Have I Done to Deserve This?* is stylistically Almodóvar's most neo-realist film (Smith 1994: 58). In addition, he himself calls it 'la película más social que he hecho' ('the most social film I've made') (Strauss 1955: 66). In the Strauss interview on the film, Almodóvar comments: 'Among the modern Europeans, the neo-realists were the biggest influence' (Strauss 2006: 44). Although deeply appreciative of earlier German expressionist cinema, Hitchcock only experimented once in this primarily European export style of neo-realism. The major exception was *The Wrong Man* (1956), which he based on a contemporaneous true case. The respective neo-realist films of Hitchcock and Almodóvar vividly represent domestic trauma and offer social critique, for Almodóvar, of the sad economic conditions of the working class during the transition to democracy, and for Hitchcock, of the witch-hunt political atmosphere of 1950s America. Making their critiques more enduring, neither director portrays a full recovery of the female protagonist in his respective films. Gloria in *What Have I Done to Deserve This?* contemplates suicide and appears alienated and alone at the film's end until her youngest son returns to take over as the man of the house. Manny's wife in *The Wrong Man* remains in the insane asylum even after he is cleared of charges, although in the real-life case she did fully recover.

14   Acevedo-Muñoz contrasts Pepa (Carmen Maura) to Jeffries (James Stewart) and Lisa (Grace Kelly) and concludes: 'Pepa retains "directorial control" control for a moment before choosing to enter the action and claim narrative agency, something Grace Kelly (as Lisa) is not allowed to do since she is "directed" by Jeffries to enter the action in Thornwald's apartment' (2006: 108).

15   Just as Almodóvar has become more politically outspoken in recent years, notably participating in the *Hay motivo* ('There's a reason') campaign to discredit President José María Aznar's implication that Basque terrorists were responsible for the 2004 Madrid train bombing, so too is the reinterpretation of *Women on the Verge of a Nervous Breakdown* becoming more political. The 2010 musical in English staged on Broadway in New York gave added meaning to Candela's fears. See Isolina Ballesteros (2013) '*Women on the Verge of a Nervous Breakdown*: From Madrid (1988) to New York (2010)' in Marvin D'Lugo

and Kathleen M. Vernon (eds) *A Companion to Pedro Almodóvar*. Chichester: Wiley-Blackwell, 367–86.

16 Hitchcock was infamous for practical jokes. Donald Spoto cites them as proof of his 'sadistic' side. At one time Hitchcock bet a cameraman a week's pay he could not last overnight in the studio chained to a camera. Hitchcock laced a flask of brandy he gave him with a strong laxative. In the morning the man was found in an embarassing state soiled in his clothes. Hitchcock paid off the bet. McGilligan notes there are 'wild, disparate versions' to this story (2003: 99). He identifies the victim as Richard 'Dickie' Beville, the floor manager, and says the laxative was in a coffee, but observes that the cinematographer Jack Cardiff in his autobiography identifies the man as Harry, says that the laxative was in a beer, that the soiled Harry was pushed out of Hitchcock's car 'in the middle of nowhere', and that Harry was arrested 'on suspicion of being an escaped convict' (ibid.).

17 See Richard Allen on the 'doubled dandy-villain' in *Rope* (2007: 112–3) and Boris Izaguirre on *Rope*'s 'absolute normality' of the 'sexuality, strangeness and intimacy of the Brandon-Philip couple' (2005: 115).

18 See Moral 2005: 26–39. Hunter protested in a letter to Hitchcock, '*I firmly believe it is out of place in this story. Mark is not that kind of person. Marnie is obviously troubled, but he realizes it. Stanley Kowalksi might rape her, but not Mark Rutland*' (2005: 39).

19 A chapter of *¡Almodóvar: Exhibition!* is devoted to stills of family cameos in his films.

20 Whether film noir constitutes a genre is controversial, as indicated in Richard Brody's article, '"Film Noir": The Elusive Genre,' in *The New Yorker* (23 July 2014); http://www.newyorker.com/culture/richard-brody/film-noir-elusive-genre-2 (accessed 2 September 2014). In Spain the situation is similar, as the most widely distributed book on 'cine negro' or 'black cinema' is a diverse collection of essays and recollections, *Noir* (2013), by the filmmaker and critic José Luis Garci, who directed *El Crack* (1981) and *El Crack Dos* (1982), examples of film noir as well as the Academy Award-winning melodrama, *Volver a empezar* (1982). Spanish booksellers categorize *Noir* as a work on genre. In terms of Almodóvar I refer to film noir as a genre rather than as merely influences because what was at stake in the case of *Live Flesh* was not only a matter of historically determined film allusions but also a shift in the generic parameters and tone that he deployed in his cinema. Another way to denote this generic approach is to call *Live Flesh* a crime film.

21 Interestingly the Mexican film critic Francisco Sánchez Aguilar cites from the novel *La Femme et le Pantin* on which Buñuel based *That Obscure Object of Desire*, the following line: 'Even lately, taking a quick mental count, I observed that I'd never had a blonde lover. I always ignored those pallid objects of desire' (2004: 118). Sánchez Aguilar views the last phrase as the source of Buñuel's title, which in Spanish-speaking countries was *Ese oscuro objeto de deseo*. In Spanish, 'oscuro' can mean either obscure or dark.

22 Again recalling *Vertigo*, a monumental Titian nude reappears in *The Skin I Live In* among the paintings hanging over the staircase of Dr. Ledgard's (Antonio Banderas) palatial home, El Cigarral.

23 In Alberto Iglesias, Almodóvar found his Bernard Hermann. Just as Hermann was an essential element to Hitchcock's mid-career successes like *North by Northwest*, *Vertigo* and *Psycho*, Iglesias's full orchestral score was the element that allowed Almodóvar's *All About My Mother* to be the distinctive international success that it was. Before working with Almodóvar, Iglesias had composed scores for successful films of Julio Medem, such as *La ardilla roja* (*The Red Squirrel*, 1993). He continued to work with Medem on *Los amantes del círculo polar* (*Lovers of the Polar Circle*, 1998) and *Lucía y el sexo* (*Sex and Lucia*, 2001). Of all composers working in Spain, he has the greatest international stature. Almodóvar's official web page describes the collaboration on the score to *All About My*

Mother as if they were making a fine wine: 'At a first tasting, Almodóvar urged Iglesias to lighten up the score because the story was already hugely dramatic on its own. This filter let the sonorous must [see below] compensate and brillantly balance the sequences and the orquestral strings, which evoked Shostokovich as much as Puccini' (http://boulevard-descapuccins.wordpress.com/2011/10/page/2/ accessed 20 May 2014).

The second sentence of this passage is complex in Spanish because it combines musical and wine-making terminology. Roughly it means that Iglesias should lighten up the score, as if he were filtering freshly pressed grapes, called the must. From *The Flower of My Secret* to *Los amantes pasajeros* (*I'm So Excited*, 2013) Almodóvar worked exclusively with Iglesias to craft his 'vintage' film scores.

24 This film was pulled from theatres early in the liberal town of Northampton, Massachusetts, as the female theatre manager of Pleasant Street Theatres explained to me when I tried to see it based on a listing in the *Amherst Bulletin*.

25 He won the Goya for Mejor Actor de Revelación, best new actor.

26 Marsha Kinder discusses how Almodóvar in his mature phase has revisited themes and aesthetics of his own work, for example, reworking the theme of brain death across a triology of films. See Kinder (2005: 257–68).

27 *Mygale* was released with several different titles in English translation: *Mygale* (City Lights, 2002), *Tarantula* (Serpent's Tail, 2005) and *The Skin I Live In* (Serpent's Tail, 2011).

28 As the 2012 *Sight & Sound* survey that proclaimed *Vertigo* the best film of all time demonstrates, it is a reference point for many transnational directors and world film critics. Almodóvar's friendship with the Argentinean director Lucretia Martel and his collaboration with her as co-producer on her film *La mujer sin cabeza* (*The Headless Woman*, 2008), which significantly alludes to *Vertigo* as well, shows both the global reach of his production company El Deseo and his enduring obsession with Hitchcock.

29 See Kercher (2013: 59–87).

CHAPTER THREE

Drawing on a Darker Humour, Cultural Icons and Mass Media:
Álex de la Iglesia's Journey from Outer Space to the Spanish Academy

I. INTRODUCTION: AN OPENING SHOT OF ARANTZAZU IN EUSKADI

On the DVD director's track for his film *Día de la Bestia* (*Day of the Beast*, 1985) Álex de la Iglesia says that he insisted on getting an opening shot at the Arantzazu Sanctuary in northern Spain despite his producer's objections that it was not worth the trip up there.[1] The rest of the complex opening scene was constructed on a film set in Madrid. Because of a legendary sighting of the Virgin by a Basque shepherd, Arantzazu has been a pilgrimage shrine since the sixteenth century. The existing stone basilica, a beautiful modern structure dating from 1951, represents the ancient roots of Catholicism in Euskadi, the Basque Country.[2] On the one hand the Arantzazu shot may remind us that De la Iglesia, whose last name means 'of the church', was born and raised in the

Establishing shot from *Day of the Beast* of the Arantzazu Sanctuary in Oñati, Gipuzkoa, Spain.

Basque country, in Bilbao, its major industrial city. He studied philosophy there at Deusto, a prestigious Jesuit college. To recall, Hitchcock was also educated by the Jesuits, an order founded by Ignatius of Loyola in northern Spain. Hitchcock even counted the number of churches in his films – fifteen – as confirmation of a religious leitmotif in them (see Fernández Cuenca 1974). Yet in insisting on filming on location at the Arantzazu Sanctuary, De la Iglesia asserted something more than a respect for his own roots. He invoked the force and mystique of cultural icons – religious or secular – and foreshadowed the crucial role that a sense of place, cinematographically understood via *mise-en-scène*, would play in his films and artistic vision. As in the inclusion of churches, De la Iglesia followed in Hitchcock's path. Most significantly in *Day of the Beast* and later in *La comunidad* (*Common Wealth*, 2000) he adapted Hitchcock's famous climactic scenes on monuments. Indeed he once told me in an internet chat sponsored by the Spanish newspaper *El Mundo* that he 'stole' the climax of *Common Wealth*, a fall from the beaux art statue on top of the BBVA Bank in Madrid, from Hitchcock. In this chapter we will explore how De la Iglesia referenced this element of Hitchcock's aesthetics, as well as many others, to build a crossover career in Spain, the US and the UK.

Like Almodóvar, Álex de la Iglesia (b.1965) never went to film school, but learned filmmaking by studying others, Hitchcock above all, and then experimenting, inventing the means to get the shots he wanted. A child of late Francoism who lived through the Transition, De la Iglesia received his early cinematographic education through State TV.[3] His father was a professor of sociology at Deusto, and a film and theatre critic for *La Gaceta del Norte*. Eschewing soccer, the whole family gathered to watch movies together. For 'good' films, such as John Huston's *Freud* (1962), which De la Iglesia saw at age five, sometimes the viewing was obligatory, but it was also permissive, as he was allowed to see even those films rated for 18 years and up. Television marked his life, especially the toughest blows. When he was twelve his father had a heart attack and died while they were watching the dubbed British sit-com *Un hombre en casa* (*Man About the House*, 1973–1976).[4] De la Iglesia notes that Carl Theodor Dreyer's *La palabra* (*Ordet*, 1955), a film about faith and miracles, became 'an essential film in my life', since he watched it with his mother and brother right after his father had died (Angulo & Santamarina 2012: 102). Later, while he was still in high school, De la Iglesia received 'an electric shock to the neurons' when he attended a film series called 'The Essential Hitchcock' of remastered copies of Hitchcock's classics in a commercial theatre in Bilbao (Angulo & Santamarina 2012: 124–5). The high quality, especially because of Technicolour, so surpassed anything he had ever seen that it motivated him to draw and publish a fanzine with friends. They dedicated the first issue to *Vertigo*.

Both Hitchcock and De la Iglesia could be considered what we call today in reference to technology, early adopters or technophiles. Hitchcock, for instance, did a 3-D version of *Dial M for Murder*, which was one of the first 3-D films intended to be shown in Spain.[5] De la Iglesia evokes this Hitchcock film, whose Spanish title was *Crimen perfecto* in his own *Crimen ferpecto* (*Ferpect Crime*, 2004). With *Day of the Beast* De la Iglesia became among the first in Spain not just to incorporate digital effects and complicated make-up, but also to make a digital master of a whole film. His first film, the short *Mirindas asesinas* (*Killer Mirindas*, 1991), showed both his general interest in the media and a penchant for the thriller genre.

II. SITUATIONAL HUMOUR IN *KILLER MIRINDAS*: A GUY WALKS INTO A BAR IN ERANDIO

Álex de la Iglesia made his first film, the twelve-minute black comedy *Killer Mirindas*, in 1991 in the Basque country, in Erandio. He co-wrote it with Jorge Guerricaechevarría, a long time friend from his early school days, with whom De la Iglesia would go on to co-write almost all of his subsequent films. Together the pair scrounged the money for the short at a party by pretending to be a theatre troupe (see Vera et al. 2002b: 39).

Killer Mirindas tells the story of a guy who goes into a bar for Mirindas, a Spanish orange soft drink. When the bartender and patrons do not understand him as literally as he expects, he morphs into a serial killer. In the first confrontation the sad sack protagonist (Alex Ángulo) tells the bartender (José Antonio Alvarez) to give him a Mirinda. When the bartender asks him to pay 120 pesetas, the man argues that he had asked the bartender to give it to him, not to charge him for it. He takes out a huge gangster's gun and shoots the bartender. The casuistry of the argument reflects De la Iglesia's Jesuit education. The killer then asks a poor guy (Saturnino García), trembling as he sits at the bar drinking coffee watching the mayhem unfold, to serve him another Mirinda. The hapless chap does as told, goes behind the bar and begins to serve as a bartender. Then the killer asks a different patron who was talking on the telephone (Oscar Grijalba) if he had the time. When that patron does not take the question seriously, the killer shoots him, too. Finally, a dapper man (Ramón Barea) comes into the bar excited after a good day and orders a drink from the substitute bartender. He turns on a small TV set on the bar and tunes it to watch bullfighting. Blithely intent on the TV screen, he ignores the killer's requests for the time and a light for his cigarette. The killer takes out his gun but holds his fire. A deep focus shot shows the situation in spatial planes. In the foreground the bullfighting fan's gripped immersion in the television leaves him oblivious to the body of the dead bartender splayed out over the bar,

The dapper client
(Ramón Barea) watches
a bullfight on the bar's
TV oblivious to dead
bartender or the
killer (Alex Ángulo)
in *Killer Mirindas*.

and to the killer in the background. The bullfighting enthusiast gets up, tells the bartender to put the drink on his tab and walks out. The killer drinks more sodas and then leaves without killing anyone else.

The narrative of the short has a classical structure that plays like a variation on the *Conde Lucanor* story from which *The Taming of the Shrew* derives.[6] To recall, in that tale a young husband orders a series of animals to bring him water, then kills them when they do not. Finally he orders his headstrong bride to bring him water and she does. The repetition of requests in *Killer Mirindas* leads the viewer to expect that every one will do whatever the irrational killer orders. However, in *Killer Mirindas* the power of television changes the dynamics. The short shows both De la Iglesia's concept of comedy as situational, which he elsewhere argues he took from Hitchcock, and his ironic placement of the screen within the screen. The short film comments on how television and popular culture has a pacifying effect on Spaniards. Marshall McLuhan called this media's 'cool' effect. The bullfighting preference not only makes the dapper guy an archetype of Spanish males but they also characterise the inheritance of state-controlled Spanish cultural production in the 1980s. According to *La cultura española durante el franquismo* (Spanish Culture during Francoism), edited by by Manuel Alcalá, Norberto Alcover Ibáñez and the Equipo Reseña, Franco's regime gave the people soccer, bullfighting and consumerism – 'para el pueblo, el fútbol, toros y consumo' ('for the people, soccer, bullfights and goods to buy') as the slogan went – while ignoring the creative potential of the medium (1977: 212). The emphasis on media history, through the representation of the effects of television in film, reappears at important junctures throughout De la Iglesia's career.

Killer Mirindas has the situational humour that Hitchcock deployed in his television series *Alfred Hitchcock Presents*. In 'Lamb to the Slaughter', for instance, a mild mannered housewife makes an unlikely assassin of her husband. De la Iglesia adapts an archetypical humorous situation – so many jokes begin with 'A guy walks into a bar' – through *mise-en-scène* using elements of local specificity; that is, a bar in Erandio that serves a typical Spanish soda.

III. CAPTURING DARK HUMOUR IN POLITICAL TERRORISM IN *ACCIÓN MUTANTE*: HOW A POLICEMAN FROM OUTER SPACE CONVINCED ALMODÓVAR TO BACK DE LA IGLESIA

Like Hitchcock, De la Iglesia came to filmmaking with a design background. Hitchcock's was in artistic design; De la Iglesia's was in graphic arts, drawing comics for publication, then later in artistic design.[7] His first cinematographic jobs were as artistic designer for Pablo Berger's short *Mamá* (1988), then for Enrique Urbizu's feature film, *Todo por la pasta* (*Anything for Bread*, 1991). These were not common avenues of *entrée* into filmmaking. However, because of his strong drawing skills, honed through the crafting of individual comic panels, De la Iglesia took Hitchcock's characteristic working method to heart. He storyboarded almost everything, certainly all action scenes, which was not the usual method in Spain. He began doing this for his first feature film, a science fiction comedy, *Acción mutante* (*Mutant Action*, 1993).

De la Iglesia's debut was an exceptional project for Spanish cinema. Given the high budgets and technical expertise necessary for special effects, in the 1990s science fiction was made in Hollywood, seldom in Spain. Pedro Almodóvar had seen and liked *Killer Mirindas* and contacted De la Iglesia with a tentative offer to produce his next short at El Deseo, the production company of Pedro and Agustín Almodóvar. De la Iglesia sent them a script for a short called *Piratas del espacio* (*Space Pirates*). The project's originality and its unique sense of humour led them to sign on as producers, first for a three-part television series based on the story, then two years later, for its revision as the feature film *Mutant Action*.[8] This marked one of the first instances in which El Deseo moved beyond producing only Pedro's films to support promising new filmmakers. *Mutant Action*, which was made for about $2.5 million, had all the characteristics of what would become a cult film.

Set in a future world ruled by good-looking people, the film tells the story of the kidnapping of the daughter of Orujo, a wealthy executive, by a terrorist group, the mutants who seek to assert the rights of the ugly. Ramón Yarritu (Antonio Resines), the group's leader, tries to kill the other members of his gang and keep all the ransom for himself as they escape from the police in a spaceship. The caper ends abruptly when they crash into Axturiax, a planet where no woman lives. Though played as a dark comedy, *Mutant Action*'s plot parodied real-life historical and political events – that is, the ETA kidnappings of businessmen and politicians for ransom that were taking place in the Basque country at that time. The characters' names, in the suffix 'ritu' for example, and the planet's spelling with two 'x's scan as Basque. The industrialist's name, Orujo, evokes Galicia, region in northwestern Spain, and yet another distinctively Spanish beverage like the Mirinda.[9] Orujo is a traditional Galician liqueur made from the residue of wine production.[10] In the early 1990s a humorous film about a kidnapping by Basques was still possible – that is, a tale of revenge against an industrialist's family could generate sympathy.[11] Everything changed in 1997 with the kidnapping and killing of the young political deputy Miguel Ángel Blanco which mobilised Spaniards for the first time to protest against ETA in mass demonstrations in major cities across Spain. By then *Mutant Action* was doubly politically incorrect as it camped up both violence against women and terrorist kidnapping.

In 1993 *Mutant Action* won three Goyas, for special effects, make-up and production. Though this was a strong national debut, the film received limited international distribution until its rerelease a decade later. The style of *Mutant Action*, as well as the national specificity of the story that alluded to Spanish political events, made De la Iglesia's first film an acquired taste.

Although *Mutant Action* could not be further from Hitchcock's genre preferences, or the general Almodóvarian typology either, as a career step this debut film did follow the Hitchcockian model of beginning filmmaking through design.[12] De la Iglesia created extravagant costumes for a terrestrial wedding scene, as well as a bizarre extra-terrestrial world, on a shoestring budget. The mutants, sitting on platforms suspended by strings, float around in a lotus position looking like the Fates of Goya's black painting 'Las Parcas' ('The Fates', 1820–23). Like Hitchcock he also identified a group of other talented artists with whom he would work repeatedly throughout his career. José Luis Arrizabalaga and

The extra-terrestrial costumes for a terrestrial wedding scene in *Mutant Action*.

Arturo García, co-artistic directors on the film, tell how De la Iglesia imagined and then created a fantastic policeman to convince Almodóvar he could carry off the film. He then went to El Deseo in Madrid with still photos of the policeman he had taken on the streets of Bilbao. When Almodóvar was still doubtful, De la Iglesia found an extremely tall friend, dressed him in the policeman's costume, and sent him into the El Deseo offices (see Vera et al. 2002b: 59). It is ironic that the Almodóvars became believers in De la Iglesia's abilities and artistic vision through the real-life visit of a fantastic, larger than life, policeman. Famously Hitchcock's father traumatised him as a youth with a visit to the police station (McGilligan 2003: 7–8).

IV. REACHING FOR THE HEIGHTS OF *VERTIGO* AND *SABOTEUR*, DANGLING FROM THE ICONS OF MADRID IN *DAY OF THE BEAST*

De la Iglesia's second feature film, *Day of the Beast,* was even more ambitious in artistic design and *mise-en-scène* than *Mutant Action.* He called upon his knowledge of Hitchcock to reach a wider audience, and of all of his films *Day of the Beast* is the one that most directly alludes to specific scenes and techniques from Hitchcock films. Moreover De la Iglesia attributes the dark sense of humour in this film, which was marketed as 'una comedia satánica' ('a satanic comedy'), to Hitchcock's concept of comedy. Close analysis of *Day of the Beast* and the criticism that it provoked shows the pivotal role Hitchcock played in transforming De la Iglesia's career from that of a marginal cult director to a mainstream commercial one.

Day of the Beast tells the story of Angel Berriartúa, a Basque priest and Jesuit theologian, played by Alex Ángulo from *Killer Mirindas*, who discovers a prediction of the Apocalypse, according to which the world will end in Madrid on 25 December 1995 when the Devil will appear and kill a baby. Signs of impending doom are already apparent in how vigilantes are torching immigrants in the streets and tagging the area with the slogan 'Clean Madrid'. The priest tries to avert total catastrophe by confronting the Devil. To invoke his presence, Berriartúa commits evil deeds on purpose. He curses a dying man, robs a suitcase and self-mutilates the soles of his feet in the sign of the Cross. To understand the dark side, he teams up with José María (Santiago Segura), a record store clerk and heavy metal fan. Together they kidnap Professor Cavan (Armando de Razza), a television personality with a programme on the occult, to force him to teach them how to summon the Devil's presence. When they conduct ancient rituals in Cavan's apartment, the Devil appears as El Gran Cabrón, a huge goat. The trio escapes out the window onto the Capitol building's facade. A chase ensues throughout Madrid until they spot the almost completed KIO twin towers. They interpret the profile of these skyscrapers that lean inward towards each other as the image of the Devil's signature, a cloven hoof. They rush to engage him there. In an ensuing battle on the rooftop the Devil throws José María off the building to his death. Meanwhile the 'Clean Madrid' vigilantes set fire to the homeless who have sought refuge at the ground level of the construction site. The priest saves the baby of a homeless woman while Cavan suffers severe burns when he tries to staunch the flames. Reminiscing some time later in the Retiro Park, Cavan and the priest look like scruffy homeless people, too, as they incline their faces disfigured from the fight to take the sun on a bench under Benlliure's statue 'The Fallen Angel'. They lament that no one else understands that they saved the world.

Day of the Beast was wildly successful both among Spanish critics and at the box office, especially among younger viewers. It won six Goya awards, including that for Best Director, and catapulted De la Iglesia's commercial career to a different level. For most of the public the film characterised his style for years after. He received adamant requests from his fans for a sequel, which he refuses to do.[13] Reflecting its attraction for a young, hipper audience and its value as a career-building model, *Day of the Beast* became the subject of the second volume of *Como hacer cine*, a 'how-to' guide for aspiring Spanish filmmakers. In the book's introduction De la Iglesia explains the origin of the idea for the film, marketed as 'a satanic comedy', and attributes his concept of comedy directly to Hitchcock:

> The idea of combining an apocalyptic horror story with a comedy was original, but even more original was to take the story seriously. I believe that the basis of comedy is a serious and rigorous treatment. The characters never should laugh at what is happening, their life is tragic and conflicted – if it isn't, there isn't a story. It's the situation that appears comic to the eyes of a third person. However more terrifying the situation in which the characters are involved, ever more entertaining it'll be to see them get out of it. We find the key to this in a phrase from Hitchcock speaking of *Vertigo*: a common man inserted in a tremendous story. (Vera et al. 2002b: 9)

There is probably no situation or leitmotif more characteristic of Hitchcock's cinema than the chase that ends in danger at great heights. Even those whose business is manoeuvering through Wall Street can list the films in which they occur – *Saboteur, To Catch a Thief, North by Northwest*, and *Vertigo* – as did H. Rodgin Cohen, profiled in 2009 as 'The Trauma Surgeon of Wall Street' in the *New York Times*.[14] The two climatic confrontations on Madrid monuments, first, on the Schweppes sign on the façade of the Capitol Building, and second,

In *Day of the Beast* Father Berriartúa (Alex Ángulo) stands before the KIO Towers in Madrid acknowledging them as the sign of the Devil.

on the top of the KIO Towers, are iconic Hitchcockian moments in *Day of the Beast*. Although the Capitol Building and the KIO Towers were identifiable landmarks in Madrid before De la Iglesia set key scenes on them – even if the Capitol building was known primarily as just another movie theatre and hotel on the Gran Vía, and the KIO Towers were seen part of an expanded business district on the Castellana marked by foreign investment – the film singled them out and transformed them into icons of their respective environments.[15] As Juan Manuel de Prada argued in his article in a special issue of *Nickel Odeon* on Madrid and the movies, De la Iglesia's film made its denizens see the city anew: 'Seldom has Madrid been depicted in such a hallucinogenic manner and metamorphosed into a city with laws on the margins of physics and reason' (1997: 196). The level of ambition in these scenes on transformed landmarks – that is, to transport the viewer beyond the laws of physics and reason – makes it worth interpreting these Hitchcockian allusions to climatic scenes on heights in detail.

Professor Cavan, Father Berriartúa and José María climb out the window of Cavan's apartment in the Capitol Building onto the Schweppes sign to escape the Devil whose presence they conjured and who is now chasing them. In a segment of an interview entitled 'Vértigo', De la Iglesia explains that during the actual filming of the sequence in Madrid, Armando de la Razza who plays Professor Cavan was genuinely terrified and kept saying he had vertigo:

The Capitol Building on the Gran Vía of Madrid, given landmark prominence in *Day of the Beast*.

In the sequence on the sign Armando de la Razza had awful vertigo and I was particularly cruel with him. But I think that it was worth the effort because I wasn't going to ruin a whole sequence because Armando had vertigo. He began to say that he wasn't going to act, and I told him that I didn't care if he didn't act, that he only had to be there and pretend like he was talking. Then I began to film while he was saying, 'I have vertigo, I have vertigo.' And that's what he's really saying. I dubbed him later. (Vera et al. 2002b: 28)

These comments, which also speak to how a director should assert his will over actors, connect the film in terms of the situation most directly to *Vertigo*, and Scottie's fear of heights as depicted early in that film. De la Iglesia's dubbing is so effective that it is difficult for even a careful viewer to tell if Armando is in fact saying 'vertigo'. That De la Iglesia tortured his actor to get the reaction he wanted is entirely plausible, and a lesson for up and coming young directors. Although Armando's desperation in the situation is evident, so, too, is the articulation of De la Iglesia's desire for viewers to see him as a Latin Hitchcock. Indeed De la Iglesia 'dubbed' *Vertigo* into the *mise-en-scène* as much as he erased its presence in the soundtrack. The film cuts from close-ups of the trio escaping out the window of Cavan's apartment onto the huge neon Schweppes sign on the façade of the Capitol Building, to progressively longer and higher-angle shots that show the Callao movie theatre and the night-time Gran Vía boulevard. These initial shots also position the characters as if they were in dark outer space as their backdrop is a giant billboard with an ad for Kodak featuring a man walking on the moon. The composition not only breaks the laws of physics but also imprints *Day of the Beast* with De la Iglesia's own signature, a connection to the outer space *mise-en-scène* of *Mutant Action*.

After these establishing shots the perspective shifts to a vertigo shot that shows the trio from above. When the madly laughing and footloose José María, who appears to enjoy the danger of the situation, slips and falls, as had Scottie's

In *Day of the Beast* the moonwalker on a Kodak billboard adds to the sense of being in outer space to the plight of Professor Cavan, Father Berriartúa and José María on the neon Schweppes sign.

The madly laughing José María (Santiago Segura) in *Day of the Beast* is about to let himself slip and plummet over street markings, motifs that recall Scottie's dream sequence in *Vertigo*.

police partner in *Vertigo*'s initial chase scene, Cavan and Berriartúa barely catch José María's hands. He is left dangling. When they pull him up, he manages to grab on to the sign again. The night-time scene has a graphic minimalist quality as the coloured neon bars of the Schweppes sign echo the stripes of the cross-walks painted on the street far below. This design or pattern repetition increases the vertigo effect, especially as the coloured lights pulse, recalling Scottie's dream.[16] The two shots are classic examples of the Hitchcockian blot, named by Slavoj Zizek, 'to describe a characteristic visual design of Hitchcock's films in which a place in the visual field, usually at the central, vanishing point of the image, contains a privileged "object" that functions as a kind of stain or blot that cues the spectator to the disruptive, threatening presence of the shadow or chaos world that subtends the everyday world of appearances and social respectability' (quoted in Allen 2007: 205). The Schweppes sign above, and the plaza gathering area for the movie theatre spectators below, produce a dynamic tension as they both 'centre' the scene, or produce a vortex, and push the signifiers of urban capitalism into the spectators' consciousness. As Malcolm Compitello explains when he discusses this scene among others in 'From Planning to Design: The Culture of Flexible Accumulation in Post-Cambio Madrid', *Day of the Beast* 'articulates a vision of urban consciousness that is cognizant of how capitalism forms space as well as how it intervenes in the dialectical tension between

The spectators in the 'Hitchcockian blot' of *Day of the Beast*.

No longer the proper sleeve length: Barry Kane grasps the villain Frey's sleeve as it gradually tears away in *Saboteur*.

Frey plummets off the Statue of Liberty in *Saboteur*.

space and place that Harvey masterfully unravels in *Justice, Nature and the Geography of Difference*' (1999: 205–6).

To return to our close analysis and more specifically to Hitchcock, José María in his mad state or heightened sense of 'urban consciousness' falls again, this time taking Cavan down with him and leaving the trio dangling in a row. This improbable result and alignment, more commonly found in a comic book, changes the dynamics and the tone of the sequence. Significantly, with Cavan now the low man on the totem pole, the film shifts from *Vertigo* to *Saboteur* (1942). To recall, in the iconic climax of *Saboteur* on the Statue of Liberty, the jacket sleeve of villain Fry (Norman Lloyd) gradually tears away from the grasp of the hero Barry Kane (Robert Cummings) and Fry plunges to his death. For this, the most ambitious shot of the film, Hitchcock invented a complicated mechanised platform to stage the fall. In *Day of the Beast* Cavan assumes the position of the villain Fry. From an overhead shot, the film cuts to a point-of-view shot of Cavan looking down at his feet dangling. Close-ups of Cavan's hand slowly slipping out of José María's grasp are intercut with shots of the gawkers, including Asian tourists looking up at the scene from the street. Analogous to *Saboteur*, Cavan's desperate suspenseful grasp

Cavan's hand slowly slips out of José María's grasp in front of the Hitchcockian motif in *Day of the Beast*.

Cavan's fall in *Day of the Beast*.

Cavan's comic book bounce with sparks that saves him in *Day of the Beast*.

and screaming plunge are shown via a bird's-eye view. In *Day of the Beast* the converging patterns on the street give the effect of a vortex into which a splayed-out man tumbles. Unlike the *Saboteur* villain who dies in the fall, Cavan is saved as he bounces onto a lower sign, creating sparks that radiate around him as in a comic book image. The scene ends as Cavan looks down at the police and his buxom girlfriend Susana (María Grazia Cucinotta) who have arrived to rescue him. José María and the priest climb off the building into another apartment where a little girl is watching a Christmas television show. Reflecting De la Iglesia's take on Hitchcock's sense of comedy, that humour is created when a desperate situation is taken seriously, she mistakes the bedraggled, scruffy José María for 'Papa Noel'. In its narrative and in its emphasis on design, the climatic scene 'Colgados' ('The Hanging Ones') reveals its antecedents in Hitchcock's archetypical scenes.

As we have seen, allusions to graphic novels or comic books interrupt this key sequence and change its tone. This comic overlay, which reflects De la Iglesia's passion for sequential art developed over many years, represents his unique interpretation of Hitchcock. In *La bestia anda suelta: ¡Álex de la Iglesia lo cuenta todo!* (The Beast is Loose: Álex de la Iglesia Tells All!, 1997), an interview book by Marcos Ordóñez, De la Iglesia recounts how he not only avidly consumed his brother Agustín's collection of comics, but also how he associated Hitchcock with the world of graphic novels of his youth. He tells how the two brothers planned a special issue of their fanzine 'No' to show comparisons between Hergé, the creator of the Tintin series, and Hitchcock:

> The relationship between Hergé and Hitchcock is exciting to explore as we end up discovering tons of similarities. From their character, two Puritans with a hidden dark side, full of obsessions and mysteries, to the most insignificant stylistic forms. Hatred of birds, for example, is a constant in Hergé and in Hitchcock. And from the beginning, from Hitchcock's British period, from Hergé's first albums. From the birds of 'Tintín in America' to the magpie of 'The Jewels of Castafiore'
>
> [...] It is fascinating how he manages to construct a plot that is sustained by a succession of minimal, insignificant intrigues ... A step that breaks time and again, a telephone line that always connects to the wrong number ... All of that is the essence of Hitchcock. There's the most pure Hergé, the essential Hergé, of the 'Jewels' and 'Tintín in Tibet,' another great masterpiece, and later there are, of course, the great adventures: 'The Scepter of Ottokar', 'The Tornasolo Affair' ... 'The Tornasolo Affair' is 'North by Northwest'. It is the height of action comedy, and the storyboarding is very similar. And '39 Steps' and 'Foreign Correspondent' ... also are pure Tintín. It's impossible not to think of Tintín seeing Joel McCrea pursuing, through a wall of umbrellas, the assassin who shoots with his pistol hidden in a camera, an image that ... yes, also appears in 'The Scepter of Ottokar'.
>
> Pure Tintín, except in respect to the relationships with women. Although if one were to look for a feminine partner for Tintín I think that his relationship would be like that of Robert Donat and Madeleine Carroll in '39 Steps': handcuffed and quarrelling during the whole episode. (1997: 43, 45–6)

This extensive comparison shows that De la Iglesia 'read' Hitchcock through the filter of Tintín. From his adolescent years on he saw them as superimposed visual storyboards, composed of 'dramas of minimal actions'. They served as foundational texts for his filmmaking.

The two climaxes on heights from *Vertigo* and *Saboteur* evoke very different main themes for these respective Hitchcock films. According to Richard Allen, the vertigo shot represents 'the implosion of the boundary between self and world' (2007: 207). Moreover, Scottie's fear of heights in *Vertigo* is often interpreted psychoanalytically as a manifestation of a psychic crisis over his masculinity. Yet *Day of the Beast* is devoid of *Vertigo*'s romantic tensions. Father Berriartúa is not a romantic hero. Furthermore as Marsha Kinder points out in *Blood Cinema: The Reconstruction of National Identity in Spain* (1993), the sexual politics of *Day of the Beast* are disturbingly misogynistic. The major female characters establish a Manichean paradigm; either they either perpetuate sexual violence in the case of the rooming house owner Rosario (Terele Pavez), who acts as a castrating mother figure when she comes at Father Berriartúa with a shot gun, or they fall victim to violent sexually inflected crimes in the cases of Professor Cavan's girlfriend Mina (Nathalie Seseña), and the daughter of the rooming house owner, both of whom are accosted in order to draw blood for demonic rituals. Nonetheless De la Iglesia's comment that he wanted to force the actor Armando de la Razza to suffer in order to get his shot suggests a different psychoanalytical interpretation for this scenario. The paradigm derives not from the hesitations and romantic longings of *Vertigo*, but from the excruciating drama of the Statue of Liberty sequence of *Saboteur*. To recall, *Saboteur* tells the story of a young factory worker Barry Kane wrongly accused of sabotage. He becomes a fugitive, while pursuing Fry, the real perpetrator of the crime. Following the clue of a letter he saw addressed to Fry at Deep Springs Ranch, he goes there and meets the owner Tobin (Otto Kruger), who denies knowing Fry, but who is in fact the kingpin in the whole scheme. Tobin turns Barry over to the police, but he escapes. While on the lam he meets up with a girl, Pat (Priscilla Lane), whom he forces to accompany him. They seek refuge in a train car full of circus performers, who prove to be generous souls and good judges of character. In a democratic moment they vote to hide the couple from the police. The chase ends on the crown of the Statue of Liberty where the villain Fry, despite an attempt by Barry to pull him back by his sleeve, falls to his death.

The gradual tearing of Fry's sleeve is generally seen as one of the supreme illustrations of Hitchcock's mastery of suspense. Nonetheless, when Truffaut praised the 'climatic force in your way of going from the smallest to the greatest, from the trivial to the all-important' Hitchcock rejoined with his doubts about whether he had reached the highest possible climax: 'Still, there's a serious error in this scene. If we'd had the hero instead of the villain hanging in mid-air, the audience's anguish would have been much greater' (1984: 147). In *Hitchcock's Romantic Irony* Richard Allen observes that in *Saboteur* the conspiratorial ringleader Tobin is one of a series of dandy figures in Hitchcock's films, like Vandamm

(James Mason) in *North by Northwest*, and that furthermore, 'The "perversity" of the figure of the dandy then issues in part from the resulting fusion of masculine and feminine traits that bestow upon him a kind of hyperbolic, almost demonic knowledge of and power over another' (2007: 84). Since Fry is Tobin's lackey, he represents a surrogate for the dandy and his fusion of masculine and feminine traits. Questions about his sexuality preface the final scene since Fry rebuffs Pat's flirting in the interior observation deck of the Statue of Liberty before Barry and he stage their final scene on the crown's exterior. There is no strong masculine hero in *Saboteur*. Speaking to Truffaut, Hitchcock confessed his supreme disappointment with the casting of Robert Cummings as Barry because the actor had little gravitas. Barry/Cummings' weak screen presence as protagonist deflects our attention elsewhere and opens *Saboteur*, and by extension, *Day of the Beast*, to an interpretation in terms of a gender continuum. Although Allen looks to Tobin as a dandy, Boris Izaguirre in *El armario secreto de Hitchcock* (The Secret Closet of Hitchcock, 2005) detects homoeroticism, 'a classic homosexual erotic dream' in Barry the handcuffed fugitive finding 'a mature, solitary, blind protector' in Philip Martin's (Vaughn Glaser) cottage (2005: 174).

To return to *Day of the Beast*, Cavan's fall resembles Fry's in that in both cases spectators identify with the predicaments, but less so with these characters. As Hitchcock noted regarding *Saboteur*, the villain falls, not the hero. In *Day of the Beast* Professor Cavan acknowledges himself to be a charlatan, not trustworthy in his knowledge of the occult. He is moreover a foreigner representing the incursion of trash international media in Spain. Cavan is a dandy analogous to Fry, the pawn to a dandy in *Saboteur*.

It is fitting that De la Iglesia turned not just to *Vertigo* but also to *Saboteur* for his iconic climaxes in *Day of the Beast*, since *Saboteur* complexly entwines gender and politics. Since Hitchcock habitually claimed disinterest in political arguments for his films, few viewers recognise that Hitchcock intended to go beyond a generic defence of American values in *Saboteur* and specifically unmask pro-German Fascist elements, called America Firsters, in the US in 1941 (see

Professor Cavan, the dandy of *Day of the Beast*, in his apartment decorated in best internationalist, self-aggrandizing style of Berlusconi.

Truffaut 1984: 145). Conversely, *Day of the Beast* has been read, with considerable difference of opinion, in terms of Spanish politics since its release. On the one hand, Marsha Kinder interprets *Day of the Beast* as a condemnation of the excesses of Socialist neoliberal policies that prefigured the change in government to Partido Popular (PP) and the right in 1996. For her the 'Clean Madrid' vigilantes represent the thugs of the Grupos Antiterroristas de Liberación (GAL) campaign in the Basque country, the covert war of Socialist prime minister, Felipe González; Cavan alludes to Berlusconi's media empire; and overall 'Madrid's corruption is inextricably linked with the drive toward European convergence' (1993: 21). On the other hand, Compitello takes issue with Kinder and argues that *Day of the Beast* is not just a political allegory but 'truly radical':

> It articulates the processes that contribute to the urbanization of consciousness at a particularly important juncture in Spanish history. It is a resistance to the kind of political thinking that attributes all responsibility for Spain's ills to the policies of the central government in Madrid and the corruption that ensued from those policies. While the Socialists bear blame for their policies that made land speculation profitable, others hold a great responsibility as well. By the time the movie was made, we must remember the right had held the reins of local government in Madrid's municipal government as well as the government of the Comunidad de Madrid for some time. (1999: 213)

Compitello does not see the 'Clean Madrid' vigilantes as an image of the Socialist GAL secret police but as a possible transmutation of the PP's vision of Madrid.

De la Iglesia's later film *Common Wealth* supports the latter reading. Although Compitello makes a case for a more theoretical, overarching reading of *Day of the Beast*, as 'a filmic challenge to the discourse of postmodernization' (1999: 214), he too acknowledges the irony that the film as a successful commodity participated in the very process it critiqued.

In *Saboteur* the villain's fall from (the Statue of) Liberty extends the ideological symbolism to the end. The film's political effect, however, was quite different and focused on the lead up to the Liberty climax. The US Navy demanded the censoring of the image of their disabled ship Normandie lying in the New York harbour, with the cut to the villain's smirk, as wrongfully implying that the Navy could successfully be targeted for sabotage on US shores (see Truffaut 1984: 146). These images were restored in a 1948 US reissue (see McGilligan 2003: 303). As we have seen in our Spanish reception chapter the film never even opened in Madrid until 27 December 1945, after the end of World War II. Even Fascist censors found it too incendiary for wartime.

For Compitello *Day of the Beast* images how 'the role of urban planning is diminished under flexible accumulation' (1999: 216) and through the transition urban planning becomes only urban design, especially through the transition between the two historical eras that the Capitol and the KIO Towers represent. Yet both Hitchcock and De la Iglesia excel in richly exploiting this element of design cinematographically. A close analysis of these scenes shows De la Iglesia's aesthetic heritage and also reveals, when Hitchcockian criticism is taken into account, significant gender, political and ideological nuances in De la Iglesia's film.

V. ONCE BURNED IN THE WEST, EVEN WITH SOME *NORTH BY NORTHWEST*: THE CROSSOVER DISASTER OF *PERDITA DURANGO*

The success of *Day of the Beast* brought De la Iglesia to the attention of Hollywood. The Spanish producer Andrés Vicente Gómez offered him the opportunity to direct a big-budget English-language crime drama, *Perdita Durango* (1997), after the veteran Spanish director J.J. Bigas Luna had left the project. Rosie Perez was already cast in the starring role. Like *Rebecca,* Hitchcock's first crossover project, *Perdita Durango* was also an adaptation of a novel, in this case one of the road novels by Barry Gifford that was based on a real event in Austin, Texas. Gifford also co-wrote the film's script as he had done when he worked with David Lynch on *Wild at Heart* (1990) in which Perdita Durango was introduced as a minor character.[17] For De la Iglesia this film marked the first time he did not work from a script he had written. He would rue the day. Subsequently he complained that the script, even as reworked by David Trueba, did not represent his preferred point of view, that of a loser:

> In fact, one of my biggest problems I had to confront was that the original novel of *Perdita Durango* didn't tell the story of a downtrodden person, but of a hero. If the movie had been closer to my vision, I would have told the adventures of a poor disillusioned fellow who lives on the Mexican border, who they say practices *santería*, but who really doesn't have any power. Nonetheless he finds himself caught up in a scheme and forced to simulate acts of witchcraft in front of a series of people. (Heredero 1997: 473)

The project presented multiple challenges. De la Iglesia not only had to insert himself into Hollywood cinema, to respect the classic Hollywood narrative arc, but also to represent a bilingual Latino perspective and direct an already established Latina star. This double bind was difficult for a Spaniard at first try. Whereas in *Rebecca* Hitchcock imported and staged a comfortably familiar

British manor life in the US, in *Perdita Durango* De la Iglesia did not stage a Spanish or Basque *mise-en-scène* for Hollywood. The Spaniards De la Iglesia and Javier Bardem, in his first major acting role in English, immersed themselves in border culture.

The film tells the story of two psychotic killers, Perdita Durango (Rosie Perez) and Romeo Dolorosa (Javier Bardem) who meet, fall in love and undertake their illegal activities together on the road. Romeo, a witch doctor, leads *santería* rituals. In a state of possession he chops up a human cadaver, throws the limbs into a cauldron, and then blows blood from the brew onto the faces of the other attendees. Romeo also robs a bank dressed as the legendary Mexican wrestler and actor El Santo. To settle a large debt, Romeo agrees to drive a truckload of human foetuses destined for the cosmetics industry across the US/ Mexican border to Las Vegas for his mob boss Santos (Don Stroud). Before setting off Romeo feels compelled to practice more human sacrifice in order to bless his trafficking mission.

Together with Perdita they randomly kidnap a pasty white teenage couple, Estelle and Duane (Aimee Graham and Harley Cross), vacationing in Mexico. Perdita rapes Duane who then is forced to watch Romeo rape Estelle. Perdita and Romeo take the couple on their journey to Las Vegas and continue to abuse them psychologically and sexually. Woody Dumas (James Gandolfini), a DEA agent, and the father of the kidnapped girl track the outlaws, but Reggie San Pedro (Carlos Bardem), Romeo's cousin, is set up to settle scores. The mobster recruits Reggie to receive the contraband cargo for a handsome pay-off if he double-crosses Romeo. In a warehouse Reggie shoots Romeo and is himself shot by Perdita, who runs out when she hears an explosion. As Romeo lies dying, Dumas stands over him. In the final scene, in the version of the film shown everywhere but in the US, Romeo melds into the image of the soldier of fortune Joe Erin (Burt Lancaster) in the Robert Aldrich classic *Vera Cruz* (1954), a favourite western of his childhood. In Romeo's imagination Dumas transforms into Ben Trane (Gary Cooper), another soldier of fortune in *Vera Cruz* who is revealed to be nobler and less materialistic in the film's showdown.[18] After Perdita sees Romeo's body taken away in an ambulance, she strolls down the neon-lit Vegas boulevard.

Perdita Durango pays direct homage to *Vera Cruz*, as well as to a sheaf of other Hollywood movies – Orson Welles' *Touch of Evil* (1958), Robert Aldrich's *The Grissom Gang* (1971), Sam Peckinpah's *Bring Me the Head of Alfredo García* (1974), Quentin Tarantino's *Pulp Fiction* (1994), Oliver Stone's *Natural Born Killers* (1994) and Robert Rodriguez's *From Dusk Till Dawn* (1996), but only minimally to Hitchcock; yet a few allusions to *North by Northwest* do stand out. One, after Romeo and Perdita have raped Estelle and Duane, Romeo

A jet plane circles around
a phallic Saguaro cactus
in *Perdita Durango*.

asks them sarcastically, 'What are your plans for the future?' The film cuts to a
low-angle shot of a Saguaro cactus around which a jet plane's trail circles. The
image punctuates sex with modern transport just as the phallic entrance into the
tunnel did at the end of *North by Northwest*, an ending that Almodóvar also
cited in *Labyrinth of Passion*. Two, more generally the cargo that Romeo trans-
ports, foetuses, is a savvy joke on the Hitchcockian MacGuffin, the element that
drives the action but is not important in itself. By diminishing the importance
of the foetuses by making them only the MacGuffin, the film executes a double
critique of major US cultural issues, that of abortion and the obsession with
youth culture. These two Hitchcockian motifs are acknowledged in the opening
title sequence. Three, in the turning point sequence when Romeo takes fateful
possession of the truckload of foetuses in Tijuana the music on the soundtrack
strongly alludes to the chase theme of *North by Northwest*.

Like Hitchcock, De la Iglesia in *Perdita Durango* pushed the boundaries
of sex and violence, mixed genres and incorporated humorous dialogue, but he
couldn't master the mix, especially the border culture. For an American audience, De la Iglesia did not get American pop culture right, particularly in his
use of music. For instance the citation of the Tijuana Brass, as a favourite of
Estelle's father, is so over explained that it makes the scene itself lame rather
than funny or parodic. Furthermore, though spectacular in his actions, a mag-
netic presence in the film, Bardem in his first English-speaking role is hard to
understand, for example when he waxes philosophical about 'big questions',
and is not convincing as a Latino either when he speaks Spanish with hints of a
Castilian accent. More problematic, however, is the unsure tone with which the
Latin culture of *santería* is presented. Carlos Heredero rightly observed to De la
Iglesia himself: 'It isn't at all clear if the *santería* rites, with that excess of "gore"
of the heart ripped from the cadaver, are filmed seriously and in a sensationalist
manner or from an ironic and disbelieving perspective' (1997: 493). Since all
of these aspects – soundtrack, dialogue clarity and *santería* – come off as un-
naturally forced, the film's pace is plodding, rather than action-packed. When
David Rooney first reviewed *Perdita Durango* for *Variety*, he called for 'serious
re-editing', since 'this trashy comic-strip saga of apocalyptic sex, violence and

voodoo rituals is not quite fast or fun enough to fully satisfy in its present shape'
(6 October 1997).

This postmodern pastiche effectively underwhelmed an international audience, too. In Spain the *ABC* critic E. Rodríguez Marchante lamented 'what a
waste' after he saw *Perdita Durango* at the San Sebastián Film Festival:

> The great attraction of this festival, the return to the big screen of that win-
> ner Álex de la Iglesia, the most highly awaited film of the year, turns out
> to be, with a swift kick I'll say, a chestnut filmed with utmost attention to
> detail: great actors, great shots, great visual pretensions, spectacular action,
> sex, violence, real life excess, Las Vegas ... In sum, everything rolled into a
> big movie – all show, no content. (26 September 1997: 130)

In short, Rodríguez Marchante saw pure surface. Even though De la Iglesia has
said on the DVD commentary track that he learned to be a better filmmaker
from making *Perdita Durango* – for example, he definitely learned to manipulate more sophisticated tools such as specialised cameras used on helicopter
shots – his first encounter with Hollywood did not go smoothly. Although the
film was a box office hit outside of the US, the film hit a snag in the US. The
executors of Burt Lancaster's estate blocked its theatrical release citing a US
law that images of deceased celebrities cannot be altered without the consent
of their respective estates. Bardem could not supplant Burt in his heroic death
scene. Trimark Films, which was set to distribute the film, would not pay what
the Lancaster estate demanded. Hence for the US market the clip of *Vera Cruz*
was removed, the title changed to *Dance with the Devil* (because, according to
Barry Gifford, *Perdita Durango* was 'too Hispanic and people wouldn't know
what the movie was about') and the film went straight to video.[19] Symbolising
the film's fate in the US market Perdita Durango indeed walked away disconsolately in the lights of the Vegas strip at the end. The fact that the cuts to the film
varied so greatly across the globe also indicates that its cultural sensibilities – in
terms of sex, violence and media references – were neither as finely tuned nor as
commercially viable as Hitchcock's were in his crossover to the US.

In the director's cut of
Perdita Durango Javier
Bardem supplants Burt
Lancaster in his dying
role in *Vera Cruz.*

Perdita Durango (Rosie Perez) walks away disconsolately into the lights of the Las Vegas strip at the end of *Perdita Durango*.

VI. THE CRITIQUE OF SPECTATORSHIP AND HITCHCOCKIAN SERIOUS COMEDY IN *MUERTOS DE RISA*

> I discovered the cinema through television, and this symbolizes a little my way of seeing things. (Álex de la Iglesia, interview, Heredero 1997: 469)

The legal issues around *Perdita Durango* as well as its lukewarm critical reception soured De la Iglesia on a cross-over career. He turned down offers to direct *Alien IV* and *The Mask of Zorro*. It was not until *The Oxford Murders* (2008) that he made another movie in English. Instead after *Perdita Durango* he returned to known territory, to Spain and Spanish television history, to make *Muertos de risa* (*Dying of Laughter*, 1999), the story of the comedy act of Nino and Bruno. With this film he continued to develop his own unique style, inflected by comic book art. One improbable comic book action scene occurs in *Dying of Laughter* when Nino's mother discovers her dead cat in the freezer. She flops over dead backwards like a plank. Although Hitchcock, too, certainly had fun with frozen meat in the television episode 'Lamb to the Slaughter', these comic book scenes are too broad and parodic to be considered allusions to Hitchcock.

As I have argued elsewhere, the essence of *Dying of Laughter* is its serious reinterpretation of television history.[20] Like Hitchcock in *Rear Window* and many other films, De la Iglesia critically explores the notion of spectatorship. In

Comic book action in *Dying of Laughter*: Nino's mother flops over dead backwards like a plank when she discovers her dead cat in the freezer.

recreating television history, he underscores how the sense of a nation emerges now through spectatorship. Like Hitchcock he values the role of the spectator and appreciates popular culture.

Dying of Laughter explores spectatorship through two significant scenes that negotiate national identity: one, the failed Tejero coup of 23 February 1981, and two, the 1992 Barcelona Olympics opening ceremony. In the first case a sergeant (Jesús Bonilla) just doing his duty occupies a television station. There he and his conscripted troops watch the violent takeover of the Congress, called F-23 in Spain, by Coronel Tejero, as well as an animated series, unfold on television. They fraternise with the television station workers and act like 'good ole boys', who are following orders, but who are not invested in overthrowing the State. In the second case, the character Nino is inserted into footage of the Olympic parade in the 1992 Barcelona Olympics as the Royal Family, and the world, watch in the stands. Both scenarios, which were situated at the moment Spain first entered the European Union, link spectatorship to issues of nationhood.

De la Iglesia continues to present his reinterpretation of Hitchcock's notion of comedy as black humour. He takes seriously comic situations of ordinary types that grow out of all proportion. For instance in an early sequence the effeminate Nino performs in a down-at-heel bar to a rowdy troupe of soldiers who force him to interact with their mascot, a goat. He valiantly tries to sing on, but

In *Dying of Laughter* the 'good ole boy' sergeant pauses for a whiskey, a smoke and some TV watching, as his troop takes over the television station during the F-23 coup in Madrid.

Nino as Zelig in *Dying of Laughter*, inserted into the opening ceremony parade of athletes, next to Prince Felipe de Borbón, as a member of the Spanish delegation during the Barcelona Olympics.

finally kills the goat, setting off a brawl. The soldiers set upon Nino and burn the bar down.

Dying of Laughter disappointed at the box office when it first appeared. However, its interpretation of the media has gained increased critical appreciation over the years. Also since Santiago Segura, known for his politically incorrect *Torrente* films, and the Gran Wyoming, who now has a TV talk show, have grown in popular consciousness, the film now ranks high in DVD viewings.[21] In 2012 in Spain *Dying of Laughter* stood at number one among De la Iglesia's films for box office returns (see Angulo & Santamarina 2012: 56).

VI. OUTWITTING THE TENANT BLOCK FROM *REAR WINDOW* TO *COMMON WEALTH*, STEALING THE MONUMENTAL CLIMAX OF *NORTH BY NORTHWEST*

De la Iglesia's return to Madrid in *La Comunidad* (*Common Wealth*)[22] was likewise a return to Hitchcock – to the genre of a suspense thriller, a Hitchcockian *mise-en-scène*, a mix of drama and humour, and a continued exploration of spectatorship. Filming in enclosed urban spaces, for this is 'a suspense movie with only one set' as De la Iglesia self-designates the film in the DVD liner notes, suggests the challenge Hitchcock met in *Rope*, *Dial M for Murder* and *Rear Window*. Indeed as he told Jesús Angulo and Antonio Santamarina, De la Iglesia and his co-scriptwriter Jorge Guerricaechevarría had Hitchcock in mind for the movie's original concept: 'The idea came about because suddenly Jorge and I reached the same conclusion as Hitchcock – that is, that the fewer elements you use, the more powerful the film is' (Angulo & Santamarina 2012: 233). However, *Common Wealth* also looked back to other 1950s classics, specifically to the Neorealist urban setting, dark humour and oppositional politics of Marco Ferreri's *El pisito* (*The Little Apartment*, 1958) and *El cochecito* (1960). Situating these films in the history of world cinema in his review of these Spanish films upon their release on DVD in 2005, Carlos Losilla argues in *Dirigido* that they should be considered more global than local, for Ferreri together with Antonioni, Fellini, Visconti and Bertolucci are 'melancholy chroniclers of a bourgeoisie in the midst of extinction' (2005: 71). De la Iglesia aspired with *Common Wealth* to a similar global profile and critical stance at the turn of the twentieth century. As it had been in *El pisito* the catalyst was again real estate.

Common Wealth tells the story of Julia (Carmen Maura), a forty-year-old real estate agent who discovers a cache of 300 million pesetas in the building of a Madrid flat she is showing, and where she stays illegally with her husband. Checking out the source of a rain of cockroaches onto their bed, she goes up to the attic flat with another tenant. They find a decomposed body; and she lifts a wallet from the body. Later using a map she found in the wallet, she returns to locate the money. She buys a 1950s-style plaid suitcase and stuffs the money into it. The other tenants of the building, who have been waiting for years for the old man in the attic to die to get his lottery winnings, band together and try every trick possible to get the money away from Julia. To get her drunk, the neighbours stage a party that only hops into action when she walks in. When she tries to leave the building with her suitcase of money, the tenant who accompanied Julia to discover the old man's body, whom the other tenants therefore consider suspect, gets on the elevator with her. The elevator gets stuck between floors. He gets caught half in and out of the elevator and is cut in half when the cage falls. The police cursorily investigate the scene.

Periodically potential buyers arrive for a tour of Julia's flat. By making scissors gestures, implying lesbian sex, she horrifies and thus gets rid of two mature women. Her husband comes home after having lost his job as a club bouncer. When she is about to tell him about the money he brings the conversation back to his lament that he is a loser. He breaks off their relationship and leaves. A Cuban tenant tries to woo her romantically, but Julia discovers that he is in cahoots with the others. They fight violently. Charly (Eduardo Artuña), a young man obsessed with *Star Wars* who dresses like Darth Vader, spies on Julia's struggles from his courtyard window. Finally the neighbours break into her apartment and tear it apart. Coming to the rescue, Charly manages to get Julia and her suitcase out via a secret way to the roof. Just as Julia crawls up the ladder, he changes the suitcase with the money for a similar one with fake bills. The neighbours pursue them with shotguns. Dressed in full Darth Vader regalia and proclaiming 'Long live the Republic!', Charly tries to stop them but is punched senseless. The chase continues over the rooftops of central Madrid to the huge statues of horses leading chariots on top of the BBVA building. After a prolonged struggle Ramona (Terele Pavez), Julia's long-time adversarial neighbour, tells Julia she must admit that they are alike. Julia refuses to say so and throws the suitcase to her, which causes Ramona to fall backwards spectacularly to her death.

'Long Live the Republic!': Charly (Eduardo Artuña) takes his stand as Darth Vader on a Madrid rooftop with the apocalyptic BBVA horses in the background in *Common Wealth*.

Some time later Julia sees a newspaper ad from a Jedi who needs a princess and recognises that it is from Charly. She figures out that the meeting place is a Madrid bar and reunites with him there. While tipping the waiters handsomely with the old bills, he tells Julia about the suitcase exchange. Charly and Julia dance as the local bar crowd joins in and celebrates their good fortune.

In significant ways *Common Wealth* returns to the successful *mise-en-scène* and aesthetics of *Day of the Beast*. For one, both films exploit enclosed spaces to manipulate the language of the thriller genre. Scenes of *Day of the Beast* are set in Rosario's bleak rooming house as well as in Cavan's luxury apartment, just as *Common Wealth* takes place primarily inside the apartment building. For another, both *Day of the Beast* and *Common Wealth* allude extensively to Hitchcockian scenes staged at heights.

In addition, both *Day of the Beast* and *Common Wealth* critique unfettered consumerism, as Spain expanded in the early years of its European Union membership and easy credit led to rampant building. Fittingly, no character in *Common Wealth* is depicted as blameless or devoid of avarice. The film's topic seems prescient in the Spanish economic real estate downturn post-2008. During the boom in Spain many apartments were renovated with cash, especially pesetas from the underground economy that had been hoarded. To change them into Euros through official channels would have exposed their owners to government scrutiny and taxes. In *Common Wealth* the MacGuffin, a 1950s-style suitcase full of pesetas, is as well conceived and critically astute as was *Perdita Durango*'s cargo of foetuses. The dark humour and critique of consumerism in *Common Wealth* also draws on the Franco-era films of Marco Ferreri, *El cochecito* and *El pisito*. In those films families coveted and fought over consumer possessions, a motorised wheelchair and a flat respectively.

The *tour de force* rooftop chase in *Common Wealth* extensively copies the aesthetics, if not the depths, of the romantic relationship, of the Mount Rushmore scene of *North by Northwest*. The citations were noted in the Spanish and international press. José Enrique Monterde in his review 'Los "quiméricos inquilinos" de Álex de la Iglesia' ('The "chimerical tenants" of Álex de la Iglesia') in *Dirigido* observed that Hitchcock was in 'extreme close-up' in the *mise-en-scène* of *Common Wealth* and that the final chase emulates the finale of *North by Northwest* (2000: 32).

Common Wealth adapts Hitchcockian aesthetics to the Spanish situation. *North by Northwest* is Hitchcock's most American movie since it envisions the US on a gigantic scale, open to the future. The open plains never end and Mount Rushmore depicts humans as mountains. The contrast in scale is similar in *Common Wealth* as Julia emerges from the apartment building to walk across the sunlit roof on the Madrid skyline. This was a successful commercial move as well. De la Iglesia showed that he could create a spectacle. Like Hitchcock

Julia (Carmen Maura) emerges from her apartment to walk across the roof between the monumental statues of the BBVA in *Common Wealth*.

in all of his scenes staged on heights, De la Iglesia built a huge production set of the rooftop in addition to filming on the actual BBVA building. Spectacular effects that convey increasing danger and suspense were created through editing, particularly to close-ups and point-of-view shots. In *Common Wealth* one neighbour dies by falling off a flagpole over the building's entrance to land at the feet of American tourists carrying a common guidebook.

Movies show us what we cannot normally see. For example the decisive moment when Cary Grant implores the bad guy to help him save Eva Marie Saint. We see the whole panorama of the modern house and the valley behind on a diagonal in the frame that indicates tension. Then the film cuts to show the bad guy step on Grant's hand, slip and fall down the mountain, breaking the coveted pre-Colombian vessel with film inside. In *Common Wealth* De la Iglesia reverses the confrontation and unlocks the Latin film inside *North by Northwest*. First the crazed Ramona and Julia are aligned in a diagonal that shows the danger of Julia's situation as she dangles from the front hoof of the equestrian statue. Then Ramona demands that Julia admit that she is as avaricious as Ramona. She commands: 'Say that you're like me. Say it.' When Julia refuses and throws the suitcase to her, Ramona falls to her death. Although her fall, breaking through several clotheslines, and bouncing off roofs recalls an improbable cartoon sequence, Ramona's death, 'like a flower' as De la Iglesia says on the DVD track, 'not my idea', recaptures the serious tone, and recalls a similar overhead shot of Julia exhausted on the checkered floor in the attic where she had located the

On the precipice of Mount Rushmore, Roger Thornhill (Cary Grant) appeals to the bad guy Leonard (Martin Landau) to help him pull Eve (Eva Marie Saint) up in *North by Northwest*.

In *Common Wealth* Julia Carmen Maura) dangles from the front leg of the equestrian statue as her mad neighbor Ramona (Terele Pávez) approaches her.

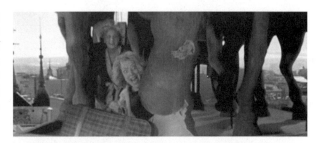

In *Common Wealth* Ramona demands of Julia, 'Say that you are like me. Say it.'

In *Common Wealth* the dead body of Ramona is arrayed like a flower whose center is the suitcase of cash which caused her fall.

Another allusion to *Topaz*'s 'flower shot': Julia lies exhausted on the checkered floor in the attic where she had located the money in *Common Wealth*.

money. The original citation is both Hitchcockian and Latin American, for both images in *Common Wealth* reference Juanita's death in *Topaz*, seen from above splayed out on a checkered floor. In *Common Wealth* Julia's swoon foreshadows Ramona's death. As discussed previously, Almodóvar in *Flower of My Secret* also quoted this same image from *Topaz*.

Common Wealth changes the conventional morality of *North by Northwest* to a darker view. In that film good and evil are clearly demarcated. When asked to show respect for human life by Grant the good guy, the bad guy steps on his

Fake money and a joker's card scatter like confetti over the Madrid skyline in the final shot of *Common Wealth*.

hand. In contrast, Julia only has to show, and does, that she is not motivated purely by money. Some critics ascribed the same diminished standards to the movie itself. Monterde found the film itself vapid and too commercial, calling it with disdain and considerable rhetorical flourish 'ese guiñol esplendoroso y comercial pero a la postre excesivamente vacío' ('that splendorous and commercial, but in the end excessively empty puppet show') (2000: 33).

Just as we can go to Mount Rushmore but cannot get Hitch's view, likewise we can go to the Calle Alcalá in central Madrid, but we cannot get De la Iglesia's splendid skyline view of the fake money and a joker's card scattering in the wind like confetti over the skyline in the film's final shot. These impossible views and the monumental scale of the spectacle show how the two films resemble each other.

Like *North by Northwest*, *Common Wealth* debuted at the San Sebastián Film Festival, with similar results at the competition, a Best Actress prize, for Carmen Maura, just as Eva Marie Saint had won for *North by Northwest*. Though certainly not the physical type of a *svelte* Hitchcock blonde, Maura's image evoked Hitchcock's women as much as humanly possible. She appeared as a blonde and stood out in every scene because of her 1950s-style pink suit, similar to those worn by Kim Novak in light green in *Vertigo* and Eva Marie Saint in light brown in *North by Northwest*. Maura was the life of the party, perhaps never more so as during fiesta time as the neighbours hold her up for the money. This was the first film for De la Iglesia with a female protagonist and he turned to Hitchcock for ideas for every aspect of *mise-en-scène*.

The fake fiesta: Julia is the center of attention in *Common Wealth* as her neighbors try to get her to hand over the money she has discovered hidden in the building.

VIII. CONSUMED BY VENGEANCE: THE UNFORESEEN CONSEQUENCES OF IMPERFECT CRIMES FROM *STRANGERS ON A TRAIN* TO *EL CRIMEN FERPECTO*

Though he cast Carmen Maura once again, for his next film after *Common Wealth* De la Iglesia turned to a completely different genre, the western in *800 Balas* (*800 Bullets*, 2002). This film tells the story of a former cowboy stuntmen in a failing western amusement park called Texas, Hollywood in Almería, Spain. They fight to keep the park open and its cinematographic memory alive when an executive (played by Carmen Maura) scouts the area as a site for a Disney-style theme park. Through these sad-sack cowboys De la Iglesia continued to refine his reputation for comedy, as well as his obsession with 'felices perdedores' or happy losers.[23] Moreover in *800 Bullets* he resurrected the place of Spain, specifically the southern region of Almería, in world cinema history as the place where both Spaghetti westerns and several top Hollywood films, such as *Lawrence of Arabia* (1962), *Doctor Zhivago* (1965) and *Patton* (1970), were made. In several ways he sets the record straight. By putting Spain back into the history of the western he took vengeance on those who had made it impossible to show *Vera Cruz*, and consequently to release *Perdita Durango* in his director's cut in the US. But it left him still waiting and wanting to make it big in Hollywood some day.[24]

With his subsequent film *Ferpect Crime* (2004), De la Iglesia returned to a more familiar Hitchcockian genre, the crime drama. The title directly recalls, with a small transposition of letters, the Spanish title of Hitchcock's *Dial M for Murder*, *Crimen perfecto,* the story of a husband who unsuccessfully plots to kill his wife. In both its plot and *mise-en-scène Ferpect Crime,* whose spelling was 'corrected' to *El crimen perfecto* (*The Perfect Crime*) by some distributors and many reviewers of the film, alludes more strongly to another Hitchcock film about a would-be perfect plot that failed, *Strangers on a Train.*[25] In the principal setting of 'el centro comercial', or shopping mall, De la Iglesia transposes these tales of vengeance into a broader critique of global consumer culture.

Ferpect Crime tells the story of Rafael González (Guillermo Toledo), a cocky, womanising clerk in the women's section of a major Spanish department store called Yeyo's. He makes out with women in the dressing rooms, sells a woman a fur coat she cannot afford and celebrates by having sex with a female clerk after-hours in the store when he provisionally receives his desired promotion to floor manager. But when the woman returns the coat, he insults her in front of his rival Don Antonio (Luis Varela), head of the men's section who then gets the promotion. Don Antonio fires Rafael. In a fight in a dressing room Rafael kills Don Antonio. Lourdes (Mónica Cevera), an ugly duckling clerk, witnesses the murder but keeps the information to herself in order to blackmail Rafael into being her lover. She acts as Rafael's accomplice in disposing of Don Antonio's body, which they cut up and incinerate in the store. Rafael finally becomes floor manager, but Lourdes has the upper hand. She remakes the store in her own image, firing the pretty women whom Rafael romanced and substituting them with her homely compatriots.

Lourdes arranges for Rafael to meet her mother and narcoleptic father at an excruciating dinner at their house. Rafael takes Lourdes on a date at the amusement park. Profoundly embarrassed at being seen by a co-worker with Lourdes and injured when trapped on one of the rides, he buys a plane ticket to get away. When she discovers his escape plan, she visits the policeman who investigated Don Antonio's death but still says nothing about the murder. Rafael begins to go mad and hallucinate. He talks with Don Antonio, now a smoking green phantasm who not only haunts him but also eggs him on repeatedly in his quest to escape Lourdes' control. Dressed as a bride she ambushes him with a reality TV show crew at the store. He has to respond live to her wedding proposal. He finally says 'yes' to her on camera, although in his mind he says, 'Yes, I will kill her.' They marry and Lourdes demands sex on her terms.

Rafael buys DVDs to find out how to rid himself of Lourdes: Buñuel's *Ensayo de un crimen*, Isaac-Pierre Racine, Agustí Villaronga and Lydia Zimmermann's *En la mente del asesino* (*Aro Tolbuknin in the Mind of a Killer*, 2002), and, of course, Hitchcock's *Crimen perfecto* (*Dial M for Murder*). When he pays for the films, *Crimen ferpecto* with its misspelling pops up on the cash register screen. At their home Lourdes shows Rafael designs for her new concept for the store – sad clown clothes – which Rafael must present to the store management. Rafael

With great satisfaction Lourdes (Mónica Cevera) reviews her newly chosen motley crew of women of all body types in *Ferpect Crime*.

Bridezilla multiplied: On a reality TV show staged in the department store the emcee asks Rafael, 'Will you marry Lourdes?' in *Ferpect Crime*.

Rafael jumps into an elevator shaft and onto a sexy ad board to escape a fire, a police inspector and Lourdes in *Ferpect Crime*.

takes her out to the amusement park again. When they ride the Ferris Wheel and stop on top, she begins to talk about having children. He lures her into leaning out to see a family below. She falls out of the car and is left hanging on. Seeing how many other people, including the police investigator, are watching them he pulls her back into the car.

At work in the department store he tricks Lourdes into going into a sound-proof room and starts a fire that makes the sprinkler system go off. When the fire spreads rapidly, pandemonium breaks out in the store and on the street. Still Lourdes (Enrique Villén) gets out of the enclosure and attacks Rafael. They struggle. The investigator arrives and arrests both Lourdes and Rafael, but Rafael slips into an open elevator shaft and saves himself by landing on an ad board he had placed there. Everyone thinks he has died in the fire, but he escapes.

Five years later with a new identity Rafael tends his own tie store. He watches the street in front of his store fill with clowns who cheer adoringly as Lourdes exits the department store and slips into a waiting limousine. A huge billboard says 'Clown Fashion Hits Big'.

Hitchcock's motifs and irony reverberate throughout this film. One, they hide Don Antonio's body in plain sight, as a mannequin (a motif in Buñuel's *Ensayo de un crimen*) dressed in ski clothes. This recalls Hitchcock's light comedy, *The Trouble with Harry* (1955), whose whole plot deals with the hiding of Harry's body after he dies unexpectedly. Two, the idea that it is not so easy to kill is a theme associated with the prolonged murder of the Russian spy in the kitchen scene of *Torn Curtain*. After hiding Don Antonio's body, Lourdes and Rafael belabour the butchering of the body. Three, the film's title, *Ferpect Crime* with its misspelling on the department store cash register is a direct citation of Hitchcock's *Dial M for Murder*. As we have seen, that film tells the story of a husband plotting to kill his wife, just as Rafael plots to kill Lourdes. In *Dial M for Murder*, Margot (Grace Kelly) grabs scissors to defend herself from the in-truder's attack. In *Ferpect Crime* this story is repeated in a flashback to the case of Howard Green, murdered by his wife with scissors. Posters for *Dial M for Murder* featured the scissors murder. Notably Hitchcock used gigantic props for his film, which *Ferpect Crime* alludes to in an insert shot of immense bloodied

The insert shot of giant bloodied scissors in *Ferpect Crime* recalls the murder weapon in *Dial M for Murder*.

scissors. Finally, and most significantly, *Strangers on a Train* is repeatedly cited and parodied in *Ferpect Crime*.

To recall, the extensive opening sequence of *Strangers on a Train* introduced the two main characters by showing only their shoes and legs as they arrive to catch a train. The suave Bruno (Robert Walker), who comes to town with the crisscross plot for murder, wears fancy two-tone wingtip shoes. When Bruno and Guy (Farley Granger) bump up against each other's shoes under the table of their train car – the 'footsies' encounter is shown in a low-angle shot – the whole vengeance plot, which Bruno calls 'the perfect crime', is set in motion. Likewise *Ferpect Crime* introduces Lourdes through her white Camper shoes, which Rafael sees beneath the dressing room door after killing Don Antonio. This point of view shot sets the blackmail plot in motion.

A crisscross first meeting: Bruno's flashy two-tone shoes touch Guy's conservative wingtips under the table in *Strangers on a Train*.

First impression through shoes: Rafael spies Lourdes' white Camper shoes under the dressing room door after he has killed Don Antonio in *Ferpect Crime*.

Insert shot of Bruno showing off his gaudy tie, a gift from his mother, to Guy when they first meet in *Strangers on a Train*.

Ferpect Crime parodies Hitchcock's characterisation and classic narration for humorous effect using the white shoes as a leitmotif. Lourdes' shoes, though white like Bruno's and ostensibly in fashion, are as ugly as she is. Moreover, the effect is heightened with a first mistaken sighting of white shoes on a red carpet. Rafael accosts a woman shopper in the store wearing similar white Camper shoes before finding out that Lourdes is his 'guardian angel'. They meet in the cafeteria. In a point-of-view shot he checks her shoes out under the table. Even the epilogue of *Ferpect Crime* references fashion in *Strangers on a Train*, since Rafael survives by selling ties, a piece of clothing intimately associated with Bruno. To recall, when Bruno first meets Guy on the train, he showed off the loud tie his mother gave him.

It is worth pausing for a moment, given that we have brought into the discussion the archetypal obsession of the gay Bruno with his mother, to consider gender representation in *Ferpect Crime*. As Boris Izaguirre in his chapter 'Pasajeros en un mismo tren' ('Passengers on the same train') notes about a subsequent encounter between Bruno and Guy:

> They are lovers in the night, the criminal image of gayness, which relates perfectly to the late Victorian education of Hitchcock. Caught in the dark, their attraction for each other is confirmed. And Hitchcock knew how to photograph it better than anyone. (2005: 100)

Perhaps because of Hitch's Victorian moral limitations, homoeroticism makes *Strangers on a Train* the beautiful, engaging and witty film that it is. Heterosexuality does not fare as well in *Ferpect Crime*. The stereotyping of women either as bimbos or sex-crazed losers, brought to a climax in the emphatic and unrelenting cruelty in representing Lourdes, makes the film misogynistic and often alienating for a female spectator. Many critics, including Tania Modleski in *The Women Who Knew Too Much: Hitchcock and Feminist Theory* (2005), have interpreted Hitchcock's films in gender terms. Modleski in particular strives to 'save his female viewers from annihilation at the hands not only of traditional male critics but of those feminist critics who see woman's repression in patriarchal cinema as total, women's "liking" for these films as nothing but masochism' (2005: 122). For Modleski, the role of Hitchcock's daughter Patricia as Barbara Morton in the film, who when she appears looks like the dead Miriam and hence evokes guilt in the villain, is key, for her haunting presence puts 'the blame for crimes against women where it belongs' (ibid.). In *Ferpect Crime* this blame should not only fall on Rafael but would be directed at him by the gaze of Lourdes' lookalikes. Following Modleski's critical approach, we need to examine how guilt both enters his mind and how it slips away.

Ferpect Crime most significantly evokes *Strangers on a Train* in the *mise-en-scène* of the amusement park that they share. To recall, in that film Bruno kills Guy's homely wife Miriam in an amusement park. It is also in the amusement park that the most iconic scene of surprise, cruelty and ironic humour takes place when Bruno chats with a young child, then pops his balloon on purpose. Later Bruno is killed in the same amusement park by a runaway merry-go-round after a fight to the death with Guy. This sequence was Hitchcock's *tour de force* in the film for his combination of live action and shots of architectural models. In *Ferpect Crime* Rafael has vengeance and murder on his mind, and perhaps Bruno's success, when he takes Lourdes to the amusement park the second time. Riding the Ferris Wheel to the top, Lourdes slips out of their car, but Rafael pulls her back in. The rescue is almost more of an accident than Lourdes' fall. Women in the other cars, like Patricia Hitchcock's character in *Strangers on a Train*, stare at Rafael in horror and generate a sense of guilt in him. The repetition of the Hitchcockian archetype of a climatic scene on heights, in De la Iglesia's most widely-circulated films, *Day of the Beast*, *Common Wealth* and *Ferpect Crime*, shows the sustained importance of Hitchcock in De la Iglesia's film over his commercial career.

In his review, 'El Crimen Perfecto: An Imperfect Crime Comedy', Roger Ebert also noticed 'hints of Hitchcock' in the film. However for Ebert the film failed as comedy:

Second time around: in their second visit to the amusement park Lourdes falls out of the Ferris wheel car and grasps toward Rafael in *Ferpect Crime*.

The endless view of consumerism: Rafael surveys the main floor of Yeyo's department store in *Ferpect Crime*.

'El Crimen Perfecto' has energy, colour, spirit and lively performances, but what it does not have are very many laughs. In a month that has seen 'The 40-Year-Old Virgin,' a wonderful comedy about romance in retail, this one seems oddly old-fashioned; it has a 1950s feel. (2005)

Ferpect Crime did mine 1950s aesthetics through Hitchcock's films of that period, but with less genuine humour and certainly little romance.[26] At the same time as *Ferpect Crime* parodied global consumer culture and archetypal dreams such as spending a night in a perfectly appointed department store, it became caught in its own web.[27] When multiple location shots of major department stores in central Madrid, Barcelona and Sevilla were seamlessly edited together, urban Spanish viewers were sutured into the film in another vortex of perspective to recognise their own shopping habitat on screen. Unlike De la Iglesia's earlier urban locations, however, these sites were all too common and mass produced and, hence, the film only reaffirmed its status as a commercial object through the *mise-en-scène*.

With a budget approaching five million Euros, *Ferpect Crime* was an expensive movie for the Spanish industry and, though it disappointed some critics, it performed well at the box office. Moreover, it opened in more international markets than De la Iglesia's previous films had, perhaps due to the accessible combination of Hitchcock and shopping.

IX. THE MAN WHO KNEW TOO MUCH AND BLOGGED ABOUT IT: THE ROOFTOP CHASE OF *BLACKMAIL* AND HITCHCOCK'S HERMENEUTICS IN *THE OXFORD MURDERS*

Does the perfect crime exist? For years, writers have speculated on this idea, time and again, and murderers, too. Some even managed to put the idea into practice. Like the case of Howard Green, in London. (Seldom in Voice Over, Exterior Flashback. Howard Green. Street – Day 63, Script of *The Oxford Murders*, 204.)[28]

Coming off his homage to *Strangers on a Train*, Álex de la Iglesia took on another story of a perfect crime, Guillermo Martínez's novel *Los crímenes de Oxford* (2004), a mystery thriller with a mathematical theme. The Argentinean novel had been a best-seller in its original Spanish version as well as worldwide in translation. Gerardo Herrero, a Spanish producer with a strong international reputation – he was also responsible for J.J. Campanella's *El secreto de sus ojos* (*The Secret in Their Eyes* (2009) – encouraged De la Iglesia to take on the project, a primarily European co-production funded by Eurimages, NBC Universal and Telecinco. To be shot on location in the UK this film would be De la Iglesia's second attempt in English. Its $10 million budget doubled what he had for *Ferpect Crime*. Although far from the scale of a Hollywood blockbuster, it still gave him the chance to put the partially aborted *Perdita Durango* behind him and assume a more global profile.

In an interview with María Güell at the film's Spanish opening in Barcelona, published in *ABC-Sevilla*, De la Iglesia adamantly dismissed any hint that *The Oxford Murders* was 'un encargo', or contract work (Güell 2008: 76). Taking three years preparation for filming, De la Iglesia wrote the script himself with his long-time collaborator Jorge Guerricaechevarría. Asked in the same interview 'What references did you find useful for weaving the plot?' he replied, 'Mankiewicz, Hitchcock ... Everything is in my head.'[29] We will explore the numerous Hitchcockian references and what they meant to De la Iglesia at a more mature stage of his career. Symbolically, De la Iglesia's crossover move to the UK recalled the late career shift of Hitchcock, who returned to the UK to recharge his career with *Frenzy*. Nonetheless, the challenges posed and the eventual solutions were far more international than those Hitchcock faced in his homecoming. Like Alejandro Amenábar who directed the megastar Nicole Kidman in his first English-language film *The Others* (2001) at a critical moment in her career when her marriage to Tom Cruise was ending, De la Iglesia was called on to help Elijah Wood, best-known for playing Frodo in *The Lord of the Rings* series (2001, 2002, 2003), transform his image from asexual idol of adolescent fantasy to mature dramatic actor able to pull off a sex scene. De la Iglesia cast the Spaniard Leonor Watling, known internationally for her role as the sleeping beauty in Almodóvar's *Talk to Her*, as Wood's character's romantic interest for his sexual awakening. The sex scene, slurping spaghetti off of Watling's body, which restages the kiss scene from Disney's *The Lady and the Tramp* (1955), helped him make the leap from G-rated to R-rated cinema. Importantly, like Amenábar with *The Others*, De la Iglesia brought his own Spanish technical crew on board for the project.

The Oxford Murders tells the story of Martin (Wood), an American grad student who comes to Oxford with hopes of studying with Professor Seldom

An 'R' version of the kiss scene of *The Lady and the Tramp*: Martin (Elijah Wood) slurps spaghetti off of Lorna's (Leonor Watling) body in *The Oxford Murders*.

(John Hurt), a famous mathematician, now retired, whose work compared mathematical series and serial murders. Martin meets Lorna (Watling), a nurse, playing squash and falls in love with her. When Seldom gives a public lecture, Martin asks him a question and is ridiculed. Later Seldom and Martin together stumble upon the murder of Martin's landlady, Mrs. Eagleton (Anne Massey), whose daughter Beth (Julie Cox), a cellist, took care of her. Seldom tells the police he had received a note that suggested that the murder was the first of a series. Cryptic mathematical clues lead to several other murders that the police investigate. First, a terminally ill patient in the bed next to that of Seldom's incapacitated and mad former student is found dead. Second, at a Guy Fawkes Night concert, which both Martin and Seldom attend to hear Beth play, a percussionist grabs his throat and dies. Finally, chased by Martin and Seldom, Frank (Dominique Pinon), the father of a child who needs a transplant drives and crashes a busload of mentally incapacitated children, killing several in a desperate attempt to get the organ his daughter needs.

Martin goes to the airport to leave on a vacation with Lorna, but becomes engrossed in a photo of the first crime scene that reveals that Mrs. Eagleton's scrabble word 'Kreis' ('circle') had given Seldom the idea for the first symbol and the diversionary theory. Martin misses the flight but Lorna leaves on it. Shortly after Martin meets Seldom in the gallery of reproductions of the Victoria and Albert Museum. Seldom confesses that he planted clues to suggest that the deaths were connected to cover for Beth, who murdered her mother to be free to love Martin.

The moral dilemmas posed by this story required a more serious, dramatic tone than De la Iglesia's previous films had demanded. As in Hitchcock's *Blackmail*, the moral message of the film, or 'la vuelta moral' ('moral twist') as De la Iglesia wrote regarding the film's final museum scene, was that no one is blameless:

> You have to pay to play. The most surprising thing is that some people believe, or more justly, that some of us believe, that we are free of guilt, and it isn't so. We aren't witnesses to a drama; we are integral pieces in the game

of suffering, and capable of knowing it and taking it on. No one is on the other side of the window. The very act of observing transforms reality and converts you into a protagonist, into the one guilty of the crime. No one is innocent. (De la Iglesia & Guerrichaechevarría 2008: 69)

Befitting the philosophical subject matter the film had the most serious tone, and fewest examples of humour, of any of De la Iglesia's movies. His comic spirit and characteristic sardonic wit found an outlet in his blog, quoted from above. After the film's release he published the blogs, entitled 'Blasfemando en el vórtice del universo' ('Blaspheming in the vortex of the universe'), along with Spanish and English versions of the script, some storyboards and copious photos. To read the blog, you have to turn the book over and upside down. In a typically irreverent post, he complained that in Elijah Wood's contract for the film three pages specified how many shots of Wood's posterior the director could take and how much he could show (De la Iglesia & Guerrichaechevarría 2008: 5).[30]

Most significantly De la Iglesia blogged about how both the budget and producers limited his artistic vision. Over the years he had learned to use a full range of cinematographic tools. He now knew almost too much about what was possible. For instance he was vetoed in using spider-cams to film a shot between two buildings, noting 'We only have enough money for cucaracha-cams' (De la Iglesia & Guerrichaechevarría 2008: 24). In his opinion, working on the *Harry Potter* films (2001, 2002, 2004, 2005, 2007) had spoiled his British technical crew into expecting too high a budget. In another post he mocks the excessive caution and control that security inspectors exercised on his use of pyrotechnics and his choice of camera placements on heights, one of the signature Hitchcock shots De la Iglesia often cited. For *The Oxford Murders* they only allowed him to shoot halfway up a building. In coarse language he recounts his exasperation:

In Greenwich five guys came with us to oversee the security measures for the shoot. We had to do a test of the fireworks, and the idiots looked at the stones to see if they got hot from the sparks. It was so ridiculous they gave us permission. But in the matter of placing cameras on the roofs, it's like they keep plucking hairs off their genitals with tweezers. They're almost giving me a heart attack. Later a leak turned up. Well, it seems the matter has turned into something terrifying because it's back to being a question of security. And what if the roof falls? It made me laugh, but the location shot depends on that stupidity. The director's assistant says that he can't risk his job for a leak ... I understand that they want to control everything, but you don't make movies that way, you make collections of picture cards. (De la Iglesia & Guerrichaechevarría 2008: 26)

The invitation to look on high was already in the novel in the concert scene. In some ways the novel itself was already cinematic, that is, either evoking well-known filmic narratives or perhaps even written with an eventual adaptation to the screen in mind, as several other novels in Spanish have been, such as those of Arturo Pérez Reverte.[31] In the novel *The Oxford Murders*, the way a triangle player dies at a concert recalls the concert hall dénouement of *The Man Who Knew Too Much*.

De la Iglesia continued to think of Hitchcock to inject suspense in the filmic adaptation. However, he unfortunately made a joke out of the concert scenario. He set the scene on Guy Fawkes Day. When the percussionist struggles and falls dead, every one looks up to search for an assassin on high. A rooftop chase ensues. Martin, Seldom and the police follow a costumed Podorov (Burn Gorman), Martin's resentful officemate, up stairs and across the rooftops. The shots from this chase scene, of a spiral staircase, recall the spiral motifs of climatic chase in Hitchcock's *Blackmail* at the British Museum, as well as, of course, *Vertigo*. To recall, in *Blackmail* the suspect Tracy (Donald Calthrop) runs through the reading room with its desks set out in a spiral pattern; he proceeds through the maven of corridors to climb out onto the dome. Podorov carries a long wrapped package, which the viewer thinks could contain a rifle. When they finally pin him down on the roof they open the package to reveal an innocuous banner with the irreverent word 'Bastards'. The effect is to deflate the tension rather like a gun shooting out a flag that reads 'Bang'. De la Iglesia embellished *The Oxford*

After the percussionist dies at a Guy Fawkes concert, Seldom, Martin and the police chase a suspect, a costumed Podorov, across the rooftops as fireworks explode in *The Oxford Murders*.

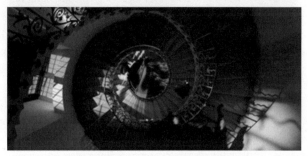

Chase on a Hitchcockian spiral staircase in *The Oxford Murders*.

Climatic chase in the rotunda of the British Museum in Hitchcock's *Blackmail.*

Murders with Hitchcockian motifs, particularly from his British period. But although humour, especially irony, abounds in the script, most of it falls rather flat in the film.

One particular humorous situation alludes to Hitchcock's *Frenzy*, which is also evoked on a more sombre note with the close-up of the face of the first victim Mrs. Eagleton (Barbara Leigh-Hunt) in *The Oxford Murders*. It resembles the morbid shot of the strangled Brenda. A closer citation to *Frenzy*, in the humorous spirit of Hitchcock, is when the police inspector offers his own theory that the symbols they have found associated with the first two cases look like a conventional menu, starting with soup, then fish, so that the third would be dessert. To recall, one of *Frenzy*'s funnier running gags is the foreign-inspired dinners the police inspector's wife serves him as he tells her about the case. He prefers plain food. Notably one day she announces 'soupe de poisson' (fish soup). Finding it too exotic for his liking, he dumps his serving back into the pot when she goes into the kitchen. In the same spirit the mathematical ruminations of Seldom and Martin, with their foreign mumbo jumbo, are all too pretentious for the plainspoken Inspector Peterson (Jim Carter) in *The Oxford Murders*.

In his blog entitled 'Five minutes of free association' as he plans the next day's shoot of the final scene at the Victoria and Albert Museum, De la Iglesia writes both specifically and philosophically on the importance of Hitchcock to his own vision:

> Let's see, it's my last day in the museum. I have to film two traveling shots, of Martin and Seldom. I prefer to use tracks rather than the steady cam, but since we can't move anything, because a hundred alarms go off, I can't lay tracks down. So I'll let it go. After that, enter into the third space, where Seldom sits down, in front of the Portico of Glory. General shot, and cuts, but Kiko says not at once, OK, as God wills, we'll have to take care of that.

Fine. Tracking shot: Martin gets up and close-up when Seldom calls him. Maybe I'll look for another way to do it, but finally this is terribly effective, it's what fits. Think about it. Super close-up in the final phase: lips, ear, like in *The Man Who Knew Too Much*. Hitchcock isn't just a director, he's a way of thinking, an attitude. It's like belonging to a group of Dwarves, it's a hermeneutics. One doesn't try to write like Jung, or Eliade. The point is that you are CONVINCED that they are on the way to the truth, YOU PARTICIPATE in their way of understanding the world. Weltanschauung, that's the concept. He isn't a director, he's a way of thinking. (De la Iglesia & Guerrichaechevarría 2008: 70)

In *The Oxford Murders* De la Iglesia used more close-ups than he had in any previous film. In the museum finale first there is a sequence of extreme close-ups, of Seldom's lips, then Martin's ear and eyes. As we see from his blog entries, Hitchcock, and specifically *The Man Who Knew Too Much*, inspired De la Iglesia to see the close-up as the most efficient aesthetic solution to telling a mystery story about murders foreshadowed. In Marrakesh the dying Louis Bernard (Daniel Gelin), an FBI agent costumed as an Arab, whispers his final secret into Dr. Ben McKenna's (Jimmy Stewart) ear, that a statesman will be assassinated in London soon.

The Oxford Murders challenged De la Iglesia to adapt a global bestseller and direct major English-language stars. In Spain the film was a big success and topped the box office in 2008. *The Oxford Murders* received six nominations for the 2009 Goyas, including Best Director and Best Film, but won for more minor categories – score, editing and production. Even though this was the first time a dubbed English-language film competed for the major prize in Spain, it did

The techniques of *The Man Who Knew Too Much*: extreme close-up of Seldom's (John Hurt) lips in *The Oxford Murders*.

Repetition of the techniques of *The Man Who Knew Too Much*: extreme close-up of Martin's (Elijah Wood) eye and ear in *The Oxford Murders*.

Final words in extreme close-up in *The Man Who Knew Too Much*: the dying, costumed Louis Bernard (Daniel Gelin) whispers his secret to Dr. Ben McKenna's (Jimmy Stewart).

not make the language breakthrough that Danny Boyle's multilingual *Slumdog Millionaire* (2008) did in winning the Best Motion Picture Academy Award in 2009. In the UK, moreover, *The Oxford Murders* won little praise for innovation or artistry. Many online critics savaged it.[32] Among newspaper and journal reviews, Carlos Boyero for *El País* was fairly typical when he wrote, 'This intelligent movie intrigues me, but I don't love it.'[33] In *Fotogramas* the 'pro' or in-favour-of review by Fausto Fernández highlighted British Hitchcock: 'It vindicates Alfred Hitchcock, but not the most cerebral one, but the clever, ironic, British father of McGuffins'; whereas writing in 'contra', or opposed to, Jordi Costa put the blame on the novel itself as a 'a scandalously simple enigma'. In the US *The Oxford Murders* was launched in 2010 first for Xbox Live, Playstation, Amazon, Vudu and Pay Per View, before opening for theatrical release.

The aesthetics of *The Oxford Murders* drew on the close-ups of *The Man Who Knew Too Much*, the *mise-en-scène* of *Blackmail* and the humour of *Frenzy* among many other references. In his production blog De la Iglesia articulated more extensively that he had ever done previously his debt to what he called Hitchcock's hermeneutics – that is, an efficient way of drawing the spectator into the film. Everyone becomes caught in a moral web in *The Oxford Murders* even without spider-cams. De la Iglesia's production blog shows not only how media has evolved but also how De la Iglesia himself endeavours to manipulate and exploit his public image as Hitchcock did.

X. A PUBLIC ROLE OR PERSONA: THE PRESIDENT OF THE ACADEMY ON STAGE, ON TV AND ON THE WEB

Many factors – early adopter status, commercial success and a strong fan base, respect and knowledge of film and media history, a sense of humour – led to De la Iglesia's election as the President of the Spanish Cinematographic Academy in 2009.[34] One of the duties of the President is to organise and preside over the

'The Force Be with You!':
Álex de la Iglesia at the
2009 Goya ceremony.

Goya award ceremony. To generate interest in the TV broadcast, which was losing viewers in recent years, he redesigned the Academy website, using his own
drawings and distinctive lettering style, and added online polls. At the actual
gala, he gave a stirring address defending the rights of creators. When he exited
the stage he gestured and exclaimed, 'A la Fuerza,' roughly evoking *Star Wars*'
'May the force be with you.' Later he would return to the stage to bring off a
surprise coup. He managed to stage the reconciliation of Almodóvar with the
Academy and sneak him on stage to receive a standing ovation during the Goyas
ceremony. To accomplish this coup, he deployed Hitchcock.

Almodóvar had left the Academy ostensibly to protest voting procedures
five years earlier. His absence also responded to a personal snub of his work
and more generally to the Academy's inefficiency in promoting Spanish cinema
globally. To carry off the surprise appearance of Almodóvar, De la Iglesia hid
him in a nearby hotel under the alias Roger Thornhill, Cary Grant's name in
North by Northwest. Almodóvar and De la Iglesia share a sense of humour and
irony, as well as good timing. Fundamentally they share a desire to transform
Spanish cinema according to Hitchcock's model and achieve artistic and commercial success as Hitchcock did. De la Iglesia has become the most public face
in Spain of this transnational project. For this reason the Spanish Ministry of
Culture awarded him the 2010 Premio Nacional de Cinematografía (National
Film Award) for lifetime achievement.[35] The official proclamation by Ángeles
González-Sinde, Minister of Culture, cited his 'innovative and transgressive
professional trajectory' that had 'enriched the language of our cinema' as well as
his negotiating efforts as President of the Academy to bring together the Spanish
film community and the general public (2010: 66465). Whether he was more
transgressor or conciliator in his public role would soon be tested.

For approximately a year public debate raged over the proposed 'Ley
Sinde' or Sinde Law, as the Sustainable Economy Act was known after Ángeles

González-Sinde. The law set out new provisions designed to fight internet piracy. The web community, which aligned with De la Iglesia's fan base, had objected that the Sinde Law stipulated excessive penalties for violations of intellectual property rights when in Spain there were not sufficient legal avenues to download content. De la Iglesia had tried but failed to broker a truce between content creators and users, both through face-to-face meetings with film exhibitors and distributors, and through an active presence on Twitter. When it became clear that the major congressional parties would approve the law, De la Iglesia announced he would resign as President of the Academy after presiding over the Goya gala. How he would perform at the ceremony was much anticipated. That night he gave a passionate speech, which was the hit of the telecast. De la Iglesia defended his vision of Spanish cinema in the new media world: 'The rules of the game have changed; the internet is the salvation of our cinema' (De la Iglesia 2011). González-Sinde, who was in the front row of the audience, made for a perfect cutaway shot as he spoke.

XI. CONCLUSIONS: REMAKES, TELEVISION AND HITCHCOCKIAN HEIGHTS IN *BALADA TRISTE DE TROMPETA* AND *LA CHISPA DE LA VIDA* AND A TRANSNATIONAL LATIN JOURNEY

For many decades Hitchcock was known to more people from his TV series *Alfred Hitchcock Presents* than his movies. In a similar manner De la Iglesia's many television projects, *Plutón B.R.B Nero* (2008–9), a 24-episode-long sci-fi series and a made-for-TV horror film full of monitoring devices, *La habitación del niño* (*The Baby's Room*, 2006), part of a series 'Películas para no dormir' ('Films to keep you awake'), have bolstered his cultural profile or 'Q score'. As we have seen in this chapter, the primary role of 'new' media, whether TV or the web, as the transmitter of culture and history has long preoccupied and intrigued De la Iglesia since his first short *Killer Mirindas*. He returned to this obsession in *Balada triste de trompeta* (*The Last Circus*, 2010) and in *La Chispa de la vida* (*As Luck Would Have It*, 2011). Both films, which were far more overtly political than his previous work, showed and critiqued how television marked life in Spain.

The Last Circus tells the story of a love triangle in which Natalia (Carolina Bang), a young trapeze artist, chooses between rivals Sergio, the Happy Clown (Antonio de la Torre), an attractive but abusive lover, and Javier, the Sad Clown (Carlos Areces), the initially timid friend. The film, which functions as a political allegory of the two Spains, Nationalist and Republican, depicts the brutality of two historical periods: first, the Spanish Civil War (1936–9) when the Republican Army invades the circus and enlists Javier's father; and second, the final years of Franco's dictatorship (1973–5) when Javier witnesses the assassination by a car bomb of General Carrera Blanco, President of the Government and anointed successor to Franco. This act is considered the most significant terrorist act by ETA, the armed Basque separatist organisation. Javier follows its rebroadcast on TV when he visits and shoots up a roadside bar. For the first time in his film career De la Iglesia represented ETA violence openly on screen. As with the Tejero coup in *Dying of Laughter*, De la Iglesia showed the role of the media in creating historical memory.

As Luck Would Have It focuses on a later period, the extreme economic and political crisis that hit Spain after 2008. Roberto Gómez (José Mota), an unemployed advertising executive who thought up the Coke slogan 'La chispa de la vida' ('the spark of life'), cannot get another job. He has a catastrophic accident that he turns into a media spectacle in order to provide for his family, especially his wife, played by Salma Hayek. Until Hayek, no major Latin American star had appeared in De la Iglesia's films. Since her appearance his movies have been given prominent slots in Latin American film festivals. *As Luck Would Have It* closed the 2012 Festival of Cartagena de las Indias, Colombia and the first Panamanian International Film Festival. *Las brujas de Zugaramundi* (*Witching and Bitching*, 2014) opened the 2014 Panamanian Film Festival. Furthermore, in 2014 he shot *Messi*, a documentary on Lionel Messi, in Rosario, Argentina.

At a mature stage of his career, De la Iglesia is also conscious of his impulse, which he traces to Hitchcock, to remake or perfect his films:

> This is something that happens to a lot of directors, we're always making the same movie. Hitchcock, for example, seems to be trying to achieve the perfect movie throughout his career, such that he remakes the same movie over and over. It's an understandable goal, which Hitchcock takes to the limit when he repeats movies, such as *The Man Who Knew Too Much*, and which Hawks imitates in *Rio Bravo* (1959) and *El Dorado* (1967). (Angulo & Santamarina 2012: 156)

De la Iglesia observed that he repeated his formulas, which always mine television history, in the following pairs – *Mutant Action* in his sci-fi TV series *Plutón B.R.B Nero* (ibid.), *Dying of Laughter* in *The Last Circus* (2012: 221), and *Day of the Beast* in *As Luck Would Have It* (2012: 184).

Although his own authorial style is now well developed and easily recognisable,[36] certain elements of Hitchcock's artistry remain part of his stock and trade, none more so than their shared obsession with heights in iconic settings, which we have seen in this chapter. As De la Iglesia explains in regard to his own repetition of this scenario in *Day of the Beast*, *Common Wealth* and

The Last Circus: 'when you take the characters to the Heights, it's as if you raised them up to Olympus, as if you purified them. Unconsciously the spectator also feels that sensation and believes that when on high the person is telling the truth and can't lie' (Angulo & Santamarina 2012: 238). The climax of *The Last Circus* unfolds at the Valle de los Caídos (Valley of the Fallen), the gigantic monument on the outskirts of Madrid that Franco had built to commemorate the Spanish Civil War. From its inception it has enflamed the passions of the two Spains.[37]

In *As Luck Would Have It*, the catalytic event of the story occurs when the protagonist falls from a high point of the Roman amphitheatre in Cartagena and impales himself on an iron bar, where he remains immobilised for the whole film. The fascination for the set, which is generally technically complex, and often filmed in a manner that reveals multiple planes of details, underscores most of his filmic production. Although he has not been able to make the leap yet to film a Hollywood blockbuster, De la Iglesia's characteristic genre mix, which in the spirit of Hitchcock is always underpinned by a unique sense of humour, has proved commercially viable and increasingly attractive to European and Latin American audiences.[38]

NOTES

1   Director's commentary, *El día de la bestia*, remastered DVD in *Colección Álex de la Iglesia*, PAL, Region 2.

2   Previous churches on the site were burned repeatedly over the centuries, sometimes for political reasons. The current stone structure, which brings together work of major Basque architects, sculptors and painters, represents a fusion of the ancient and the modern. The official website is http://www.arantzazu.org/. Information on the legend appears on http://www.turismoa.euskadi.net/s11–12375/en/contenidos/h_cultura_y_patri-monio/0000010902_h5_rec_turismo/en_10902/10902-ficha.html.

3   See Jesús Angulo and Antonio Santamarina, *Álex de la Iglesia. La pasión de rodar* (2012: 102–3).

4   This series about a young man and two women cohabiting was adapted for US TV as *Three's Company* (1977–1984).

5   Correspondence in the USC Warner Bros. Archives discusses the existence of a 3-D copy and the need for special publicity in Spain. However, as Dave Kehr notes in 'It Leaps (Gasp!) Off the Screen', his review of a Classic 3-D series at the NY Film Forum: '"Dial M for Murder" was held back by Warner Bros. until May 1954 in the US, when it was released only in conventional prints' (*NY Times*, 12 August 2010: C1). The 3-D copy was almost certainly never shipped to Spain either.

6   See Don Juan Manuel, 'Exemplo XXXV, De lo que contesçió a un mançebo que casó con una [mujer] muy fuerte y muy brava' ('Of What Happened to a Young Man on His Wedding Day') (1969: 187–92).

7   Carlos Heredero asserts in *Espejo de miradas* that De la Iglesia's talent for drawing comes from his mother who was a portrait painter: 'He inherited from his mother a talent for

drawing, thanks to which he started to create his own comics from early on (including the character 'The Thing of the Tidal River', a kind of shark-river eel that terrorizes Bilbao's Tidal River) and to publish comic strips in the magazine *Trokola*, in *La Gaceta del Norte*, in *El Correo Español* and in publications such as *Euskadi* and *La Gaceta del Ocio*. During a time period in which comics reasserted their maturity as art for an adult public, Alex was moving between his comic strips with as much ability as imagination, all the while keeping up his university studies in philosophy.' (1997: 456)

8 See 'Entrevista con José Luis Arrizabalaga y Arturo García,' *Como hacer cine 2: 'El día de la bestia,'* (Vera et al. 2002b: 58. De la Iglesia's artistic co-directors on *Day of the Beast* recall his early career in this interview.

9 De la Iglesia agrees with his interviewers that the name Orujo recalls Cayetana Martínez de Irujo, the daughter of the Duchess of Alba, the richest person in Spain, thus an obvious kidnapping target (Angulo & Santamarina 2012: 157).

10 The high-proof Orujo is seeped in tradition and is used to make a fiery drink: 'From *orujo*, Galicians traditionally make a drink called *queimada*, in which bits of lemon peel, sugar and ground coffee are put into a clay pot. Then the *orujo* is poured on top and the pot is lit on fire until the flame turns blue. This ancient tradition dates back to Celtic times and includes a ritual where the *queimada*-maker recites a "spell" as he makes the drink' (Lisa and Tony Sierra, *About.com Guide*, http://spanishfood.about.com/od/drinks/a/orujo.htm).

11 The identification of the industrialist as Galician suggests a political allegory for the film, as a leftist revenge against Manuel Fraga Iribarne (b.1922), Galicia's most famous and fierily reactionary politician who 're'-founded the Partido Popular in 1989 and then promoted José María Aznar's election as president representing the Partido Popular. Aznar was the first President on the right since the end of Franco's dictatorship.

12 De la Iglesia takes a contrary view in his interview with Carlos Heredero in *Espejo de miradas*. He claims that he was trying to exaggerate and make fun of Almodóvar's style in the wardrobe design in *Mutant Action*, but that neither Almodóvar nor any one else caught the reference: 'I tried to imitate in a satirical way the wardrobe, colour palette and archetypes of his movies. It seemed obvious to me. During the shooting of the film I thought Pedro was going to come by at any moment and would think that we were making fun of him, but the worst thing is that it didn't turn out as planned and still every one was thrilled' (Heredero 1997: 483).

13 Comments made during the Director's Q & A after the Harvard Film Archive screening of *Common Wealth*, 5 May 2007.

14 Alan Feuer wrote: 'Earlier this fall, after a busy month of shuttling to Washington, H. Rodgin Cohen, the dean of Wall Street lawyers, settled into a table upstairs at the Red Hat, a favorite restaurant overlooking the Hudson River here in the Westchester village where he lives. He and his wife of 40 years, Barbara, ordered modestly (and identically) – salad, swordfish steak, glasses of Chardonnay – and the table talk was undemanding in a casual, nerdy way. Mr. Cohen, who is known as Rodge, wondered at one point how many Hitchcock films revolved around "high places" as a leitmotif. Barbara did not know – and did not seem to care – so he rattled them off himself with enthusiastic detail: "Saboteur," "To Catch a Thief," "North by Northwest," and, of course, 'Vertigo."' According to Feuer, Cohen 'played perhaps the largest role of all in the gruesome doings of the Wall Street bailout last year' (13 November 2009: MB1).

15 Malcolm Compitello gives an extensive history of both buildings in 'From Planning to Design: The Culture of Flexible Accumulation in Post-Cambio Madrid', *AJHCS*, vol. 3, 1999: 199–219. He explains: 'The Edificio Capitol is one of the anchors of the first major modernization project in Madrid, the expansion of the Gran Vía from the Calle de Alcalá to the Plaza de España' (1999: 206), a significant urban planning project undertaken between 1914 to 1936. Moreover, Compitello notes: 'The building was one of the first to combine a movie theatre and other public spaces with living and office space. The Capitol Building also introduced a number of structural innovations imported from buildings designed in other countries. The large concrete beams that allow for the great spans of space in the building were imported from Germany. The architects and their collaborators traveled to a number of European cities to examine the latest in building design in general and cinema design in particular to assure that they incorporated all of the latest in technology' (1999: 207). On the other hand the Torres KIO, later the Torres de Europa, 'Madrid's equivalent of the twin towers of the World Trade Center ... form the symbolic northern opening of the Paseo de la Castellana whose southern flank is also graced by a redesigned architectural monument, Rafael Moneo's Atocha train station now called the Puerta de Atocha' (1999: 208), which was the central axis of Madrid's urban development from the 1970s onwards. Compitello also gives a detailed history of the Torres KIO and the role of the Kuwaiti Investment Office and its local representatives in Spain's economic boom. The unfinished towers, whose plans date from the mid-1980s, were put up for auction in 1993, as investment scams came to light.

16 See also Rothman on what he terms 'Hitchcock's signature motif /////' in *Must We Kill the Thing We Love?* (2014: 154, 180).

17 On the evolution of *Perdita Durango*'s script see Angulo & Santamarina 2012: 200–5.

18 As Brad Stevens shows in '"Perdita Durango": A Case Study', the film circulates internationally in at least three major versions, none of which can be described as definitive because all are either dubbed (in the case of the longest Spanish version) or severely cut to take out rape, child oral sex, nudity, drugs and violence including a re-imagined Crucifixion. An Australian version removes a clip of the *Mary Tyler Moore* show. As noted, the US version removes the final flashback to *Vera Cruz*. The extensive flashbacks, a technique used throughout *Perdita Durango*, probably tested as too confusing for US audiences.

19 Edward Guthman, 'Sexy, Violent "Perdita" Finally Arrives in U.S. / Tiny unauthorized "Vera Cruz" clip held up release', *San Francisco Chronicle*, 16 January 2000.

20 See Kercher 2005: 53–63.

21 TV also gives a sense of the global popularity of the film. In 2014 *Dying of Laughter* was broadcast on Señal Colombia, Bogotá, in the program 'En cine nos vemos' with an introduction by Judieth Restrepo.

22 The English title of the film does not convey adequately the meanings of the Spanish, which is a much more common word than 'commonwealth' is in English. 'Comunidad' means community as well as the political entity of a city such as Madrid.

23 On 'happy losers' see the *El País* interview by Elsa Fernández-Santos (2002) and Angulo & Santamarina (2012: 36). *800 Bullets* received some devastatingly negative criticism in Spain as pure self-indulgence. Ramon Freixas wrote in *Dirigido*, 'The worst of Álex de la Iglesia is brought together in this babbling and good-for-nothing film, which, yes, is tremendously personal, but that shouldn't be confused with excellence' (2002: 13). The film marked an inauspicious debut for De la Iglesia's own production company, Panico Films. As with *Perdita Durango*, another initial box office flop, he only recouped his investment in *800 Bullets* much later through international sales (see Angulo & Santamarina 2012: 64).

24 When De la Iglesia finished *800 Bullets*, Stephen Spielberg called and asked for a private screening of the film in Los Angeles because he had filmed *Empire of the Sun* (1987) and *Indiana Jones and the Last Crusade* (1989) in Almería. During the screening Spielberg questioned De la Iglesia intently about how he made the film. When they finished Spielberg asked him what he'd like to do in the future and the following conversation ensued. De la

Iglesia: 'I wouldn't mind working in Hollywood.' Spielberg: 'Why do you want to do that since you can make films perfectly well in your own country?' De la Iglesia: 'Man, I don't know, for the money.' De la Iglesia is still waiting for a call back from Spielberg (Angulo & Santamarina 2012: 257)

25　De la Iglesia anticipated these changes to his title and considered the title 'risky', as he explained on the film's official site: 'It's a risky title. They're going to correct it in the majority of the media where they talk about the film. There's a wink to Hitchcock, of course, and another one to Gozcinny: When Obélix would get drunk in "Caesar's Laurels" he always used to say: "Ferpectly!"; http://www.clubcultura.com/clubcine/clubcineastas/delaiglesia/ferpecto_claves.htm (accessed 20 July 2012). Gozcinny and Uderzo, *Les Lauriers de César*, 1971 (trans. *Astérix and the Laurel Wreath*, 1974).

26　The contrast in tone could not be greater between *Ferpect Crime* and Woody Allen's *Match Point*, a steamier homage to *Strangers on a Train*, both from 2005.

27　Dana Stevens saw the film as a 'sly critique of consumerism' as he celebrated it as 'a bright, gaudy and tremendously satisfying ride' in his *New York Times* review (2005: B8).

28　The nineteenth-century period flashback quoted in the epigraph, a scene described in the script in these terms – 'We see some black boots walking down some stairs, frightening away a black cat' – is a minor homage to Hitchcock's early London period of *The Lodger* (1929).

29　In particular, see Joseph Mankiewicz's *Sleuth* (1972).

30　Wood discovered the blog's existence in the middle of the shoot. Director and star had to clear the air about how De la Iglesia had written about Wood's girlfriend online.

31　See *Alastriste* (2006) based on his *Alastriste* novel series (1996), Román Polanski's *Ninth Gate* (1999) based on *Club Dumas* (1993), *Territorio Comanche* (1997)/*Comanche Territory*, (1997) based on the eponymous novel (1994), *Uncovered* (1994) based on *The Flanders Panel* (1993) and *El maestro de esgrima* (1992) based on *The Fencing Master* (1998). De la Iglesia did not find Guillermo Martínez's novel inherently cinematic since 'all of it takes place in the characters' heads and there's no action' (Angulo & Santamarina 2012: 275).

32　See Jonathan Holland for *Variety*, Stella Papamichael for *BBC.com* and David Lewis for *The San Francisco Chronicle*. The 'Rotten Tomatoes' critics' rating was 10%.

33　See Barry Bryne for *Screen International*, Henry K. Miller for *Sight and Sound*, and also Alex Cox in *The Guardian* on his experience acting in the film.

34　José Quetglas, the make-up artist on his movies, nominated him. De la Iglesia credits his election purely to the movie technicians (Angulo & Santamarina 2012: 311).

35　Since 1980, nineteen directors have received the prize, which is accompanied by 30,000 Euros. Almodóvar received it in 1990. No woman director has ever received it. In 2011 the selection process caused a national scandal. The chosen jury had to be disbanded and a new one convened because the former did not conform to the 2007 gender parity law which stipulated that at minimum 40% of all Spanish government panels had to be women; http://www.elmundo.es/elmundo/2011/07/18/cultura/1310990260.html.

36　See Boyero 2010, and the discussion of De la Iglesia as a 'popular auteur' in Buse et al. 2007: 4–7.

37　De la Iglesia was refused permission to film at the actual site (see Angulo & Santamarina 2012: 288). Most likely the on-going controversy over the forced interment of Republican soldiers at the Valley of the Fallen, and a wider debate over other sites of Spanish Civil War dead which continued to be discovered, entered into the calculation of the National Patrimony's decision.

38　*The Last Circus* received the Silver Lion for best director and the screenwriting prize at the Venice Film Festival, and the Silver Condor for best Ibero-American film from the Argentine Film Critics Association.

CHAPTER FOUR

Against Hitchcock: Alejandro Amenábar's Meteoric Career

I. INTRODUCTION: MUTUAL DISSATISFACTION

Alejandro Amenábar flunked out of film school. Today his sanitised biography in the US college textbook *Cinema for Spanish Conversation* says he left because he was not being challenged by the curriculum (McVey Gill et al. 2006: 260). But Amenábar was bitter as a student. He definitely held a grudge against the professor who failed him in his screenwriting class. In his successful debut film *Tesis* (*Thesis*, 1996), Amenábar took his revenge by parodying his nemesis through the character of Professor Castro (Xabier Elorriaga). Although Castro speaks the 'dirty' truth about the abysmal state of Spanish cinema in the 1990s in the global market, he is not only pompous and self-absorbed, but also an accomplice to murder. To say the least, this professor makes a scary thesis adviser for the protagonist Angela (Ana Torrent).

There is a spirit of rebellion against authority, and in particular, against father figures, in all of Amenábar's films. To state this solely in terms of Amenábar's personality is to engage in pop psychology; nonetheless, it can also serve as a metaphorical guide for exploring his career strategy within the industry and for defining the *zeitgeist* in which his films first appeared. Our ultimate goal is to interpret the films themselves within their cultural context. This chapter will explore how Amenábar built his career *against* Hitchcock; each of Amenábar's first four films took Hitchcock's classics as models of inspiration to work, or rebel, against. Amenábar adapts Hitchcock's films to show and correct the errors Hitchcock made in them. For him, the anxiety of influence, to cite Harold Bloom's eponymous text (1996), has always been a matter of rebelling against the father, or certainly against the 'strong' father's work.[1] Of all the directors whose work is considered in this book, Amenábar is the one for whom psychoanalysis and dreamwork play the most prevalent role in his films.

II. AMENÁBAR'S EARLY EDUCATION

Alejandro Amenábar was born in 1972 in Chile to a Chilean father and a Spanish mother. They came to Spain in 1973 days before the fall of Allende. According to Carlos F. Heredero, they did not flee Chile because they feared direct political repression for their beliefs, but rather because the turmoil reminded his mother of the upheavals of the Spanish Civil War (1997: 80). Ironically they now sought a more tranquil environment in Spain as that country anticipated the uncharted post-Franco era. Speaking of his own generation, Amenábar called himself apolitical, as did Almodóvar early in his career (Heredero 1997: 95). Almodóvar famously denied the relevance of Franco. He did, however, acknowledge the dictator's impact on his decade of Catholic private schooling in which 'se respiraba una especie de regustillo nostálgico por la época anterior' ('one breathed a kind of little nostalgic aftertaste for the earlier era') (Heredero 1997: 87).

Amenábar's early cinematic education came primarily through seeing movies on video with his neighbours, an American couple who were friends of his parents. Passionate about music as a youth, he played guitar and organ. He wrote short stories that he illustrated and set to music. Despite having no formal musical training, Amenábar is unique among Spanish filmmakers in that he composes major parts of the scores to his films himself using a computer programme connected to an organ. As a work method he often imagines the music for a scene before writing the dialogue.

Another youthful passion was his voracious reading of all of Agatha Christie's novels. In high school as he began to see horror movies at the Cine Covadonga in Madrid and read the film magazine *Fotogramas*; he developed a taste for 'cine que da miedo, no el que da asco' ('movies that inspire fear, not revulsion') (Heredero 1997: 86). Since a career in the film industry seemed a natural match for someone with his interests, he enrolled in the Facultad de Cinematografía e Información in Madrid. While there Amenábar met Mateo Gil, another student and important future collaborator with whom he would co-write his first two feature films. Together they began to film shorts not connected to their assignments with a video camera. These early short films, *La cabeza* (*The Head*, 1991), *Himenóptero* (*Himenopterus*, 1992) and *Luna* (1994), explored the link between violence and voyeurism later developed in *Thesis*.[2] The short films caught the attention of the Spanish filmmaker José Luis Cuerda, whom Amenábar calls 'mi padre cinematográfico' ('my film father') (Heredero 1997: 99) for giving him his first big break. *Thesis* was a double debut: Amenábar's first feature film and Cuerda's first attempt at producing.

III. *THESIS*: THE LESSONS OF HITCHCOCK'S COMMERCIAL CINEMA AND THE HUMOROUS IRONIES OF *PSYCHO*

The great irony of Amenábar's career, given that he did not finish film school, is that his debut film has become the model, literally a textbook case for film school aspirants, of how to succeed in filmmaking in Spain. A study of his career began a series of 'how-to' books called *Cómo hacer cine* ('How to make movies'). The first volume contains extensive interviews from all the major partners in this production. The tone of almost all of the exchanges is direct, what one could call 'no nonsense'.[3]

Although Amenábar was, by 2002, the model in Spain for independent filmmaking, at the time he made *Thesis* he was taking his lessons from Hitchcock, all the while deflecting attention from the connection with false leads. For the *Espejo de miradas* interview Carlos Heredero probes Amenábar with the question, 'Is it true that some shots were taken directly from a film called *The Changeling*? It caught my attention that you'd be referring to that movie, and not to some other film of Hitchcock...' To which Amenábar responds:

> Yes, in fact. It's a movie that's foremost in my mind because I think it communicates really well what I mean by suspense, by horror. It plays a lot with sound. How it uses music has influenced me not only in *Thesis*, but also in my shorts. (Heredero 1997: 103)

Amenábar goes on to comment that he also was influenced by *The Night of the Hunter* (1955), *The Spirit of the Beehive* (1973) and *JFK* (1991), but deflects any implication that Hitchcock was his model. He hides the influence of Hitchcock, yet it is strongly present in *Thesis* and in the shaping of his career, both in direct allusions and in broad terms of genre definition.

The attraction for Hitchcock is explained in part in Professor Castro's remarks. Spanish cinema of the 1990s was not commercial enough. Amenábar saw Hitchcock, who was so often criticised for being too commercial, as a way out of this dilemma, a way to find new audiences against the Hollywood juggernaut.

According to Amenábar's comments in the 'Making Of' feature on the DVD, he intentionally chose to make a genre film with *Thesis* because its more 'mathematical' structure was easier to construct for his debut. How Amenábar 'imitates' Hitchcock in *Thesis* lies above all in his working methods, in an almost overbearing attention to planning and detail in order to replicate American, or especially, Hitchcockian genre standards.[4] For example, as the veteran cameraman Hans Burman who shot *Thesis* comments in the 'Making Of', there are a very high number of shots per sequence for a Spanish film of its time. *Psycho*'s

After a long chase through the university corridors, Bosco (Eduardo Noriega) catches Angela (Ana Torrent) from behind and she turns to face her pursuer in *Thesis*.

shower scene is not only the most obvious reference for the thriller genre, but moreover the gold standard of an incredibly high number of shots per sequence. In the scene in which Bosco (Eduardo Noriega) chases Angela (Ana Torrent) throughout the *Facultad*, or school of the college, Amenábar aspires to surpass this standard. He not only storyboarded the sequence, following Hitchcock's meticulous working methods, but also composed the sequence with a high number of shots, including inserted close-ups. Because of the number of shots the sequence, which ended with Bosco catching Angela by surprise from behind, took two days to shoot.

Thesis broke new ground in Spanish terror films through its reliance on strings and piano in its soundtrack to the exclusion of brass instruments. Like Bernard Herrmann's soundtrack to *Psycho*, which famously employs discordant string instruments to evoke terror and suspense, Amenábar attempted a similar effect in his composition. Despite its embedded technology which tries to capture the attention of a youth audience, for instance the way the music that Angela (classical) and Chema (Fele Martínez) (heavy metal) listen to through ear plugs in the school's cafeteria is used to characterise them, *Thesis* still evokes older films, and their *mise-en-scène*, as well. In the opening credit sequence the ticket collector comes on the train personally to announce a death on the tracks

Don't look now!: The ticket collector (Walter Prieto) faces the passengers to tell them not to look at the dead body on the tracks as if they were an audience at a horror movie in *Thesis*.

and to tell the passengers not to look at the body. He poses in the train car like the announcer at the theatre in *The Thirty-Nine Steps* or the one who appears to introduce *Frankenstein* in *Spirit of a Beehive*. A more likely contemporary scenario would have been for the announcement to come only over the loudspeaker system. The official is lit slightly from below as were those stage announcers. His clear enunciation and resonant voice recalls theirs. This direct address creates the retro atmosphere of a horror film.

Amenábar refers to Hitchcock directly when he comments on how he and Mateo Gil conceived of *Thesis*'s plot. For example, he says the snuff film was 'a good pretext, almost a "McGuffin" to construct a thriller with' (Heredero 1997: 105). Also he mentions that they struggled with how to present multiple assassins and still sustain the suspense of the film, since they had a Hitchcockian admonishment in mind that Hitch hated whodunits. Both *Psycho* and *Thesis* construct their mysteries and build suspense in the flight from psychopaths by relying on subjective point-of-view shots. These shots mimic the glances of the impatient young women – the sisters Marion (Janet Leigh) and Leila (Vera Miles) in *Psycho*, and Angela and, to a lesser extent, her sister Sena (Nieves Herranz) in *Thesis*.

Thesis evokes *Psycho*'s Norman Bates in the characterisation of both the young male protagonists Bosco and Chema. As strong characters they presented Amenábar and Gil with a dilemma in their attempt to avoid making the film a whodunit. Casting an attractive Anthony Perkins as the psychopath Norman Bates was considered one of the more daring elements of the film in its time. The sexy Noriega, who resembles a heavier Perkins, as Bosco challenges the viewer in *Thesis* to accept a young, attractive and well-mannered killer. Yet the characterisation of the outcast Chema also picks up on elements of the less than confident Norman Bates in the *mise-en-scène* of Chema's creepy apartment and in the witty bantering of the Chema and Angela.

In its visual tricks and its dialogue *Thesis* evokes and adapts *Psycho* through its profound appreciation of Hitchcock's humour. Amenábar comments that his original concept for *Thesis* moreover was to depict metacritically the aesthetic devices of cinematographic violence and humour:

> In the beginning I was more focused on showing the mechanisms that movies are made with and the techniques that are used to communicate humour or violence. It's an idea that I've put aside for the moment because I'd like to do a movie about how you make a movie within a movie. (Heredero 1997: 105)

Although Amenábar claims to have abandoned his grander metacritical project, Hitchcockian humour remains central to *Thesis*'s style and tone, and critical success.[5] To give one example, Angela cautiously enters Chema's apartment

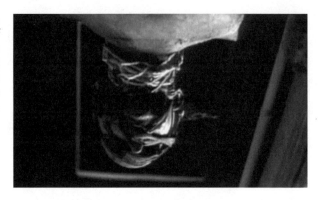

House of horrors:
The dark corridor of
Chema's apartment is
decorated with bound
mannequins suspended
upside down from the
ceiling in *Thesis*.

just as Marion entered Norman's parlour. The settings make the viewers fear their owners. Norman has his taxidermy, with an impressive owl hung from the ceiling. In a similarly frightening decoration Chema has mannequins of bound bodies suspended in his dark corridor. In these sequences, the male protagonists explain and defend their unusual hobbies as they simultaneously implicate the female visitor in them. In *Psycho* Norman begins by complimenting Marion that she eats like a bird. He then takes a dominant role by making a joke of the saying and asserting his knowledge when he explains that birds actually eat a lot. Likewise Chema first invites Angela to have a bite to eat before he shows her the videos she has come to see, but she refuses, hence being an even lighter eater than Marion. Rebuffed, he stuffs his face from the refrigerator, and says 'al grano' ('to the point', or literally, 'to the grain') to her as they move to his bedroom where he matter of factly lists all the kinds of exploitation videos he has. The spectator is left to tease out the sexual innuendoes of the courtship dialogue reminiscent of Norman skirting around the topic of Marion being on the run. She, in turn, treads lightly around the topic of his insecurity. To deflect the tension, he affirms his manhood by saying of his taxidermy: 'A man should have a hobby.'

The humorous tone that is created by playing off the respectability of domestic situations is common to both films. Before the lovebird couple get ready to go their separate ways from the cheap hotel in an opening sequence of *Psycho*, Marion describes her dream of respectability in great detail. She wants them to have dinner at her house with the picture of her mother on the wall, even if they have to turn the picture around to make love later. Her control of domestic allusions in the dialogue gives her dominance in the scene, even though she is deeply disillusioned that her affair with this divorced man Sam Loomis (John Gavin) is not leading to marriage any time soon. She leaves the hotel room finally telling her lover he cannot follow her at that moment since he has not put his shoes on yet. This innocuous banter about a mother's portrait in *Psycho* of course accrues

Seething with resentment for having to endure a family dinner with the suspected killer Bosco, Angela turns her disdain on her clueless sister (Nieves Herranz) who is thrilled to receive Bosco's compliments in *Thesis*.

greater significance, and pleasure for the viewer, in a second viewing, when we know Norman is matricidal.

In *Thesis* Angela's mother (Rosa Avila) invites Bosco to join the family for dinner to Angela's great dismay. Angela believes that Bosco broke into her apartment using the keys she dropped the day he chased her through the college. The dinner table conversation functions simultaneously in different registers for the viewer as did the *Psycho* dialogue. To the parents and to Angela's sister, Bosco comes off as supremely well mannered and a good date for Angela, someone who makes harmless wedding videos, while Angela sees a dangerous adversary. She seethes with resentment of her family for putting her in the situation of having to have dinner with Bosco, who even has the gall to hit on her sister at the dinner table. Every time we see Bosco bite into his meat, for which he effusively compliments Angela's mother, the spectator feels Angela's frustration at not being able to reveal what she suspects about Bosco to her family. She is progressively confirming her suspicions that he makes snuff movies and may have killed his girlfriend Vanessa. The visual humour or irony is that the charming Bosco sinks deep into flesh and does not leave the female characters with an easy exit strategy.

The very title *Thesis* signals that Amenábar's debut film has an imbedded didactic purpose, to demonstrate how cinema and its spectators are implicated

The perfect, carnivorous guest: as he bites into his meat, Bosco (Eduardo Noriega) leans in to compliment Angela's mother on her cooking in *Thesis*.

in the transmission of violence. *Thesis* shows how the camera accosts Angela in her bedroom, just as in an earlier era Norman spied on Marion through a peep-hole in his office wall. In the nightmare sequences of *Thesis* the red 'on' light of the video camera blinks in the corner of the frame as Angela lies in bed. She later discovers the tapes of herself with these bedroom shots in Chema's camera. In the film's epilogue patients in the hospital crane to see the violent snuff images the television anchor warns them *not* to look at. Ironically, Chema and Angela portray the 'good' spectators as they walk away from the spectacle on television just as the screen goes black. The scene thus reaffirms a generational break – that the younger generation can walk away from the television violence that mesmerises their elders, even though they are its protagonists.

The fundamental emphasis on a generalised movie experience was an important aspect of *Thesis*'s success in creating a new Spanish cinema in the 1990s. As Amenábar observes:

> The movie's theme is quite international. Its universe is fundamentally cinematic. There are no explicit references to Madrid or to any specific school, on the contrary the characters are universal and it's not hard for people to identify with them. I suppose this is the reason it's been one of the best selling Spanish movies in the whole world. (Vera et al. 2002a: 29)

Amenábar intentionally universalised *Thesis*, through location and characterisation, especially by choosing a genre film, in order to reach an international audience. These are tenets of Hitchcockian filmmaking, too.

As argued throughout this book, another one of the characteristics of Hitchcock's filmmaking appreciated by Spaniards was his humour. While *Psycho* is seldom thought of as a funny film,[6] its trailer, which ranks among the best known of Hitchcock's trailers and likewise of his on screen introductions, is a hallmark of his droll humour.[7] In it Hitchcock gives a walking tour of the *Psycho* set, pausing and making hand gestures that ostensibly acknowledge the viewer's delicate sensibilities. He waves the camera away from the gothic mansion's bathroom. This moment in the trailer tends to elicit laughter from the audience.

Despite this bathroom not being the site of the shower scene, the audience, connoisseurs of *Psycho* that we are, recognise this wink not as an affirmation of Victorian sensibilities but rather as a compliment to our status as knowledgeable viewers, if not voyeurs, who are part of the overall game. Hitchcock's humorous, *gemütlich* tour plays with and diffuses the tension that he built up around the marketing of *Psycho*. This famous strategy would lock the audience in for the film's duration.

In the trailer to *Psycho*, Hitchcock waves the camera away from visiting the mansion's bathroom, ostensibly to protect the sensibilities of the audience.

The trailer for *Thesis* has none of the storyline of Hitchcock's tour although it does share a certain Hitchcockian bravado in that Amenábar intended from the start to include the line 'What is cinema?' in the trailer.[8] He saw this movie as a treatise on film itself. To understand his position, or thesis, the climactic wave scene deserves interpretation, as it furthermore underscores Almenábar's debt to Hitchcock's use of humour. Part of this scene is featured in the trailer, which opens with Ana saying to the camera, 'Hello. I'm Ana and they're going to kill me.' Right before Bosco begins to film Ana who is tied to a chair (like a spectator in a movie theatre), to create his snuff movie of her death, he opens a door to a closet in the garage. From screen left in the frame out falls Yolanda's body. Bosco picks up her hand and makes it wave, limply, saying 'say hello to Ana'. It is a bizarre gesture that reveals to Ana and to the audience that Bosco killed his girlfriend Yolanda, as well as his friend, the missing Vanessa, and plans to kill again. The gesture's ambiguity stands out. Throughout the film Bosco has played the suave, well-mannered, wealthy kid. The macabre and cheeky wave of Yolanda's hand breaks the pattern and suggests that he is actually a psychopath.

In a macabre gesture Bosco lifts the hand of the dead Yolanda and waves it saying, "Say 'hi' to Ana." in *Thesis*.

Bosco pushes the hand back into the closet. While I do not mean to suggest a direct allusion to *Psycho*'s trailer here, both films continually exploit and explore the concept of voyeurism, and in how they incorporate humour into this pursuit. *Thesis* relies on humour not just in the climactic scene but also throughout the film. Chema's banter with Ana and other characters, like the security guard whom he bribes with pornographic tapes, is exemplary.

Thesis discloses how Amenábar mastered the art of Hitchcockian suspense punctuated with humour. This mastery paid off. The film made one of the most successful artistic and commercial debuts in the history of Spanish cinema, sweeping the Goya prizes in 1997, winning seven, including best film, best script and best new director.

IV. *ABRE LOS OJOS*: *VERTIGO* 'CORRECTED'

Because of the success of *Thesis*, Amenábar's second film *Abre los Ojos* (*Open Your Eyes*, 1997) was much anticipated. Given the accolades for *Thesis,* he now had the funding to fully realise his talent and aim for even bigger prizes in the global film market. Not the least part of the anticipation for *Open Your Eyes* was due to its announced reprise of both the thriller genre and the themes of audiovisual violence and voyeurism. Alongside the sexy Eduardo Noriega, Amenábar cast Penélope Cruz, a rising star internationally, coming off her role as the youngest sister in Fernando Trueba's Academy Award-winning *Belle Epoque* (1992), which traced her first love and sexual initiation. The stakes were high. Amenábar and his co-scriptwriter Mateo Gil turned to Hitchcock – in this case, one might even say, with a vengeance.

Open Your Eyes tells the story of César (Noriega), a handsome womaniser with family money and a huge modern Madrid apartment. In his bedroom he has an alarm clock that wakes him with an insistent recording of the title line, 'Open your eyes'. César falls in love with Sofía (Cruz), an aspiring actress, when his best friend Pelayo (Fele Martínez) brings her as his date to a lavish birthday party at his apartment. At the party's conclusion he leaves with Sofía and spends the night at her apartment. They talk, he sketches her, but they do not have sex. When his current, now former, steady girlfriend Nuria (Najwa Nimri), who was shunned at the party, comes by to pick him up the next morning at Sofía's, she drives the car into a wall in an angry attempted murder/suicide. César survives the crash but his face is horribly disfigured, so much so that he has to wear a mask. The film moves in and out of César's subjective world, in flashbacks and dreams, as he tries to make sense of his life. It follows his attraction for the two women, but especially to Sofía, the love of his life, for whom Nuria doubles visually in his dreams.

César is particularly confused to find himself in a psychiatric penitentiary for a murder he doesn't remember committing. There, under protest, he undergoes therapy with a psychiatrist and discusses possible reconstructive surgery with a team of doctors. Part of the puzzle he puts together from his subconscious dreamwork leads him to uncover a corporation called Life Extension, represented in television ads by the mellifluous Serge Duvenois (Gérard Barray), with a dubious scheme for cryogenic preservation of bodies. In the film's final scene on a skyscraper rooftop, which brings together the film's overarching themes of life and death, César confronts all the major characters from the film. Duvenois reveals that the characters are only figments of his imagination, for when César despaired at never having his face reconstructed, he committed suicide and was then frozen until 2045, which is supposedly the current moment. Duvenois tells César that he has been living a nightmare of his own creation, but that he can choose a different dream if he commits suicide again. After a brief hesitation on the precipice to observe that he suffers vertigo, César jumps from the building.

Though it is difficult to disentangle the plot of *Open Your Eyes*, which confused critics and viewers alike, no one missed the message that this was a supremely ambitious film.[9] Simply put, in *Open Your Eyes* Amenábar remade *Vertigo* in a contemporary setting and corrected Hitchcock's 'errors'. In the press Amenábar was vocal about his intentions and his judgement of Hitchcock. He gave the most complete exposition of his argument to the critic Carlos Heredero for the latter's interview book *Espejo de miradas*. Because it so directly concerns Amenábar's relationship to Hitchcock, it is worthwhile reviewing the relevant exchange in its entirety. Heredero asks Amenábar, 'Dreams, the obsession with the gaze, the reality or irreality of death ... there are many elements, besides a quite explicit quotation, that refer to *Vertigo*. What motivated you to use this reference and how does this relate to your film?' Amenábar answers:

> *Vertigo* is the story of a man obsessed with transforming one woman into another one, and *Open Your Eyes* tells the story of the protagonist César's obsession to separate the images of two women who he mixes up, to the extent that when he's fucking one of them, she suddenly transforms into the other one. In this sense it could be said that my movie is a kind of *Vertigo*, but backwards, taking into account that mine can also be considered, basically, an explicitly romantic love story. (1997: 109)

Significantly Heredero pursues this line of questioning to ferret out Amenábar's Hitchcockian intentions: 'Do you realise then that you've tried to make a Hitchcockian movie in spite of the fact that you think Hitchcock is overrated?'

Amenábar replies not only with an extensive critique of *Vertigo,* but also with a generalised complaint about Hitchcock's status as filmmaker:

> Of course it's a very Hitchcockian movie, but this doesn't take away from the fact that I think the whole beginning of *Vertigo,* that attempt to communicate the progressive obsession that Scottie is feeling there, is handled very awkwardly. That movie had great possibilities, but I think it was a great error on his part to allow the viewer to find out the solution to the mystery in the middle of the film. I think it would've been much more effective if the audience wouldn't have known until the end whether Judy was or wasn't the same woman as Madeleine. I realise that I can be even more inept in my own films, but some of Hitchcock's little tricks leave me cold and he doesn't always seem all that skillful. (Ibid.)

As a follow-up Heredero moves to probe how Amenábar's recognition of *Vertigo*'s defects – in Spanish Amenábar uses the word 'torpe', meaning awkward or clumsy, to describe them – influenced his concept for *Open Your Eyes*: 'This very particular reading that you make of *Vertigo* can explain the fact that in *Open Your Eyes* you almost always try to control the identity of César's gaze and what the viewers can see...'. Amenábar agrees, elaborating on his intention in the film:

> What I intend is for the viewer to live exactly the same deception that César does, and for this reason the spectator's position coincides with that of the protagonist for at least eighty percent of the film. With this in mind, in this case I've had to very carefully plan out the point of view from which to film each situation and where to place the camera. This way just as César has trouble understanding what is happening to him, so, too, the viewer has trouble understanding what's going on. Even in the actual climax we see and hear what César sees and what they tell him. They don't leave him any other choice but to believe or not believe it, and the viewer ends up in the same position as him then. This is what the game's about. It's precisely the reason why the end of the film is told, but not seen. (1997: 110)

Amenábar's comments were so explosive that Oti Rodríguez Marchante in the introduction to *Amenábar, voluntad de intriga* (Amenábar: Will for Intrigue, 2002), the first interview book on Amenábar in Spain, almost feels the necessity to come to his defence and downplay them in order to reassert Amenábar's precocious genius:

Besides showing his precocious and natural talent, his ability to create controversy appears put together with an explosive mix of sincerity, meditation, ingenuity and dynamite. Only with this temperament and a clear conscience would a young, strong-willed film director get the idea to question openly and publicly some classic movies and their untouchable directors. Amenábar has had to dedicate a good part of his public interactions with the press to nuance and contextualise some declarations he made about the movie *Vertigo* by Alfred Hitchcock. (2002: 15)

It goes without saying that allowing Judy to reveal the ruse in a letter at *Vertigo*'s midpoint, which lets the spectator appreciate her point of view and torment almost as profoundly as Scottie's, does not have to be considered a falling off in quality on Hitchcock's part. The American Film Institute ranks *Vertigo* number one as the best 'mystery film' ever; the 2012 *Sight & Sound* survey ranks it as the best film of all time. Yet what is clear, putting this bluster over Hitchcock's reputation aside for a moment, is that Amenábar wanted to reconfigure *Vertigo* in two important ways; one, to delay the revelation to the audience, and two, to focus exclusively on the subjective reality of the male protagonist, to limit himself strictly to what he calls 'first person narration' (Rodriguez Marchante 2002: 67).

Amenábar calls his reconfiguration a 'reversal' of *Vertigo*. This can be understood in different ways. For one, in general terms where Scottie tried to make two women into one, Judy into Madeleine, César tries to separate Sofía from Nuria. For another, more specifically *Open Your Eyes* does reverse the order of the defining events of Hitchcock's film. *Vertigo*'s plot is a spiral as is the film's overall artistic concept, from Saul Bass's credit sequence of a swirl superimposed on a red open eye, to Hitchcock's famous stairwell vertigo shot. The end of the film circles back to the beginning as it positions Scottie between life and death on the bell tower as he was on the edge of the city roof. *Open Your Eyes* on the other hand places Nuria's suicidal crash, which is analagous to Judy slipping off the bell tower, towards the beginning, but it ends with a rooftop scene, the opening and original setting for Scottie's vertigo. This is the reverse order of *Vertigo*'s plot.

As a prelude to discussing the plot intricacies in even more depth, and probing the psychoanalytical interpretation of the film, it is instructive to acknowledge the existence of, and to explore the place the director's cameo has in, Amenábar's *Vertigo* remake. *Open Your Eyes* is the only Amenábar film in which he appears on screen. The presence of a director's cameo has always been associated with Hitchcock and Amenábar adheres to the convention of this well-known feature. As Richard Allen writes regarding 'The Author in the Film'

In his cameo in *Open Your Eyes*, Amenábar laughs at César (Eduardo Noriega) and the line Amenábar's co-scriptwriter Mateo Gil has just said ('Fix your face') as César exits the men's room of a club.

in *Hitchcock's Romantic Irony*, Hitchcock's cameos 'playfully draw attention to Hitchcock, the director, as a presence behind the work, by inscribing that presence, not as a character in his films but as the flesh-and-blood director who populates his own film as an extra' (2007: 21). In *Vertigo* Hitchcock appears crossing a street carrying a horn case. In *Open Your Eyes* Amenábar and his longtime buddy Mateo Gil cross paths with the protagonist César at a nightclub. They appear as nameless extras, as Hitchcock did in *Vertigo*. Amenábar and Gil taunt César as they are exiting the men's room as César is urinating. When Gil tells César 'Fix your face,' Amenábar looks directly at César and laughs in his face.

This scenario cleverly acknowledges the role of Gil as assistant director and co-scriptwriter. In addition, as in Hitchcock's cameos, which often took place at bus stops or on the sidewalk, Amenábar/Gil's cameo occurs in a public place. Whether the twosome make fun of themselves, as Hitchcock does in *Lifeboat* where he stares longingly out of an ad for a diet aid, is less certain. Perhaps the men's room set and male duo indirectly refer to Amenábar's coming out as a gay man; however, he only made that revelation public in *Shangay Express*, a free Spanish newspaper for the gay community, in 2004, seven years after the release of *Open Your Eyes*.[10]

More significant to our reading of the film is the relationship of the authorial cameo in *Open Your Eyes* to the interpretation of the narrative, especially its structure and pace. As Richard Allen, citing Michael Walker, remarks: 'Hitchcock's cameos are often carefully timed interventions in the story which signal a decisive shift in the action as the protagonist "crosses a threshold" into the shadow world' (2007: 22). Allen further explains:

> These appearances achieve their most self-conscious form when Hitchcock actually seems to acknowledge his role in orchestrating or precipitating the narrative action. This is nicely illustrated in his cameo appearance in *Rear*

The Janus shot in *Open Your Eyes*: César (Noriega) in profile facing one way with his mask on the back of his head facing the other.

Window, where the attentive viewer will observe Hitchcock repairing the clock in the apartment of a composer who is struggling to write the song that will become the love theme of the film. As John Falwell has argued, Hitchcock through this gesture identifies himself with the composer as the orchestrator of his film. (2007: 22–3)

To a certain degree Amenábar and Gil, through their mocking do 'precipitate' the narrative action and mark a shift into a 'shadow world' for César. The extensive nightclub sequence and the parting on the way home lead César to a crossroads in his life, the decision to actually take his own life. This is symbolised artistically through what I am calling the Janus shot, in which his profile faces one direction and the mask on the back of his head faces another. When César leaves the men's room after being laughed at by Amenábar and Gil, his ego is too deflated to continue trying to resume his old life. He is surrounded by the club crowd rave dancing. He picks up his mask where he had discarded it and places it on the back of his head. The camera frames César's profile in a shot that symbolises his dual consciousness as old and new selves.[11] He makes himself so drunk he returns to the men's room to throw up. The Janus shot is repeated a second time here as we watch him vomit. Afterwards César stares at

Sofía (Penélope Cruz) and César (Noriega) in a Janus shot talk at the nightclub's bar.

'Open your eyes':
Nuria (Najwa Nimri) in
close-up as if seen from
the angle of César lying
on the pavement.

himself in the mirror as if taking stock of his life. The Janus shot is repeated yet again as *leitmotif* when he joins Sofía, and later Pelayo, too, in conversation at the bar. Throughout the bar sequence César stands off to the right side of the frame with his face and mask in profile.

Pelayo, Sofía and César exit the club together and say their late-night good-byes in the street before going their separate ways. Sofía leaves first, and then Pelayo hurries off after her. A jealous César cannot bear the thought that after Pelayo rounds the corner out of sight he is actually reuniting and hooking up with Sofía. César runs after them and collapses. The film cuts to a black fade. A female voiceover says: 'Open your eyes.' This sequence, which begins with the black fade, is key to understanding how Amenábar revises *Vertigo*. In it the order of shots limits the perspective to that of César. First Nuria appears in blurred close-up as if from the angle of César lying on the pavement, then the film cuts to a reaction shot of César gasping at the vision of her, and finally the film quickly cuts again to a close-up of Sofia from the same low angle. The black fade accompanied by a female voiceover in *Open Your Eyes* functions as far more than a simple transition. Not only does it significantly disorient the viewer, but it also acknowledges the role of the moviegoer as an interpretative subject in this play of doubles. In psychoanalytical terms, the black fade sutures the viewer into Amenábar's obsession for *Vertigo*. Specifically it revises the crucial revelation at *Vertigo*'s midpoint, which is another female voiceover, as Judy mentally composes her confessional letter to Scottie. *Open Your Eyes* delays the *Vertigo* revelation through how the female doubles are depicted. In *Vertigo* Scottie forces Judy to become Madeleine, and she acquiesces. Judy tears up the confessional letter and decides to become Scottie's lover, the object of his obsession, no matter what the consequences. On the other hand, in *Open Your Eyes* César desires Sofia, but Nuria blocks this desired transformation and interposes herself in his dreams. This blockage appears in the pavement sequence, just discussed, and in a later sequence in Nuria/Sofía's apartment, to be analysed shortly. First, however, it is important to take stock in more general terms as to how *Open Your Eyes* both reconfigures *Vertigo* while it uncannily repeats the latter's artistic leitmotifs.

There are few films that can benefit from formalist interpretation of story-telling in terms of *fabula* (the complete chronological story) and *syuzhet* (the reorganised version of events that plays out on screen) as much as *Open Your Eyes*.[12] The first half of the film almost lulls the viewer into thinking that the two develop simultaneously, and consequently the plot develops in a linear fashion. Only one early scene signals a possible disjunction, through the presence of the uncanny. César discovers a deserted Madrid, specifically an empty Gran Vía in the morning. The sequence hints at the existence of another reality, or at least the genre of a sci-fi film. Yet an educated viewer, the same kind of viewer Hitchcock took on Madeleine's obsessive visits to the gallery of the Legion of Honor to see Carlotta's portrait, might recall how the Spanish artist Antonio López García, considered a supreme figurative or realist painter, depicted precisely this avenue as devoid of people after stationing himself on the Gran Vía at dawn day after day over a period of years, in order to record this tableau. The desolation of the familiar is considered one of the characteristics of López's work that received its first major exhibition in Madrid in 1993.[13] However after the nightclub scene, where Amenábar appears to assert his directorial presence through the cameo, *fabula* and *syuzhet* diverge, and the sense of the film as a dream world is much stronger. In the movie's final scene, called 'Final Realization' on the DVD, the representative of the Life Extension corporation, Serge Duvenois, tells César that a 'empalme', or splice, was made in César's life the night of the nightclub visit. It was the night of Janus because he led two lives thereafter. Duvenois explains that after that night a reclusive César gave up on restoring his face, signed a contract with Life Extension to be frozen, and committed suicide by taking pills. Duvenois encourages César to commit suicide again to enter into a different dream.

The film's narrative from the dividing point of the nightclub sequence is a different nightmare. It is far more disorienting, more synchronous, than the first half of the film. Moreover, as *Open Your Eyes* transitions from what in classical formal analysis would be from exposition to complication, Hitchcock's *Vertigo* assumes a more prominent role artistically as the model for César's wish fulfill-ment that was signalled by the female voice intoning 'Open your eyes'. At the same time as the correction of *Vertigo*, with the interference between the female doubles, becomes more prominent, so, too, does the emphasis on César's sub-jectivity increase. As he lies in the street, César wakes up to the image of Sofía over him. They proceed to have sex in her apartment. The duality of the situa-tion, as reality and dream, and the primacy of César's subjectivity to the film's interpretation, is signalled in another bathroom scene. This one is in an apartment rather than in a nightclub. César wakes up once during the night and heads to the bathroom. There he sees his disfigured face in the mirror. Frightened he goes back to bed with Sofía. He wakes up again to repeat his trek, but the second time he sees himself in the mirror restored to his former handsomeness.

In this second half of *Open Your Eyes* César's dual consciousness becomes synonymous with his condition of romantic love. Two sequences, both of which convey romantic love, directly allude to Hitchcock's *Vertigo* and employ his well-known cinematographic techniques. César goes to an apartment, which we identify as Sofía's from the figurines of mime artists that appear in the foreground. All he encounters, however, are photos of Nuria where before he had seen ones of Sofía. As he ransacks the place in fury, Nuria hits him over the head with a bottle and he falls down. He wakes up to Nuria standing over him saying apologetically that she thought he was a robber. The close-up of Nuria's face is hazy. At his request she goes to get him a glass of water. The film cuts from a close-up of César prone on the floor to a medium shot of Sofía in a haze coming through the door and framed by it. The sequence alludes to the transformation sequence in *Vertigo* in which Judy enters the hotel room where Scottie is waiting for her after her daylong makeover in the image of Madeleine. Judy as Madeleine, platinum blonde and wearing the grey suit Scottie picked out for

Open Your Eyes alludes to *Vertigo*: a medium shot of Sofía (Penelope Cruz) in a haze coming through the door and framed by it, as she appears to César.

Green haze in *Vertigo*: Judy (Kim Novak) coming out of the hotel bathroom to reveal to Scottie her transformation into Madeleine's image.

Romantic rotating close-up shot of Sofía and César kissing in *Open Your Eyes*.

Scottie kisses the transformed Judy in *Vertigo*'s hotel room sequence.

her, enters the hotel room in a fog of light. She has realised his romantic dream. Amenábar's adaptation of *Vertigo* here is straightforward. César's desire, like Scottie's, is to possess the innocent or aloof, romantic partner—not the slutty, sexually available Nuria/Judy. They realise their desires.

As the sequence progresses, César embraces Sofia. Their kiss is filmed in a rotating shot that recalls the hotel kiss in *Vertigo* in which Scottie's memory of taking Madeleine to the mission stable is a background projection. The soundtrack to this sequence, which culminates in César and Sofia naked, making love, is one of the most symphonic moments in the film's score. Unlike *Vertigo*'s score for the hotel room transformation, which repeats the romantic musical theme of the film, and hence emphasises the image of Madeleine as the sublime Other, the music in *Open Your Eyes* conveys an ominous tone through the minor key punctuation of piano and violin phrases. It more resembles the eerie theme music that accompanies *Vertigo*'s credit sequence. The music reinforces the ever-present threat in *Open Your Eyes* that Sofía will again be revealed in César's consciousness as Nuria. Whereas for most of *Open Your Eyes* the desire to separate Sofía and Nuria is prevalent, and in this the film differs markedly in emphasis from *Vertigo,* that strives to conflate the two women, this particular bedroom sequence points the way towards a common interpretation of the two films. Both Hitchcock and Amenábar are concerned with the role of loss in the symbolic order.

To explore Amenábar's interpretation it is helpful to consider Slavoj Žižek's analysis of the two losses that befall Scottie in *Vertigo*:

> Hitchcock's finesse consists in the way he succeeds in avoiding the simple alternative: either the romantic story of an 'impossible' love or the unmasking that reveals the banal intrigue behind the sublime façade. Such a disclosure of the secret *beneath* the mask would leave intact the power of fascination exerted by the *mask itself*. The subject would again embark on a search for another woman to fill out the empty place of Woman, a woman who, this time, will not deceive him. Hitchcock is here incomparably more radical: he undermines the sublime object's power of fascination *from within*. Recall the way Judy, the girl resembling 'Madeleine', is presented when the hero runs into her for the first time. She is a common redhead with thick makeup who moves in a coarse, ungracious way – a real contrast to the fragile and refined Madeleine. The hero puts all his effort into transforming Judy into a new 'Madeleine', into producing a sublime object, when, all of a sudden, he becomes aware that 'Madeleine' herself was Judy, this common girl. The point of such a reversal is not that an earthly woman can never fully conform to the sublime ideal; on the contrary, it is the sublime object herself ('Madeleine') that loses her power of fascination. (1993: 85)

Žižek elaborates on this 'second loss' in which 'the whole fantasy structure that gave consistency to his being falls apart' (1993: 86):

> Madeleine's 'second death' functions as the 'loss of loss': by obtaining the object we lose the fascination dimension of loss as that which captivates our desire. True, Judy finally gives herself to Scottie, but this gift of her person 'is changed inexplicably into a gift of shit': she becomes a common woman, repulsive even. This produces the radical ambiguity of the film's final shot in which Scottie looks down from the brink of the bell tower into the abyss that has just engulfed Judy. This ending is at the same time 'happy' (Scottie is cured, he can look down into the precipice) and 'unhappy' (he is finally broken, losing the support that gave consistency to his being). This same ambiguity characterizes the final moment of the psychoanalytical process when the fantasy is traversed; it explains why a 'negative therapeutic reaction' always lurks as a threat at the end of psychoanalysis. (Ibid.)

César's disillusionment in the final scene, his learning that Sofia (further idealised by her white gauzy dress) and his psychoanalyst Antonio were figments of his imagination, is likewise a loss of a loss, as explicated by Žižek.

Though we have seen here how *Open Your Eyes* alludes to specific shots from *Vertigo*, of the fog and the kiss, and thus adapts Hitchcock's artistic vision most directly or formally, it is important to consider how *Open Your Eyes* incorporates indirectly, in the logic of the film, the famous tracking shot from Hitchcock's film. Again Žižek's *Looking Awry*, especially the section entitled 'The Hitchcockian Blot', may serve as an important guide to our comparisons of the two films. Since the exposition of Žižek's text is a rather dense detour, it may be helpful to preview our argument. Significantly, the black fade in which a female voice intones 'Open your eyes' is analogous to what is commonly called the vertigo shot. Both black fade and vertigo shot represent the gaze turned back upon the respective film's spectator and announce the maternal superego.

Žižek analyses films in terms of three stages – oral, anal and phallic. In formal terms for Žižek, 'if montage is the "anal" process *par excellence*, the Hitchcockian tracking shot represents the point at which the "anal" economy becomes "phallic"' (1993: 95). He explains, '"phallic" is precisely the detail that "does not fit," that "sticks out" from the idyllic surface scene and denatures it, renders it uncanny' (1993: 90) and further, referring to Lacan:

> This is the way Lacan defines the phallic signifier, as a 'signifier without signified' which, as such, renders possible the effects of the signified: the 'phallic' element of a picture is a meaningless stain that 'denatures' it, rendering all its constituents 'suspicious,' and thus opens up the abyss of the search for a meaning – nothing is what it seems to be, everything is to be interpreted, everything is supposed to possess some supplementary meaning. The ground of the established, familiar signification opens up; we find ourselves in the realm of total ambiguity, but this very lack propels us to produce ever new 'hidden meanings': it is a driving force of endless compulsion. The oscillation between lack and surplus meaning constitutes the proper dimension of subjectivity. In other words, it is by means of the 'phallic' spot that the observed picture is subjectivized; this paradoxical point undermines our position as 'neutral,' 'objective' observer, pinning us to the observed object itself. This is the point at which the observer is already included, inscribed in the observed scene – in a way, it is the point from which the picture looks back at us. (1993: 91)

Žižek details how several artistic innovations in Hitchcock's films, among them the vertigo shot, function as the 'phallic' spot or 'blot'. A black fade with a voice-over is nothing new. However, the disembodied voice saying 'Open your eyes' after we have witnessed César's fall likewise acknowledges our voyeurism, the essence of cinema. We may have closed our eyes to avoid seeing death. Thus, we

Bird's-eye-view of César
on the edge of the roof
in the climactic scene of
Open Your Eyes.

In an overhead shot in
Open Your Eyes César
bends backward on
the roof's edge, body
foreshortened, as in the
optical illusion of Dalí's
'Crucifixion.'

have been, in Žižek's words, pinned to the observed object, and inscribed in the scene, afraid of our own death as well as of César's. The voice of the maternal superego speaks and asserts her power over life and death.

Although the two black fades in *Open Your Eyes*, at the suture of the 'empalme', or splice, at the film's midpoint, and at the film's end, are structurally analogous to the disorienting the vertigo tracking/zoom shot shot, neither a black fade or a female voiceover are particularly innovative as cinematographic techniques, as was the vertigo tracking/zoom shot shot in its day. Nonetheless, it is worth noting that Amenábar does experiment artistically and challenge Hitchcock's status as innovator and cinematographic artist in the end sequence to *Open Your Eyes* in a different way. As he declared to Heredero in the interview quoted above, Amenábar intentionally maintains the perspective of César, with a far greater consistency than Hitchcock does for Scottie in *Vertigo*. However, right before the film cuts to show César jumping, in the image of Scottie's psychedelic nightmare, there is a bird's-eye, or God's-eye, shot of César. This shot breaks with the consistency of representing César's perspective. He is then shown bending backwards, which gives us an unusual perspective. His whole body is foreshortened and he looks up. As in the uncanny Gran Vía sequence, the reference here is to other well-known Spanish paintings, in this case of Salvador Dalí. Dalí experimented with perspective to represent both the Crucifixion and the

Ascension, in a manner that merged Christian iconography with his personal mystical mythology based on 'the metaphysical spirituality of the substantiality of quantum physics' (quoted in Ades 2000: 164). The paintings 'Crucifixion (Hypercubicus)' and 'Ascension' show the Cross floating in space with the observer left in a 'dizzying' sense of space. The two later Crucifixions, two stereoscopic panels, 'Gala's Christ' (1978), depict Christ precisely from the angle that the back-bending César is shown in *Open Your Eyes* (see Ades 2000: 182–3).

A reference to Dalí at this point in the film, as a dual allusion to Hitchcock whose *Spellbound* included a dream sequence designed with Dalí, seems particularly appropriate, as Duvenois has just explained that Antonio the prison psychiatrist (Chete Lera) was only a 'necessary' character in César's 'first' dream, and hence should not be believed. Hitchcock vocally dismissed psychoanalysis as a bogus practice, thus striking out at his 'father'/benefactor the producer Selznick, who avidly believed in it. In *Spellbound* the character John Ballantyne (Gregory Peck), who has assumed a false identity as Dr. Anthony Edwardes, undergoes analysis to discover the buried guilt for his brother's death in childhood. In his dreams César, too, has been uncovering his guilt, not for killing a woman as the prison psychiatrist suggests, but rather class guilt. Sofía caricatured him as a soulless tycoon. He imagines their sexual climax as dependent on him putting money into her body as if she were a life-size bank. Previously in the film we have seen her strike a frozen pose as she solicits money as a street mime. To interpret the suicide sequence as a crucifixion emphasises the moral tone of the film, something that Amenábar shares with other Latin directors who have creatively translated Hitchcock's films. Amenábar in the director's notes to the US DVD of *Open Your Eyes* further personalises the moral message when he observes: 'I might even agree with my producer, José Luis Cuerda, who suggested that César was a kind of punishment for the spoiled rich youth in my film *Thesis*.'

To conclude and underscore how Amenábar revised Hitchcock in *Open Your Eyes*, we may revisit the differences between the two films as seen in their endings. *Vertigo* universalises themes in the religious setting of the dénouement in which the Mother Superior appears to frighten Judy and precipitate her fall; *Open Your Eyes* in evoking Crucifixion iconography also makes a similar gesture. However, *Open Your Eyes* at the same time presents a more secular, relativistic option. It contextualises the climax as corporate scandal. César's belief or lack of belief in Life Extension, and consequently his willingness to jump off the roof, is bracketed by the suggestion, uttered by the psychiatrist Antonio in that final scene, that César's business partners plotted his demise to take over the catering firm and forced him into signing the Life Extension contract and committing suicide to carry it out. *Vertigo* had its Gavin Elster as evil manipulator of Judy's fate, but his business was the prosaic shipping, never a whole corporation based on bogus science like Life Extension. Neither ending, of *Vertigo* or *Open Your Eyes,* however, can be interpreted as definitive closure. *Vertigo* had two different endings, for example, though the casual moviegoer would not have been aware of the duality since only one was ever shown at any given screening. Nonetheless, because it implies a rereading of all of the 'events' of the film as dreamwork, the ending of *Open Your Eyes* throws the spectator into a postmodern questioning of the integrity of subject, which is far removed from the classical Hollywood dictum that by the finale all plot elements be clearly resolved. This questioning is how Amenábar aggressively 'corrected' Hitchcock.

With its ending at the Spanish mission, and castanets giving the beat on the soundtrack to Scottie's psychedelic nightmare, *Vertigo* stands out in its *mise-en-scène* as one of Hitchcock's most atmospherically Spanish films. Even so Spanish audiences gave *Vertigo* only a bemused polite reception when the film was shown in competition at the San Sebastián Film Festival. They far preferred Hitchcock's witty interviews to the actual film (see Bolín 1958). It took decades for the film to find the place in world film history that it has attained today.

It is unlikely that these more folkloric Spanish touches are what drew Amenábar to this classic in the first place. Nonetheless, *Open Your Eyes*, with in its setting in contemporary Madrid, is a uniquely Spanish interpretation of *Vertigo*, rooted in Spain's cultural history, of urban architecture, home design and modern painting. Even more so than the original *Vertigo*, *Open Your Eyes* did not fare terribly well at gathering invitations to the official competition sections of the major film festival circuit. Still, it did win the Panorama award in Berlin, a lesser award than the Golden Bear, and best film prizes in Tokyo and Guadalajara. In Spain it was nominated for ten Goyas, but won none. Simply put, it was too dense. Yet even without the accolades, given that *Open Your Eyes* was a French/Italian/Spanish co-production with a budget of '300 milliones de pesetas'[14] the film achieved considerable international distribution in theatrical and DVD release over a period of years. Finally, it is worth noting the timing of the film's release was a particularly good career move since it was poised to feed off an increased interest in Hitchcock at the time.[15] *Open Your Eyes* was launched on its international run in 1998, the year preceding the Hitchcock centenary. Already film magazines were gearing up in with special essays, such as Carlos Losilla's 'Hitchcock a la sombra del cine negro' ('Hitchcock in the shadow of film noir') in *Dirigido*'s June 1998 issue. In the US in 1998 Gus Van Sant directed and produced the remake of Hitchcock's *Psycho* for Universal Studios, which was met with a considerable backlash.[16] During this decade Universal also oversaw the lucrative franchise of *Psycho* sequels – *Psycho II* (1983), *Psycho III* (1986) and *Psycho IV: The Beginning* (1990), all of which had different directors. Amenábar was not in the running to direct either a remake or a sequel, but his own film was ready for a Hollywood remake.

V. A REMAKE VIA THE STAR SYSTEM: TOM CRUISE'S *VANILLA SKY*, BETWEEN SCI-FI AND TRUE ROMANCE

Amenábar's film caught the eye of someone with deep pockets and Hollywood insider knowledge – namely Tom Cruise. Cruise bought the rights to remake *Open Your Eyes* with the money he had made through his roles in *Mission Impossible* (1996) and *Mission Impossible II* (2000). As Stephen Holden wrote in 'Plastic Surgery Takes a Sci-Fi Twist' in the *New York Times*:

> 'Vanilla Sky' has been faithfully adapted from the Spanish filmmaker Alejandro Amenábar's 1997 romantic thriller 'Abre los Ojos' ('Open Your Eyes') into a star vehicle for Mr. Cruise, its story transplanted to New York City from Spain and amplified by a blockbuster budget. Redemption (by true love or a heroic exercise of will) has been the theme of some of Mr. Cruise's biggest hits, and here it takes on a more personal resonance than in any of his previous films. (14 December 2001)

Launching into the Hollywood saga of *Vanilla Sky* (2001), a star vehicle if ever there was one, was Amenábar's crossover moment. Though Amenábar told Carlos Heredero he did not believe in the Spanish star system as a means of making a box office hit, he certainly had a different opinion of the potential of the Hollywood star system to further his career and to break into bigger budget markets.[17] Amenábar and Gil received joint script credit for *Vanilla Sky* with its director Cameron Crowe. Cruise entrusted the project to Crowe as the latter had previously written and directed *Jerry Maguire* (1996), a huge hit in which Cruise starred.

It is entertaining to speculate what attracted the scientologist Cruise to *Open Your Eyes* – the sci-fi or the love story? His jet-set love affair with Penélope Cruz during the filming of *Vanilla Sky*, as a possible rebound from the end of his marriage to Nicole Kidman, was tabloid fodder and will always be associated with the film.[18] As we saw above in Holden's comments, most critics considered *Vanilla Sky* a faithful scene-by-scene adaptation of *Open Your Eyes*. To give just one example of the transposition, Cruise as David Ames wanders an empty Times Square, for instance, whereas César looked askance at the empty Gran Vía. The director Crowe in his DVD commentary expresses special pride at this Times Square sequence because they managed to empty out the heart of New York and do the scene without the assistance of CGI, as Amenábar likewise had

Faithful adaptation of the Gran Vía: David Ames (Tom Cruise) wanders an empty Times Square in *Vanilla Sky*.

when he imitated the uncannily realistic atmosphere of López García's paintings. When we think of sci-fi and romance, it is worth a pause to contemplate that Amenábar may have perceived a melding of genres already in Hitchcock's *Vertigo*, particularly when Madeleine wanders into the redwood forest and traces her life backwards and forwards, which others had not noted.[19] However, the uncanny moment for which *Vanilla Sky* will perhaps be most eerily remembered today is for transposing the final leap from a skyscraper in Madrid to one in New York City. In *Vanilla Sky* the World Trade Center towers from which so many leapt to their deaths in 2001 are clearly visible.

Despite the ominous premonition of its ending, the overall tone of *Vanilla Sky* is infinitely lighter than that of Almenábar's original. For instance, when Sofia Serrano (Penélope Cruz) calls Juliana Gianni (Cameron Diaz) the 'saddest girl to ever hold a Martini', somehow the drink and Diaz's coquettish image displaces the sadness. Shot from the back in her tight satin slacks as she holds her glass over her head, Diaz is a cute and sexy jilted lover, not the noir femme fatale that Najwa Nimri was in her red *cheongsam* in *Open Your Eyes*. The party is just livelier, more fun in *Vanilla Sky*.

This change in tone is in some ways ironic, since humour was one of the main selling points of Amenábar's *Thesis* for a college-age audience. To recall, *Vertigo* confined, or even segregated, its humour to the sessions between Scottie and Midge, generally in her apartment and with cocktails. Who can forget Scottie staring at the cantilevered brassiere on a pedestal and Midge asking Scottie rhetorically if his mother didn't teach him about women? Since Amenábar intentionally concentrated on César's subjectivity and restricted the woman's presence in *Open Your Eyes*, he eliminated the option of a Midge character, and with it most of the opportunities for humorous banter. Pelayo and César pick up the slack a little in their buddy humour about scoring with women, but these exchanges fall flat in comparison with *Vertigo*'s zingers. One notable exception of a joke that does work occurs in an interior apartment scene. When César asks

Sofía what she does for a living, she replies she is an 'arms dealer'. It's so implausible, it's funny. In *Vanilla Sky* Sofia uses the exact same line that she is an 'arms dealer', but it comes off even better because it fits the overall lighter, happier tone. The effect is moreover amplified as the early party scenes with the charming duo of Cruise and Cruz run twice as long as those in *Open Your Eyes*.

There are many ways in which *Open Your Eyes* was a particularly good candidate for a remake, and making it into a comedy was not one of them. *Open Your Eyes* was a relatively inaccessible art house film. Viewers got lost – though many enjoyed the confusion – in its postmodern markings in the indecipherable suspension of meaning. Hollywood smoothed out or clarified the plot. Motivation was made clearer, and more conventional cinematic techniques were used to signal to the viewer when a sequence is a hallucination.

What is much clearer in *Vanilla Sky* is the conspiracy of the Board of Directors against David to declare him incompetent due to the accident with Juliana. In *Open Your Eyes* César's 'socios' or business partners are only mentioned in passing, never seen. *Vanilla Sky* adds a boardroom scene. Every one of the 'Seven Dwarfs', as the trust fund company managers are called, has an on camera introduction by Disney dwarf name. Likewise the Life Extension scheme is given an extensive on-screen sales pitch by the actress Tilda Swinton, playing Rebecca Dearborn, who explains the special option of a 'Lucid Dream' upgrade to the contract. In general *Vanilla Sky* makes the corporate structure visible with these humorous villains, whereas *Open Your Eyes* outlined the workings of capitalism more vaguely, as distant tentacles in César's subjective world. Because they are presented overtly as seedy elements within a corporate structure, as opposed to David's faithful, though still corporate, lawyer who wrests the company back for him, *Vanilla Sky*'s critique of capitalism is more easily dismissed.

The clarity of *Vanilla Sky*, whose title, as David explains, describes the sky in a Monet painting that he inherited, is not necessarily a virtue. There were jokes in the press about the film being plain vanilla compared to Amenábar's film.[20] With rare exceptions, Hitchcock remaking his own *The Man Who Knew Too Much* among them, remakes have horrible reputations in film history. Gus Van Sant's *Psycho* is a key example of a lesser version of a classic. Lucy Mazdon in *Encore Hollywood: Remaking French Cinema* (2000) notes that the 1980s and 1990s marked a heyday for remakes of French films. Most well-known remakes of the time were comedies, such as *Three Men and a Baby* (1987) of *Trois hommes et un couffin* (1985) and *The Birdcage* (1996) of *La cage aux folles* (1978), though the thriller *Nikita* (1990) was also remade as *The Assassin* (1993) to considerable attention. Mazdon argues: 'The act of remaking the films and the various ways in which they are received should be seen as related components of a wider process of cross-cultural interaction and exchange' (2000: 2). Mazdon is particularly keen on debunking a general distain of 'a much wider body of (particularly French) criticism which condemns remakes, dismissing them as "pap" purely because they are remakes and, by extension, ignoring the "vacuity" of the French films upon which they are based, terming them "fine Continental fare" simply because they are the source of a remake' (2000: 1). In short, the European intelligentsia has long looked down on Hollywood. Ironically the huge poster of Truffaut's *Jules et Jim* (1962) in David Ames' apartment, which Roger Ebert in his review finds puzzling and out of place, partially answers the Europeans and reclaims the territory. The cultural markers of the apartment, of wealth, are French, i.e. the Monet painting and the *Jules et Jim* poster. On the one hand, this French décor simply characterises David as wealthy. To love Monet or French Impressionism is not particularly esoteric. Packing the art museums for Impressionist blockbusters is a common American cultural experience and represents mainstream tastes. However, a clip from *Jules et Jim* that is shown in the concluding sequence of *Vanilla Sky* suggests that David learned how to love from the film. To recall, Truffaut was the champion of Hitchcock and stood for a re-appreciation of commercial cinema, need we say, Hollywood cinema like *Vanilla Sky*. The film's concluding sequence shows how movies, mostly American fare, gave shape to David's reality. It is a sweeping vindication of the role movies play in the cultural consciousness in general in contrast to the singular reassessment of the solitary spectator of *Vertigo* that is *Open Your Eyes*.

To return to Mazdon's call to interpret remakes in a wider context, the cinematic and cultural context from which *Vanilla Sky* and *Open Your Eyes* emerged began to position Spanish cinema broadly as European cinema. By 1998 Almodóvar had become a well-known Spanish director, but he was seen as a singular example. Moreover, because of his progressive sexual mores, Almodóvar was long seen as more French than Spanish. His films received far better press in France than in Spain, his work frequently premiered in Cannes. The remake of Amenábar's film, or the cross-cultural exchange that it represented, had a more general significance for the emerging role of Spain in the European Union, and in twentieth-century global culture. Although André Bazin, among other critics cited in Mazdon, lamented that the remake had a 'detrimental effect upon the films on which they were based' because no one bothered to re-circulate the original (2000: 4), this 'annihilation', in Mazdon's words, does not seem to have been the case with *Open Your Eyes*. It has continued in circulation, and in particular its availability in the US region code has depended more on the interest generated by Amenábar's subsequent films, which reached yet further into global markets, or the repackaging of the DVD cover in the US to show Penélope Cruz's cleavage as her career blossomed, than by any 'quasi-Oedipal' 'act of violence' by *Vanilla Sky*. In short, the cultural issues the French have with the US are of an entirely different order than those of Spain with the US. As seen briefly above, Crowe seems to acknowledge this, and perhaps even thumb his nose at the French, in the placement of *Jules et Jim* in the décor and in the sequence of clips from the movies.

In conclusion, Amenábar's career benefited from the remake, however the two films are judged. Even if it did not rise to the box office figures of a *Mission Impossible* sequel, nor satisfy Cruise fans with more of the same, *Vanilla Sky*'s success was of a different order than that of *Open Your Eyes*. Like *Open Your Eyes* it garnered numerous award nominations, particularly for Cruise as Best Actor and Cameron Diaz as Best Supporting Actress, though few major prizes. The title song composed by Paul McCartney received the most recognition. However, *Vanilla Sky* actually marked a low point in Penélope Cruz's crossover career for she was nominated for a Razzie as Worst Actress of the Year for her performance in it and *Blow* (2001).

Since he did not have artistic control over his film's adaptation, the interpretation of *Vanilla Sky*, either as a version of *Vertigo* or of *Open Your Eyes*, which we have attempted here, is perhaps less significant than the mere fact of the huge recognition that a Hollywood remake of his work represented. Some would say Amenábar sold out to Hollywood commercialism and compare him unfavourably to Almodóvar who has famously resisted the chance to remake any of his films in Hollywood – by 1998 Almodóvar had already received many offers to remake *Women on the Verge of a Nervous Breakdown*, for instance. Nonetheless buying into the remake for Amenábar led to an entirely different category of stars becoming accessible to him in casting future projects. Cruise's interest made Amenábar a known quantity at a relatively early stage in his career. The special feature 'Hitting it Hard', contained on the US DVD with clips from Cruise and Cruz adored by crowds on a world marketing tour, shows just how powerful the Hollywood marketing machine can be. The feature ends with the film's opening night in Madrid and subsequent party. Cruise tries to sing in Spanish. Almodóvar dances. Amenábar appears hugging Crowe and smiling with a rather more satisfied look than the 'Fix Your Face Dude' gave César and us in *Open Your Eyes*.

VI. *THE OTHERS*: CROSSING TO HOLLYWOOD VIA *REBECCA*

In his brief preface to the Spanish edition of the script for *Los otros* (*The Others*, 2001), an immense glossy full-colour book, Amenábar looks back on his career trajectory and compares this project to a little boat crossing the Atlantic for an encounter with 'the others':

> I wrote *The Others* in the summer of 1998 with a spirit very similar to that which took over me when I wrote *Thesis*. I just let myself get carried away with wanting to enjoy myself – that is, to frighten myself. I never thought that it would end up being my next movie, or that that little boat, that is a project when it is born, would cross nothing less than the Atlantic, and would put us in contact with 'the others,' the Americans, on a completely new journey, an unusual one I'd say, for Spanish cinema. The effort to get to port safely was intense and the apprenticeship was permanent. (Robles 2001: 7)

Using metaphors usually applied to Columbus's encounter with indigenous peoples, Amenábar expresses not only personal pride for what he learned by making the film, but also more significantly pride for what the product represents for Spanish cinema – that is, the exceptional achievement of crossing over to Hollywood as no other Spanish director had done before. Although *Vanilla Sky* showed that Amenábar's films were viable products for adaptation in a global market, *The Others*, whose script he wrote and directed, represented his true crossover moment. Not only did it gain the backing of a Hollywood studio, but it was his first, and until *Agora* in 2009 his only, English-language movie. Indeed the launching of the two English-language projects, *Vanilla Sky* and *The Others*, was intimately connected. The deal-making happened in quick succession. Sensing the international potential of *The Others* when they read the script, Amenábar's Spanish producers contacted Canal+ (France) and Miramax (US), both of which expressed interest in co-production. Subsequently when Amenábar travelled to New York City to meet Tom Cruise a few months after Cruise bought the remake rights to *Open Your Eyes,* he met Nicole Kidman there, too. Listening to Amenábar talk about *The Others* project in that initial meeting, Kidman expressed an interest in taking the lead role. Cruise then became involved as executive producer of the film, a role he had already assumed for *Vanilla Sky.*

Adding interest to the story of the deal, the story of Cruise and Kidman also continued to draw the attention of the popular press at the same time. Just as the romantic story of *Vanilla Sky* fed the tabloids a plotline for the Cruise and Cruz romance, the story of *The Others*, of a woman abandoned by her husband, drew parallels with Kidman and Cruise's rocky marriage at the time. Cruise and Kidman had starred together in Kubrick's controversial and sexually steamy thriller *Eyes Wide Shut* (1999). They separated in 2000 and later divorced in 2001. Narrative and star discourse tend to intersect in the public domain.

To recall, *The Others* tells the story of Grace Stewart (Nicole Kidman), whose husband left for war but in the present moment of the movie, 1945, has not yet returned to their home, which she believes to be haunted, on the island of Jersey off the French coast. Three servants – a housekeeper/nanny, ground-skeeper and maid – arrive looking for employment, before her advert was even printed in the paper. They are ghosts from another era of the house. Grace, whose staff has just mysteriously left, hires them to care for the house and her two photosensitive children, Anne (Alakina Mann) and Nicolas (James Bentley). To protect her children from the light, she is strict about the rules of the house. She keeps the curtains shut and locks every door behind her before opening another one. Even with all her precautions, numerous strange sounds and ap-paritions in the house disturb her and the children and provoke investigation. At one moment she witnesses her daughter, dressed in her First Communion dress transform into an old woman. Grace's husband returns, but leaves suddenly again without explanation. Afterwards servants rising from the graveyard, who resemble photos from a book of the dead that Grace has discovered, approach the house menacingly. Grace locks them out. However, she and the children find themselves on the margins of the meeting of the living and the dead at a séance in the house. A new family living in the house wants to uncover who is haunting it and why. The séance reveals that Grace had suffocated her children, and then killed herself. The new family flees the house and puts it up for sale.

To deal with these megawatt stars, Cruise and Kidman, Amenábar had to modify his directing style. This was only one aspect of the crossover transfor-mation that Amenábar underwent as a result of *Vanilla Sky* and *The Others*. Kidman, for example, expected to hear when a take was good and actively shaped her on-screen image through frequent conferences with Amenábar. It is hard not to see the predominant choices of backlighting and grey tones for all aspects of the *mise-en-scène* – in Amenábar's words, 'so that the faces of the actors stood out' (Robles 2001: 229) – as accommodations to Kidman's star status and to expectations of classical Hollywood cinema. Amenábar laments, 'I would have liked to make a movie that truly seemed filmed in the 1940s' (Robles 2001: 240). But he came close.

Not only are there significant parallels between the career paths and dealings with stars and producers of Hitchcock and Amenábar, but also *The Others* is in many ways, especially in terms of narrative structure and cinematographic art, a remake of *Rebecca*, Hitchcock's first film in Hollywood. In his own crossover moment between 1939 and 1940, which culminated in the release of *Rebecca*, Hitchcock had similarly been swept up into the maelstrom of star commen-tary based on off-screen real-life family tensions. To recall, *Rebecca* follows the nameless second wife of Maxim De Winter (Laurence Olivier) in the man-sion Manderley as she tries to fit into the larger than life image of Rebecca, the deceased but much remembered (especially by the housekeeper Mrs. Danvers (Judith Anderson)) first Mrs. De Winter. Hitchcock managed to use the implicit family rivalry between Vivien Leigh (Laurence Olivier's wife) and Joan Fontaine (playing Mrs. De Winter) to his advantage. Olivier, comparing Fontaine unfavourably to his more famous wife on set, made Fontaine cower. By not censoring Olivier, Hitchcock captured the perfect look for the insecure second Mrs. De Winter.

Hitchcock's first encounters at United Artists with David O. Selznick, the legendary producer who hired Hitch from Britain, were stormier than any resentment that Olivier brought to the set. Ironically Selznick hesitated in his choice of Hitchcock's first American project between 'Titanic', to be a star vehicle for Carole Lombard, or *Rebecca*. According to Patrick McGilligan, Hitchcock preferred the Titanic project, and was already explaining to the Board of Trade in London that the film would not stop people from going on cruises, but rather 'would glorify British seamanship and heroism, and promote recent advances in lifesaving measures' (2003: 229). Still, Hitchcock was more concerned with missing out on his income, having finished *Jamaica Inn* in London, as Selznick dallied while Atlanta burned so to speak, with *Gone with the Wind* (1939), than with the choice of which film he did first. He wanted to get on that big boat with the whole entourage – his wife Alma Reville, his daughter Pat, his personal secretary Joan Harrison, two cooks, a nanny and his two dogs to sail to America, as he eventually did when Selznick settled on *Rebecca*. He intended to stay for a while (see Izaguirre 2005: 30). Though Selznick finally moved ahead for fear of losing Hitchcock to another studio after Hitchcock won the Best Director award from the New York Film Critics for *The Lady Vanishes,* Selznick immediately began to mandate many choices, among them the casting of *Rebecca*'s lead actress, Joan Fontaine, with whom Selznick was infatuated – an attraction that neither Hitch, nor his wife Alma, shared – and the fealty to the book upon which the film is based. The mogul would not allow Hitchcock to stray from the book in the treatment. According to McGilligan, Selznick particularly 'hated Hitchcock's comic additions, and targeted them all for deletion – particularly the Hitchcockian seasickness, which the producer judged "cheap beyond words." Selznick films were solemn entertainment, and the du Maurier novel certainly was humorless' (2003: 241). It is hard to imagine it now, but Hitchcock was in a diminished role as a director in the Hollywood of that era. As he himself described his situation, he was 'a minor figure in a vast film industry made up of entrepreneurs who headed the studios' (quoted in McGilligan 2003: 233).

It is common to speak of 'British Hitchcock' when referring to the films he made in Britain before leaving to work in Hollywood. The Hitchcock criticism in English often looks at this divide 'British/Hollywood' in terms of genre. In *Alfred Hitchcock and the British Cinema* (1986), Tom Ryall characterises British Hitchcock as espionage films; but other critics also look at the divide in industrial and aesthetic terms. In a chapter of *Hitchcock's Films Revisited* entitled 'Plot Formations', Robin Wood defines the British/Hollywood opposition with considerable nuance as both a stylistic shift between 'lean economy' and 'luxuriance', defined principally by Selznick's intervention, and as a continuum of mastery of point-of-view editing and spectator identification techniques (2002:239). Crediting Michael Walker with the discovery, he notes Hitchcock's point-of-view tracking shot first appears in *Rebecca* although Wood later qualifies regarding this same 'signature' innovation: 'This must be seen, I think, as a logical continuation and refinement of Hitchcock's earlier techniques, rather than a phenomenon somehow dependent upon the move to America' (2002: 240).

What Amenábar learned through his contact with American production methods, and what can be thought of as 'a logical continuation and refinement' of earlier techniques, or as a clear break from earlier practices, is hard to pin down. In an interview with Isabel Andrade, published in the volume on the film edited by Jesús Robles, he speaks of a newfound, required intensity in directing that emerged from his relationship with Kidman, of the new and nerve-wracking experience of audience testing the film in the US before release, and especially of a creative conflict with Hollywood backers over his refusal to use surround sound for the whole film. We will consider the latter two elements in detail shortly. A comparative analysis of *Rebecca* and *The Others* yields a nuanced view of the already more than local Amenábar and the still British, yet global Hitchcock at their respective crossover moments. It is a way to grasp the overall changes in Spanish cinema and the importance of Hitchcock in this transformation. Three interconnected aspects are crucial to this understanding: the industrial or marketing choices, the narrative structure, and aspects of cinematographic style. The challenging conceit of *The Others* is to develop a story around a confined space, a Hitchcock specialty, seen in *Rear Window, Dial M for Murder, Psycho* and many others. The *mise-en-scène* of *The Others* is pure Hitchcockian Manderley. Further, Amenábar marries 'fondo y forma' (theme and structure) by making the children's photosensitivity an essential limiting factor to their confinement in the gothic, heavily curtained mansion. The essential tool of cinematography, the manipulation of light, becomes a narrative *leitmotif*.

Numerous parallels stand out between *The Others* and *Rebecca* in terms of characterisation and plot. Nicole Kidman in playing Grace becomes another Hitchcock blonde like Joan Fontaine, the star of *Rebecca*, or Hitchcock's own favorite blonde, Grace Kelly. In fact Amenábar had Kidman change her naturally reddish hair to blonde for the film, supposedly so she would not be read as Irish when she was to appear British. He has said about the transformation and her air of glamour, 'Afterwards when I saw her with her medium curls, she looked like Grace Kelly out of one of Hitchcock's movies' (Robles 2001: 229).

In *Rebecca* the new Mrs. De Winter confronts the formidable housekeeper Mrs. Danvers who is fiercely committed to the memory of her former mistress. Hitchcock never shows Mrs. Danvers walking, but rather cuts to her image so that she takes on the character of an apparition in the film. Similarly in *The Others* Grace Stewart's adversary is the housekeeper and nanny Mrs. Mills (Fionnula Flanagan). Though a ghost from the nineteenth century, Mrs. Mills controls the unfolding of events through her knowledge of the house's prior history. In both films exactly what the mystery we are seeking to solve changes throughout the film: Is it why Rebecca died? Who killed her? Or who she was in love with? Likewise in *The Others* the mystery changes: Is it who haunts the house? Or is it why Grace died? Ultimately the element of suicide links the two plots. Maxim De Winter is found not guilty of his wife's death because there is a reasonable doubt as to whether Rebecca committed suicide, due to her cancer. At the end we learn Grace killed her children and then herself in torment.

On the surface *The Others* is by most terms a far more innocent, more socially conservative film than *Rebecca*, which concerns adultery and implies lesbian attraction and power at every turn. Even the Production Code office in 1940 recognised what was implied and objected to 'the quite inescapable inferences of sex perversion' (McGilligan 2003: 249) in *Rebecca*'s script, most of which Hitchcock cleverly managed to preserve. Boris Izaguirre calls the bedroom scene in which Mrs. Danvers belittles the new Mrs. De Winter by showing her Rebecca's splendid clothes and especially her underwear 'a lesbian provocation never surpassed in any other film, a provocation charged with domination and submission, ownership and punishment' (2005: 38). Izaguirre not only terms this 'one of the most clearly gay scenes in Hitchcock' but moreover notes that in Spain it was acted out as a scene of 'vindication in 1980s bars of this type' (ibid.). Izaguirre goes much further in his interpretation of this lesbian scene:

> What Danvers proposes to the nameless one is almost a sin: to delve into the private life of a dead person. The extreme state of preservation in which everything is found seems sick. The physical proximity between those two women seems morose, diabolic and unnatural. It's more, the very idea of having consented to this coming together turns into a stigma for the new wife and into a triumph for Danvers: she has just administered the first dose of a drug to some one susceptible to addictions. (2005: 39)

For Izaguirre, Danvers is 'the voice of the betrayed wife' (2005: 42). He even attempts, less convincingly, to see her as the image of Alma Reville, betrayed by Hitchcock's fascination for glamorous blondes, and diminished, 'a simple appendage to Hitchcock' (2005: 43) when he crossed over to Hollywood

Mrs. Danvers (Judith Anderson) shows a display of Rebecca's clothes and underwear to the new Mrs. De Winters (Joan Fontaine) in *Rebecca*.

because there she was supplanted by a cadre of people as his continuity editor and co-scriptwriter, roles she filled in the UK. This is not true because as McGilligan notes, for example, in 1939 Alma received a weekly salary equal to Hitchcock's from Walter Wanger to develop the story that would become *Foreign Correspondent*, the film that followed *Rebecca* (2003: 248). While it is tempting to speculate if knowledge of the queer celebration and reenactment of *Rebecca*, evidence of a particularly Spanish cultural appreciation of Hitchcock, might have added to the attraction for the then-closeted gay Amenábar to remake this particular Hitchcock film as his first American project, there is no direct evidence in any of his interviews to support this supposition. Though Amenábar is more a product of the Madrid of the 1990s than the 1980s, simply because of his age, it is hard to imagine he would not have been aware of the cultural history of the Movida in its most important decade even if he were not a participant. Nonetheless, he does cite *Rebecca* as a direct inspiration for the melodramatic dualistic structure of *The Others*:

> For me this movie picks up on two important duels, the duel of Grace with Mrs. Mills, and the duel of Grace with the little girl. If you notice, all the sequences are planned as duels. This gives more importance to the final reconciliation. This is a story about two women, Grace and Anne, who like each other but who don't manage to get along, due to some obscure reason we don't know. It's something that has to do with melodrama, with *All About Eve, Rebecca* ... *The Others* is a women's picture, the men are subordinate. (Robles 2001: 246)

In a successful melodrama, which *The Others* is, tone is a key element. The atmosphere of *The Others* draws upon a wealth of allusions to film history, beyond that of Hitchcock's *Rebecca*. It also alludes to Victor Erice's *The Spirit of the Beehive*, another Gothic tale in which the child Ana interprets the world of the Spanish Civil War through her conversations with Frankenstein's monster she has seen in James Whale's movie, to evoke a slightly different tone of innocence and foreboding from that produced through the duel between Grace and Mrs. Mills. Amenábar acknowledges: 'All the shared intimacy that comes across in the relationship between the brother and the sister in *The Others* has a lot to do with Erice's movie' (Robles 2001: 246). The parallels between the two films are even greater. The opening credit sequence of *The Others*, which shows a children's book, resembles the credit sequence with children's drawings in *The Spirit of the Beehive*. Likewise, Amenábar's insistence on the strategic use of silence and whispering in *The Others* recalls the bedtime scenes in *The Spirit of the Beehive* in which Ana probes her sister with whispered questions about the nature of monsters. When Grace and her children read the Bible aloud or grasp the rosary in the film's early scenes, they evoke this atmosphere of childhood innocence, and perhaps bewilderment, within strict parameters whose markers coincide with Spanish culture.

Indeed the religious dimension of *The Others* was one site of global/local tensions from the film's inception, for as Amenábar observes: 'One of the things I was worried about when the story was translated into English was not to abandon its Catholicism' (Rodríguez Marchante 2002: 131). Amenábar did not want *The Others* set on the British mainland because the religious discourse would have had to be changed, out of his comfort zone, to Protestant/Anglican rather than Catholic. To recall, there is an extensive sequence regarding the preparations for Ana's, Grace's daughter's, First Communion. He was adamant upon choosing the island of Jersey off the French coast because it was Catholic, and a British territory occupied by the Nazis in World War II. Yet for the actual filming, Amenábar could have recreated the ghost mansion of *The Others* on a set anywhere. Only the limited exterior sequences in fact were real locations; the mansion was an elaborate set that Amenábar had built in northern Spain. In this he followed Hitchcock who, when he built and populated the elaborate Manderley entirely on a Hollywood set, recreated in America a distinctly British ambience, which was more comfortable for him.

The house is key to how Amenábar modelled his crossing after Hitchcock's. Again the reference to Hitchcock is explicit: 'While we were searching for locations, no one imagined that the house was in Santander, and that it was the appropriate place to reproduce the iconic images that I had seen in movies like *Psycho*' (Robles 2001: 241). It was the stairs leading up to the house that did it: 'it had, of course, the image from *Psycho*, with the flights of stairs that lead up to the house' (Rodríguez Marchante 2002: 122). By simplifying his concept to one of a confined space, and insisting on a Catholic location in the script, Amenábar paved the way for maintaining more creative control of his first Hollywood project, or at least shifting its artistic boundaries towards a European model. By filming away from Hollywood, on the margins of Europe, Amenábar managed to negotiate a transnational no-man's-land. He began by scouting limited exteriors in the island of Jersey but quickly found a more suitable mansion and working conditions in Santander, in the Cantabria region of Spain, where most of the filming eventually took place. There he could employ an almost entirely Spanish production crew. Still, like Hitchcock with Selznick, Amenábar had to fight for creative control and try not to be overwhelmed by new demands. On the one hand, he hired the award-winning Javier Aguirresarobe as his Director of Photography, whereas Hitchcock's initial request to hire a British DP was vetoed. On the other, the American studio model required Amenábar to take on Benjamín Fernández, a Hollywood veteran, as Artistic Director, too, a role that does not exist in the Spanish industry.[21] Reflecting the differences between Hollywood and European cinemas, the two differed over their artistic concept for *The Others*, as Amenábar observes: 'He always pulled towards the realistic side, and I tried to win him over towards a more oniric side' (Robles 2001: 229). Again the house saved Amenábar from grandiose plans, for he apparently won the battle: 'But the action takes place in Jersey, and that necessitated that the spaces be small. I'm very pleased with how the sets were designed' (ibid.).

Hitchcock asserted his creative control over *Rebecca* by limiting the shots that he took of any given sequence so that Selznick, who had final say on editing, did not have the extra footage to change Hitch's concept of the film. Perhaps Amenábar learned from Hitch's cat-and-mouse games with Selznick for he insisted on the right to the final cut in his contract. As Amenábar says: 'They were paying me like a European director, and a European director keeps his editing rights. Hollywood directors, who have enormous mansions, lose control over their movies and gain other things. For me, to control the final cut is fundamental' (Robles 2001: 228).

Nonetheless, Amenábar struggled through major battles with Hollywood producers over the soundtrack, which is the cinematographic aspect that most inspires and sets Amenábar apart artistically. He explains his approach to sound in the film:

I believe that that's what makes *The Others* work. That absolute nakedness of elements makes it so that when you open yourself up to the story and you enrich it, it lets loose. The movie is almost totally monaural until we enter into contact with the world of *The Others*, which is when – 'Poookk!' – Surround Sound enters. We play a lot with silence, which is what Grace herself

says in the movie. That was something that was difficult for American producers to accept. It seems extremely risky to them, *vis-à-vis* the spectator,
that there be complete silence in the movie at certain moments. But I think
it's crucial for the story, because that way when the sound does come in
(with the noise of the door or voices) we are much more receptive and attach
more meaning to it. (Robles 2001: 233)

Though the lesbian subtext of *Rebecca* makes this film seem more daring, both
Rebecca and *The Others* suggest that marital infidelity and what I am calling
performance or erotic anxiety are key motivations in their respective plots. In
Rebecca Maxim De Winter reveals to his second wife the story of Rebecca's
infidelities, their argument and confrontation, which leads to her death, in the
love cottage by the sea. These revelations come as divers discover Rebecca's
body. At this point in the film we think we have solved the mystery of Rebecca
in the figure of the cuckolded husband Maxim (Laurence Olivier). Likewise, in
The Others, Grace's husband Charles (Christopher Eccleston) returns from the
war. We are uncertain if he is a ghost or not; the fact that he refuses to eat makes
his phantasmagoric presence more likely. Interestingly, Amenábar has singled
out the episode of the husband's return as 'a point of imbalance, due perhaps
to the fact that this part can only be understood in a poetic sense' (Rodríguez
Marchante 2002: 109). Moreover, both the marital reunion in the forest fog and
the bedroom scene were the two scenes that were considered for elimination in
the audience test screenings of the film (Rodríguez Marchante 2002: 111). The
bedroom scene between Grace and her husband leads us to think we, too, have
found a possible solution to the film's mystery. While making love in bed, Grace
asks her husband if he left for war because 'I wasn't enough for you' – that is,
she was not sexual enough. She awakes to find him gone again. At this point in
the film, the spectator can trace a psychological underpinning, of sexual frustration, to Grace's motivations, and further, to the madness and isolation of *The
Others*. By looking at *The Others* from the perspective of *Rebecca,* we can note

Not sexy enough?:
Grace (Nicole Kidman)
asks her perhaps
imaginary husband
(Christopher Eccleston)
in bed if he went to war
because 'I wasn't enough
for you' in *The Others*.

how both films' narrative trajectories posit a false, or incomplete, early solution which depends upon and highlights the erotic potential of the main characters. Precisely in the marriage dynamics, we see Hitchcock's 'Victorian morality' too. Moreover, as Robin Wood concludes, the film provides 'a thoroughgoing and radical analysis of the difficulties placed on successful heterosexual union by the social structures and sexual organization of patriarchal capitalism' (2002: 50).

Turning points of both *Rebecca* and *The Others* underscore the similarities of cinematic style in these films. In *Rebecca* Maxim escapes punishment for Rebecca's murder because a plausible motive for her committing suicide is revealed. To recall, Rebecca mocked Maxim in the cottage telling him she was pregnant with another's child. The major male characters of *Rebecca* meet in Rebecca's doctor's office where they learn Rebecca was not pregnant but dying from a cancerous tumor. She thus had a clear motive to commit suicide, given that cancer was a death sentence in that era. The scene of the surprising twist in the plot, which sets Maxim and his new wife free from legal punishment but not from Catholic guilt, is distinctively filmed. Leonard Leff in his DVD commentary notes that the sparse, dimly-lit *mise-en-scène* connotes the office of an abortion doctor, a scenario that could not be openly disclosed at the time. All the participants arrange themselves in a circle.

In *The Others* the surprise dénouement likewise occurs in a circle around a table in a dimly-lit room. Years in the future from the time in which Grace and her children lived in the house, these same children reveal in the séance that they were suffocated and killed by their mother Grace, who immediately committed suicide. Amenábar himself sees the ending as a judgement scene, harkening back to his Catholic upbringing: '*The Others* starts off in a *naïf* tone, and ends being serious, although luminous. The Catholic religion presents all the Biblical stories as if they were of superheroes, so that they end up being interesting, and

In *Rebecca* the male protagonists gather in a circle around Dr. Baker (Leo G. Carroll), Rebecca's doctor, in his office to learn she was dying from cancer.

The final séance in which the children reveal that they were killed by their mother, who then killed herself in *The Others*.

I, since I was brought up in a school run by priests, have this deeply engrained' (Robles 2001: 229). In sum, not only do both films unfold around the dynamics of a young woman confronting a housekeeper, but also some key turning points or climactic moments, which are filmed in starkly similar fashion, share psychological implications of sexual inadequacy.

In these films it is also significant to interpret the accents of the characters. In the séance scene the renters of *The Others* mansion with their spoiled son Victor (Alexander Vince), who are driven out by the ghosts (in DVD Chapter 18, 'This House is Ours') have modern, slightly Americanised accents, in contrast to the Commonwealth accents of Grace and her children. Apparently whoever is sitting at the table is in control. Yet in the final shot of the film, in which Grace peers over a distant For Sale sign on the mansion's gates, *The Others* banishes the modern/Americanising presence from Europe and reasserts a British Hitchcockian voice. This ending can be interpreted as Amenábar subtly favouring a British- or European-inflected voice for the Spanish film industry. Just as *Rebecca* was Hitchcock's first big-budget American film, *The Others* was Amenábar's risky entrée into Hollywood's 'made in English' world. Whereas Amenábar did keep his comfort level high by working with familiar Spanish crews in Cantabria, his home territory, he also made a savvy decision to follow Hitchcockian models and career path. Hitchcock himself said that *Rebecca*, although made in the US, was a classic British film, at heart a gothic period piece. As Wood notes, no less than seven of the films of Hitchcock's American period were set in the UK (2002: 45). *The Others* likewise is not only a gothic period piece, but it is also classic Hitchcockian *Rebecca*, with a British accent to boot.

The gothic genre limited even Hitchcock. One of Hitchcock's famous comments about *Rebecca*, as told to Truffaut was that 'it's not a Hitchcock picture; it's a novelette really. The story is old-fashioned; there was a whole school of feminine literature at the period, and though I'm not against it, the fact is that the story is lacking in humour' (Truffaut 1984: 127). While there are a few moments of comic relief in *Rebecca,* Hitchcock is right that humour is less

Nicole Kidman takes
control of the shot
in *The Others*.

significant to the film's overall tone than in almost any other of his pictures. Humourlessness also characterises *The Others*, with a few notable exceptions, particularly the dead-on honest comments spoken at the dinner table by the child Nicolás, who has been interpreted as Amenábar's alter-ego in the film (see Rodríguez Marchante 2002: 119).

Both Hitchcock and Amenábar made extensive use of special effects in their respective films to create a gothic atmosphere and communicate the 'luxuriance' of a Hollywood production, too. For this they needed fog to envelop the haunted house in long shots, and in the case of *Rebecca* for it to envelop the mystery of the boat in which her body was found as well. The digital techniques to create the fog in *The Others*, and the global status of the Spanish special effects firm Daiquiri, were extensively commented on in the Spanish press.[22]

Neither the distinctive camerawork used by Hitchcock in *Rebecca* to develop the character of the new Mrs. De Winter, such as Hitchcock pulling the camera away from her to emphasise her fragility, nor the editing associated with Mrs. Danvers, which is almost a jump cut because she tends to appear in frame without an establishing shot, is present in *The Others*. Simply put, the dynamic of the duel changed in *The Others* with Kidman, who is portrayed as a much stronger character than Fontaine. Kidman did indeed control the camera angles. Upon her objection, Amenábar and the DP Aguirresarobe reshot the initial scenes to put the camera on her eye level rather than in a low-angle according to their plan (Rodríguez Marchante 2002: 154). Grace, rather symbolically, was capable of a duel on equal footing, parallel to Mrs. Mills. Framed in profile holding a shotgun trained on Mrs. Mills, she demands the keys to the house back. Only once in the film does *Rebecca*'s characteristic pulling-back shot appear, when the power balance shifts to the ghostly trio, which includes Mrs. Mills. The similarities in the camera techniques of the two films concern mostly the evocation of suspense. Throughout both films, shots of doorknobs, particularly at eye level, signal uneasy anticipation. We see this when the new Mrs. De Winter dares enter Rebecca's study, and likewise when Grace enters the piano room and is then thrown back by supernatural forces. Staircase scenes are shot similarly in both films, too, such that the overhead high-angle view upon the respective female protagonists evokes delirium. Although Amenábar did not copy Hitchcock's trademark techniques of the Mrs. De Winter/Mrs. Danvers duel, he reluctantly admits he has his own trademark technique for terror effects in *The Others*: 'I've used the zoom, before a traveling shot, because it seems to me the zoom generally creates more fear. I've reached that conclusion, perhaps it's absurd. For this reason in the moments of terror I've turned to the zoom' (Robles 2001: 238–9). The zoom/travelling shot is a variation on the *Vertigo* shot, Hitchcock's most famous trademark.

The Others was an enormous hit in Spain. It won almost all the significant Goyas in 2002 – for best picture, best director, best screenplay, best photography and best music. More significantly, *The Others* was invited to the main competition of the Venice Film Festival. Though it did not win there, it also garnered other significant international awards from sci-fi organisations to those of critics, and hence broadened Amenábar's international recognition. His rise was meteoric as *The Others* was only his third feature film. Moreover the film grossed close to one hundred million dollars in the US alone for a film made on a budget of around seventeen million. No Spanish director had ever made a box office success of this magnitude with an English-language film.

Amenábar built his career on a sound foundation of his knowledge of film history. As he remarked regarding *The Others*, he chose to make a contemporary film in the style of Hollywood classics of the 1940s. Duelling with Hitchcock's legacy of *Psycho*, *Vertigo* and *Rebecca* allowed him to succeed transnationally.

VII. *MAR ADENTRO*: INDEPENDENCE WITH A GLANCE AT *REAR WINDOW*

Although Amenábar has long been a cinephile, which has been key to his success, he has said that he is not much of a reader. For this reason it is odd that he chose the real-life story of Ramón Sampedro, a paraplegic poet who fought a thirty-year battle for his right to die, as his next film after *The Others*, *Mar adentro* (*The Sea Inside*, 2004). If anything, Amenábar was following at this point in his career in the footsteps of the Mexican director Guillermo del Toro, who alternated between English-language blockbusters and smaller Spanish-language films after his initial crossover to a Hollywood production, rather than remaking Hitchcock. As Sampedro (Javier Bardem) is confined to bed for much of the film, the situation recalls tangentially that of Hitchcock's *Rear Window*. Both Jeff Jefferies (Jimmy Stewart) and Sampedro are witty raconteurs and have active love lives, with blondes. But Amenábar had already explored the implications of voyeurism earlier in his career with *Thesis*. *The Sea Inside* is thoroughly original.

Bringing the story and political cause of euthanasia to the screen was a risky decision made somewhat less so by casting the critically acclaimed Javier Bardem in the lead role. For *The Sea Inside* Amenábar explored expensive cinematographic techniques, such as underwater scenes and major helicopter landscape shots which were new to him and uncommon for Spanish national cinema due to their cost. The script, written by Amenábar and Mateo Gil, played to Amenábar's strong point – his original love of composing a film score. The incorporation of well-known classical music, especially 'Nessun dorma' from *Turandot*, becomes 'the sea inside' and allows the film to connect to the international art house audience.[23] In the climactic dream sequence, Sampedro imagines himself getting up from his bed and flying out the window over the landscape. The music soars with him. It is a supreme gesture of independence through music.

The Sea Inside marked another triumph for Amenábar, as he became only the third Spanish director to win the Academy Award for Best Foreign Language Film. In Spain the film also swept the Goya prizes at the same time as it generated controversy over the issue of assisted suicide, a position vehemently opposed by the Catholic Church. Admiration for the film and for the real-life Sampedro marked a cultural sea change in Spain of secular liberalisation. The new positions of the Zapatero Socialist government towards gender equality, gay rights and the secularisation of education were framed in ethical terms. Amenábar's earlier films all take into account moral implications, from his earliest explorations of voyeurism in *Thesis,* but they never entered into the national debate as clearly as in *The Sea Inside* did before.

VIII. *AGORA*: MEGALOMANIA OR A WOMEN'S PICTURE?

To say that Amenábar's 2009 film, the historical drama *Agora*, represented a new genre for the major director is an understatement. He certainly did not look to Hitchcock's career for inspiration. This film tells the story of the female philosopher and astronomer Hypatia (Rachel Weisz) in fourth-century Alexandria with whom a slave falls in love. It takes Amenábar's interests in ethical questions to the larger realms of historical allegory. In *Agora* Roman Egypt faces the hardening positions of religious groups; this can be seen as analogous to critical political situations of the early twenty-first century in Iran, Iraq and Afghanistan. Overall *Agora* represented a new stage for the internationalisation of Amenábar's career, and not just because it marked his second film in English with a major Hollywood star, in this case Rachel Weisz in the lead role. In terms of location and set design, Amenábar let his ambitions soar well beyond what he had done for *The Others* and its Jersey island location that was replicated in Cantabria. For *Agora* huge urban sets were created in Fort Ricasoli, Malta, at the same spot where *Gladiator* (2000) was filmed. That blockbuster would have seemed a successful model in recreating the glories of the era of MGM's classic epics.

Though Hitchcock's Hollywood classics were his longest film – with *North by Northwest* at 136 minutes, *Rebecca* at 130 and *Vertigo* at 129 – Hitchcock seldom received the critique that *Agora* frequently did, that at 141 minutes initially, then cut to 128 for its Cannes screening, it was far too long. Simply put, the film was tedious and left many critics, even those like Carlos Boyero of *El País* who appreciated the challenge that Amenábar had embarked on and the overall merits of his now prestigious career, found the film at best 'laborious and thoughtful, well written and well filmed, more than worthy' (2009).

In terms of gender representation the film marked an additional new direction in Amenábar's career. Upon *Agora*'s lukewarm Cannes reception Todd McCarthy commented in *Variety* (22 May 2009): 'Alejandro Amenábar's non-competing "Agora," [is] an unusual epic about the fourth century female scholar Hypatia that, from conversational evidence, may find its commercial key through its appeal to women.' Even though Amenábar's previous films alternated between male and female protagonists, the main audience for these dramas was arguably male. Among the aspects perhaps calculated to appeal to a female public, *Agora* included the well-known story of the historical Hypatia presenting her menstrual cloth to her student/aspiring lover to dissuade him of pursuing her. The presentation of the cloth, originally a philosophical lesson, is left unexplained in the film. This discussion of the cloth leitmotif in the film's dialogue led Stephen D. Greydanus to observe that along with other filmic anachronisms, Hyapatia often 'sounds more like Jane Austen than a neoplatonist'.[24] For any audience, male or female, Rachel Weisz as the intellectual Hypatia will never supplant Elizabeth Taylor as Cleopatra as classical film goddess.

Agora was not the epic success that Amenábar would have wished after his Academy Award triumph with *The Sea Inside*.In Spain it initially topped the box office and made roughly half of its estimated $70 million budget back by 2010. But *Agora* faced difficulties getting international distribution, and as a result by 2014 for the world-wide box office the film had only recouped $39 million of its initial budget (http://www.boxofficemojo.com/movies/?id=agora.htm Accessed 7 September 2014). It was 'a box office disaster' (Antonio Diéguez, *El Mundo*, 2 February 2014).[25]

This fiasco caused Amenábar to rethink his next project. Since then he has returned to the thriller genre. Working from his original screenplay, the film *Regression*, slated to be released in 2015, stars Ethan Hawke and Emma Watson. Set in Minnesota, although filmed in Toronto, *Regression* tells the story of a detective (Hawke) investigating the case of Angela (Watson) who accuses her father (David Dencik) of murder. When the father 'unexpectedly and without recollection admits his guilt', a famous psychologist, Dr. Raines, is brought in to help him recover his memories. The solution, according to John Hopewell in *Variety*, 'unmasks a horrifying nationwide mystery' (10 June 2014). With this international English-language film, co-produced by Telefónica Studios, MOD Productions and Amenábar's own company Himenoptero, among others, Amenábar looks back as much to his own success with *The Others* – whose $200 million worldwide box office made it one of the most highly grossing Spanish films ever – as to Hitchcock's film of repressed memories, *Spellbound*.

IX. A CAREER AGAINST HITCHCOCK

In conclusion, Amenábar has built his career against Hitchcock. Arguing to diminish Hitchcock's reputation in Amenábar's early years of filmmaking was not only a smart marketing ploy but also the sign of a serious student of Hitchcock's career and filmography. In some ways Amenábar has now assumed the role of professor. He curated a series of nine of his favourite films to help launch the Turner Classic Movie HD Channel in Spain in September 2013, presenting each film with an on-camera introduction. The series concluded with an hour-long interview on his own career. His commentaries received wide circulation beyond the reach of the paid cable channel since they were reviewed in the culture section of *El País* and were available on YouTube. For Hitchcock, 'the director who has most influenced him',[26] he chose to present *Rear Window* and concluded his introduction by giving advice to future filmmakers: 'I recently read in William Friedkin's autobiography that Hitchcock is the best director to learn how to make movies from. You don't have to go to any school. It's enough to see his movies and ask yourself why did he do that' (*El País*, 20 September 2013). As we have seen in our interpretations of his films, his own debt to Hitchcock is enormous. Most significantly, he remade *Vertigo* in *Open Your Eyes* and *Rebecca* in *The Others*. These two films represent Amenábar's most significant crossover moments, and his biggest breakthroughs. Seeing these films as remakes, or intentional 'misreadings' in Harold Bloom's terms of influence, and appreciating the traces of Hitchcock in Amenábar's other films, enables us to appreciate how Alejandro Amenábar, working against Hitchcock's legacy, launched himself into risky original projects that led to career breaks unsurpassed by any other contemporary Spanish director. Of all the directors profiled in this book the Chilean-Spaniard Amenábar is perhaps the most transnational as he continues

227

to reach out from the realm of Spanish national cinema to make global English-language productions.

NOTES

1   In his preface to the second edition of *The Anxiety of Influence* Bloom disavows framing influence as an Oedipal complex: 'I never meant by "the anxiety of influence" a Freudian Oedipal rivalry, despite a rhetorical flourish or two in this book' (1997: xxii). One of those Freudian 'flourishes' in his writing, primarily on Romantic poetry, was to point out 'the uncanny effect' that 'the new poem's achievement makes it seem to us, not as though the precursor were writing it, but as though the later poet himself had written the precursor's characteristic work' (1997: 16). Bloom clarifies that he focuses on anxiety caused by the 'strong' writer's works upon 'strong' successors: 'Any adequate reader of this book, which means anyone of some literary sensibility who is not a commissar or ideologue, Left *or* Right, will see that influence-anxiety does not so much concern the fore-runner but rather an anxiety achieved in and by the story, novel, play, poem or essay. The anxiety may or may not be internalized by the later writer, depending upon temperament or circumstances, yet that hardly matters: the strong poem is the achieved anxiety. 'Influence' is a metaphor, one that implicates a matrix of relationships – imagistic, temporal, spiritual, psychological – all of them ultimately defensive in their nature. What matters most (and is the central point of this book) is that the anxiety of influence *comes out of* a complex act of strong misreading, a creative interpretation that I call 'poetic misprision' (1997: xxiii). Bloom did not discuss film, however his writings on influence, and his definition and defence of a Western literary canon, have had enormous impact on cultural discourse, or the so-called 'culture wars' in the US.

2   Barry Jordan states: 'On the whole the shorts recycle but also significantly re-engineer the classic, "shock inversion" template of the Hitchcockian thriller. Here the wholesome everyday world of the "wrong person, in the wrong place at the wrong time" is turned upside-down and his/her life is catapulted into a spiraling nightmare' (2012: 31).

3   The book opens with a photo of Amenábar looking like a bored, 'too cool' adolescent with his hand on his cheek and holding the scene marker board for *Thesis* with Ana's line 'Hola' ('Hi') on it. In the interview below the photo he explains his dissatisfaction with the state-run film school: 'I didn't finish my degree: I left in the fifth year, when I got the opportunity to make *Thesis*. I have courses from the third and fourth years outstanding. I'll have to take them the canisters of *Thesis*, to see if I pass or not … It's an excessively theoretical degree program, which is very far removed from the reality of the profession. It's good as a way of meeting people who want to do the same thing as you do. It helped me meet friends, but it wasn't worth it for much else' (Vera et al. 2002a: 17).

4   'A really thorough preparation for the film was important for me. I think that's the key if that European cinema, or in our case, Spanish cinema, is to compete with American cinema' (Vera et al. 2002a: 21).

5   Mateo Gil, co-scriptwriter of *Thesis*, affirms: 'The tone is the most important part of a script, besides the structure and characters. I think *Thesis* could've worked very well if the tone had been harsher, but it wouldn't have been the major hit that it was. A friend told us, even if you make a really serious movie, you have to punctuate it with humour so that the public is with you' (Vera et al. 2002a: 33).

6   By genre *Psycho* is categorised as a thriller, or as Jim McDevitt and Eric San Juan argue in *A Year of Hitchcock*, '*Psycho* can rightly be called a horror film, a unique distinction in

Hitchcock's works' (2009: 314). Hitchcock discusses his intentions in *Psycho* in terms of tone and genre: 'If Psycho had been intended as a serious picture, it would have been shown as a clinical case with no mystery or suspense.' He continues, 'In the mystery and suspense genre, a tongue-in-cheek approach is indispensible' (Truffaut 1984: 202). David Thomson in *The Moment of Psycho* sees that laughter had a part in the film's effect on audiences from its initial reception, but that the laughter was a defensive strategy to fend off the subversive impact of sex and violence: 'Anyone with any sense of film knew not just that *Psycho* changed "cinema" but that now the subversive secret was out – truly this medium was prepared for an outrage in which sex and violence were no longer games but in fact everything. *Psycho* was so blatant that audiences had to laugh at it, to avoid the giddy swoon of evil and ordeal. The title warned that the central character was a bit of a nut, but the deeper lesson was that the audience in its self-inflicted experiment with danger might be crazy, too. Sex and violence were ready to break out, and censorship crumbled like an old lady's parasol. The orgy had arrived' (2009: 2–3). This is not to say that some critics, or many viewers (certainly the five directors studied in this book are among them), have not seen *Psycho* as 'funny'. The controversy has a long history. Famously Robin Wood had his first article rejected by *Sight & Sound* with the comment that 'Mr. Wood had failed to see that the film was intended as a joke' (Grimes 2009: B15). Wood's article, which launched his career as a film critic, was subsequently published in *Cahiers du cinéma*. Wood was foremost among those critics who took Hitchcock's films seriously, even when acknowledging the humour in his work. His citation of Hitchcock – 'You have to remember that *Psycho* is a film made with quite of a sense of amusement on my part. To me it's a *fun* picture. The processes through which we take the audience, you see, it's rather like taking them through the haunted house at the fairground…' (2002: 142) – was repeatedly quoted by other critics, such as David Bordwell and Linda Williams. See Wood 2002: 56–7, 142–51, and Williams, 'Discipline and Fun: Psycho and Postmodern Cinema', 2004: 164–204.

7   David Thomson states: 'The tongue-in-cheek trailer was a signal of a devastating move yet one with a strange, sardonic flourish. The advertising was intimidating, but it carried a new respect for movies and those who made them' (2009: 96). Amenábar likewise acknowledged a new attitude toward cinema in *Thesis*.

8   Eduardo Noriega remembered Amenábar's comment to the actor during filming: 'For example, in a scene when Xabier Elorriaga asks what is cinema, Alejandro asked me to please lower my voice when I said my line because he wanted to use that phrase in the film's trailer. It's an example of how he had the whole movie under control. He had it all in his head' (Vera et el. 2002a: 114).

9   Peter Stack of the *San Francisco Chronicle* was fairly typical when he wrote: 'One comes away with glazed eyes and a puzzled frown' in his review 'Thriller Goes From Eye-Opening to Eye-Glazing: Absurd plot sinks promising story' (30 April 1999).

10   The website Cooperativa reported the following on 31 August 2004 in an piece entitled 'Alejandro Amenábar: "No me importa reconocer que soy gay"' ('Alejandro Amenábar: "I don't mind admitting I'm gay"'):' The Chilean-Spanish director Alejandro Amenábar admitted his homosexual status in an interview he granted to the magazine *Shangay Express*, a publication about the gay world which is distributed free in Spain.

> 'The form in which any one acts depends on the person and the image you want others to have of you. I've always tried to be consistent and to act normally in everything, as well as with considerable discretion. It frightens me that people can meddle in my private life, but on the other hand, I don't mind admitting I'm gay,' declared the director of films such as 'Thesis,' 'Open Your Eyes,' and 'The Others.'

He stated, 'I was worried about saying I was gay more because of some of my older relatives who possibly could have been especially affected by the news, so I told them first. Finally I didn't have any problems with anyone.'

Amenábar had some critical words for the press that spends its time on gossip and romance in Spain, and which to his mind 'doesn't show respect for anything or anybody.'

He concluded, 'Although I realize the topic of TV garbage has already been talked to death, the general state of the country frightens me. That this is what defines our country on a daily basis is terrible'; http://www.cooperativa.cl/p4_noticias/site/artic/20040831/pags/20040831125516.html

11 The shot also recalls the famous superimposed shot of the Elisabet (Liv Ullman) and Alma (Bibi Andersson in Ingmar Bergman's *Persona* (1966).

12 For more on this critical distinction, see Maria Pramaggiore and Tom Wallis, *Film: A Critical Introduction* (2008: 66).

13 This exhibition at the Museo Reina Sofía, and consequent book-length catalog *Antonio López: Pintura, Escultura, Dibujo, Madrid, Mayo-Julio 1993*, came after the international success of Victor Erice's film *El sol de membrillo* (*The Quince Tree Sun*, 1992). Before this film, which depicted López's creative process, he had been ignored, if not disparaged by Spain's cultural elite, for at the time more abstract art was considered to better represent the hip mood of this rapidly modernising country. Quoted in the catalog is the following portrait of the artist from the article 'La decisión de la verdad' ('The decision of the truth') by Antonio Muñoz Molina that appeared in *El País* (20 March 1993): 'A recent photograph shows Antonio López García, dressed as an explorer or peddler, standing at the corner of Gran Vía and Calle de Alcalá, at the exact spot where for years he took up his station as day was breaking to paint the dawn coming up on the deserted streets of Madrid. With his greying hair uncombed, and wearing a gabardine a shade too large for him a pair of boots for country pursuits and a kind of knapsack strapped to his chest by a crossbelt, he takes to the streets of Madrid like a healthy, venerable pilgrim who has journeyed on foot from his provincial home to see the mysterious dawn of the capital for himself; and you can tell at a glance that he will never cease to be a stranger and that he will never leave the place. Antonio López García has something about him of the astonished traveler, of the countryman uprooted and transplanted to Madrid, of the absorbed peasant and artist who is capable of spending hours and hours engaged in his task, and so engrossed in it that he is deaf to sounds and voices, so taken up with the material perfection of things that he cannot tell in the end whether he has spent just a few short hours or whole years contemplating them, so bent on reproducing them in detail that they will ineluctably escape from him to the secrecy of their unmoving mutations' (López 1993: 33–4). His well-known paintings of Madrid are 'Gran Vía' (1974–81) and 'Gran Vía' (1977–90) (López: 1993: 232–3). 'Gran Vía' is also reproduced in Cheryl Brutvan, *Antonio López* (2008: 116).

14 Anon. (1997) 'El cine en España', *Dirigido*, 258, 74.

15 See also Dan Aulier on the 1996 restoration and re-release of *Vertigo* (1998: 189–96).

16 See James Francis, Jr., *Remaking Horror* (2013: 19–32).

17 'I don't believe that in our cinema a specific actress or actor is going to save a movie at the box office, so I always try to select the actors who are best suited to interpret each role' (Heredero 1997: 111).

18 See 'Penélope Cruz y Tom Cruise', *Hola* (30 January 2002); http://www.hola.com/cine/2002013032858/cine/am/cruzcruise/. On the Kidman/Cruise separation and divorce see Alex Tresnlowski, 'Hearts Wide Shut', *People* v.55, n.7 (19 February 2001); http://www.people.com/people/archive/article/0,,20133675,00.html.

19   The whole idea of Life Extension may have been suggested by yet another *Vertigo* scenario. The *mise-en-scène* of the walk in the park is yet other significant direct allusion to *Vertigo* in *Open Your Eyes*. In the first part of *Vertigo* when Scottie accompanies Judy masquerading as Madeleine in her 'wanderings' at the behest of Gavin Elster, they drive up the coast to a redwood forest. In the forest Madeleine stops before a display of a tree's cross-section, traces her life in the rings implying even that she does not know when she has lived before, but that she senses her death is imminent. She then begs off from answering Scottie's questions about her life. It is in this second outing of Madeleine/Judy and Scottie that they first fall in love and kiss. *Open Your Eyes* repeats a similar *mise-en-scène* in the several sequences in the park where a path between tall trees dominate. The psychoanalyst Antonio observes that César's park dreams in which he strolls with Sofia, never Nuria, are his most pleasant. In both films the space of the forest or park is an idealised *locus amoenus* that is removed from a linear timeline.

20   See, for example, Brian McKay, 'These Skies are not only Vanilla, but a bit too familiar'; http://www.efilmcritic.com/review.php?movie=4641&reviewer=258.

21   Although IMDb credits Benjamín Fernández for Art Design, and lists him as 'uncredited' for Art Direction and Set Design on *The Others*, in an interview about their conflicts, Amenábar refers to Fernández as 'director artístico' or artistic director; see Rodríguez Marchante 2002: 122, 215. For Fernández's first-person account of his collaboration, see 'Dirección artística,' Amenábar 2001: 182–201.

22   Carlos Boyero calls Amenábar 'a creator of atmospheres' (*El País*, 9 October 2009). In *Dirigido* Hilario J. Rodríguez viewed Amenábar's filmic techniques more negatively. He implied that Amenábar's 'pedigree of a videogame addict' caused him to overload *The Others* with possibilities: 'However many more tricks, so much better the spectacle' (2001: 41).

23   On music in Amenábar's films see Thomas Deveny (2010). Deveny notes that Amenábar prolongs the usual length of 'Nessun dorma' for *The Sea Inside* (2010: 213).

24   For a serious analysis of the errors and anachronisms of *Agora*, see Steven D. Greydanus http://www.decentfilms.com/articles/agora.

25   For a discussion of *Agora*'s distribution woes within the context of global economic trends see Jordan (2012: 235–46).

26   'Alejandro Amenábar selecciona sus películas favoritas para TCM HD'; http://www.audio-visual451.com/alejandro-amenabar-selecciona-sus-peliculas-favoritas-para-tcm-hd/.

PART II

LATIN AMERICA

Latin American Openings of Hitchcock's Films: The Reception History for Mexico City

I. INTRODUCTION

Throughout the decades of Hitchcock's career, the Mexican film industry constituted the strongest, most productive counterpoint to Hollywood in Spanish-speaking Latin America. As Paulo Antonio Paranaguá states in *Tradición y modernidad en el cine de América Latina* (Tradition and Modernity in Latin American Cinema, 2003), 'the Mexican film industry was the principal cinematographic phenomenon in Latin America during the first half of the twentieth century; such primacy would belong to Brazil's New Cinema in the second half' (2003: 15). That its cinema represented a high level of expertise evoked considerable national pride in Mexico, often precisely because it kept the Colossus of the North at bay, although according to Seth Fein in 'Myths of Cultural Imperialism and Nationalism in Golden Age Cinema', during World War II the actual relationship was more 'collaborative' than confrontational.[1] Regardless of the particularities of US-Mexican interactions at intergovernmental levels, the processes at play on screen signalled profound social changes. According to Jesús Martín-Barbero, Mexican cinema connected with 'the hunger of the masses to become socially visible' (1987: 181). Hitchcock entered the Mexican market as a wedge – associated with Hollywood because of English-speaking familiar stars, but different from Hollywood as a representative of British/European filmmaking. To look ahead in our study, the enduring importance of British Hitchcock, for which the Mexican director Guillermo del Toro expressed a specific preference in his book *Alfred Hitchcock* (1990), constitutes one of the most fascinating parts of the Mexican reception story. Furthermore given the early representational triangulation, how and when Hitchcock crossed over to represent Hollywood in Mexico also marks an important transition in Latin American film history that we will explore and interpret in this chapter.

Many scholars and critics, including Paolo Antonio Paranaguá, Carlos Monsiváis, Emilio García Riera and Guillermo del Toro to name just a few, have written extensively not just on Mexican cinema, but also on world cinema. However, while they place Hitchcock in a global perspective – understood here more accurately as universal or standardising – they have not addressed his reception within a specifically Mexican context. Del Toro, for example, never mentions any premiere of a Hitchcock film in Mexico nor does he cite any critic writing in Spanish. His references are French – Truffaut, Chabrol and Rohmer – and American – principally, Spoto – whom he is introducing to his Spanish-speaking audience. The Argentinean critic Nestor García Canclini, who works and publishes in Mexico, in his chapter on Latin American cinema in *Diferentes, desiguales y desconectados: mapas de la interculturidad* (Different, Unequal and Disconnected: Maps of Interculturality, 2004) notes that he never respected Hitchcock's work until Truffaut wrote about him. As a response to García Canclini's call to examine hybridity in local inflections of global popular culture, this chapter will explore the initial reception of Hitchcock's films through a case study of their premieres in Mexico City.

Not only were most of Hitchcock's films released in Mexico, first in the capital, but also they were commented upon contemporaneously within the context of a vibrant film culture, and within the context of local interpretations of world events. As Humberto Mussacchio documents in *Historia del periodismo cultural en México* (The History of Cultural Journalism in Mexico, 2007), the dialogue around cinema extended across diverse popular and literary magazines and included such titles as *Revista Elhers* in the 1920s, the sports magazine *Esto* and *Cine Mundial* from 1953, and the controversial *Nuevo Cine* in 1961, after which a veritable plethora of new film magazines appeared, *Premiere*, *Cinemanía* and *24 por Segundo*, oriented towards the more commercial offerings, as well as *Cine, Intolerancia Divina, Primer Plano, Nitrato de Plata* and *Estudios Cinematográficos* of UNAM, which focused on art cinema as well (2007: 142–3). However, these journals and magazines appeared sporadically. In order to trace Hitchcock's Mexican reception more consistently in its historical context, this chapter focuses on the two most important daily newspapers in Mexico City during Hitchcock's lifetime, *El Universal* and *Excelsior*. Although both periodicals, which are still in existence today, received some government support, they were considered independent voices. By looking at film reviews, advertising and caricatures, as well as editorials and general reporting of news in these papers of record, our approach repeats the model of the Spanish case study of the Madrid newspapers *ABC* and *Vanguardia* in chapter one, and hence invites comparisons between Spain and Latin America. Furthermore, studying the initial reception history of Hitchcock's films in Mexico City lays the groundwork for appreciating the context in which the contemporary Latin Hitchcock directors arose and for highlighting local differences. Subsequent chapters will explore whether the traits in evidence at the original release of his films found echoes in the work of later Latin American auteurs.

II. PREMIERE DATES AND A COMPARISON OF SPANISH TITLES

Knowing the dates for the premieres of Hitchcock's films is a precondition for studying the reaction to them in a contemporaneous context, but this information is not easy to find. No searchable electronic database yet exists for any major Latin American newspaper for the period of Hitchcock's career.[2] These newspapers are only accessible on microfilm. Neither do the movie archives in the US where Hitchcock papers are held, the Warner Archives or the Academy of Motion Pictures Archives among others, have an independent record of release dates for Latin American capital cities. Thankfully, Mexico City is a singular exception because significant research supported by UNAM on film release dates has already been done on the capital.[3] The following chart of premieres of Hitchcock's films is based on the four-volume series of books *Cartelera cinematográfica*, which documents the release of films in Mexico City during the periods 1930–1939, 1940–1949, 1950–1959 and 1960–1969.[4] Information for the original titles and premieres is from Jane E. Sloan, *Alfred Hitchcock: The Definitive Filmography*.

Original Title	Mexican Title	Original Opening	Mexican Opening	Cinema in Mexico City
Champagne	*Champaña*	August 1928	4 April 1930	Cine San Juan de Latrán
The 39 Steps	*Treinta y nueve escalones*	Sept. 1935	14 Nov. 1935	Cine Palacio
The Secret Agent	*Cuatro de espionaje*	Jan. 1936	18 Sept. 1936	Cine Rex
Sabotage	*Sabotaje*	Dec. 1936	11 Feb. 1937	Cine Palacio
Jamaica Inn	*La posada madita*	May 1939	2 May 1940	Cine Alameda
Rebecca	*Rebeca*	March 1940	1 August 1940	Cine Alameda
Foreign Correspondent	*Corresponsal extranjero*	August 1940	23 Oct. 1940	Cine Alameda
Mr. and Mrs. Smith	*Casados y descasados*	Jan. 1941	12 April 1941	Cine Magerit

Suspicion	La sospecha	March 1940	25 Dec. 1941	Cine Olympia
The Lady Vanishes	La dama desaparece	Oct. 1938	16 July 1942	Cine Rex
Saboteur	Saboteador	April 1942	4 August 1942	Cine Teresa
Shadow of a Doubt	La sombra de una duda	Jan. 1943	8 April 1943	Cine Alameda
Lifeboat	Náufragos	Jan. 1944	4 Jan. 1945	Cine Alameda
Spellbound	Cuéntame tu vida	Oct. 1945	13 June 1946	Cine Alameda
Notorious	Tuyo es mi corazón	July 1946	12 Feb. 1947	Cine Alameda
The Paradine Case	Agonía de amor	Dec. 1947	24 June 1948	Cine Cosmos (inauguration); Orfeón
Rope	La soga	August 1948	19 May 1949	Cine Palacio Chino
Under Capricorn	Bajo el signo de capricornio	Sept. 1949	19 Jan. 1950	Cine Alameda
Strangers on a Train	Pacto siniestro	June 1951	7 Dec. 1951	Cine Alameda
Stage Fright	Desesperación	Feb. 1950	25 Dec. 1951	Cine Alameda
I Confess	Mi secreto me condena	Feb. 1953	30 Dec. 1953	Cine Las Américas
Dial M for Murder	Con M de muerte	April 1954	11 Nov. 1954	Cine Alameda
Rear Window	La ventana indiscreta	July 1954	5 May 1955	Cine Chapultepec
To Catch a Thief	Para atrapar al ladrón	July 1955	22 Dec. 1955	Cine Chapultepec
The Man Who Knew Too Much	En manos del destino	May 1956	8 Nov. 1956	Cine Chapultepec
The Wrong Man	El hombre equivocado	Dec. 1956	25 April 1957	Cine Las Américas
The Trouble with Harry	Al tercer tiro	Oct. 1955	25 April 1957	Cine Chapultepec
Vertigo	De entre los muertos	May 1958	5 March 1959	Cines Alameda y Polanco
North by Northwest	Intriga internacional	July 1959	2 Oct. 1959	Cines Roble y Ariel (prem); Roble (normal)
Psycho	Psicosis	June 1960	29 March 1962	Cine Chapultepec

The Birds	Los pájaros	March 1963	18 July 1963	Cine Chapultepec
Marnie	Marnie	June 1964	28 Jan. 1965	Cines Latino y Continental
Torn Curtain	Cortina rasgada	July 1966	2 Feb. 1967	Cine Chapultepec

This information suggests that many of Hitchcock's early British films – *Woman to Woman, The Lodger, The Ring, Blackmail, Waltzes from Vienna, The Man Who Knew Too Much, Young and Innocent* – which did open in Madrid, Spain, did not receive any comparable, contemporaneous screenings in Mexico. On the other hand, the early *Sabotage*, which did not open in Spain in its original version until 1983, was released more or less on schedule in Mexico in 1937.

The interval between the British or American release and the Mexican release is generally under a year for those films in the above chart. Subtitling, and later dubbing studios in Mexico efficiently prepared the copies for national release. Dubbing, initially called 'duplicación', was first introduced theatrically with the premiere of *La Luz que Agoniza* (*Gaslight*) starring Charles Boyer and Ingrid Bergman on 3 January 1945. According to the film scholar Fernando Peña, *Gaslight* was also the first film to appear dubbed in Buenos Aires.[5] There are a few Hitchcock films that were released more than a year and a half after they opened in the US: *Champagne, The Lady Vanishes, Suspicion, Stage Fright* and *Psycho*. Why their Mexican release was delayed beyond a year merits further study, particularly in the case of *Psycho*, since it was an enormous box office draw in Spain where it opened much closer to the time of its US release.

For half of Hitchcock's films the titles in Spanish are considerably different in Mexico and Spain, as the following chart illustrates:

Original Title	Mexican Title	Spanish Title
The Secret Agent	Cuatro de espionaje	Agente secreto
The Lady Vanishes	La dama desaparece	Alarma en el expreso
Mr. and Mrs. Smith	Casados y descasados	Matrimonio especial
Spellbound	Cuéntame tu vida	Recuerda
Notorious	Tuyo es mi corazón	Encadenados
Under Capricorn	Bajo el signo de capricornio	Atormentada
Strangers on a Train	Pacto siniestro	Extraños en un tren
Stage Fright	Desesperación	Pánico en la escena
I Confess	Mi secreto me condena	Yo confieso

The Man Who Knew Too Much	En manos del destino	El hombre que sabía demasiado
Dial M for Murder	Con M de muerte	Crimen perfecto
The Wrong Man	El hombre equivocado	Falso culpable
The Trouble with Harry	Al tercer tiro	Pero...¿Quién mató a Harry?
North by Northwest	Intriga internacional	Con la muerte en los talones

Generally one Spanish-speaking market opted for a more direct translation from English than the other. The exceptions – that is, those films whose Spanish titles highlighted different aspects of the respective films – were *North by Northwest*, whose narrative reference few English-speaking audiences understood, and *Notorious*. In these cases the Spanish-language titles referred to the respective genres. Correspondence in the Warner Archives at USC documents that there was considerable discussion within the studio over the choice of appropriate Spanish titles for these five films Hitchcock made for Warner Bros. – *Rope, Stage Fright, Strangers on a Train, Dial M for Murder* and *The Wrong Man*.

Of Hitchcock's silent films the only one for which I have evidence of release in Mexico is *Champaña* (*Champagne*). It received no significant reviews. Its ads were positioned in *Universal* alongside of those for *La dama más inmoral* (*A Most*

Sexy ad for *Champagne* with no mention of Hitchcock in *El Universal* (4 April 1930) but with the tagline 'romantic story with exciting adventures in a torrent of champagne and love.'

240

Inmoral Lady) and hence marketed like a version of the Follies Bergère, a type of live entertainment also found in Mexico City in the 1930s. *Champagne* was overshadowed, both in the placement of its ad in *Universal*, and in sensational-ist, nationalist copy – 'triumph of the language!' – by the innovation of the day, *Sombras de Gloria* (*Shadows of Glory*, 1930), the first foreign-language feature produced in the US with live dialogue in Spanish. Nonetheless, the box office hit and most significant film of the day was the sound film directed by Alfred Santell *El romance del Río Grande* (*The Romance of the Río Grande*)(US, 1929), 'an ex-ceptionally beautiful plot developed in Mexico and among Mexicans in which our characters and customs are not ridiculed, but on the contrary are presented with complete justice compared to what has happened until now in cinema' (*Universal*, 4 April 1930). It is certainly ironic that the first Hitchcock film to be promoted in Mexico City, as in Madrid, Spain, was the lightweight *Champagne,* whose plot and aesthetics Hitchcock himself scorned and whose reception was blithely removed from the cross-border developments of the day. However, if one pays attention to the immediate period of its release one notes how nationalist identity framed the reception of US cinema despite its transnational complexity and it allows one to understand how his more aesthetically significant movies of the 1930s were re-ceived as British once they were inserted into the narrative of Mexican history.

III. HITCHCOCK'S BRITISH SPY FILMS: *THE THIRTY-NINE STEPS, SECRET AGENT* AND *SABOTAGE* AND THE NEWS OF THE SPANISH CIVIL WAR AND TROTSKY IN MEXICO

We tend to forget when we think of Hitchcock in terms of his most influential films, such as *Vertigo* and *Psycho,* that his British sound films of the 1930s – *The Thirty-Nine Steps*, *Secret Agent* and *Sabotage* – were spy movies that had at least a skeletal relationship to the geopolitics of the moment. From 1935 to 1937 a Hitchcock film opened annualy in Mexico City and was announced in the two major city papers against the backdrop of headlines of news of unrest, then war in Spain, that was to lead to the most important wave of Spanish immigration to Mexico since the Discovery of the New World or 'the Encounter'.

In Mexico City in the 1930s there were already sizeable expatriate and busi-ness communities who were interested and involved in world events. Reflecting their presence as well as the proximity of the US, both *El Universal* and *Excelsior* carried a regular section in English that was not merely a translation of articles in the respective papers. In the 1930s the English section included cultural news, whereas in later decades it evolved into a current events synopsis with classified ads about accommodation. In *El Universal*, whose English section was called 'News of the World', columns about Hitchcock appeared on the front page of the English section alongside news of the Spanish Civil War. The rest of the paper in Spanish included different reviews and ads for his movies.

When *The Thirty-Nine Steps*, the first Hitchcock movie to receive major coverage in Mexico City, opened, Mexican movie theatres were in the midst of a fiscal crisis according to coverage in *El Universal*. Fewer European films, including Spanish films, were being made due to wartime conditions. To compensate theatrical runs were extended and the public's interest would wane by the end of the run. As a sign of Mexican nationalism, the fanaticism for American/ Hollywood stars was blamed, too, both for aberrations at the box office and for encouraging too thin a body type for women, whereas European movies were praised for representing a healthier body image. In 1935 to stimulate the film exhibition sector in Mexico a new law was passed that lowered taxes on film exhibition by sixty per cent. The law also included a new prohibitive tax on the importation of 'discos para cinematógrafo', or movie records, to force movie theatre owners to buy modern equipment to be able to show talkies. Some Mexican exhibitors resisted the equipment change since sound film stock deteriorated faster. Problems with new technology reoccurred as a theme in the published reports regarding Hitchcock, too. A *Universal* review in English for *Woman Alone* quoted Hitchcock imagining the sound equipment breaking down:

> The creed that I chalk up in front of me today is that we are making motion pictures. Too many men forget that I try to tell my story so much so in pictures that if by any chance the sound apparatus broke down in the theatre, the audience would not fret and get restless, because the pictorial action would still hold them! Sound is all right in its place, but it is a silent picture training which counts today. (11 February 1937, Section 2: 8)

For Hitchcock the possibility of a technical glitch justified the primacy of the visual over the aural in 'making a Hitchcock picture'. The 1935 film law regarding the modernisation of equipment implies that Hitchcock's scenario had indeed occurred in Mexico. As a sound film and a British import *The Thirty-Nine Steps* represented a turn to the modern. Superlatives abound in the ad for the 'mystery' film, which was stylised in a black reverse image (*Universal*, 17 November 1935, Section 1: 8). *El Universal* film critic Fidel Solis felt the publicity hype proclaimed in superlatives in the ad was justified as he effusively praised the film:

> *39 Steps* is an exciting film, full of mystery, with a great deal of subtlety to the action and plot.
>
> But truly at this moment we can't come up with the exact phrase to describe this movie. The word emotion is right when one speaks of *39 Steps*.

Modern stylised reverse ad for *The Thirty-Nine Steps* in *El Universal* (17 November 1935).

It isn't a concept most used in the publicity, but it's a reality plastered all over the screen.

It succeeded – cleverly, with technical perfection – to follow the tangled action in an interesting way. It isn't a crime film in which fantasy exchanges punches with reality, but rather it's a logical process, stupendously realized in such a way that it holds the audience's attention for extended periods.

The locations where the action unfolds, the characters, the photography, with great technical advances, all of this stands out in the film we are reviewing. ('La pantalla y sus artistas', *El Universal*, 17 November 1935, Section 1: 5)

Solis does not interpret *The Thirty-Nine Steps* as a solo directorial triumph for Hitchcock, who is never mentioned in the substantial featured review, but rather as a sign of the cutting-edge quality of British cinema in contrast to Hollywood's product:

British filmmaking – in this new creative phase – is showing us its great advances. Its laboratories don't produce crime films like those we're accustomed to seeing from Hollywood, but rather film reels full of interest, with great visual attributes, with perfect coherence in all the scenes.

The objective of the production, so unexpected for the audience, is a demonstration of what cinema can achieve when one has such an attractive plot at hand as well as when one manages to find the exact manner to realise it. (Ibid.)

After praising the acting, too, Solis concludes by again identifying *The Thirty-Nine Steps* as 'a demonstration of the progress of British cinematography' (ibid.).

Cuatro de espionaje (*Secret Agent*) was Hitchcock's next film to open in Mexico City. When it premiered in September 1936, it had stiff competition from MGM's Academy Award-winning *Motín a bordo* (*Mutiny on the Bounty*, 1935) at whose opening night gala British and American ambassadors appeared.

Wartime advertising of *Secret Agent* in *El Universal* (19 Sept. 1936).

Next to Spanish War News telling of the defence of Madrid and the rebel occupation of San Sebastián, *Cuatro de espionaje* received coverage with articles both in Spanish and in English. John Gielgud, who was featured throughout, lauded 'Alfred Hitchcock's brilliant technique' in direction (*El Universal*, 19 September 1936, Section 2: 8) but none of the other coverage mentions Hitchcock. The review, though not on the society pages, assumes that tone: 'An exclusive audience filled the hall of the elegant theatre on Madera Avenue, and the movie was very entertaining' (ibid). The ad for the film showing the aerial bombing of a train as well as the embrace of the male and female spies along with the line 'The most passionate and strange film that has been made to this day' seems to indicate that the film defied generic classification.

When *Sabotaje*, promoted bilingually with the US English title *Woman Alone* in Mexico, not the UK original title *Sabotage*, opened in Mexico on 11 February 1937, to the day's headline of 'Alcalá de Henares Bombed', it was advertised as a war movie. Several articles that day speculated about Germany's intentions to invade Poland imminently. For the first time in the Mexican promotion and reception of his films, Hitchcock's name now figured front and centre in the coverage. Internationally, *Sabotage* was one of the more controversial of Hitchcock's movies because of his manipulation of the audience's reactions through suspense. In the film a twelve-year-old boy unwittingly carries a bomb that goes off and kills him. To recall *Sabotage* in more detail, Madame Verloc and her husband run a movie theatre, his cover for his anarchist political activities. In an act of sabotage the power goes out across the city of London and customers angrily demand their ticket money back. When Mr. Verloc comes under scrutiny of Scotland Yard, and their undercover agent Ted who is falling in love with Mrs. Verloc, Mr. Verloc hands the task of delivering a package with a ticking bomb along with film canisters to Mrs. Verloc's young brother Stevie. The boy's errand is so fraught with delays that the package explodes and kills him. At dinner Mrs. Verloc intuits her husband's guilt and kills him with a knife. An explosion of another bomb, hidden in a birdcage in their apartment, destroys the evidence of her crime.

Hitchcock later admitted to Truffaut that making a child die in a picture was 'a grave error'. He elaborated:

I made a serious mistake in having the little boy carry a bomb. A character who knowingly carries a bomb around as if it were an ordinary package is bound to work up great suspense in the audience. The boy was involved in a situation that got him too much sympathy from the audience so that when the bomb exploded and he was killed, the public was resentful. (Truffaut 1984: 109)

Yet none of the contemporary Mexican newspaper criticism of *Sabotage* criticised the plot, or the killing of a child. In fact, like Guillermo del Toro who wrote in 1992 in *Alfred Hitchcock*, republished in *Hitchcock por Guillermo del Toro* (2009), 'of having made purée out of Verloc's little brother-in-law ... for me personally it is one of the film's greatest achievements' (2009: 81), the reviews celebrated the tension created in the film. The *Excelsior* review, entitled 'The Movie "Sabotage": Indelible Impressions on the Soul', praised the film, and British cinema in general, for its economical but effective exposition, including the child's fateful mission:

With an entirely British reserve, with an atmosphere of crime, of mystery played out through the facial expressions and technical artistry of the principal actor Oscar Homolka, the movie *Sabotage* deserves to be given a top ranking. It doesn't have the popular tricks of most crime films. It reaches the soul of the spectator in ways that are natural and humane, such as in that scene of wandering through the streets without knowing that he is carrying a deadly bomb, which creates moments of intense emotion. Nonetheless, the technique is simple, but it causes remarkable effects. (*Excelsior*, 12 February 1937: 6)

The only criticism the reviewer has is that Mrs. Verloc does not cry more over her brother's death, but rather impassively kills her husband: 'The scene of the murder of her husband is carried out with a masterful hand, and it is a shame that the suffering for the death of the younger brother is not shown in those moments. It isn't the fault of the actress, but of the situation' (ibid.). Perhaps a Mexican interpretation required more melodrama, a good cry over the little brother. Yet overall the reviewer judges the film 'a good type of sensationalism, of those which enslave the audience, such that no one can take his eyes off the screen, which is the great secret of good movies' (ibid.). Indeed *Sabotage* was judged to be setting the standards for contemporary cinema. *Excelsior*'s English reviewer gives particular credit to the director by name: 'Again must the reviewer pay his compliments to director Hitchcock who seems to have that master's touch in bringing to the screen real people with appropriate sets and surroundings. "The

Woman Alone" is a vital and human document' (*Excelsior,* 12 February 1937). It occasioned the publication in the English section of *Excelsior* one of the most comprehensive presentations of Hitchcock's cinematographic philosophy found at any time in these newspapers. In the article, 'Thorough Emotional Shake-Up is What Alfred Hitchcock Aims to Give Public in His Thrillers', Hitchcock notes the importance of comedy in the film's balance:

> Next to reality, I put the accent on comedy. Comedy, strangely enough, makes a film more dramatic. A stage play gives you intervals for reflection on each act. These intervals have to be supplied in a film by contrasts, and if the film is dramatic or tragic, the obvious contrast is comedy. (*Excelsior,* 11 February 1937, Section 2: 8)

This pronouncement on the importance of comedy in a film's balance becomes one of the key tenets of Hitchcock's Latin reception from the 1990s onwards. Likewise in the film review in *Universal,* 'La pantalla y sus artistas' ('The screen and its artists'), which appeared next to even more extensive coverage of bull-fighting, Fidel Solis remarked on the public's enthusiastic response at the film's premiere and noted: 'With this film [Hitchcock] has crystallised his great knowl-edge of technique as a director ... The principal characteristic of this film lies in the excellent interconnections achieved in order to present ... a harmonious whole, blending the tragedy of passions with human suffering' (*Universal,* 15 February 1937). Putting this review next to bullfighting coverage may be one of the most appropriate placements for any review of this film. Hitch felt the 'best scene' was Mrs. Verloc's killing of her husband. Truffaut compared it to the dramatic pro-cess of Mérimée's staging of Carmen's death, 'with the victim thrusting her body forward to meet the slayer's final stab' (1984: 110); Hitchcock concurred and explained how he created the scene's tension around the attraction of the knife. Hitch makes Mr. Verloc seem like the bull in his description:

> Verloc stands up and walks around the table, moving straight toward the camera, so that the spectator in the theater gets the feeling that he must re-coil to make way for him. Instinctively, the viewer should be pushing back slightly in his seat to allow Verloc to pass by. Afterward, the camera glides back toward Sylvia Sidney, and then it focuses once more on the central object, that knife. And the scene culminates, as you know, with the killing. (Truffaut 1984: 111)

Hitchcock felt it was important that Sylvia Sidney not show her inner feelings on her face. Perhaps for this reason, critics, including Solis, had a hard time reading her. Solis makes one of the strangest comments anywhere about Sidney, noting her 'extraña atracción mezcla de china y europea' ('strange attraction [due to her] mixture of Chinese and European [looks]') (ibid.). This is bizarre ethnic stereotyping, but less cruel than Truffaut's later observation that the actress reminded him of Peter Lorre because of her eyes (ibid.).

On less of a tangent, Solis nonetheless agreed with what Hitchcock left out of the adaptation from Conrad's novel: 'In the film adaptation it was necessary to eliminate superfluous material, and in so doing the work turned out perfectly balanced' (*Universal*, 15 February 1937). This directly conflicted with Jorge Luis Borges' view of the film that appeared in *Sur*, one of Borges' rare film reviews in that journal, and only one of two of Hitchcock's films. Borges pithily and dismissively opined, 'Destreza fotográfica, torpeza cinematográfica: tales son los juicios tranquilos que me "inspira" el último film de Alfred Hitchcock' ('Photographic skill, cinematographic blunder: such are the assured judgments that the latest film of Alfred Hitchcock "inspires" in me').[6] Overall Solis saw Hitchcock's films, as British products, as economical in their exposition. Borges, on the other hand, expressed a more conservative, literary view and preferred Conrad's novel.

The headlines during *Sabotage*'s run described the siege of Madrid. On February 12 the main news was 'All Foreigners Can Leave Madrid'. Yet in the mid-1930s Mexico had its own share of clandestine activities going on that were intertwined with the actions in Europe. The very week of *Sabotage*'s

Ad for *Sabotage/The Woman Alone* from *Excelsior*, showing the foreign look of the actress Sylvia Sidney.

Wartime framing in the ad for *Sabotage/The Woman Alone* in *El Universal*.

Mexican City opening Trotsky began his exile there. *Excelsior*'s coverage of Trotsky's arrival, which Mexico City denizens excitedly followed, was extensive. Although Trotsky spoke of freedom, as *Excelsior* headlined its interview with him 'Trotsky now knows what freedom is' (12 January 1935), he and his family still faced peril and continued pursuit. Three days before Hitchcock's *Sabotage* opened in Mexico City, *El Universal* reported on its front page that Trotsky's son Sergio was arrested without known cause. On 10 February, the day before the film's opening, a headline read 'Trotsky "Disappears" While Audience in Hippodrome Waits'. The lack of explanation for these events only underscored for the general reader or potential moviegoer their probable connection to Mexican and European intelligence activities. On the day after *Sabotage* opened, a regular cultural column in *Excelsior*, 'Ayer, Hoy y Mañana' ('Yesterday, Today and Tomorrow') gave a particularly Mexican spin on sabotage in its commented on the long delay before Trotsky's appearance at the Hippodrome lecture, then known to have occurred because he was waiting for a phone call:

> There is no mystery about why Trotsky wasn't able to talk on the phone with his New York supporters the night of the announced speech. Managers of the telephone company are clarifying things, by saying the following, 'Some machines on the line weren't working right. There wasn't any sabotage or intervention of any kind. It was only a technical defect in the main office in Mexico. When it was fixed it was too late to continue. It was nothing more than one of those unfortunate things that go wrong at the most inopportune time.'
>
> That is to say, 'things' happened the Mexican way. There was a blunder [torpeza], that's the way the failure is explained.
>
> The public here is already accustomed to 'the lines are not working right,' precisely when they ought to work well; but for people in New York these 'things' aren't understandable. (*Excelsior*, 12 February 1937: 5)

Through the Trotsky commentary *Sabotage* became associated with Mexicans' gripes about their inferior phone system. This Hitchcock film vividly demonstrates how different Hitchcock's initial reception was in Latin America. Not only did *Sabotage* become enmeshed in a historical/political narrative, but also many key elements of Hitchcock's aesthetic reception in Mexico came to light through it: the recognition of the place of comedy in his films, as well as the foreshadowing – in the lament over the impassive, perhaps Asian Mrs. Verloc – of the filter of melodrama through which Hitchcock's movies of the 1940s and 1950s were seen.

IV. HITCHCOCK'S FILMS OF THE 1940s AND EARLY 1950s: FLYING DOWN TO MEXICO CITY, JOUSTING FOR A PLACE WITHIN THE GOLDEN AGE OF MEXICAN CINEMA

How was the reception of Hitchcock's films unique to Mexico in the 1940s and 1950s? Did his move to Hollywood have an impact, and if so, when? These decades coincided with the Golden Age of Mexican cinema, although scholars vary in setting its exact parameters.[7] Internationally Mexico exported its films throughout the Western hemisphere and challenged Hollywood's hegemony. Domestically the rise and evolution of Mexican cinema, particularly in a grow-ing acceptance of a capitalist model, and in its aesthetics, which showed an increased emphasis on melodrama, strongly affected the reception of Hitchcock's films during this period. Carlos Monsiváis interprets the place of melodrama in these dynamics:

> The founding project of the Mexican cinema was the 'nationalisation' of Hollywood. Although imitation was unavoidable, differences between the two industries abound. For example, certain Hollywood genres were impos-sible to translate: the screwball comedy, the thriller and, in the last instance, the western. Melodrama was more important in Mexico than in the USA because, traditionally, Mexican popular culture is premised on the peren-nial confusion between life and melodrama and the corresponding illusion that suffering, to be more authentic, must be shared publicly. (1995: 117)

Though Monsiváis's thesis describes how Mexican cinema selectively adapted Hollywood genres, it could equally be applied to explain how Hitchcock's films during the Golden Age were positioned generically for a Mexican audience. When Hitchcock's *La dama desaparece* (*The Lady Vanishes*), which was still one of his British spy period films that preceded his move to Hollywood, opened in Mexico in the early 1940s, generically it was given a different treatment than his other British films had received. By the time that *The Lady Vanishes* opened, Hitchcock had already moved to Hollywood and Mexican cinema was in its ascendance. Although the ad in *Universal* on 16 July 1942 promised a sensation-alist mystery film, with Hitchcock's name prominent in the selling, the featured review in that same paper, entitled 'Cuando un joven penetra a la alcoba de una dama' (literally, 'When a young man penetrates a lady's bedroom'), was about sex and social mores, a version dripping with melodrama. The ad came from the main office; the review copy was local.

One of the more important ways to gauge the Latin reception of Hitchcock is to study how his move to Hollywood was framed, especially to note when this

Mystery like you've never felt
it before, it will take your breath
away: Sensationalist ad for
The Lady Vanishes in *El
Universal* (16 July 1942).

move to become what we now call a crossover director was celebrated. The marketing of *The Lady Vanishes* only reveals a small part of the overall picture. As seen in chapter one, in Spain *Rebecca* was the flashpoint for a celebration of modernising aesthetics and for a debate over questionable morals. Yet in Mexico City newspapers *Rebecca* barely caused a stir. There were ads but it did not receive any commentary either in *Universal* or *Excelsior*. On the other hand, *Casados y descasados* (*Mr. and Mrs. Smith*), a comedy regarded today as one of his lesser films, Hitchcock's second film after *Rebecca*, was the centrepiece of a huge event that transformed his reception in Mexico and definitively associated him with Hollywood. *Mr. and Mrs. Smith* premiered on 12 April 1941, Sábado de Gloria (Easter Saturday) and opened to the general public on Easter Sunday. The religiosity of Mexicans was reflected in the titles of other movies that opened during the same Easter period: *Creo en Dios* (*Believe in God*) by Fernando de Fuentes, and even *El cielo y tú* (*All This and Heaven Too*) starring Bette Davis and Charles Boyer. *Mr. and Mrs. Smith* fell from above as their secular counterpoint. *Universal*'s headlines read, 'A Rain of Stars Fell Upon Mexico Yesterday' with the subtitle 'Existe una vía rápida de conexión' ('There's a rapid air connection'). Three Pan Am planes filled with Hollywood stars flew down in a trip that lasted only twelve hours to inaugurate the air connection between Mexico City and Los Angeles. Both major newspapers covered their stay for days with copious photos and lists of the stars. For *Universal* the event presaged the rise of international tourism: 'The transcendence of this trip is enormous if one takes into account that it shows in the US the existence of a rapid route to connect the two countries and with this the advantages for international tourism become abundantly clear' (*Universal*, 12 April 1941). Although the stars' official programme included High Mass at the Cathedral, the main event was a reception at the Cine Magerit where the programme for the stars featured the premiere of *Mr. and Mrs. Smith*.

Allusions to the film's plot were woven into the coverage. For instance, the public was compared to 'los descasados', or the unmarried, for they were as impatient waiting for the stars to appear as Mr. and Mrs. Smith were acting out their marital disagreements: 'This same public showed signs of impatience to see the "luminaries" of North American cinema as soon as possible' (ibid.). When the stars finally came out, Mickey Rooney tried to speak Spanish, and Norma Shearer made the crowd swoon. *Excelsior* reported on 13 April, 'Norma Shearer Conquered the Sympathies of the Metropolitan Public through her Refined Manners'; on 14 April 1941 the exchange, and the consciousness of Hitchcock's film in a Mexican context, even made it into the featured satirical cartoon in the *Excelsior*, a fixture of the editorial, on page 4, in which Mr. and Mrs. Smith became a long-time Mexican married couple sniping at each other. The husband sinks back in his easy chair and wistfully remembers the Easter weekend, 'Me río de Norma Shearer, teniéndote a mi lado,

A list of the visiting stars and Hollywood bigwigs headed the ad for *Mr. and Mrs. Smith* in *Excelsior* (12 April 1940).

vida mía' ('I'm laughing at Norma Shearer, having you by my side, my dear'). The wife retorts, 'Gracias ... Pero si ella te ve a mi lado, se reiría de tí, corazón' ('Thanks ... But if she sees you by my side, she'd laugh at you, sweetheart'). The events of this Easter weekend helped define radical cultural changes. Whereas one part of the city reenacted 'The Traditional Burning of Judas', another new movie theatre, Cine Estrella, with the cutting-edge kinetoscope technology was 'presented to the Mexican people'. Mexicans celebrated their progress and global connections. Although Hitchcock himself was not on any of those planes flying down to Mexico City, his boss David O. Selznick was. It was this publicity event, and the self-imaging of Mexicans in the comedy *Mr. and Mrs. Smith*, that shows first, that Hitchcock in 1941 was seen as representing Hollywood, and then, that his films were integrated into a contemporary Mexican narrative, too.

Garcá Cabral's cartoon 'Casi igual' ('almost equal') in *El Excelsior* satirizes the typical Mexican couple by referring to the visit of the Hollywood star Norma Sherrer.

Nationalist discourse in the 1940s celebrated innovation, particularly technical advances, such as regular air connections. In contrast to Spain's main newspapers of this time, *ABC* and *La Vanguardia*, which carried conventional movie reviews on a regular basis, film commentary during this same period was more truncated in *Universal* and *Excelsior* and seldom rose to the level or length of what could be called a review. Instead, brief paragraphs captioned stills from the featured films. Newspaper reporting on cinema primarily took two forms – either political or policy news that affected the film industry, which often appeared on the front or editorial pages, or in *Universal* a regular column called 'Nuestro Cinema' ('Our Cinema') penned by the pseudonymous Duende Filmo, roughly 'Film Phantom'. In both cases, and as the title 'Our Cinema' indicates, the perspective was nationalist. Hence when El Duende Filmo wrote about Hitchcock, which he often did, he represented a localised reception of Hitch's filmography.

From the point of view of the papers of record during the Golden Age of Mexican cinema, *where* Hitchcock's films opened was as significant, or more so, than their content or aesthetics. This tendency skewed the coverage and made the appraisal of his films considerably different than how world film history now generally evaluates his films and ranks them according to importance.

Not only did *Mr. and Mrs. Smith* take top billing as we have seen, about which Robin Wood opined: 'Even the most dedicated auteurist is unlikely to claim it among Hitchcock's successful, fully realized works' (2002: 247), but perhaps even more surprisingly, so did *Agonía de amor* (*The Paradine Case*). McGilligan calls this film 'a lifeless picture' and 'a permanent loser' and quotes Gregory Peck, one of the film's stars, who said it was the picture of his that he'd 'like to burn' (2003: 396). Again the film's Mexican title, literally 'Agony of Love', evokes melodrama, whereas the English title sounds like a spy story. There were also full-page photo shoots of Louis Jordan, *Agonía de amor*'s leading man, an unusually strong ad presence. Importantly, the film inaugurated the Cine Cosmo. Full-page ads congratulated the owners with stylised letters, 'for having provided our capital with a movie theatre worthy of it due to its sumptuousness, splendid comfort and capacity' (*Universal*, 24 June 1948). It even had a car park, an American phenomenon. As El Duende Filmo explained in 'Nuestro Cinema', however, the Cine Cosmo represented an exhibitors' war, in which Cine Cosmo was the opening salvo from the upstart 'Cadena de Hierro' ('Iron Chain') as seen in this caricature of a joust that accompanied his article (*El Universal*, 26 June 1948). Hitchcock's films until then usually opened at the Cine Alameda. The Alameda was part of the Cadena de Plata or Silver Chain owned by Emilio Azcárraga Vidaurreta, depicted in the cartoon as the opposing knight. Azcárraga, a true media mogul, was a major investor in RKO in Mexico. He founded and until his death in 1972 headed up Televisa, Mexico's pre-eminent television network throughout the twentieth century. It remained a family fiefdom.[8] Hitchcock did not alienate Azcárraga. His films never played

The Knight of the Silver
Chain of movie theatres
and founder of Televisa,
Emilio Azcárraga
Vidaurreta, charges in
a joust against the Knight
of the upstart Iron Chain
in a political cartoon in
El Universal (26 June
1948).

the Cosmo again but continued to premiere at the Alameda and other Mexico City movie theatres.

Many other industrial changes – and resentments – affected the positioning of Hitchcock in Mexico. When *Sombra de una duda* (*Shadow of a Doubt*) opened at the Alameda on 8 April 1943, the big story that whole week was that Bette Davis was vacationing in Acapulco. In other theatres María Félix in *María Eugenia* and Pedro Amendáriz in *Soy puro mexicano* (*I'm a Real Mexican*, 1942) enjoyed successful runs. The Coliseo arena, a new venue constructed specifically for Mexican wrestling contests, had just opened three days before with a world championship fight between El Santo and Tarzán, as seen in this illustration (*El Universal*, 5 April 1943, Section 1: 14). El Duende Filmo admitted he had not yet seen *Shadow of a Doubt*, but he recommended it nonetheless because of Hitchcock's reputation 'even though this Phantom hasn't seen it the film is one THAT SHOULD BE SEEN because the director is Alfred Hitchcock, creator of *Rebecca* and *Suspicion*' (*El Universal*, 8 April 1943). Yet the film industry was in turmoil. *Excelsior* editorialised against members of the cinematographic unions committing acts of sabotage, damaging the films they were showing, and against Hollywood for sending too many war movies. Ironically there was high demand but a scarcity of movies to fill all the venues, particularly the second-run theatres. El Duende Filmo predicted, 'El derrumbe de los salones de cine se vislumbra' (roughly, 'the collapse of movie theatres is on the horizon'). Moreover in 'Nuestro Cinema' he railed against the exploitation of Mexico City exhibitors whom he depicted as captives of foreign/Yankee distributors and price collusion:

> National movies have begun to create a following for the movies among people who before used to look at this entertainment with indifference, which has benefitted foreign movies. The Yankee distribution companies are opening annexes in strategic cities of the Republic and send back huge sums

Advertisement for the Mexican wrestling championship bout between El Santo and Tarzán that inaugurated the Coliseo Arena in *El Universal* (5 April 1943).

of money to their main offices in New York. They justify their attitude because there is a national distribution company, overseen by an Israeli who is notorious for his abusive practice of taking 75% off the top of ticket sales for their films. (*El Universal*, 4 April 1943)

The anti-Semitism of the comments is striking. If the exploitation of exhibitors were not enough, however, the US had already begun to ration virgin film stock across all of Latin America. In Mexico this situation not only limited the number of movies made but also led to a government decree that only movies with Mexican themes could be made. The juxtaposition of the ads for *Sombra de una duda* (*Shadow of a Doubt*) and *Soy puro Mexicano* (*I'm a Real Mexican*), in which their respective casts moreover face opposite directions, gave *El Universal* readers a sense of the nationalist tension in the air (4 April 1943, Section 2: 6).

By the time Hitchcock's next movie *Naúfragos* (*Lifeboat*) opened in Mexico City the news again was 'Lowered production of national movies – the US has reduced its shipment of raw material by 30 per cent' (*El Universal*, 5 April 1945). The paper editorialised 'Danger for National Cinema'. Neither Hitchcock's aesthetics nor the film's plot received any attention. It is ironic that these newspapers so decried the cutbacks in film stock shipments to Mexico without mentioning the hemispheric politics, for Mexico received more such material than any other Latin American nation. In fact, as Seth Fein points out, US foreign policy was directly intervening to develop the Mexican film industry as a 'counterweight to Argentinean production' in an effort to block the possibility of Axis propaganda originating from Argentina (2001: 167). Yet the often myopic nationalist discourse of the war years did acknowledge one new technological

Political cartoon depicting the fate of 'Our Cinema' held prisoner to foreign exhibitors who take 75% of the box office in *El Universal* (4 April 1943).

development positively. The day after *Lifeboat* opened on 4 April 1945 so did *La Luz que Agoniza* (*Gaslight*) with Ingrid Bergman and Charles Boyer that was 'all in Spanish, no subtitles'. Patrons were asked to vote on whether they liked 'duplicación' – dubbing – or not. El Duende Filmo devoted two columns to the subject concluding that the experiment 'ha ido de perlas' (literally, 'had a pearly start') or went superbly. Subsequently Hitchcock movies were shown dubbed, too.

The presence of Ingrid Bergman in his next film, *Cuéntame tu vida* (*Spellbound*) was exploited way beyond the star discourse for any other of his films in Mexico. Unusually for the serious newspapers at the time there were full-page fashion spreads for local stores that promoted the film and her image as appropriate for the Mexican woman. Ironically Bergman is not glamorous in *Spellbound*; she dresses like the psychiatric doctor she plays. Generally, and certainly now in the

Casts for *Shadow of a Doubt* and *I'm a Real Mexican* face off in opposing ads in *El Universal* (4 April 1943).

Costume Museum in Madrid, Bergman is seen as a fashion plate in *Notorious* or *Tuyo es mi corazón*, but when that film opened in Mexico City in 1947 it received no fashion coverage. *Spellbound* received feature commentary in *El Universal* and had a long run in Mexico City. But unlike in Spain, Dalí's participation was never mentioned.

Another example of the way in which the Mexican reception of Hitchcock's films of the 1940s and 1950s differs from than of Spain, for example, is seen in how *Para atrapar a un ladrón* (*To Catch a Thief*) was discussed in 1955. In Europe and the US *To Catch a Thief*, since it was set on the French Riviera and starred the glamorous pair of Grace Kelly and Cary Grant, represented a moment to advertise luxury. These aspects were crammed into the newspaper ad, which appeared both in *Universal* and *Excelsior* (20 December 1955). Yet whereas the ad touted cinematographic innovation, star power and romance, the newspaper review expounded on the topic

Ad for *To Catch a Thief* in *El Universal* touts an exotic setting, cinematographic advances, star power and romance.

of thievery. El Duende Filmo began his 'Nuestro Cinema' column in which he commented on *To Catch a Thief* recalling how honeymooning tourists had been assaulted in Mexico City:

> You will remember not so long ago that there appeared in the police blotter the notice of a scandalous assault, which a pair of newlyweds were victims of robbery, in the outskirts of Teotihaucán, when in broad daylight two hoodlums led by a woman, climbed into the car of the frightened North Americans and made them return to the city to their lodging on a very busy street where they were staying. The husband stayed in the car under the guard of the woman and one hoodlum, while the other one went up to the rooms with the wife to get the money. Certainly there must have been some among you who upon reading this news must have thought that the tourists who were robbed were spineless and that they let themselves be easily intimidated, because how could it have been that they didn't call out for help anywhere along the way, when they passed by a policeman or when they were in the midst of so many cars? (*El Universal*, 20 December 1955, Section 1: 5)

Letting his readers imagine themselves as tourists abroad, he then suggested their experience seeing the movie *Terror en la noche* (*Terror by Night*, 1946) would be 'a similar assault'. He ended the piece giving his opinion on Hitchcock's film about a robbery at a tourist spot – not as good as *Rear Window* or *Rope*. What constitutes at best a superficial appraisal of *To Catch a Thief* also exposes continued fissures around the legacy of Miguel Alemán Valdés (Presidential term, 1946–1952) who endeavoured to consolidate and modernise Mexican tourism, having come to the Presidency from the Ministry of Gobernación that supervised national tourism.[9] By the mid-1950s the scenario of movie-going, if not tourism, was a generalised consumer behaviour for the Mexican Don Juan and

It can happen to you, Don Juan and Doña Mariquita, Public!: Illustration to accompany *El Duende Filmo*'s review of *Terror by Night* and *To Catch a Thief* in *El Universal* (20 December 1955).

Doña Mariquita Public. Hitchcock was enveloped in the discourse and was key to the experience.

V. HITCHCOCK'S FILMS OF THE LATE 1950s AND 1960s: STANDARISED PUBLICITY WITHIN A NEW MORAL CODE AND LOCALISED EXPRESSIONS OF FEAR

In the late 1950s and 1960s the marketing and discussion of Hitchcock's films in Mexico in both *El Universal* and *Excelsior* followed a more standardised global model that took its cues from Hollywood. Although Hitchcock continued to be touted as an example of the latest advances in technology, Vistavisión and Technicolour, which had not yet penetrated Mexican national cinema, there was less variance from the now standarised judgement and publicity line that Hitchcock was 'el amo del suspenso' ('the master of suspense'). Little direct mention was made of either humour or melodrama. His films became bound to comments on terror and suspense, which had appeared in a more arbitrary, but localised fashion regarding *Atrapar a un ladrón* in El Duende's discussion of tourist assaults. These papers featured production stills or well-known publicity photos, such as the famous stills of Hitch holding birds, before and during that particular film's theatrical run. However, their captions did hint at a more local history. They noted the long lines at the theatres or tellingly lamented that the films had only opened in Mexico after a considerable delay.

Nonetheless three films in particular – *En manos de destino*, *Psicosis* and *Los pájaros* – received more specialised attention and generated a more local commentary. *En manos del destino* (*The Man Who Knew Too Much*), Hitchcock's remake of his 1930s spy film, opened in Mexico at the same time as a major reworking of the Mexican movie code. The new 'C' classification for adult films was controversial. *Excelsior* published extensive excerpts of a letter from Luis B. Varela, President of the Mexican Institute of Intellectuals entitled 'Nos Están Moralizando' ('They are moralising us'). Varela derided the new code as a symptom of a widespread moralising atmosphere:

> Recently all entertainment venues are broke because of this so-called moralisation of the environment. National cinematographic production is stalled and it's boring with traditional *charros*, *mariachis*, fairs and country ballads. There's enough material to make something great, but we're frozen. For this reason the audience is still literally cramming itself in to see the mutilated films that come to us from abroad in spite of the fact that the budget-minded censors leave them in an artless condition. (*Excelsior*, 8 November 1956)

Varela further deems the new movie code unnecessarily puritanical. He compares the situation to Prohibition in the US, a misdirected experiment only befitting the United States that fomented tourism to Mexico.

> In Mexico alcoholic intoxication is not subject to censorship; everyone can drink until they drown. On the other hand, the angle 'of the different vision,' the ocular and auditory relaxation that doesn't intoxicate anyone, finds itself strictly censored and rationed by the organisms that acting like a mafia are trying to brainwash the minds of the race with paralysing shots of stupidly 'redeeming' mescaline. (Ibid.)

Eschewing the alcoholic analogies, El Duende Filmo in *El Universal* nonetheless shared Varela's views against the new censorship standards. Writing his 'Nuestro Cinema' column about *Los Amantes* (The Lovers), the first Mexican film to receive the new 'C' classification – 'which shows danger and indicates that only those adults who may wish to risk contamination with immorality ought to see them' – El Duende argues for the artistic merits of the film, which deals with prostitution, but decries the salaciousness of the publicity campaign for the film.

> What bothers me is that in the ads that they make for the film good taste gets lost in order to attract the public's attention. The chords of morbid curiosity are strummed by underscoring that special classification of the Directorship of Cinematography and by noting that people are scandalised, but it doesn't take away the desire to go see what scandalised the censor. For a movie like 'The Lovers,' which is a work of art, the appropriate publicity ought to be different although it may not get the market results that are sought after. After all how the movie is sold resembles how its protagonists traffic in love. (*El Universal*, 13 November 1956)

The movie ads on 8 November 1956, the day *The Man Who Knew Too Much* opened, illustrate El Duende's point about creeping salaciousness in advertising. The ads all included their classifications. Those for *Las zapatillas verdes* (The Green Slippers) and *Los Héroes Están Fatigados* (*Les héros sont fatigués*, 1955) with María Félix and Yves Montand, as seen below, suggest a Mexican celebration of eroticism. The contrast in modesty could not be greater with the publicity for *En manos de destino* (*The Man Who Knew Too Much*) with Doris Day and James Stewart, as parents searching for their kidnapped child. Hitchcock was touted not only as the latest in technology, for Vistavision and Technicolour, but also as recommended family entertainment. This attitude contrasts with his positioning in Spain during the 1950s that emphasised how he tweaked the censors.

Provocative ads in
El Universal for *Los
zapatillos verdes* and
Les héros sont fatigues
with the rating code 'C'
(8 November 1958)

The publicity campaign for *Psicosis* (*Psycho*) in Mexico carried through with the innovative, though globally standarised, warning that latecomers would not be admitted to the theatres, although sometimes with Hitchcock's softer admonishment:

> You don't begin a book at the end, or dinner with dessert and *Psycho* is a genuine banquet of emotions. My aim is, naturally, to help you to deeply enjoy this movie. See it from the beginning!

Shocked parents, Doris Day and
Jimmy Stewart, in the ad for
The Man Who Knew Too Much,
appropriate for adults
and children (*El Universal*,
8 November 1958)

Psycho's admonishment or change in exhibition rules was not discussed. What was in the news – 'La permanencia voluntaria queda abolida' ('Voluntary stay is abolished') – was that *Spartacus* (1960), an unusual 70mm film, would only be shown in two screenings with an hour to empty the theatre between them. Also tickets would be available four days in advance. Apparently in Mexico City the problem was not that moviegoers arrived late, but that they stayed on.

If on the one hand *Psycho* was overshadowed in exhibition rules by the luxurious exclusivity of *Spartacus*, it was even more significantly co-opted by two other Mexican contexts. It was paired in ads and reviews with the Mexican horror film *Espiritismo* that opened the same day.[10]

The caption for the still from Benito Alazraki's *Espirtismo* read in part, 'interminable minutes of true anguish and authentic suspense parade across the screen' while to its right on the page the still of Vera Miles screaming in *Psycho*

Juxtaposition of ads in
El Universal for *Psycho*
and *Espiritismo*.

was titled 'In "Psycho" Suspense Reaches its Climax'. The ads for the two films were prominently juxtaposed.

Espiritismo copied the graphic style of the torn page from *Psycho*. Yet *El Universal* carried the theme from this Mexican/Hollywood dialogue to editorialise on the state of Mexican cinema in 'Expectación y "Suspenso" en el Paréntesis Espectacular del Cine' ('Expectation and "Suspense" in the Spectacular Pause in the Cinema') that the government had to respond to Mexican movie producers who were running out of funds. The article concluded:

> The way that some producers found to make movies in collaboration with the workers is good: but it is only a temporary measure for the moment. Because of this it is urgent to hear the response of Mr. Secretary of Government, for the cinematographic industry is in his hands. (*El Universal*, 29 March 1962, Section 3: 7)

Although the co-opting of *Psycho* in Mexico, to sell or save national cinema, on the one hand may have diminished its impact, more likely it reaffirmed the reputation of Hitchcock in that he could serve as a fulcrum for a discussion of a national cinema crisis.

Although *De entre los muertos* (*Vertigo*) and *Intriga nacional* (*North by Northwest*) – nowadays among Hitchcock's most highly regarded films – played Mexico City to respectable runs and good crowds, neither of these films could be considered blockbusters during their release based on the news reports. The

Hitchcock film that received the most attention, and blockbuster status, was *Los pájaros* (*The Birds*). It opened in multiple theatres and played to big audiences. As the *Universal* reporter notes, Hitchcock was by then even more popular due to his television series. Moreover most people had already heard of the film from reports on its US release:

> A lot has been said about this movie, its presentation on Broadway was a reason for scandal because of the anticipation that it generated and the effects seen after the film finished, which have been discussed a lot. To create this state of anxiety producing emotion it turned to two elements for which the public feels sympathy and attraction: children and birds. Birds taken in isolation, except for predators, are innocent and cause no harm, but in a swarm and furious for whatever reason, they are terrifying. (*El Universal*, 18 July 1963, Section 3: 7)

Again these newspaper commentaries wove a story of the crisis in Mexican cinema, 'Una sección puede paralizar el cine', ('A sector of a union can paralyse the movies'), around their Hitchcock review. In fact a union strike of cinematographic workers was forecast for the day *The Birds* opened. The next day *El Universal* published a survey of comments of the people who saw the premiere. Most proclaimed astonishment along with their endorsement, as did Mr. Moisés García, a businessman: 'Me trajeron a la fuerza, pero oiga usted ¡qué peliculón!' ('They forced me to come, but listen, what a blockbuster!'). The article emphasised the opinion of Mr. Justino Blas Henríquez:

> Si lo que pasa por la pantalla fuera realidad algún día, ¡qué bomba atómica ni 'qué hacha'! Esto sí que es realmente pavoroso. Con solo pensar que eso le pudiera pasar a mi familia, 'se me pone la carne de gallina'... (If what happens on screen were to become reality some day, what an atomic bomb, or blow! This really is something dreadful. Only thinking that it could happen to my family makes my hair stand on end... (*El Universal*, 19 July 1963)

This reminds us that in 1963 the final scene in *The Birds* could be thought of in terms of nuclear war, an interpretation that is seldom evoked for the film today.[11] The *Universal* headlines of 22 July 1963 – 'Advierte el Papa la Esperanza de que Haya una Tregua Nuclear' ('The Pope Expresses Hope for a Nuclear Treaty') – confirm that Mexicans were indeed aware of the nuclear threat.

Hitchcock's films of the late 1960s – *Marnie* and *Torn Curtain* – were mostly discussed in terms of the delay in their opening in Mexico. *El Universal* captioned one *Torn Curtain* still with this complaint: 'This much-anticipated film today receives the prize for the long time its opening was postponed. Such an event will happen today Thursday in the Chapultepec, finally putting an end to the public build-up that anticipates the success that this film will receive in Mexico' (*Universal*, February 2, 1967). Although in other eras delays signalled censorship, these probably reflected diminished expectations for these films' commercial potential.[12] When *Torn Curtain*, the more political of the two films opened, most attention was dedicated to Sophia Loren in *Judith* (1966) and the excitement around and countdown to the Mexico City Olympics: '617 days are left.' *Marnie*, and all other entertainment news, was rather lost in the extensive coverage of Churchill's death, mourning and funeral that coincided with *Marnie*'s release and opening week. For the ex-pat Hitchcock, then perceived to be in decline, this was perhaps fitting.

VI. CONCLUSIONS

Our readings of the historical and cultural record in *El Universal* and *Excelsior* have brought to light important trends in the Mexican reception of Hitchcock's films. First, his films of the 1930s, that is, British Hitchcock, had a significant impact in Mexico and even entered into the political discourse of those years of the Cárdenas administration (1934–1940) as events from Trotsky's exile in Mexico were envisioned as *Sabotage*. In this period, moreover, Hitchcock's films were viewed as generic hybrids and praised for their humour as well as for their spy or police plots. Second, during the subsequent decades of the 1940s and early 1950s, the reception changed as Hitchcock's films were inflected by the context of the Golden Age of Mexican cinema and its emphasis on melodrama. Most significantly, Hitchcock's crossover to Hollywood was framed differently in Mexico than in Spain. Whereas *Rebecca,* a pseudo-Old World drama, marked the transition elsewhere, Mexico celebrated *Casados y descasados (Mr. and Mrs. Smith)*, a comedy of modern marriage, in a Hollywood extravaganza that promoted the new aerial link between Mexico City and Los Angeles. Third, throughout his career Hitchcock was synonymous in Mexico with innovation and progress, such as improvements in sound or the advent of colour, which became increasingly important as upscale theatres expanded in the capital. Fourth, especially later in Hitchcock's career, from the 1960s on, his advertising was copied to market Mexican film and serious newspaper commentary grabbed onto the now familiar, reductive vision of Hitchcock as 'master of suspense' to create interest in their headlines about the financial crisis in Mexican cinema. Overall our analysis here has shown that the appraisal of Hitchcock's films in newspapers was far more widespread and its characterisation most distinctive in the earlier part of his career than in what we now consider his mature period.[13]

Finally, it is important to reiterate that what constituted film criticism or film commentary in Mexican newspapers throughout Hitchcock's career was different from what was practiced in other Latin American capitals, or what we expect and understand today from major news sources. For instance Buenos Aires had and continues to have a strong tradition of film criticism including bylined reviews in *La Nación*. With rare exceptions in Mexico City film critics were anonymous. Film commentary was a popular service like a restaurant review. Serious commentary was devoted to the discussion of national policies or the financial state of the industry, seldom to aesthetic or narrative cinematographic interpretation. This type of commentary, however, situated Hitchcock within the cinematographic industry and often identified him as an industrial model.

Further study of contemporaneous literary and popular magazines, many of which began during the 1960s, a decade which marked a mini-boom in cinema magazines, would complement our focus on major newspapers and would likely reveal other aspects of Mexican reception of late Hitchcock. They may provide reasons for the delay in the release of several Hitchcock films, which newspapers lamented. Likewise it would be important to discover if Hitchcock's classic films such as *Psycho, Vertigo* and *North by Northwest*, later *The Birds* and *Frenzy*, received significant attention in Mexican cinema magazines or whether they were shunted aside as too 'commercial'.

To begin to expand our analysis to these other sources, we can conclude by turning to Francisco Sánchez Aguilar, a screenwriter and film critic, and above all the well-respected film critic for *Esto* (1972–1980), a high circulation sports paper, and consider his remarks on Hitchcock in *Cinefilia es locura* (2004), a memory of his cinema-going experiences. In *Cinefilia*, which includes Sánchez' published interviews, he praises *Psycho* and *Rear Window*, but finds his pet peeve with Hitchcock's kisses:

> I've never understood why Hitchcock liked kisses so much. A kiss always stops the action. Buñuel detested them as kitsch; I, because they're anti-cinematographic. Juan Antonio de la Riva understood it very well.[14] Hitchcock, on the other hand, never understood it. (2004: 210)

Sánchez is an important Buñuel scholar, author of *Todo Buñuel* (1978) and *Siglo Buñuel* (2000), among other film books, so it is not surprising that Hitchcock ranks below Buñuel in Sánchez's estimation here. Nonetheless, even a Buñuel scholar, who says 'La pasión por el cine es mi tema' ('Passion for cinema is my obsession') when asked to choose an example of a kind of film about which he feels passionately, cites not Buñuel, but Hitchcock.

> I tend to like boxes that contain a box, which contains another box, etc. To give them a name, I'll call them *matrioska* movies. These are the ones that excite me. An example: *The Birds*. This notable film by Alfred Hitchcock encompasses at least three schemes: the birds' attack, the love story and the transposition of feminine personalities. Not satisfied with that, the film-maker even adds parables like the following: The hero (a term which with respect to this film has to go between quotation marks) is a lawyer and his little sister calls him a defender of crooks. There are protests and the young girl counters with her point of view: 'Now you're defending – she says – a guy who killed his wife with six shots to the head.' And she adds, 'It's something terrible! An outrage!' There's a pause. Everybody in the room supposes that the girl is justifiably terrified, but – oh, surprise! – the reasons for her anxiety are of a more pragmatic sort, for as she right away explains: 'I think two shots were more than enough.' Tippi Hedren in turn asks for the reason why the man killed his wife so savagely. With his touch of black humour, the answer is as simple as it is eloquent: 'Because she turned off the television while he was watching a baseball game.' (2004: 201–2)

Sánchez's passionate choice, and defence of *The Birds* underscores the importance that this film had in Mexico City. His comments on the film's dialogue moreover bring into relief the enduring role of humour in the reception of Hitchcock in Mexico, whose presence the Mexican filmmaker Guillermo del Toro was to note and exploit in his own films in subsequent decades.

NOTES

1   Fein summarises, 'the Golden Age of Mexican cinema resulted not from nationalist (as usually asserted) but collaborative policies that evolved out of the particularities of US-Mexican interactions at a variety of transnational and intergovernmental levels between the 1930s and 1950s. Chief among these was the direct intervention of the US government in Mexican film production organized by Nelson Rockefeller's Office of the Coordinator of Inter-American Affairs (OCIA), responsible for U.S. cultural and economic relations with Latin America during World War II' (2001: 164).

2   *La Nación*'s electronic archive begins in 1998; *Universal*, in 1999. LAN (Latin American Newspapers) advertises itself as 'the first collection of the World Newspaper Archive, a partnership between the Center for Research Libraries community and Readex, a division of NewsBank, to systematically create an extensive Web-based collection of international newspapers'. However Readex only focuses on nineteenth- and early twentieth-century newspapers. In emails they responded that the company did not have plans to expand

their timeframe; http://www.crl.edu/collaborative-digitization/world-newspaper-archive/latin-america.

3   Violeta Nuñez Gorritti published a partial record, for the 1940s only, for Lima, Peru.

4   I thank Jenny Romero of the Special Collections of the Margaret Herrick Library, Academy of Motion Picture Arts and Sciences, Beverly Hills, CA, for calling these sources to my attention.

5   Peña, who is responsible for the recent discovery of the complete copy of *Metropolis* (1927) in Buenos Aires (see Rohter 2010), provided me with this information in email correspondence.

6   Borges' review is republished in Edgardo Cozarinsky, *Borges y el cine* (1974: 51).

7   Carlos Monsiváis defines the Golden Age as c. 1935–55 (1995: 117), whereas Seth Fein sets the era as beginning in 1940, to coincide more closely with the onset of World War II (2001: 164).

8   For a brief history of Televisa and the Azcárraga clan, see Omar Hernández and Emile McAnany, 'Cultural Industries in the Free Trade Age: A Look at Mexican Television' (2001: 392–4).

9   See Alex Saragoza, 'The Selling of Mexico: Tourism and the State, 1929–1952' (2001).

10   Rafael Aviña notes the exuberant exoticism of Mexican horror films. He suggests that Alazraki's and other Mexican horror films place themselves in an uncertain alignment with the 'foreign': 'In an always derivative genre, plagued with scientists with foreign last names – Malincheism or xenophobia? – and cardboard laboratories with pulsating burners, pre-Cortesian reliquaries and Aztec reincarnations, and a delirious exoticism in which all kinds of witches, priests, zombies, hypnotists and voodoo fit, there is an abundance of films like *Muñecos infernales* (1960), *Espiritismo* (1961), both by Benito Alazraki, and *Misterios de la magia negra* (Miguel M. Delgado, 1957)' (2004: 206).

11   The 'not quite documentary', *Double Take* (2010) by Johan Grimonprez tries to recapture 'the ambient weirdness of the times' through Hitchcock in the 1950s and 1960s (A. O. Scott, 'Recasting the Cold War as the Hitchcock Years', *NY Times*, 2 June 2010).

12   See Marién Estrada, '"¡Corte!... ¡corte!... ¡y más corte!": La censura en el cine mexicano' ('"Cut!... Cut!... and More Cuts!": Censorship in Mexican Cinema'), Fundación Manuel Buendía; http://mexicanadecominicacion.com.mx/fmb/foromex/censura.htm. Surveying the history of film censorship in Mexico, Estrada notes: 'Morality has served as a pretext for governmental cuts, but politically incorrect topics have kept the authoritarian Mexican system much busier.' She notes that censorship had a strong revival in the waning years of Miguel Alemán's presidency. Several films were cut, denied exhibition licences and/or delayed in their releases. She concludes: 'What is certain is that censorship has a thousand ways to operate that go beyond the clumsy and cynical open prohibition, and those methods are much more dangerous because they operate in silence, without any way to prove their existence, as in the selection of scripts, the RTC classification, and the bad marketing and exhibition of a film.'

13   Since the *Cartelera cinematográfica* volumes published by UNAM, which served as a basis for the research charts in locating opening dates of Hitchcock films included here, did not include a volume for the decade of 1970s, *Frenzy* and *Family Plot* have not been included in this study.

14   Juan Antonio de la Riva is a Mexican writer and filmmaker, born in 1953 in San Miguel de Cruces, Durango, where his father was an iterant film exhibitor, whose story the son told in his break-through movie *Vidas errantes* (*Wandering Lives*, 1984). Two of his other significant films are *Elisa antes del fin del mundo* (*Elisa Before the End of the World*, 1997) and *El gavilán de la sierra* (*The Mountain Hawk*, 2002).

CHAPTER SIX

Guillermo del Toro's Continuing Education:
Adapting Hitchcock's Moral and Visual Sensibilities to the World of Horror

I. INTRODUCTION: CAREER PATTERNS

Before 2006, when Guillermo Del Toro released his international mega-hit *El laberinto del fauno* (*Pan's Labyrinth*), the Mexican director, born in 1964, had made five feature-length films, all within the horror or fantasy genre, that alternated between small-budget Spanish-language films in Mexico and Spain – *Cronos* (1993) and *El espinazo del diablo* (*The Devil's Backbone*, 2001) – and Hollywood productions – *Mimic* (1997), *Blade II* (2002) and *Hellboy* (2004). Conventionally this alternation makes Del Toro the epitome of a successful crossover director. Unlike other Latin crossover directors, such as Álex de la Iglesia, Del Toro has consistently been successful at the box office. This success can be credited to his study of Hitchcock and a single-minded focus on the horror genre. But it is little known that Del Toro has assiduously studied not just a few classic Hitchcock films, but every one he ever made. In 1990 while he was a film professor at the state university in Guadalajara, and before he directed his first feature film, Del Toro published a well-researched book on Hitchcock. The monograph *Alfred Hitchcock* (1990) comprehensively surveys all of Hitchcock's films, television programmes and unfinished projects.[1] Undertaking this academic study gave him not only intimate knowledge of cinematic techniques, but also gave him insight into Hitchcock's career in its entirety, as an industrial model. This chapter will explore Del Toro's writings, specific allusions to Hitchcock's films in his work, and their shared career patterns. Throughout we will speculate on to what extent Del Toro has gone beyond the notion of cross-over in the transnational scheme of contemporary cinema.

The paradigmatic importance of Hitchcock for Del Toro's career can be sensed in the following passage from the section on Hitchcock's *Frenzy*:

> The product of the 'new Hitchcock,' as critics and publicists hastened to call *Frenzy*, has the privilege of being the most perfect work of the last stage of the director, and the energy he needed to carry it out is equivalent to that which a young person would need in his first work, but, while all this may be true, it is ridiculous to proclaim a 'new Hitchcock.' Let's not be mistaken, the movie is driven by the dark vision of a sceptical and skilful old man; the 70 years of frustration of Hitchcock and the 50 he spent being a 'good boy' in the industry, vomit out a savage work, which could pass for the fresh work of a young, rebellious, and furious filmmaker, but neither fury nor rebellion are exclusive to youth. *Frenzy* is the darkest, most personal and admirable creation of an old and tired poet of brutality. (1990: 474)

Del Toro's profound admiration and understanding of Hitchcock as 'the poet of brutality' is evident in this passage. As he contemplated the hard road to his directing debut, he looked to Hitchcock for energy and inspiration. He writes as if the old man were advising the young Turk to persevere.

Structured as a critical biography of Hitchcock, Del Toro's introduction to *Alfred Hitchcock* functions as a virtual aesthetic manifesto. Moreover, when he compares British and American Hitchcock, Del Toro defines his own values and reveals his career aspirations. Del Toro strongly defends the British period: 'The films shot by Hitchcock during his so-called British period have received much less distribution than they should have and tend to be seen negatively – even by their creator – when in reality they are as interesting, and at times even more so, than those of his North American work, since they treat ideas and situations with an intensity and purity infinitely superior to the works which succeeded them' (1990: 26). Del Toro chooses *Blackmail* to illustrate his notions of intensity and purity arguing that it is 'more complex and subversive', and in particular, more misogynist, than other British works, such as *The Lodger*. He cites examples in *Blackmail* from the attempted rape/murder scene in the artist's studio. Interestingly, since Del Toro was struggling towards making his own debut film at the time he was writing, he agrees that the complexity of *Blackmail* was 'a little overdone' finding that a common defect of 'first works' (1990: 27). Although Del Toro is a firm defender of British Hitchcock, he does appreciate Hitch's motivation to work in Hollywood: 'He yearned to learn all the details of the foreign industry in order to achieve his total independence later on' (1990: 29). Again this reads like a pep talk for Del Toro's own career path: try to get to Hollywood to learn, but make enough money to have creative control on your own projects, or as it worked out for Del Toro, film *Mimic* to be able to make *The Devil's Backbone*. Del Toro makes a particularly impassioned defence of Hitchcock being able to create masterpieces with few resources, a situation Del Toro himself faced in Mexico: 'There are those who commit the stupid error of trying to wipe out with a stroke of the pen the importance of this era of the director, alleging that Hitchcock's narrative, that is, his pyrotechnics, were still not fully developed due to the lack of resources in that era and that for this reason his filmic expression appeared very limited' (1990: 27–8). Again foregrounding the *Blackmail* painter's sequence, as well as citing others in *The Man Who Knew Too Much* and *Young and Innocent*, he dismisses anyone who doesn't see these films as he does as 'hydrocephalic' (1990: 28). Apart from the minor impact of these comments in a longstanding critical debate, it is hard not to read these passages as Del Toro's cry for recognition of his own project, for his own early career and for an emerging new Mexican film industry.[2]

After his introduction to Hitchcock, Del Toro devotes a short chapter to each film, beginning with a story synopsis and ending with a note on the place of Hitch's cameo in the respective film. Because Del Toro pays detailed, careful attention to selected cinematic techniques of each of the films discussed, the book serves as undeniable evidence of Hitchcock's influence on the filmmaker in his own work, all of which postdates the book. Overall, the book stands out both as a scholarly document, and surely, as an idiosyncratic view on Del Toro's reactions to Hitchcock's films, to which we will continue to refer in our discussions of the individual films. Offering one preview here will attune the reader to Del Toro's voice in the book. While noting what the critics Leonard Leff and Donald Spoto, then the directors Eric Rohmer and Claude Chabrol, have to say about *Saboteur*, Del Toro adds: 'It is impossible for me to overlook mentioning here the profound irritation that Robert Cummings, the prognathous (sic) actor to whom Hitchcock would later give the role of Grace Kelly's lover in *Dial M for Murder*, causes me. In both films the "hero" gains in stature only because of the generic convention' (1990: 227). Del Toro expresses what can only be called colloquially 'pet peeves' about many of the films through the discourse of an educated man, epitomised here by the Greek word choice 'prognathous', chiefly used in physical anthropology, meaning with a prominent or protruding lower jaw (*OED*). The preferences he developed watching Hitchcock, however, are deeply felt – a profound irritation or discomfort – and long held, indications of the tenacity that has enabled Del Toro to survive both in a studio system and in the world of independent film. To avoid what Del Toro saw as Hitchcock's errors in settling for Cummings, a 'B list' choice according to McGilligan and whom

Hitch himself called merely a 'competent performer' (2003: 301), Del Toro resolved early not to compromise on casting. In interviews on his film *Hellboy*, Del Toro prides himself on casting Ron Perlman as the hero. Perlman had supporting roles as the nephew of the evil businessman in Del Toro's debut film *Cronos,* and as the leader of the Bloodpack in *Blade II.* When Kellvin Chavez asks Del Toro if he had any problems casting Perlman, Del Toro replies:

> Yeah, we went through the usual song and dance. I just didn't want to give in, I think the best thing in a movie is when you're sharing the weight of the movie with someone that you trust completely and that you feel is capable of delivering the part perfectly. I think that for *Hellboy*, Ron Perlman was the only actor to do it really. And the studio was suggesting other, bigger names. That's why it took me 5½ years to get it made, because I was very stubborn and I just stuck by my chosen actor. (http://latinoreview.com/films_2004/sonypictures/hellboy/guillermo.html)

Del Toro's study of Hitchcock's negotiations with the studios that led sometimes to lamented casting choices prepared him for his own prolonged battle over Perlman. Del Toro saw in Perlman the perfect actor for horror/fantasy films, which had fascinated him since childhood.

Like Almodóvar, Del Toro began filmmaking through trial and error with a Super-8 camera. Significantly, whereas Almodóvar was already a self-supporting worker in Madrid, precocious Del Toro was only eight years old when he began experimenting with his father's camera, making movies with ketchup and his *Planet of the Apes* action figures. He refers to them as horror movies and that one 'was filled with exploitation elements' (Daniel Epstein Interview, 2003). At eight, he dressed up as a vampire sucking his sister's blood for a family photo. The impact of his early films, such as *Matilda,* starring his mother as an invalid devoured by a giant foetus, resurfaces both in *Mimic*'s giant insects and in his obsession with demonic foetuses in jars in *The Devil's Backbone* and *Blade II.*[3] Del Toro credits his parents' large, eclectic collection of art books, which included volumes on European masters as well as on comic book artists, with inspiring his visual abilities. Later in his teenage 'film geek' years (Epstein, ibid.), Del Toro spent seven years as the projectionist for a cinema club that each week showed two or three movies, including world cinema, in 16 or 35mm. This was before the advent of video in Mexico. Del Toro clearly has a broad-based knowledge of global film culture.

Unlike Almodóvar or Hitchcock, however, Del Toro was not just self-taught, but had formal university training in fields related to film. Del Toro attended his home town University of Guadalajara where he studied visual arts and opted especially to concentrate on short films and theatrical make-up. In 1984 he worked as producer on Jaime Humberto Hermosilla's *Doña Herlinda y su hijo* (*Doña Herlinda and Her Son*, 1985) in which his mother Guadalupe Gómez de del Toro starred as Doña Herlinda. In 1985 he wrote and directed his first professional short film *Doña Lupe*. From there he moved to work in television. In 1986 he made his major directing debut with episodes of *Hora marcada* (1986–1990), a Mexican equivalent of *The Twilight Zone*. His friend Alfonso Cuarón, who would later make *Y tu mamá también* (2001) and *Gravity* (2013), also debuted on this series.[4] Del Toro calls the *Hora marcada* experience 'like a film school' (Director's Interview, *Cronos* DVD). Also in 1986 he began to storyboard what would become *Cronos*, his first feature-length film, which took eight years to make. Though coming at a different stage, before rather than after his feature film breakthrough, Del Toro's career followed Hitchcock's in working for a sustained period of time on a commercial television series.

Significantly Del Toro's career both parallels and intersects with the development of film studies as an academic discipline. While he was imagining *Cronos*, Del Toro taught film at the University of Guadalajara between 1986 and 1992 and wrote *Alfred Hitchock*. According to Clara Cisneros Michel, a professor of literature at Guadalajara, who was involved in new programme development, Del Toro's years at the University of Guadalajara coincided with the creation of a film degree there, a first in Mexico. The programme encompassed film production and cinema studies. This is particularly important because the recognition of film not only as an academic discipline, but also as a career track, happened not in the huge main state university, UNAM, in Mexico City, but at the campus of Mexico's second largest city, Guadalajara. The presence of multinational tech companies, such as Hewlett Packard, in Guadalajara at the time added to the sense of the possible. Guadalajara had a ready market for those students with audio-visual skills.

Even though Del Toro's main interest from his student days was special effects, as expected for someone with his longstanding interest in horror, this is one area where formal training was not available in Mexico. Looking elsewhere, he took Dick Smith's US correspondence course to receive his Certificate of Special Make-up Effects Artistry. Today Smith, who did the make-up for *The Exorcist* (1973), posts Del Toro's testimonial on his website: 'Your course has been the catalyst for everything I dreamed to do.'[5] In 1985 Del Toro founded Necropia, his own special effects company in Mexico. In an article in *Dirigido*, Quim Casas emphasised Del Toro's pioneering spirit with this move:

> Del Toro simply reasoned: at the moment of beginning the pre-production of *Cronos* there wasn't in all of Mexico any company that could develop

the types of effects, trick photography, and special make-up that he required. Hence, he decided to form his own team of technicians and invent everything he needed for his first feature film as he went along, just like the pioneers of cinematography and the creators of the most modest B-movies. (2004: 48)

Over the long gestation period of *Cronos*, Del Toro did special effects make-up on major films of top Mexican directors, such as Arturo Ripstein's *Mentiras piadosas* (*Love Lies*, 1987), Luis Estrada's *Bandidos* (*Bandits*, 1991), Nicolás Echevarría's *Cabeza de vaca* (1991) and Paul Leduc's *Dollar Mambo* (1993). Through these productions he made significant contacts in the industry, especially with Guillermo Navarro, who later served as his director of photography on *Cronos*, *The Devil's Backbone* and *Hellboy*. These early projects depended on family ties, for Guillermo Navarro's sister, Bertha Navarro, served as producer for *Cronos*.[6]

Whereas Hitchcock's entry into the film industry was via set design, Del Toro's was special effects make-up. Both specialised areas, which emphasise the role of the visual component in film, are unusual career paths into directing. Moreover, the high level of technical knowledge, which both Hitchcock and Del Toro acquired from an early stage in their careers, allowed them to invent new distinctive looks for their subsequent films. Both pursued these careers quite relentlessly, too. Undoubtedly Del Toro's talents and know-how in special effects and make-up in the world of fantasy have enabled him to move in and between multiple industries, where others have failed. This background makes his work extraordinary, especially in Latin American cinema, since it has been a commonplace that peripheral industries cannot do horror well because the genre requires special effects, which in turn means high production values beyond their usual budgets. In sum, all of Del Toro's films, which we will now consider individually, touch on the horror or fantasy genre.

II. HUMOUR, VISUAL PYROTECHNICS, AND MORALITY: FROM *YOUNG AND INNOCENT, THE TROUBLE WITH HARRY, THE BIRDS, SABOTEUR* AND *PSYCHO* TO *CRONOS*

Over eight years Del Toro poured everything he had learned into his first feature film *Cronos*. The result was a thoughtful, not particularly gory, vampire tale with visually rich and complex sets. When it was made, its $2 million budget ranked it as the second-most expensive Mexican film ever made, after *Como agua para chocolate* (*Like Water for Chocolate*, 1992). Although *Like Water for Chocolate* broke new ground internationally, Mexican cinema had a long track record with period costume dramas. Audiences connected easily with their melodramatic strains reminiscent of Mexican *telenovelas* or soap operas. Yet *Cronos* represented different generic conventions and technical aspirations altogether. It was quite a surprise that *Cronos* became a huge critical success, winning the 1993 Critic's Prize in Cannes and nine Ariel awards, the Mexican equivalent of the Academy Awards, including those for best picture and best director. Just like Hitchcock, who was known, and often derided throughout his career, for his commercial aspirations, Del Toro aimed to make a commercial film viable in a global market beyond Mexico. To increase the film's viability, he targeted different markets with specific language versions: one, an unsubtitled, bilingual version of Spanish with some English, primarily in the dialogue of the American actor Ron Perlman, for most markets; two, a version of Spanish with English subtitles for the world art-house market; and three, a dubbed, Spanish-only version for the US Latino market. Del Toro was so committed to this experiment he did some of the dubbing voices himself.[7]

Cronos begins with a voiceover narration telling how in 1535 an alchemist makes the Cronos device, a special golden timepiece in the form of an egg-shaped mechanical insect for a Mexican viceroy. Four hundred years later the same alchemist, who has survived as a vampire, is found dead in the wreck of a bank building. A beam from the building's collapse has stabbed him through the heart. Fastforwarding to modern-day Mexico, Jesus Gris (Federico Luppi), an Argentine antiques dealer, discovers the magic device in an angel statue he buys. Playing with it like a toy in front of his granddaughter Aurora (Tamara Shanath), he sets the ancient mechanism in motion. When it pierces him, he turns into a vampire. In the meantime Dieter de la Guardia (Claudio Brook), a dying industrialist, relentlessly quests for this same Cronos device, which he knows to be a source of eternal life. De la Guardia lives over his factory in an apartment full of religious relics, books on alchemy and preserved organs. He orders his goon-like nephew Angel (Ron Perlman) to wrest the time machine away from Gris. Like De la Guardia, Gris himself begins to understand the powers of the device. Rejuvenated by periodic fixes or piercings, he now begins to crave human blood and follows a man with a nosebleed at a New Year's party into the men's room. There the nephew Angel kidnaps Gris. He later pushes him over a cliff in a car. After a funeral Gris rises from the dead. Only the granddaughter Aurora understands what has happened and hides him in her toy chest. She accompanies Gris to a showdown with De la Guardia at his factory. She kills the old man. Angel and Gris struggle and fall to their deaths. Instead of seeking rebirth this time, Gris destroys the device by smashing it with a rock. His wife and Aurora mourn his subsequent death, but human order, embodied and portrayed by this nuclear family, has been restored.

Cronos alludes to such a wide range of international cinematic classics, beginning with the threatening machinery of Fritz Lang's *Metropolis,* which morphs into the machinery inside the Cronos device, that it is hard to isolate only Hitchcock's presence in the film. In fact, Victor Erice's *The Spirit of the Beehive* is more of a consistent backdrop than any other one film. *Cronos*'s opening repeats the Rembrandt colouration and lighting of *The Spirit of the Beehive.* In both films a little girl befriends a 'monster'. In the latter he is an escaped soldier to whom she unwittingly gives her father's musical watch. Her father is a beekeeper. The Cronos device combines these motifs of watch and insect hive. However, both Erice and Del Toro appear to have looked back to Hitchcock for inspiration in terms of the role of nature. Interestingly, Del Toro refers to Erice several times in his book on Hitchcock, most consistently when he discusses the meaning of *The Birds.* He writes: 'For Victor Erice, the presence of "a series of obsessions deriving from the notable Catholic education" of Hitchcock becomes evident in the film, and suggests the intervention of chaos can have a divine origin' (1990: 431–2). Erice reads Hitchcock's *The Birds* in terms of a markedly Catholic allegory. This allegorical approach manifests itself in the many layers to the structure of *The Spirit of the Beehive,* which *Cronos* repeats. *The Spirit of the Beehive*'s indirect metaphorical language, linking Franco and Frankenstein, allowed it to critique patriarchal society and avoid censorship. In *Cronos* capitalism, as symbolised by the industrialist de la Guardia, receives the brunt of the critique.

As Erice engages the imagination of the child Ana (Ana Torrent) in *The Spirit of the Beehive,* a child obsessed by seeing the film *Frankenstein,* Del Toro enters completely into a child's fantasy in *Cronos* through the relationship between grandfather and grandchild. The desire to do so appears autobiographical. In the director's commentary to the tenth anniversary DVD edition of *Cronos,* Del Toro says that his film is an *homage* to his childhood relationship with his own grandmother Josefina Canbreros who died a year before the film was finished.[8] Her portrait appears on the bedroom wall in the final death scene of the movie.

Hitchcock did significantly incorporate children in dangerous situations into some of his films. In both versions of *The Man Who Knew Too Much,* a child is kidnapped. The schoolhouse and the children's party scenes are key locations for terror in *The Birds.* In *Sabotage* the young boy Stevie unwittingly carries a bomb in a film canister that explodes and kills him. Yet Hitchcock's films rarely acknowledge the child's point of view to the extent that *Cronos,* or even more so *The Spirit of the Beehive,* do. In a notable exception, the child's point of view allowed for the frame structure of Hitchcock's *The Trouble with Harry.* In this film the child Archie, while roaming the fields with his toy gun, discovers the dead body in question at the beginning and end of the film. In

contrast Del Toro's *Cronos* genuinely accedes to the pleasures of child play at
key junctures. Yet when casting children, Del Toro's point of view in *Cronos*,
as was Hitchcock's in most of his films, remains that of a sympathetic adult,
rather than that of the child herself, as in Erice's *The Spirit of the Beehive*.
When Hitchcock cast his own daughter Pat as a young daughter of a senator in
Strangers on a Train, for example, she entered into an adult world of cocktail
parties and acted as an adult. She prepared and served the drinks while making
witty small talk.

Hitchcock is most present throughout *Cronos* in the film's use of leavening
humour. Two deliciously funny sequences of the mortician working to the beat
of ranchero music illustrate the film's pacing with comedy. Tito the mortician,
moreover, serves as a Del Toro alter-ego since he is an under-appreciated macho
Mexican make-up artist, doing his best work on a body he finds out later will
be cremated. The first sequence begins with an insert shot of a lacy pincushion,
a feminine detail associated with women sewing. The camera gradually pulls
back to show the grimy mortician sewing together the now vampiric Jesús Gris's
face and jaw, as a foppishly dressed man looks on. The visual joke is gender-

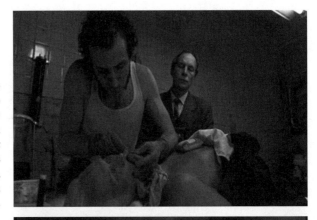

To the sound of ranchero
music in *Cronos*, Tito
(Daniel Jiménez Cacho)
the macho Mexican
mortician does his best
work sewing up Jesús
Gris (Frederico Luppi),
now a vampire, while a
foppish man looks on.

An incongruous display
is good for a laugh: A
bourgeois salesman,
who the fugitive Richard
Hannay meets on the
train, holds up a girdle in
The Thirty-Nine Steps.

based, like that of the salesmen of lady's under garments the fugitive Richard Hannay meets on the train in *The Thirty-Nine Steps*. In *The Thirty-Nine Steps* we first see the girdle held up, then the camera pulls back to show the two bourgeois salesmen in suits who are responsible for this incongruous display. The film cuts to a view of another fellow traveller, a priest overwhelmed with righteous disapproval and forcing himself to keep reading his newspaper. In this mortician sequence, as in sequence of *The Thirty-Nine Steps*, we find 'la risa por contraste', or humour through contrast (1990: 345), which Del Toro also praises when he analyses *The Trouble with Harry*. Del Toro defines it as when 'generally, the everyday, impassive *gentleman* of five o'clock tea comes face to face with an absurd and chaotic scene' (ibid.).

In the second sequence that illustrates *Cronos*'s Hitchcockian pacing, the mortuary worker tries to start the crematorium fire. The situation recalls the kitchen scene of *Torn Curtain* when Paul Newman and the spy *Frau* struggle to kill off the bad guy, finally holding his head long enough in the gas oven. Similarly, getting a gas crematorium fire going to incinerate the vampire's body is no easy task. It just will not light. The mortician has to go down into the cellar to check the gas line. In his absence Gris gets out of the coffin and leaves. The viewer not only appreciates the difficulty of a workman's task, as in the prolonged killing in a gas oven in *Torn Curtain*, but also shares a privileged point of view unknown to the film's characters. The viewer roots for the vampire's escape when the worker is away fixing the leaky gas line. The sequence ends as the mortician successfully incinerates an empty coffin. Ironically, his meticulous make-up job does not go up in smoke, but the vampire Gris removes his own stitches in the next scene.

Likewise the creation of suspense through the insertion of humour is evident in the men's room sequence at the New Year's Eve party. The idea of a holiday party with dancing, to contrast with the vampiric condition of the protagonist, itself appears inspired by Hitchcock's narrative stock in trade. Writing on Hitchcock's *Young and Innocent*, another British period film, Del Toro observes the prevalence of the party motif:

> The scene of the children's party and the already mentioned 'long takes' of the end are the first signs of a dramatic situation that will be repeated many times in Hitchcock's work: the use of a party, of music and dance (generally associated with the joy of living), in contrast to a terrible situation for the characters or a place appropriate for death and corruption. This association, which had been already outlined in *Secret Agent*, will be repeated in *Rebecca, Suspicion, Shadow of a Doubt, Notorious, Rope, Strangers on a Train, The Birds* and *Marnie*. (1990: 172)

In a low-angle shot
in *Cronos* Jesús Gris
(Frederico Luppi) as a
vampire, licks blood off
of the men's room floor
as a man with highly
polished shoes walks in.

In *Cronos* the viewer almost expects Del Toro himself to come out of one of the toilet cubicles, as in a Hitchcock cameo. Instead a husky Mexican man, who actually bears some physical resemblance to Del Toro, does. The clearest gesture to Hitchcock is how the sequence ends, however, with a low-angle shot of Gris licking blood on the men's room floor, as a highly polished pair of men's shoes walks by. This close-up recalls the characterisation through close-ups of shoes that opens *Strangers on a Train*.

Finally the climatic rooftop sequence with the illuminated company logo sign owes much to Hitchcock's innovative set creations and camera techniques. The showdown scene on high is a staple of Hitchcock thrillers, spanning from *Blackmail* (on the face of a huge statue) and *Saboteur* (on the Statue of Liberty), to *North by Northwest* (on Mount Rushmore) and *Vertigo* (in the mission bell tower). Although there are other classic allusions at play here, such as the clock sequence in Chaplin's *Modern Times* (1936), which point to a critique of capitalism implicit in a death scene on an advertising sign, it is instructive to consider what Del Toro himself comments about how critics have interpreted these Hitchcock sets. Writing on the section on *Blackmail,* Del Toro cites both Spoto and Leff, noting that in the giant monument chase sequences in *Saboteur* and *North by Northwest* 'the clearest intention is to show monuments erected to honour humanity, which remain indifferent to the human dramas that take place in front of them' (1990: 108). The giant illuminated sign 'De la Guardia' signifies honour only in a virtual, postmodern sense. Although the company is ironically called after a guardian angel, it is indeed indifferent to the human struggle, or morality play that is unfolding on it. The fall of the two characters, Angel and Jesús Gris, from the sign platform and through the roof of the factory recalls the sophisticated set and camerawork that Hitchcock created for *Saboteur*'s Statue of Liberty sequence. To recall, Hitchcock had a huge model of the Statue's hand made for the studio. The saboteur is forced to the edge of

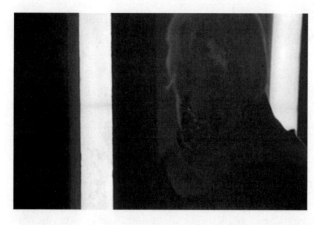

In the climactic scene from on high in *Cronos* the grandfather Jesús Luppi looks towards his granddaughter to make his enemy do the same.

the statue. He slips off but the hero catches his sleeve, which gradually tears away. Insert shots of the ripping create tension. The fall, which was done with a hydraulic seat for the actor that moved away from the camera, was an example of Hitchcock's 'pirotécnica' or pyrotechnics, as Del Toro calls these innovations. Interestingly Del Toro 'corrects' what Hitchcock told Truffaut he saw as a possible defect in that scene, namely that the bad guy falls, not the hero, thus allowing for less identification and hence suspense (Truffaut 1984: 147). In *Cronos*, both hero and bad guy take the plunge.

Yet the major difference in the suspense is how the presence of the child Aurora drives the sequence in *Cronos*. Every glance down in her direction by the two male actors signals cuts in the montage. Hitchcock employed this technique consistently. Telling actors where to look not only was a major element of his directing style, but it famously became an enormous bone of contention with method actors, such as Montgomery Clift or Paul Newman. On the set of *I Confess*, Hitchcock once told Clift to look up, and Clift, searching for his motivation, immediately asked why. Hitchcock responded with irritation 'because if you don't I won't be able to make my cut' (McGilligan 2003: 461). In *Cronos* ultimately, Gris's look toward his granddaughter makes Angel look down as well. This forced distraction allows Gris the opportunity to jump him. They plummet through the air together and break through the glass roof of the factory. Although Del Toro did not design new hydraulic equipment as Hitchcock did for *Saboteur*, the breaking roof in *Cronos* represented an expensive special effect for a Mexican film of its time.

Among directors of Del Toro's generation, *Psycho*, 'the most overly familiar motion picture in history' (McGilligan 2003: 578), is the Hitchcock film with most universal appeal and influence. *Cronos* is no exception to *Psycho*'s pattern of influence. *Psycho* is embedded specifically in *Cronos* in its score, which like Herrmann's creates tension through the use of violins, and in subtle visual allusions to *Psycho*'s climactic sequence. To recall, when Lila (Vera Miles) discovers Mother's corpse in the Bates' house basement, the psychopathic son Norman attacks her dressed as Mother. Shown in an early sequence in Gris's shop, the head of the antique statue that contains the Cronos device resembles the mummified Mother who spins around in *Psycho* both in colouration and physical structure. In *Cronos*, the insects, which attract Gris to probe the statue and eventually find the Cronos device, come crawling out of the deep-set eye socket of the carved statue. The sunken eye sockets are what give Mother her fright power in *Psycho*.

One of the most distinctive elements of the *Psycho* basement sequence is the effect achieved with a bare hanging light bulb. Coming into the basement, Lila hits it and sets it swinging. The camera stays on the bulb through its oscillations, which add to the sense of Lila's disorientation and unease in the situation. Hitchcock insisted on getting a lens flare from the light. The cameraman went through many takes to achieve the flare, which under normal circumstances is generally considered a defective shot. In *Cronos* Del Toro does not go so far as to use the lens flare effect. However, a swinging bare light bulb figures prominently in the aftermath of the climactic fall sequence and adds to the set's creepiness. After a black fade, a high-angle shot reveals the broken bodies of Gris and Angel as a single light bulb swings in and out of the frame. A bell-like sound in the score accompanies the motion and tolls for death. The film then cuts to a low-angle shot that shows Aurora, who is symbolically the light herself, approaching her grandfather's body. Whereas the swinging light bulb disorients Lila in *Psycho*, the same death image in *Cronos* does not deter Aurora. She resuscitates her grandfather with the Cronos device she carries hidden in her teddy bear.

Mainstream US critics such as Roger Ebert, who gave *Cronos* a 'thumbs up', did not note the presence of *Psycho*, or any other Hitchcock film in *Cronos*, as they did later in the case of *The Devil's Backbone*. Rather, Ebert finds *Cronos* distinctive as a horror film for its religiosity, which he attributes to a Latin culture:

In *Psycho* when Lila (Vera Miles) comes into the basement to meet Mother, she hits the light bulb and sets it swinging.

Recalling *Psycho*: in the aftermath of the fall of Angel and Jesús through the glass ceiling into the basement a single light bulb swings in *Cronos*.

What Latin horror films also have is a undercurrent of religiosity: The characters, fully convinced there is a hell, may have excellent reasons for not wanting to go there. The imagery is also enriched by an older, church-saturated culture, and for all its absurdity 'Cronos' generates a real moral conviction. If, as religion teaches us, the purpose of this world is to prepare for the next, then what greater punishment could there be, really, than to be stranded on the near shore? (http://www.rogerebert.com/reviews/cronos-1994)

What Ebert sees as 'Latin' is the Catholicism whose values Del Toro and Hitchcock shared. Del Toro argues that ethical and moral concerns were essential to Hitchcock's melodramas:

> Chabrol and Truffaut have adapted the rules of the master to their own filmic universes, comprehending that the basis of suspense (understood as the extreme interest of the viewer in a subject that is presented) is sustained with solid and interesting characters, even if they are everyday people, among whom a melodrama of genuine moral and ethical weight is generated, as it always occurs in Hitchcock. The creations of Richard Franklin, Brian de Palma and Spielberg lack this weight, in spite of their enviable use of narrative resources. (1990: 47)

For Del Toro, to create a successful film, and further, to stand above these major directors in the industry, solid characterisation must be accompanied by moral and ethical dilemmas. *Cronos* presents the moral dilemma of an ordinary man having to choose between living forever as a vampire or causing his own death. We relate to Gris as a caring grandfather and multifaceted underdog. He is savvy enough to take on and play a game with a master of the universe, the industrialist De la Guardia.

Aurora bludgeons the villain to death to save her grandfather in *Cronos*.

Donald Spoto argues that 'the added dimension of Hitchcock's best work – its moral as well as its aesthetic sense' can only be explained by referring to Hitchcock's 'training in Catholicism' (1994: 504). Spoto illuminates: 'Hitchcock's moral sense thus reveals the shallowness of ordinary judgment – for nice people do commit murder. In this regard, the Catholic sensibility triumphs. Everyone is capable of sin' (1994: 505). Although the granddaughter Aurora in *Cronos* is not the cultured villain like Uncle Charlie in *Shadow of a Doubt*, it does comes as a shock in *Cronos* when the final act of violence is committed, abruptly and straightforwardly, by a little girl in a cute red raincoat. She kills the industrialist with the man's club to save her grandfather. There is no sentimentality in this bludgeoning or in her role overall. All of the characters of *Cronos* are depicted as cultured and refined. Federico Luppi, who plays the protagonist/vampire/antiques dealer Gris, is known for an on-screen presence of dashing elegance. Even the supporting characters, such as the heavy/nephew (Ron Perlman) who is intent on choosing the right profile for his nose job, are striving to move up in the world through makeovers. Regarding the paradoxical role of aesthetics, Spoto is accurate to point again to Hitchcock's Catholicism: 'the director's Catholic roots and deep moral sense as an artist insisted that the split in style and act (elegance versus crime) was the clue to the fragility of the human condition' (ibid.). Del Toro not only understands this point of view, but also puts it on the screen in *Cronos*.

III. THE HOLLYWOOD GENIE OUT OF THE BOTTLE: FROM *THE BIRDS* TO *MIMIC*

After the international critical success of *Cronos*, Guillermo del Toro was offered contract work in Hollywood to direct scripts of film projects, especially horror films, already under way. He turned them all down, including the fourth installment of the *Alien* series.[9] Interestingly he did collaborate with John Sayles on the script for Sayles' Spanish-language film *Men with Guns* (1997). He also helped Sayles contact Federico Luppi to star in his film. In the meantime four of Del Toro's own treatments for science fiction films were rejected in Hollywood until his treatment of a story by Donald A. Wolheim about a mutant species that attacks humans was accepted. *Mimic* tells the story of Dr. Susan Tyler, played by Mira Sorvino. To halt the spread of a deadly disease, she genetically fashions a new species of insects out of cockroaches, beetles and flies. Although the creatures are supposed to be sterile, they reproduce and become monster bugs when she releases them into subterranean New York. Their scariest trait is that they mimic humans. An autistic child Chui (Alexander Goodwin), son of a shoemaker, in turn mimics their sounds on the spoons he plays with. As they are pursued through the subways, in the course of the film the bugs devour the boy's father, as well as many members of the NYC police. Finally Susan's husband Peter (Jeremy Northam) sets off an explosion that annihilates most of the insects. When the crucial male insect threatens the child Chui, Susan distracts the monster bug by cutting herself. The male bug is then run over by a train, which ends the insect plague. Susan, her husband and the orphaned Chui are reunited above ground in the film's final tableau.

As with *Cronos*, *Mimic* is about letting the insect genie out of the bottle. Ironically, these bugs became much more complex and more independent than Del Toro wanted. One has to remember that *Mimic* was given its go-ahead in the shadow of *Jurassic Park* (1993), which wowed audiences with its computer-generated/digital dinosaurs. Hollywood always wants to remake its last success. Although Del Toro himself had done the drawings for the mutant insects, the Hollywood production model metaphorically let them get away. The Spanish critic Quim Casas describes Del Toro's disappointment with his first foray into Hollywood as if Hollywood itself were *Mimic*'s underworld of giant insects:

> *Mimic* can be seen as a practical experience of apprenticeship in the twisting and slippery territories of Hollywood. Del Toro didn't like how the movie ended up, since his intention was to make a B movie with much simpler giant insects than the investors finally decided on. Since then he does not work with a designated second unit, thus taking charge of everything that is filmed in his movies. (2004: 50)

Nonetheless, Casas argues that Del Toro did still succeed with *Mimic* in making a B movie as he originally wanted:

> The B movie series is not only a particular aesthetic of cheap production, sets that stand out, bad actors, abbreviated narrative forms and imaginative

shots, but also a quality, a concrete manner of dealing with the cinemato-graphic story. In *Mimic* Del Toro is closer to it than to the Hollywood fan-tasy movie of high production values.

In contrast to his movies in Spanish and *Hellboy,* in *Mimic* the characters lack dramatic, or authentically coherent, hooks. They could be called mi-nor, in terms of how their basic characteristics are sketched out, compared even to that *Blade* that was about to enter into Del Toro's domain. In this manner the film also resembles certain B movies, although it isn't consistent in drawing the connection simply in one stroke. The protagonists of the film wander aimlessly under the asphalt, ambushing, attacking, defending themselves or surviving in the ventilation ducts, the sewers, the abandoned subway cars and the rust of the iron labyrinths that served to run the sub-way, but which now are the home of mutant insects. (2004: 52)

For Casas, minimal characterisation in *Mimic* – often the lack of 'agarraderas drámaticas' or dramatic hooks – distinguishes the film from Hollywood's grand productions. Since Casas points to characterisation as the critical element where Del Toro expresses an authorial perspective, that of a B film, in *Mimic*, it is worth exploring this aspect of the film in the context of Hitchcock.

Along with *Pan's Labyrinth, Mimic* is the only one of Del Toro's films with a female protagonist, although Marisa Paredes in *The Devil's Backbone,* and Leonor Varela in *Blade II,* come close in their supporting roles. Of all the casting choices for *Mimic,* US critics most faulted that of Mira Sorvino as Dr. Tyler. James Bernardinelli finds her 'miscast' compared to her previous roles, arguing that 'maybe the problem is that she's so good at playing bimbos (as in *Mighty Aprhrodite* and *Romy and Michelle's High School Reunion*) that it's hard to accept her as an egghead' (http://www.imdb.com/reviews/84/8497.html). He neglects to mention that Sorvino played Marilyn Monroe in *Norma Jean and Marilyn* (1996) the year before *Mimic*. All these 'bimbos', of course, are blondes. Is there a Hitchcock blonde here? In fact, yes. Sorvino's casting can be appreciated as an updating of Hitchcock's female icon. *Mimic*'s plot recalls *The Birds* in which Melanie Daniels (Tippi Hedren) is seen as responsible for unleashing a freak of nature, albeit above ground. Indeed, the culpability of Melanie in unleashing the plague of birds in Santa Rosa has long been one of the most debated aspects of *The Birds*. Her sexuality, symbolised by the lovebirds, which she secretly drops off at Mitch Brenner's ranch, is often portrayed as the catalyst for the avian plague. Although Janet Maslin (1997) in her *New York Times* review faults *Mimic* for general lack of motivation in characterisation, she is one of the few critics to note the irony of Dr. Tyler and her husband having trouble conceiving children while 'Susan's malevolent bugs spew fecund foam

Melanie Davis (Tippi Hedren) on her way across Bodega Bay to drop off a pair of lovebirds at Mitch Brenner's (Rod Taylor) ranch in *The Birds*.

beneath the Delancy Street subway station'. Dr. Tyler in *Mimic* is the sexually frustrated, and by extension, culpable catalyst of nature in *Mimic* as Melanie was in *The Birds*.

Not surprisingly, Del Toro is a big fan of *The Birds*:

> *The Birds* is Hitchcock's most spectacular movie, one of the most impressive technical and filmic exercises in all of film history and the perfect narrative and thematic continuation of the most *sophisticated* Hitchcock of *Psycho*.
>
> Within his 'catalysing' cycle, the film takes the obsession that Hitchcock felt for birds as 'heralds of chaos' (Spoto's words) to its perfect conclusion. They are used in a fitting manner that brings to bear upon human beings the ultimate and grandest evidence of their coexistence within chaos itself. (1990: 425–6)

As we have seen, *Cronos* alludes frequently to *Psycho*, hence *The Birds*, Hitch's next film, appears as a logical pattern to follow for *Mimic*. As Del Toro notes, Hitchcock settled on *The Birds* after the studios rejected three of his suggested projects, a situation similar to what happened to Del Toro's first four proposed treatments in Hollywood. Both films are essentially nature parables.

Yet it is in the treatment of the female role in particular that *Mimic* resembles *The Birds*. Scientific authority in a female voice was already envisioned in the role of the amateur ornithologist Mrs. Bundy (Ethel Griffies) in the diner sequence of *The Birds*. She carries the lengthy expository scene as she lectures on birds while others speculate on the reason for the bird attacks. In *Mimic* Dr. Tyler is a similar voice of authority in an early sequence in which she presents her Judas strain of insect in a press conference. Not surprisingly either, the feminist critic Camille Paglia in her BFI monograph on *The Birds* (1998) finds

Female voice of authority in *The Birds*: Mrs. Bundy the ornithologist (Ethel Griffies) lectures Melanie and the other diner patrons on birds.

the film's meaning in the role of woman's power in the 'nature parable'. This is evident in her reading of the film's publicity campaign:

> In a print ad, Hitchcock tried sexual innuendo: 'There's a terrifying menace lurking right underneath the surface shock and suspense of *The Birds*. When you discover it, your pleasure will be more than doubled.' It's the familiar Shakespearean paradox of shadow versus substance, but for Hitchcock the menace is archetypal woman, who is the mistress of surfaces." (1998: 88)

Paglia notes that Tippi Hedren as the protagonist Melanie Daniels was probably unjustly criticised in reviews of the time because in making her debut, Hedren represented a new sensibility in the line of Hitchcock blondes. This freshness is what comes across in the casting of Sorvino as Dr. Tyler in *Mimic*, too. Overall, Paglia views *The Birds* 'as a perverse ode to woman's sexual glamour, which Hitchcock shows in all its seductive phases, from brittle artifice to melting vulnerability' (1998: 7). *Mimic* is by no means about fur coats and nail polish – wardrobe elements that Paglia analyses. However, Eve's responsibility for chaos is critical to both films. *Mimic* makes this connection clear in an early scene at home between Dr. Tyler and her husband right after the viewer has just seen some of the first giant bugs. As her husband plays the piano, he tells her she is responsible for the insect plague: 'They were designed to die; they are breeding.' In *The Birds* when Melanie comes to dinner at Mitch's house, she sits down to play the piano. Shortly thereafter, birds invade the house by swarming down the chimney.

In reading the 'psychological dynamics of the finale' Paglia sides with Margaret M. Horwitz's view:

> Lydia certainly appears 'victorious' and that she and the birds have 'achieved dominance'. It's like the Pompeiian wall panels of the Villa of the Myster-

ies, where the exhausted, flagellated acolyte buries her face in the receptive maternal lap: rogue vixen Melanie has been whipped back to her biological place in the pecking order. Horwitz sees Melanie's eclipse in the film's treatment of her car: first, it gives her the 'power to come to Bodega Bay', then Mitch 'ends up driving it', and finally she's 'banished to the back seat' – becoming one of two children to Lydia as mother and Mitch as father (and Oedipal son). (1998: 86)

In *Mimic*'s finale, Dr. Tyler is similarly shunted aside by her husband. Crawling out of the crater of the explosion, in a last suspenseful revelation, he resurrects the family Trinity and reasserts a conventional dominance as he towers over Susan and Chui in their embrace. The blessing of the absent father, Chui's dead father, is silently given in the sign of the cross, the shoemaker's necklace draped over the new father's back.

Many other Hitchcockian motifs are prominent in the film. The child Chui always identifies beings, human or a mimicking insect, according to their shoes. The deadly male insect is 'Mr. Funny Shoes', for example. Chui's obsession with men's shoes, though logical for the son of a shoemaker, and a humorous touch, also alludes to the opening of *Strangers on a Train*, which characterises the main characters by close-ups of their shoes. The sinister, yet dapper protagonist Bruno will always be known for his 'funny' two-tone shoes. Other motifs from *Strangers on a Train* also find inventive new uses in *Mimic*. One of the famous shots of *Strangers on a Train* is of Miriam's glasses that fall and break when she is strangled by Bruno. In *Mimic*, the shoemaker's glasses fall off when he is devoured by a giant insect. As in *Strangers on a Train*, the glasses are all we see of the brutal killing of a major character. But in *Mimic*, Dr. Tyler's husband picks them up and later uses them to complete the electrical circuit in an abandoned subway car and to enable the trapped good guys to escape.

In *The Birds*' family scene finale, beaten down Melanie is put in her subservient place in the arms of mother Lydia (Jessica Tandy) in the back seat of the car.

In *Strangers on a Train* the shot from within a storm drain creates extra suspense as Bruno (Robert Walker) drops and tries to retrieve the incriminating lighter.

Finally, in *Mimic* we begin to see Del Toro imitating some of Hitchcock's classic techniques and motifs to create suspense.[10] This is especially prominent in scenes with lighters. The archetype is the sequence in which Bruno drops his purloined lighter down a street grate in *Strangers on a Train*. It falls further from his grasp as he tries to retrieve it. The viewer is dying with suspense as she watches Bruno's efforts from a shot from within the storm drain. In *Mimic*'s ending in subterranean New York, Peter opens a gas line and tries to get his lighter going to create an explosion, but the lighter – shall we say, predictably – falls out of his grasp. The film cuts to a shot showing the lighter from below, just as in Hitchcock. *Mimic*, however, adds extra suspense, for the lighter appears to fall through water, which we think will eliminate the possibility of a saving explosion. Hence, the big final blow-up comes as even more of a surprise.

In conclusion, interpreting *Mimic* in the context of Hitchcock's *The Birds* sheds light on the role of gender in the film, which critics have disparaged or simply overlooked in *Mimic,* as well as the importance of religion in the film. Del Toro's interpretation of *The Birds*, in which chaos is the sign of divine intervention, forefronts the shared Catholicism of the works of the two directors. This convergence is especially evident in the prominent place of Catholic religious symbols in *Mimic*'s finale. The dead shoemaker's cross necklace adorns the new family, survivors of the explosion, as a blessing from God. Also, we have seen how *Mimic* exploits and reintegrates in its own discourse of suspense significant Hitchcock leitmotifs, particularly of glasses and lighters from *Strangers on a Train*. Unquestionably, the presence of Hitchcock's work in the narrative and *mise-en-scène* of *Mimic* shows that it supported and enabled Del Toro's transition between his first Mexican and US films.

IV. FROM HITCHCOCK'S 'DUALITY FILMS' AND *PSYCHO*'S SWAMP TO *THE DEVIL'S BACKBONE*

After *Cronos* Guillermo del Toro wanted to make *The Devil's Backbone* in Mexico as his next project, but he found it difficult to get funding for the film, so went ahead with *Mimic*. In an interview with Gabriel Lerman in *Dirigido* after *Mimic*'s release in Spain, Del Toro discussed how the obstacles he was encountering to get *The Devil's Backbone* underway impacted his long-term career plans. To Lerman's suggestion about the difficulties of filming in Mexico, 'but perhaps it may be more difficult to continue filming in Mexico', Del Toro replied:

> I don't think so. My long-term plan is to be able to become sufficiently prestigious so that people recognise my name. Then I'll be able to make a movie in Mexico and nobody will care if I film it in Spanish or English ... When the time comes I'm sure that there'll be people who will put up the necessary funds. I don't want to make a $30 million movie in Mexico, I want to make a movie that lets me have the freedom that $2 million or $3 million gives. I want to have, whenever possible, total autonomy. (1997: 52)

When later Lerman asks why he wants to film in Mexico, Del Toro argues strongly for cultural specificity:

> Because the stories one tells have particular characters that belong to specific places. I know that I can't tell the story of *Mimic* in Mexico the same way that I tell it in the United States so that it has the same characteristics. There are things in *Mimic* that are simply North American and Anglo-Saxon. The traits of the characters from *The Devil's Backbone* are exclusively Mexican, and have a very Latin American magic about them. In this film that I'm about to shoot there's going to be a kind of festival of colours and sensations that I can only get in Mexico. (ibid.)

This Mexican folkloric festival, however, never happened. He never could get sufficient backing for the film in Mexico. Moreover in 1998 his father Federico del Toro, an automotive entrepreneur, was kidnapped and held for ransom in Guadalajara, a situation that was still not resolved when he and Bertha Navarro arranged to meet Pedro Almodóvar at the Guadalajara International Film Festival (see Cruz 2008: 49). Del Toro later negotiated his father's release, but he himself continued to receive death threats, which forced him into self-imposed exile, primarily in California, for the safety of his family. He stated that because some of the criminals responsible for his father's kidnapping were never caught, he could never film in Mexico again, only act as a producer of others' projects there.[11] For *The Devil's Backbone* he took up the co-production offer from Almodóvar's El Deseo company, whose terms meant filming in Spain with a Spanish crew. Respecting cultural specificities, he rewrote the script and transposed its original backdrop of the Mexican Revolution to the Spanish Civil War.[12]

Although this new alliance of Almodóvar/Del Toro was much commented on in the press of the time, their common admiration for, and mining of, Hitchcock's work went unnoticed. As this book demonstrates, there is a significant, defined class of Latin directors inspired by Hitchcock. The association with Almodóvar's production company, which produced films by Álex de la Iglesia, Daniel Capalsoro and Guillermo del Toro, also links a significant number of them.

The Devil's Backbone, which was released worldwide in 2001, is a ghost story. It tells the story of a boy Carlos (Fernando Tielve) who is left at an orphanage near Madrid supposedly to protect him from the Spanish Civil War. The orphanage is run by a pair of Republican sympathisers, Dr. Casares (Federico Luppi, again) and Carmen, the directress with a Buñuelian prosthetic leg, played by Marisa Paredes, known for her work in Almodóvar's *All About My Mother*. Jacinto, the young caretaker and Nationalist sympathiser, who is the heavy of the orphanage's staff, is played by the Spanish heartthrob Eduardo Noriega, known from Almenábar's *Open Your Eyes* and *Thesis*. Jacinto has sex with the directress in exchange for one of her keys with which to try to open the orphanage's safe. The safe contains some of the fabled Republican gold bars, which act as the film's 'Macguffin'. Dr. Casares has his own cache. He keeps foetuses with prominent spines pickled in huge glass jars. Drinking the liquid from the jars, as Casares does, fortifies the brave imbiber with the devil's backbone. Del Toro explains the title: 'Devil's backbone is essentially poverty and disease, something that destroys childhood' (DVD commentary).

By talking with the other boys and studying a book of drawings by one of them, the new boy Carlos gradually discovers that a young boy Santí (Junio Valverde), who died under mysterious circumstances, haunts the orphanage. When Carlos sneaks into the kitchen to get water one night, Santí scares him with his appearance. Jacinto later beats Carlos for the night-time intrusion. Jacinto, himself an orphan, is caught by the directress trying to steal the gold hidden in the orphanage's safe and is expelled from the orphanage. He sets the building on fire and flees in a truck with some of his buddies. The directors die as a result of the confrontation and Jacinto and his cronies set siege to the orphanage. The boys rally to defend it. In a tableau that echoes Mother in a chair in *Psycho*'s basement, they position the dead director's body with a gun in a visible window to scare off Jacinto and partners. Though finally abandoned by the other men, Jacinto takes possession of the gold and wears it around his belt. He and the boys confront each other near the cistern pool. Jacinto is wounded and falls into the pool. Refusing to let go of the gold, he is pulled under the water by Santí's ghost. With this vengeance behind them, the boys set out on the road away from the orphanage.

Of all of Del Toro's films, *The Devil's Backbone* is the one in which Hitchcock's motifs, desire for innovative pyrotechnics and narrative structure are most strongly apparent.[13] The film is an ode to Hitchcock. The evidence for this is clear and convincingly presented by Del Toro himself in his 'maiden voyage into DVD commentary', the voiceover track made in excellent conversational American English for its US release. Early on in the commentary Del Toro explains that he owes the narrative structure to Hitchcock's duality films:

> This is the movie I made I love. One of the reasons is because it was structured in a free environment. The movie is constructed like a rhyme, something I have been trying to do for many, many years. The movie opens and closes with similar images and a similar epilogue and prologue. In the movie we will be quoting many images in pairs. This comes from me watching and enjoying the duality films of Alfred Hitchcock, where in order to establish a certain rhythm in the poetry of a movie and a certain commentary in pairs, like *Shadow of a Doubt, Suspicion, Strangers on a Train*, where duality is important, he would repeat and quote himself, and quote situations. Like this image, for example, the kid kneeling or crouching by the water will be repeating much later with another character for the purpose of being resonant.

Indeed the basement scenes by the cistern pool, which begin and end *The Devil's Backbone*, function like *Psycho*'s swamp. To recall, the final image of *Psycho* is of Marion's car being pulled out of the pond.

Given that his director of photography Guillermo Navarrro accompanies Del Toro for the DVD commentary, many remarks concern the lighting and mood of the picture. Del Toro faced a challenge for *The Devil's Backbone* in central Spain near Madrid similar to that Hitchcock faced for *The Birds* in the bay area of northern California – how to deal with an area 'drenched in sun' to create a mood of horror. In choosing to introduce the ghost Santí in midday light in the courtyard door, Del Toro makes a gesture to Hitchcock's spirit of poetic, and finally technical innovation. In *The Birds* the first time a bird attacks Melanie she is out in a motorboat on the water in broad daylight.

The colour of the sky was subdued in the post-production lab to get the right effect (see Paglia 1998: 19). As Del Toro writes:

The ghost Santí appears in broad daylight in the courtyard doorway of the orphanage in *The Devil's Backbone*.

In *The Birds* the first bird attack is against Melanie as she crosses the sunny Bodega Bay.

Much has been said that it's in the horror genre where an artist free of the ties of 'the real' can create his purest reflection about the world, approaching what in literature is the equivalent of poetry. *The Birds* is the *only* horror film (in the most fantastic and purest sense of the term) that Hitchcock made. It's his film of the freest conceptual and artistic creation. (1990: 432–3)

Another example of the 'construction in pairs' is the repetition of a shadow on a curtain, done with digital effects as discussed in the DVD commentary. In noticing the shadow without an object to cast it, Carlos senses Santí's presence near his bed in the cavernous orphanage dormitory, first in an early sequence, which is later repeated. For Del Toro, these poetic images, *The Devil's Backbone*'s shadows, and those in *The Birds*, 'succinctly define what it means to be human'. In both films to be human means the ability to receive and interpret sensations. The frequent use of strong expressionistic shadows in *The Devil's Backbone* recalls moreover Hitchcock's Germanic tutelage so evident in his British period, which Del Toro both admires and defends.

Another one of Del Toro's Hitchcockian 'dualities,' which link formal and symbolic elements, concerns a camera movement associated with classic 1930s films. Moving between two rooms of a set, the camera shows the set wall in its transition, and thus violates the illusion of reality. (Almodóvar used this movement to great success in the bedroom scene of *What Have I Done to Deserve This?*) In *The Devil's Backbone* Dr. Casares declaims love poetry to his mirror on the wall in his room. The camera moves parallel to the set, showing the wall between his room and that of the directress. The wall symbolises his unrequited love for her. Reprising the motif of unrequited love, Casares will later recite Tennyson to her as she lies dying in the aftermath of the explosion. Yet in this initial scene with the wall, we move around the wall between their two rooms to an equally brutal scenario. We see Jacinto having violent sex with her to get a key to access the gold. Del Toro says: 'I wanted the key, being a fan of Hitchcock. I always loved the way he did the huge crane in *Notorious* with Ingrid Bergman with the key to the cellar.' While his comment about the key reaffirms the importance of Hitchcock to the interpretation of this sequence, the filmic transgression, of showing the artificiality, the theatricality of the set, is far more significant. Hitchcock, in showing, for example, an obviously fake set wall at the end of *Marnie,* for which even Almodóvar criticised him, pushed the boundaries of filmic discourse to their limits, made the spectator aware of them without losing her interest in the narrative. *The Devil's Backbone*, in the use of a retro camera movement, revels in the history of film, and especially in Hitchcock's place in it, and in the artificiality of the medium.

Subtle moodiness in *The Devil's Backbone* is achieved by expressionistic shadows and digital particles that signal the ghost's presence, but also through measured yet free-moving camerawork that allows for most information to be gradually transmitted visually to the spectator, rather than through dialogue. The camera functions as another witness. Like Hitchcock, Del Toro implicates the spectator. He shows us the elements for an explosion, to cause suspense, before the explosion occurs, as in the case of the gas cans in the orphanage, or in the case of the bomb in the courtyard, which never does explode. Another good example of this well-paced visual reveal is how the presence of Dr. Casares helping an injured boy is shown, even after Casares has died, and hence is another ghost. We only see Casares' handkerchief on the hall floor but know that he, and metaphorically, the good guys too, live on in good deeds. Likewise in Hitchcock's *Rope*, the hat of the murder victim left behind is discovered, and reveals the presence of the body in the apartment.

In his DVD commentary to the sequence in which huge crosses and paintings are hauled out and displayed in the orphanage, Del Toro is defensive about the interpretation of the presence of religious imagery in *The Devil's Backbone*:

Conchita (Irene Visedo) receives 'a grain of strength' vitamin from an orphan as if it were a communion wafer before she sets off to seek help in *The Devil's Backbone*.

> Most people think it is me and my Catholic obsessions. No, as the Fascists came back and wanted to reign in Spain, the Republicans put up religious imagery to say to leave them alone.

While the information is historically accurate, his choice of this material, as well as that of the teacher Conchita (Irene Visedo) giving daily vitamins to the orphans as if they were communion wafers saying 'un granito de fuerza', or 'a grain of strength', as she places them on their tongues, argue precisely for the perception of Del Toro as a director 'obsessed' with Catholicism. The importance of the vitamin communion is stressed by its being repeated, inverted, when an orphan gives her a vitamin before she sets off to seek help after the building has been torched. On the road Conchita encounters Jacinto who stabs her to death. Her death is hence framed as martyrdom. Del Toro and Hitchcock wove numerous Catholic motifs into their films with full understanding of the Catholic worldview. In *The Devil's Backbone* the jars of foetuses are a crucial image of visceral, political unease of our age. The Catholic Del Toro calculated their effect well.

The Devil's Backbone does not shy from the representation of violence, nor did *The Birds*, or *Frenzy*. Del Toro's 'walk out scene' merits discussion in the context of terror techniques. He calls the sequence in which Jacinto cuts Carlos's face as a punishment for trespassing in the kitchen 'a walk out' – that is, 'anybody who isn't with the movie is going to walk out' (DVD commentary, *The Devil's Backbone*). He is aware of transgressing a taboo, which is especially strong in Hollywood, to actually show violence against children. Analogously, a 'walk out scene' for Hitchcock would be the sordid strangling sequence of *Frenzy,* one of Del Toro's favourite Hitchcock pictures due to 'precisely the film's "bad taste"' (1990: 463).[14] As in the case of the directress's prolonged death later in *The Devil's Backbone*, Del Toro's half-in-jest remark applies here, too: 'As a

The 'walk out' moment
in *The Devil's Backbone*:
Jacinto cuts Carlos's
(Fernando Tielve)
face with a knife
as punishment for
trespassing into
the kitchen.

Catholic fat boy, I like the characters to suffer' (DVD commentary, *The Devil's Backbone*). The film represents Jacinto consistently throughout as someone who can only communicate through violence. Casting the 'teenage idol' Noriega against type as Jacinto – 'the equivalent of having Brad Pitt play a psychopath' – follows Hitchcock's effective lead of casting the handsome Anthony Perkins as Norman Bates in *Psycho*.

In conclusion, many other techniques and motifs associated with Hitchcock's suspense vocabulary, such as the reverse tracking/forward zoom *Vertigo* shot, the distinctive violin sounds of *Psycho*'s soundtrack, and the placing of the dead body of Dr. Casares in a chair for a scare like Mother's in *Psycho*, are also used in *The Devil's Backbone*. Yet what is most significant about the film is Del Toro's acknowledgment that he constructed it with Hitchcock's poetic 'rhythm' in mind. The sounds of that 'rhythm' are convincingly there in the film – in the digital innovations that indicate the ghost's presence, in the implication of the spectator through the camerawork, and in the suggestive symbolism, Catholic and otherwise, through the film.

V. A GLOBAL MIX OF LOVE AND ADVENTURE:
FROM *NORTH BY NORTHWEST* AND *ROPE* TO *BLADE II*

When the Spanish critic Antonio Santamarina reviewed *The Devil's Backbone* in *Dirigido*, he ended with a pessimistic forecast: 'Unfortunately the new scheduled stopover for Guillermo del Toro in Hollywood, for the filming of *Blade II*, doesn't promise great results' (2001: 24). Many people were indeed surprised that Del Toro took on the sequel to *Blade* (1998), based on the eponymous Marvel comic book hero, in which Wesley Snipes was set to reprise his starring role. Since critics worldwide had overwhelmingly panned director Stephen Norrington's work on *Blade,* it was not surprising Hollywood was looking to revive the property with a change in director. But given that Del Toro had complained of loss of creative control on *Mimic,* his last encounter with Hollywood, it would seem he had learned his lesson and would duck those swirling blades this time. The fact that David Goyer, scriptwriter on *Blade* and *The Crow* (1994) who would become director for the third installment *Blade: Trinity* (2004), was already contracted to write *Blade II* when Del Toro was approached also augured for significant limits being placed on Del Toro's creative input. The likelihood that *Blade II* would catapult Del Toro's name into positive blockbuster recognition was not great. What happened to that *auteur* talk he fed *Dirigido*'s Gabriel Lerman about *The Devil's Backbone* and his 'freedom'? Why take on *Blade II* then? Money must have spoken loudly. But his longtime attraction to comic book and fantasy art was also right up there. Finally, the character Blade, also called Daywalker because he is half-man, half-vampire, represented a return to the themes and genre tropes Del Toro had spent years mulling over for his debut vampire film *Cronos.*

Blade II introduces a new breed of vampires called the Reapers, who prey on both humans and vampires. In Prague a downtrodden man with a cleft chin, the sign of the Reapers, goes to give blood for money at a clinic, which recalls all fascist fantasies about dental torture. He, however, opens his jaws wider than any of them and devours his tormentors instead. Meanwhile, also in Prague, Blade (Wesley Snipes) tracks down his partner/father-figure Whistler (Kris Kristofferson), whom the old-style vampires captured and supposedly killed in *Blade.* He rescues Whistler from a huge tank of water that looks like a game show booth. Back at their home base, they are accosted by two vampire visitors with bug-like masks, Nyssa (Leonor Varela) and Asad (Danny John-Jules). These messengers from the vampire king Damaskinos (Thomas Kretschmann) seek to enlist Blade's help in combating the Reapers. Blade joins an alliance with their squad, called the Bloodpack, led by Rheinhardt (Ron Perlman). The Bloodpack enter the disco-like House of Pain where they engage the Reapers in a subterranean fight scene. Afterwards Nyssa performs a memorable autopsy on a twitching Reaper to show both how quickly they rejuvenate and where their only vulnerable point is. Many explosions and martial arts scenes reminiscent of *The Matrix* (1999) later, several major characters – Blade's new sidekick Scud (Norman Reedus), and Damaskinos's son (Luke Goss) – go over to the darker side of the Reapers. Nyssa and Blade are ever more attracted to each other, especially as she sees him saving her in battles. Damaskinos's son betrays and kills his father. Nyssa confronts her brother and is bitten by him as well. Then in an act of self-sacrifice she asks Blade to take her out into the light so she can die before she is transformed into a Reaper herself. Blade, or Daywalker, who himself has the special power to resist light, carries her in his arms toward the sunrise until she is vapourised by the dawn's rays.

When *Blade II* was released, Del Toro proved sceptics wrong. Most critics and audiences found that he had been up to the challenge. Even Mark Holcomb (2002) of the *Village Voice*, who found the film fell short of Del Toro's 'whip-smart revisionism of *Cronos*', joined others in making puns about 'breathing new life' into the Blade franchise. Pam Grady of Reel.com states the general opinion: '[*Blade II*] only means to entertain, and that it does' (22 March 2002). Del Toro finally succeeded in making his B movie in *Blade II* and it gave him the credentials to take on *Hellboy*.

There is little in Hitchcock's 53 films that come anywhere near the vampire genre or the comic book adaptations of *Blade II* and *Hellboy*. The legendary editing of the crop-duster chase scene in *North by Northwest*, as evidence of Hitchcock's skill with adventure tropes, or his pacing, and creation of suspense in the gas station explosion sequence of *The Birds*, can only go so far as a basis for comparison. Truly Del Toro's work, and Del Toro's Hollywood, is that of another generation, marked more by the technological revolutions of George Lucas's *Star Wars* series (1977–1983). Yet there are 'big picture' comparisons, especially lessons about auteurship and cinematic style, which derive implicitly from Del Toro's study of Hitchcock's career. Reviewing *Hellboy* in *Dirigido*, Quim Casas argues that Guillermo del Toro is unique among his generation of directors without borders in achieving a 'coherencia interna', or 'internal coherence', throughout his work in three major industries (2004: 46). 'Internal coherence' is in fact synonymous with auteurist cinematic vision, which definitely manifests itself in Del Toro's work. Looking at Del Toro's career chronologically then, the jump from *The Devil's Backbone* to *Blade II*, or the disjunction between these projects, from the small-budget Spanish/Mexican film to the Hollywood megabudget action flick, is where the concept of his auteurist vision is most directly challenged. Importantly, it is also where the notion of a new global auteur is reaffirmed. *Hellboy*, so close in genre to *Blade II*, can almost be seen as part of the Blade series.

The location of *Blade II* announces the global ambitions of the film. *Blade II* was set and partially filmed in Prague, something the critic John Berardinelli found strange.[15] How strange not to recognise it as near the homeland of Dracula, and if we are talking contemporary global politics, also as one of the vibrant cultures of the new Europe? It is significant that Del Toro sets the House of Pain, *Blade II*'s party scene, in Prague. As we noted with respect to *Cronos*, the presence of a party scene, to establish the parameters of good and evil and create a sense of foreboding, was a Hitchcock narrative staple. Moreover, the club party scene that opens the first *Blade* was its most memorable, and for some, its only acclaimed sequence. In the vampire club/American slaughterhouse, blood sprays out of the sprinkler system as the dance music peaks. *Blade II* repeats the vampire party *topos* in an urban European environment. The House of Pain sequence begins with a joke about exclusivity. Blade cannot see the vampires, or find the nightclub on the city street until Nyssa hands him special glasses that make vampire markings, or graffiti, visible.

The film's global pretensions are also apparent in its language mix. It has snippets of subtitled dialogue when some vampires speak, presumably in Czech, and also in Russian. American English dominates the picture, as it does the current world. To recall, Del Toro tried mixing languages to enhance characterisation in *Cronos*.[16] He now carried these ideas forth to Hollywood's *Blade II*.

Despite an immense difference in pacing or overall rhythm between the languorous *The Devil's Backbone* and the video-game zapping of *Blade II*, the visual conceptions of these apparently disparate films have much in common. Moreover, the visual concept of *Blade II* departed radically from Norrington's *Blade*, in a manner particularly consistent with Del Toro's Catholic background, a trait, to repeat, he shares with Hitchcock. The initial film imagined the character Blade in Egyptian or biblical settings. For example, in a climactic sequence when the vampires drain Blade's blood, they half entomb him standing up as if he were King Tut on display in a museum. Del Toro's fantasies *in Blade II*, on the other hand, look Roman, if not Roman Catholic. Recalling *The Devil's Backbone*'s orphanage basement, numerous sequences of *Blade II* are set in underground catacombs, such as the rotunda of the purebred vampires. On the DVD commentary track to *Blade II*, Del Toro calls Damaskinos' chamber a 'Roman Age ruin'. Elgin marble-like carvings serve as backdrops to his indoor pool of blood, which recalls *The Devil's Backbone*'s cistern. Furthering the sense of mystery, as did the cavernous orphanage dormitory in *The Devil's Backbone*, most of the large sets of *Blade II* resemble church interiors replete with high-placed coloured windows. When Blade prowls and engages in a fight on scaffolding which bisects the interior of a church, the very scale of the space

The Elgin marble-like carvings, as in a 'Roman Age ruin,' serve as backdrop to Damaskinos's (Thomas Kretschmann) indoor pool of blood in *Blade II*.

Blade (Wesley Snipes) prowls over the scaffolding that bisects the interior of a church in *Blade II*.

questions Blade's vulnerability, just as in *The Devil's Backbone* it defined Carlos as an orphan and challenged his will to explore.[17] The visual consistency, of depicting monumental, symbolic spaces, with religious overtones, is a consistent component of Del Toro's auteurist vision. Giving it his usual mark of authenticity for the movie's freely conceived *mise-en-scène*, the *Blade II* sequence was filmed in an actual church in Los Angeles.

Yet, like Hitchcock's films, *Blade II* works not just because of the monumentality of the sets, but because viewers can understand and care about the film's story through a savvy handling of adventure and melodrama. The moviegoing experience is about the gore and the cool *vagina dentata*-style innards of the new breed vampires, but *Blade II* works because it is balanced by small sequences that involve the spectator in identification. For example, the film crosscuts between confrontations of vampire bands in the catacombs, resembling war platoons in action, to shots of the geek Scud (Norman Reedus) in his surveillance van outside. We are that guy with the box of doughnuts looking in on the wars and fighting private fears of the invading vampires. Taking Scud's almost safe position acknowledges that the viewer is conscious of, if not in control of the technology. Furthermore, the presence of the intimate closed space helps the viewer connect to the epic scenes. The interplay is made even more memorable by Blade's unmasking of Scud later in the film as himself both vampire and mole. Del Toro pulls us into caring again through an interplay of scale and a wink to his auteurist vision, which he laid out in *Cronos*. Ron Perlman, the goon-like nephew in *Cronos*, plays Reinhardt, a vampire ringleader in *Blade II*. In an early sequence Blade implants a small detonator, a Cronos-like pronged device, on the back of Reinhardt's head to control and threaten him. In the revelation sequence, Reinhardt flings the device off, calling it, and thereby Blade's powers, fakes. When Reinhardt tosses the device, Scud catches it in his hand. Taunting Blade even more fiercely than Reinhardt did, Scud reveals he is a mole

In his almost safe spectator's position the geek Scud (Norman Reedus) eats his doughnuts in a surveillance van in *Blade II.*

and traitor. The device digs into Scud's hand, *à la* Cronos device. Reasserting his power for good, Blade activates the device and blows Scud to bits.

Blade II has plenty of blood and guts and big explosions, but its pacing, of big explosions, then intimate scenes, and its narrative structure, recall lessons learned from Hitchcock especially regarding the importance of love interests to adventure films. Del Toro discusses criticism of *North by Northwest*:

> Spoto affirms and clearly demonstrates that one of the most important ideas of the film is Roger Thornhill's acquisition of an independent identity and his finding love. He even connects the reason for his journey to these two ideas. Although the quest for identity as well as the contrast between appearance and reality are fundamental ideas in the film, I think Robin Wood gets closer to the truth. He notes that what essentially ties together the journey and the obtainment of love, on Roger's part, is the transformation that responsibility brings about in him. Responsibility is the external dramatic drive, what permits one situation to evolve from another, just as love is what moves the characters. (1990: 394)

In *Blade II* Del Toro develops a significant love interest between the main characters Blade and the pure vampire Nyssa. It drives the narrative as Thornhill's did in *North by Northwest*. *Blade II* has a glamourous, sexy look, never more so than in how Del Toro establishes the chemistry between Blade and Nyssa. Their relationship plays out the classic conflict of love versus duty that Del Toro discusses when he analyses Hitchcock's *Notorious,* too. Somehow, although Nyssa is pure vampire, she does not crave blood as regularly as Blade does. She happens on Blade sitting alone in a room self-injecting a huge vial of blood into a vein in his arm, in a clear analogy for drug addiction. The film cuts to a shot of her in leaving the room. Through the half-open doorway she expresses her

Duty and love: through a half-open doorway Nyssa (Leonor Varela) looks back on Blade's need for a fix with superiority in *Blade II*.

The *Pietà* finale of *Blade II*: Nyssa chooses to die in the light in Blade's arms.

superiority, her self-sufficiency, and notes Blade's weakness for needing his fix. Elegant yet sparse sequences, such as this one, and the film's *Pietà* dénouement, in which Nyssa chooses to die by sunrise in Blade's arms rather than let the infected vampire blood change her into a lowly predator, not only balance the film's substantial martial arts sequences, but above all, inject issues of motivation and morality into the narrative arc.

All vampire movies are about blood as a marker for sex and race. With Blade, the black superhero, Del Toro stepped into a tale of black and white race relations, which as he had noted, speaking of *Mimic*, characterise America. Blade dresses as a Goth in his distinctive long leather coat. As a Goth, he appeals to a specific subculture, marked by aesthetics and especially music that is more often associated with white ethnicity, all the while being a fantasy version of blaxploitation heroes like Shaft.[18] Del Toro's solutions for *Blade II*, nonetheless, are not fixated on US racial tensions. They are as globally mixed or internationalist as were Hitchcock's spy pictures *North by Northwest* and *Notorious*, called in Spanish *Intriga internacional*, for his time. The casting of Leonor Varela as Blade's love interest in particular emphasises how the film represents a new multiethnic Hollywood, as detailed in Mary Beltrán's (2005) article, 'The New Hollywood Racelessness: Only the Fast, Furious (and Multiracial) Will Survive'. Educated in Paris at the Ecole du Passage and the Conservatoire Superieur de Paris, Varela is the daughter of a French mother and a famous Chilean biologist and philosopher father. The family escaped Pinochet's dictatorship to Costa Rica. Varela, who played Cleopatra in the 1999 US TV series of the same name, is not identified in any dialogue as Latina in *Blade II*. However, her brown hair and light bronze skin tone stands out from the white phalanx of male members of her 'pure' vampire family. Beltrán argues that the trend to a multiethnic Hollywood 'reflects contemporary shifts in U.S. ethnic demographics and ethnic identity, while subtly reinforcing notions of white centrism that are the legacy of the urban action movie' (2005: 50). Nyssa/Varela represents this new multiethnic Hollywood, as ethnically, if not racially ambiguous. However, if perceived as Latina in the US market, her messianic, heroine status, underscored in the death tableau, suggests that *Blade II* speaks to these shifts in US demographics. Her virtual martyrdom, a digitalised vapourisation as the sun strikes the female vampire's body, symbolically defuses the Latino threat to black or white audiences. Finally, it is important to note, whether Nyssa is seen as Latina or not, her blurred ethnicity speaks not just to a domestic market, but travels well internationally as a positive marker for multiethnicity in other cultures as well.

The casting of the Spanish comic actor Santiago Segura as a vampire in *Blade II* also shows how Del Toro's instalment appeals to a wider, more Latin global audience than the other films in the trilogy. Segura wrote, directed and starred in the incredibly popular *Torrente* series films about a fat, politically incorrect cop.[19] The heroic Blade and the corrupt Torrente are polar opposites. In an early sequence of *Blade II,* Segura's character is tortured by having his head held to the wheel of a motorcycle. Sporting his trademark long stringy hair and an incongruous red boa, a sign of sexual ambiguity, he returns in the film's coda to confront Blade again, this time in a convenience store. Blade sighs and rams his blade through the vampire Segura again to end the film. Del Toro points out in his DVD commentary that Spanish audiences not only recognise Segura but also react differently to *Blade II* because of his presence. Overall, Del Toro's *Blade II* lightens up Wesley Snipes' angst-driven, slightly wooden demeanour as Blade. Segura's role, and in particular the insertion of a comic coda to the film after Nyssa's death scene, is one of several examples in *Blade II* of how Del Toro incorporates humour as a foil for dramatic tension. It recalls Hitchcock's humorous coda to *Strangers on a Train*. After Bruno dies under the carousel, Guy (Farley Granger), now cleared of his wife's murder, gets on a train again, this time with his fiancée Ann (Ruth Roman). When a priest (Dick Ryan) in the carriage tries to strike up a conversation, as Bruno did in the beginning, Guy and Ann silently exchange glances and get up and move away from him. Del Toro enjoys literally winking at the audience in good humour to release tensions, as did Hitchcock in *Strangers on a Train*.

In a particularly graphic sequence about half way through *Blade II*, after Blade decapitates the Devil Priest, the eye in the half of the head that is left on the floor blinks. On the DVD commentary Del Toro explains that the film's Hollywood studio backers were not only disturbed by the violence of this close-up, but were unconvinced by Del Toro's argument that 'the audience is going to laugh'. Test screenings showed they did, and the sequence stayed as filmed. Del Toro had pushed boundaries of censorship with the studio much like Hitchcock did with the Production Code officials on the *Psycho* shower sequence.[20]

Del Toro finally enjoyed more freedom to realise his creative vision on *Blade II* than he had with *Mimic*. Two major changes put him more in control: one, filming mostly in Prague, away from the Hollywood studio's direct scrutiny, but within the $54 million budget, and two, contractually requiring that no work be done by second units, over whose work he lost the power to oversee on *Mimic*. Perhaps no visual effect is more symbolic of Del Toro's newfound freedom in *Blade II* than his homage to Hitchcock's experimentation in *Rope*. Del Toro sought a new way to film the conventions of the action genre film, one of which is the suiting up of the heroes for battle, and chose shiny black, *animé*-style costumes. On the DVD commentary, when Del Toro tells how he plotted this sequence by storyboard, a Hitchcock trademark, the producer rejoins 'this is called a shot list' as if reminding him what to do in Hollywood. The producer adds, with exasperation, that Del Toro insisted on getting his cuts, especially off the black backs of these costumes, to wipe into the next shot. Famously Hitchcock filmed uninterrupted ten-minute shots and disguised the changing of reels in *Rope* by directing the camera at an actor's dark-suited back. It was his manifesto of freedom from the studio's control. Del Toro concludes his chapter on *Rope* discussing the critical reactions to this technique. Not surprisingly, he sides with *Rope*'s enthusiasts:

> Rohmer and Chabrol object to Bazin's contempt for the film and point out that the director's interest wasn't in breaking with cinematographic language, but in 'being able to express himself in the same way he already had and as he would do in the future.' They conclude enthusiastically that 'Hitchcock possesses the unique art of being able to keep observing his model with the meticulous eye of a painter without letting that affect his narrative tempo. He can magically transmute onto the rich canvas that which originally seemed to be the inarticulate and arbitrary frame for one of his most highly planned works.' (1990: 286)

Del Toro is not so crazy as to consider using ten-minute shots nowadays. However, he still references Hitchcock in the context of his own inventions.

In *Blade II*, as Hitchcock repeatedly did throughout his career, Del Toro evokes motifs from his previous films. For instance, Damaskinos in *Blade II* has a huge eugenics chamber, with jars of foetuses floating in liquid, as Mr. de la Guardia had jars of body parts in *Cronos*, and Dr. Casares had jars of foetuses in *The Devil's Backbone*. We have already discussed the reappearance of the Cronos device in *Blade II*, and the repetition of subterranean pools. Certain camera movements, such as showing the edge of a set in *The Devil's Backbone* and in *Blade II* between subterranean levels, as well as specific digital effects, such as floating particles in *The Devil's Backbone* and scattered light flares in *Blade II*, have also become Del Toro signatures. This cannibalisation of his own work is one more sign of the realisation of Del Toro's auteurist vision in *Blade II*.

VI. HITCHCOCK'S LEGACY OF ARTISTIC SENSIBILITY: FROM *STRANGERS ON A TRAIN* AND *FOREIGN CORRESPONDENT* TO *HELLBOY*

Del Toro's commercial success with *Blade II* gave him the profile in Hollywood to be able to make *Hellboy,* another action-adventure picture, and to push for casting Ron Perlman, his favourite actor, in the main role. Briefly *Hellboy* tells the story of how a huge red monster with a tail, sawn-off horns and a giant hand is found as a youngster by American troops in Nazi Germany in the midst of a satanic ceremony. Kept as a secret weapon and assigned a boyish bodyguard, Mike Meyers (Rupert Evans), Hellboy goes on periodic missions to save the US from mostly large mollusk-like monsters that he blows up. The distinctly working-class Hellboy with a fondness for cigars and six-packs would rather not be a monster, but Rasputin and cohorts pursue him to make him acknowledge his satanic powers. Hellboy tries to romance Liz (Selma Blair), an attractive Goth psychic confined to a mental institution, whom Meyers also courts. Liz is captured and her breath taken from her. Hellboy defeats the forces of evil in battle, kisses Liz and brings her back from death. Meyer in voiceover intones the film's moral: 'What makes a man a man: the choices he makes and how he decides to end the game.'

By the time Del Toro made *Hellboy*, which is based on Mike Mignola's Dark Horse comic series, his own artistic vision and his working patterns for the fantasy genre were well established. As Hitchcock did with his beginnings in set design, Del Toro stayed true to his own roots in special effects. He took them to big-budget heights in the modelling of Hellboy, the amphibian man Abe (Doug Jones), and the myriad monsters of this comic book universe. *Hellboy* is part of a trend for Latin filmmakers like Del Toro and Robert Rodriguez to handle genre films, and thereby become part of the Hollywood mainstream. In an interview with Kellvin Chavez for *Latino Review*, Del Toro himself observes, 'It's a great sign that we can now tackle basically any genre on any franchise or any type of movie we want.'

For Del Toro this move into the Hollywood mainstream began with Hitchcock. There are several constants in Del Toro's work, repeated in *Hellboy*, that coincide with characteristics of Hitchcock: first, the use of humour in suspense films; second, the inclusion of Catholic reliquary and the emphasis on a kind of morality; third, the addition of a love interest to an action genre; and fourth, inspiration in the visual arts tradition.

In *Hellboy*, as was the case in *Cronos*'s mortician, the humour of the film is that of working class sarcasm. For instance, after arriving at a museum from his secret garbage truck with one-way mirrors, Hellboy acts as if he were an everyday pest exterminator out to apply the monthly roach spray treatment. Observed by the high-class museum curators, Hellboy's deadpan nonchalance, as he is about to be jumped by a humongous slimy beast generates humour in the face of horror. The situational humour is akin to that in *Frenzy*'s grotesque night-time truck ride when the mass murderer Bob struggles in the midst of sacks of potatoes to find his tiepin on the corpse of his victim Babs. In both *Frenzy* and *Hellboy*, the governing imagery and associations suggest a working-class milieu. Babs the corpse is just another sack of potatoes.

A second shared constant characteristic is the inclusion of Catholic reliquary and emphasis on a moral vision. An army photographer Trevor 'Broom' Bruttenholm (Kevin Trainor as young 'Broom') discovers the baby Hellboy in a tomb in an abbey in Prague. They bond. The photographer/father-figure (John Hurt as an older 'Broom') gives Hellboy a rosary, which serves as one of his talismans and figures prominently, hanging from the barrel of a rifle, in a group photograph of the army troop.[21] Hellboy is a monster that doesn't want to be one. He struggles against his dark side to be human. When Del Toro himself critiques Hitchcock's filmography, he continually notes how specific films are 'more moral'. For instance he praises *Suspicion* (1941):

> ... to my judgment one of the greatest films of Hitchcock. Along with *Shadow of a Doubt*, *Strangers on a Train* and *Notorious*, it explores in depth the themes of trust and loyalty, present already in *The Lodger,* and important in *The Thirty-Nine Steps* and in *Sabotage*. But it's in the first group of films mentioned where the ambiguity and need for trust reach their ultimate expression. The film, along with *Rebecca*, moreover begins a new direction in Hitchcock's cinema, which would distinguish the Hollywood works from the British ones. Hitchcock now shows a greater appreciation of human

In the troop's group photo in *Hellboy*, the rosary, a gift from Hellboy's 'father' the photographer, hangs prominently from the rifle next to him.

character and tends toward an 'intimate' cinema of suspense, which is more moral, less filled with 'technical pyrotechnics' (with the exceptions of *Saboteur, North by Northwest*, and *The Birds*). (1990: 217)

Unlike Hitchcock, however, Del Toro employs more pyrotechnics as he enters the Hollywood mainstream. Yet it is also true that in *Hellboy* through the insertion of the character of Mike Meyers, at Del Toro's instigation, not only is the love theme triangulated, but significant issues of loyalty and trust are also introduced, aspects Del Toro praised in *Suspicion* and viewed as signs of a successful transition to Hollywood.

A third commonality is the addition, which was discussed in the context of *Blade II*, of a love interest in the film's action narrative to emphasise Hellboy's maturation and growing sense of duty. Significantly, Mike Mignola, the creator of the Hellboy comics, points out that the love interest was purely Del Toro's idea and did not exist in his artistic vision.

A fourth commonality, seen strongly in *Hellboy*, is the importance of a European visual arts tradition to both Hitchcock and Del Toro. Although they are perceived as popular directors, the inspiration for their films often come from high art. For example, in the joint DVD commentary track from Mignola and Del Toro, the latter points out how the early sequences in the abbey ruins and later a craggy frozen landscape are 'right out of Caspar David Friedrich'. Mignola responds that he still does not know what Del Toro is talking about, but clearly Del Toro drew on his knowledge of Friedrich's romantic landscapes for artistic direction in creating *Hellboy*'s sets. Similarly, between 1999 and 2002 the New York Museum of Modern Art, Paris's Centre Pompidou and Montréal's Museum of Fine Arts all mounted exhibitions around the theme of the paintings that influenced Hitchcock. Diego Moldes in his book *La huella de 'Vertigo'* (The Trace of 'Vertigo', 2004) summarises the main points from the Centre Pompidou exhibition:

In the retrospective they showed images that directly influenced the composition of many shots and sequences of his films, images that derived from
many disparate artists: Turner, Rodin, Munch, Magritte, Rossetti, Millais,
Ernst, Khnopff, Spilliaert, Hopper, De Chirico, Beardsley, Valloton, Duch-
amp, Dalí, Man Ray, etc., even if in the exhibition symbolism and surreal-
ism certainly stood out as the two movements that most influenced Hitchcock's aesthetic education of Hitchcock. There were five Hitchcockian
themes: woman, desire and the double, the generative spaces of suspense,
terror, and performance. (2004:30)

In some cases Hitchcock's comments on his artistic inspirations are direct
and oft-cited, as in the case of Edvard Munch's 'The Scream' (1895–1910)
and Edward Hopper's 'House by the Railroad' (1925) in regard to *Psycho*.
In his chapter 'Referencias pictóricas y literarias en *Vértigo*' ('Pictorial and
literary references in *Vertigo*') Moldes analyses several compositions in the
film in the context of the Pre-Raphaelite paintings of Sir John Everett Millais.
He compares, for example, Millais's painting 'Ophelia' (1851–2) to Scottie
and Madeleine floating in San Francisco Bay during her faked suicide attempt
(2004: 33) and Millais's 'The Eve of St. Agnes' (1863) to Judy in the hotel room
silhouetted against the curtains. What Hitchcock and Del Toro share, besides
a deeply-felt appreciation for art history (no minor coincidence) is even more
specific. Their aesthetic visions, as evidenced by the citations of Millais and
Friedrich, gravitate to particular aspects of nineteenth-century art, to allow
them to represent in, Moldes's words, 'a mythification of the most tragic and
morbid romanticism' (2004: 32). Furthermore they take upon themselves, as
did the Romantic painters they admire, to find within themselves 'a new mythology, one which would be relevant and binding for the culture as a whole'
(Koemer 2009: 79). Moreover Del Toro's allusions to Friedrich's winter scenes,
many of churches or churchyards, such as 'Churchyard in the Snow (1828) or
'Abbey in the Oak Forest' (1809–10), reveal a kinship with Friedrich's con-
templative spectator position which presents in effect 'art as religion' (Koemer
2009: 161).

In *Hellboy* Del Toro does not dwell on his references to high art, but respects and directly adapts frames from Mignola's comic books as well. Scattered
throughout the film, these compositions place a main character in three-quarter
shot in the foreground against a strong and well-defined monument in the background, recalling an iconic comic book hero composition.

Finally, as we have seen, all of Del Toro's films make direct gestures to
Hitchcock's works. The most poignant Hitchcock quotation in *Hellboy* is to the

In the sea of umbrellas of *Foreign Correspondent* Johnny (Joel McCrea) witnesses the assassin, who disguises his gun with his camera, kill the diplomat Van Meer.

A sea of umbrellas, which dominates the funeral sequence of Hellboy's surrogate father, is also an homage to Hitchcock's visual 'parentage.'

umbrella sequence of *Foreign Correspondent*. In Hitchcock's film, the young American newspaperman Johnny Jones stands on a grand exterior staircase in Amsterdam. There he witnesses a man who disguises his gun with his camera to assassinate the diplomat Van Meer, then flee into a sea of open umbrellas. Johnny gives chase. In *Hellboy* a similar sea of open umbrellas dominates the funeral sequence of the professor, Hellboy's surrogate father, who is killed in his lab. As he repeats Hitchcock's motif in the *mise-en-scène*, Del Toro acknowledges his visual parentage, his own surrogate father in Hitchcock. It remains to be seen if he kills the father with his camera.

VII. CUTTING-EDGE HUMOUR IN *PAN'S LABYRINTH*: MERCEDES THE RIPPER AVENGES *FRENZY*

With *The Devil's Backbone*, Del Toro entered Spanish cinema under the aegis of the Almodóvar brand. Yet, given the hybrid geography of the casting (Eduardo Noriega and Marisa Paredes from Spain, Federico Luppi from Argentina), and the director's previous Hollywood successes, he still seemed to be an 'exotic outsider' for Spanish audiences. With *El laberinto del fauno* (*Pan's Labyrinth*) that outsider status gives way to a different view of Del Toro. The film weaves and consolidates various strands of the Hitchcock rubric, combined with a startlingly Spanish historical and cultural specificity. Perhaps that amalgam is no better crystallised than in the development of black or gallows humour in *Pan's Labyrinth* in scenes in which one character cuts another. Specifically Del Toro uses editing and intense dialogue in situations of torture or horror to simultaneously create Hitchcockian humour and suspense.

Black humour has long been not only associated with Spanish culture but considered integral to it. We can trace its roots and sensibility from the cruel pranks in Francisco de Quevedo's *Buscón*, the seventeenth-century picaresque novel, one of the main contributions of Spain to Western literature, through the nineteenth century in Francisco de Goya's satirical sketches *Los caprichos*, to the influential twentieth-century Neorrealist films of the Marco Ferreri-Rafael Azcona collaboration, such as *El cochecito* (*The Little Car*, 1960) in which a man so obsesses over owning a car for the disabled that he poisons his whole family when they refuse him the money, or later Luis García Berlanga's *El verdugo* (*The Executioner*, 1962), a comedy of Spanish life and customs, which were so stifled under Franco's dictatorship.[22] While not a comedy film, but certainly an example of black humour, Luis Buñuel's *Viridiana* (1961) mines even greater depths of repression in its beggars' orgy and mordant parody of religion. Notably, these Spanish cultural intertexts are sutured into the fabric of Del Toro's film through the more universal cinematic style of Hitchcock.

The appreciation, or more conventionally the influence, of Hitchcock in the Spanish and Latin American world differs markedly from an analogous phenomenon in US Cinema, exemplified by David Lynch in *Blue Velvet* (1986) or Christopher Nolan in *Memento* (2000), among others, whom John Orr studies in *Hitchcock and Twentieth Century Cinema* (2005), in two significant ways, especially in debut films: one, the 'Latin' or Spanish and Latin American world notices Hitchcock's humour and incorporates humour in similar situations; and two, the Latin world appreciates and adapts the moral tone of Hitchcock's films.

Regarding the moral tone, the very structure of a fairy tale dictates its presence. Del Toro himself in his DVD director's commentary observes that *Pan's Labyrinth* belongs to that genre. The film takes place in Spain in 1944 in the post-Civil War era. It tells the story of a young girl Ofelia (Ivana Baquero) who travels with her pregnant mother Carmen (Ariadna Gil) to the encampment of the Francoist army, led by Captain Vidal (Sergi López), who is Carmen's new husband. There Ofelia discovers the hidden world of the *maquis* or rebels in the forest which intersects with the subterranean world of fantasy of labyrinths, tunnels and caves. Though her mother dies in childbirth, she gives birth to a son.

Throughout the story Ofelia carries out three tests according to the instructions of the faun Pan who becomes her moral compass. In the final test she snatches her brother from his cradle to escape from Captain Vidal. He kills Ofelia, then he is killed by the *maquis*. In the end Ofelia is reborn into heaven where she completes a family trilogy. Her assumption is her reward for having sacrificed herself to save an innocent being.[23]

About halfway through *Pan's Labyrinth* the maid Mercedes (Maribel Verdú) and the doctor (Alex Ángulo), who are both moles or double agents, travel through the forest to the hardscrabble camp of the *maquis*. The doctor plans to examine and treat the wounded leg of the Frenchman, head of the rebels. Shortly upon arriving he proclaims that he has to amputate even though there is no anaesthesia. When the doctor opens his bag and takes out his saw, which looks more appropriate for a butcher than a surgeon, the spectators are faced with another 'walk-out scene' comparable to the one in *The Devil's Backbone* in which Jacinto cuts the young protagonist's face.

Through the editing Del Toro does not allow the audience to look away from the screen, but rather creates suspense as he plays with its reactions. The film cuts to a close-up of the infected leg and the enormous saw which together emphasise the visual aggression. Instead of cutting away immediately from the shot of the horrific operation, the camera pans over to the Frenchman's face, who asks the doctor to pause. Audiences regularly respond to this moment with laughter. The request is unexpected. The new intervention releases tension, provoking an outward manifestation of pleasure. By foiling expectations, the tension generated in the sequence is liberated. Playing with the audience gives them the courage to watch the horror of the amputation that immediately follows. The sequence ends with a black fade, the most abrupt, or metaphorically the most severe cut, of cinematographic transitions.

In the script of *Pan's Labyrinth* this sequence, #87 A. Int. Gruta – Noche (#87 A. Interior Grotto –Night), stands out for 'an extremely dense silence', in which the Frenchman's heroism is foregrounded for enduring amputation with

The 'walk-out' scene in *Pan's Labyrinth*: the doctor (Álex Angulo) begins to amputate the Frenchman's leg without anaesthesia.

only the weight of Mercedes and his brother holding him down. The Frenchman only says, 'Do what you have to do, doctor.' And the doctor responds, 'Don't move. I'll try to do it in as few cuts as possible' (Del Toro 2006: 69). In the script there is no notation for a humorous pause or Hitchcockian suspense. These were added in the filming. Both heighten the perception of the heroism of the *maquis*, and in addition allow the spectator to become more involved in the situation from the rebels' point of view. The editing, or specifically the cutting, of the film evokes compassion in a situation of horror.

It is significant to recognise how Mercedes is characterised in *Pan's Labyrinth* according to the action of cutting, too. The scenes in the kitchen of the mill with the group of cooks and maids are beautiful, cheerfully maternal, filmed with golden lighting, which Del Toro calls 'luz maternal' ('motherly light)', which re- calls the Velásquez painting 'Mujer cocinando huevos' ('Woman Cooking Eggs', 1618). Here Mercedes cuts turnips and upon finishing always puts her knife away in her apron, foreshadowing its use as a defensive weapon.

It is revealing that Maribel Verdú, the object of passion of the male ado- lescents in Alfonso Cuarón's *Y tu madre también* represents a role so directly opposed to that which she played in that Mexican box office hit of Del Toro's close friend. In the forests of *Pan's Labyrinth*, Verdú is transformed into the image of the castrating woman, emaciated and fierce, in the primitive style of the mother and wet nurse of the civil governor in José Luis Borau's *Los furtivos* (*The Poachers*, 1975).[24]

In *Pan's Labyrinth* Mercedes activates a proscribed interpretation. We meet her for the first time in a scene in which Captain Vidal is shaving him- self with a barber's razor.[25] Resting his hand on Mercedes' shoulder in a sign of domination, he chastises her for having let his coffee burn. Although she knows the reason for her lack of vigilance was that she had run off to meet the rebels, she keeps her face expressionless. The captain's gesture warns her that she should not stray towards the political opposition. She then returns to the kitchen to tell the others the captain's orders for dinner. Meanwhile Ofelia gets ready for the captain's dinner party and takes a bath, too. The bath sequence ends with a close-up of Ofelia examining a birthmark on her shoulder, which she interprets as a sign she is a princess. The sequence returns to a shot of Mercedes' hands cutting a turnip in rounds, and later rolling the knife up in her apron. The loud sound of Mercedes' forceful strokes on the cutting board are heard at the same time as a dog's howl, which emphasises the animalistic connection of the action. The cutting action forms part of a political economy. It is a way of resisting or avenging oneself on the powerful. While she gives the orders to the other women to prepare supper, the film cuts to a shot of one of them who smiles in reaction to the vision of Ofelia coming down the stairs and entering the kitchen in her party dress, the princess being welcomed into her maternal realm.

Whereas Mercedes hides her intentions along with her knife, Captain Vidal enjoys an overt laugh at the expense of his victims. Vidal directs his sarcastic remarks to the young rebel Tarta (Iván Massagué) who was recently captured in the rebels' assault on the Captain's storehouse. Brandishing his torture instruments in front of Tarta's face, Vidal tells him that with their every use they will become more and more like 'friends', implying that the rebel will slowly begin to squeal on his compatriots. The sequence up to this point is conventional in its dialogue and visual realisation. Frequently a torturer uses humour to humiliate his victim, making sadistic humour a weapon of torture itself. Nonetheless, what distinguishes this sequence is its resistant humour, in the ironic situation that he who should speak cannot because he is a stutterer.

DVD chapter 15, 'Torture', begins with the sound of Mercedes again cutting turnips in the kitchen, but now she is so distracted that she has amassed a huge pile of them. We see her face with a tear on her cheek. Another cook chides her for her lack of concentration, saying 'That's enough.' The action and the sound of cutting function like a cinematographic cut that presages crosscuts, as we shift between the room where the doctor is visiting Ofelia's mother confined to bed, and the warehouse where the prisoner is awaiting his interrogation. Mercedes is relieved since she saw through a crack in the doors that the prisoner is not her brother Pedro, although she still agonises over what she knows awaits him. The three settings are equally dark though the light in the warehouse falls ominously on the captain's face leaving half of it in darkness, giving him a threatening expression. When the captain begins to play with Tarta offering him a cigarette 'of the good kind', Tarta answers true to his namesake, which is the beginning of the word for stuttering, 'tartamudear', by stuttering 've-ve-te a la mierda', roughly 'go-go-to hell'. The captain himself recognises that he is witness to a cruel joke when he says to his lieutenant, 'Oye, Garcés, para uno que cogemos, resulta que es tartamudo' ('Hey, Garcés, for the one we catch, turns out he's a

The anguished Mercedes (Maribel Verdú) establishes her role as the one who cuts as she chops too many turnips in the Velázquez-like kitchen setting in *Pan's Labyrinth*.

stutterer'). The camera pans in a curve around the post to which Tarta is tied in a movement that recalls the scene of the captain shaving, which showed his domination. It positions us in Tarta's place. Slowly the captain shows him the three instruments of torture that he plans to use for the interrogation, 'to make our relationship closer, like brothers'. Upon touching Tarta's shoulder with the first instrument, a hammer, the captain comes up with the idea of promising to free Tarta if he can count to three without stuttering. Tension heightens. The film cuts between shot and reverse-shot between Tarta and the captain. Tarta counts one, then two, and at three he begins to stutter, getting stuck on the 't' of 'tres' ('three'). As he lifts his head in a pathetic gesture, we see the captain beginning to hit him with the hammer. It is immediately followed by black fade, out of compassion for the spectator.

In DVD chapter 19, 'Nothing more than a woman', the captain's troops have captured Mercedes with a bag full of products from the captain's warehouse destined for the *maquis*. The captain has her tied to the post. He dismisses his lieutenant saying, 'No es nada más que una mujer' ('She's nothing more than a woman') – that is to say, that since she is a woman he is in no danger. While the captain reviews the same instruments that he had used to torture Tarta and repeats the same speech about the different stages of becoming 'hermanos' ('brothers and sisters'), the film shows us close-ups of Mercedes' hands untying her bonds with the same knife she always carries in her apron. Afterwards we see her in long shot from behind the captain's back. Then we hear a loud noise as she drives the knife into the captain's back when he turns his back on her. Her vengeance is even greater, underscored in the dialogue, which throws his multiple negatives, a linguistic characteristic of Spanish, back at him. Mercedes tells him 'no soy ni un viejo ni un prisionero herido' ('I'm neither an old man nor a wounded prisoner') as she proceeds to stick her knife in his mouth, cutting both his mouth and cheek while telling him with great satisfaction and irony, 'You won't be the first pig I've gutted!'

There is humour, certainly irony, in this vengeance for having mistreated a whole gender. There is a double movement here in that Mercedes is also achieving a revenge on Hitchcock and his multilation of the feminine body. The explicit representation of the cut to the face alludes to the violence of *Frenzy*. As Carlos Reviriego in *El universo de Alfred Hitchcock* describes it, *Frenzy*, Hitchcock's penultimate film, features 'one of the iconic, and genuinely horrendous, images of Hitchcock's filmography: a pale feminine face with big paralysed eyes, her tongue hanging out of one side of her mouth, and a tie around her neck' (2006: 200). For Del Toro *Frenzy*'s strangulation sequence 'seems to encapsulate all the horror that Hitchcock is capable of' (1990: 472). He moreover admires its tempo and dialogue that 'has an almost unbearable intensity' (1990: 470). When Del

Mercedes the ripper
extracts her vengeance
on Captain Vidal (Sergi
López) by cutting his
mouth in *Pan's Labyrinth*.

Toro reissued his book on Hitchcock with a short prologue in 2009, he continued to affirm his absolute admiration for *Frenzy* as 'one of the most dazzling
jewels of the director' (2009: 14). To recall, Hitchcock makes his first 'cameo'
in *Frenzy* making reference to Jack the Ripper. Returning to *Pan's Labyrinth*,
Mercedes the Ripper escapes to the arms of her real brother in a good cavalry
chase scene as if *Pan's Labyrinth* were a western. Not only is there an ironic
commentary on the captain's words about 'becoming brothers', but Del Toro
also underscores the notion of brotherhood in the cinematographic intertextuality. Terror becomes humour through this chain of allusions.

Captain Vidal shows his valour as he sews up Mercedes' cut himself in front
of the mirror. It is both difficult to watch or stop watching. The act of sewing,
shown pitilessly in close-up, is an act of praise for the abilities of the special
effects crew in creating the latex prosthesis that makes possible the suturing.
Moreover the action recalls, with good humour, Del Toro's career trajectory. As
mentioned earlier with regard to *Cronos*, he began his career as a make-up artist
through a correspondence course. In *Cronos* the vampire also operates on his
own face, undoing the sutures with which the mortician had sewn up his mouth.
This reading underscores how Del Toro not only revisits his own films but also
those of his teacher in order to get them right. In the process of righting them,
cinema becomes a system of corrections or creative translations.

Captain Vidal
(Sergi López) sews himself
up in *Pan's Labyrinth*.

VIII. 'CAN'T LIVE WITHOUT' HITCH: MEXICAN BEER AND POP MUSIC IN *HELLBOY II: THE GOLDEN ARMY*

It would be absurd to claim that Del Toro's most recent films clone Hitchcock. Del Toro has more than established his own auteurial sinecure worldwide. He has moved on to direct big-budget projects in sci-fi fantasy, such as *Pacific Rim* (2013) as well as more modest ones in the horror genre, such as *The Strain* (2014), a series of TV films based on books he co-wrote with Chuck Hogan, and *Crimson Peak* (2015). Still almost every Del Toro director's track mentions Hitchcock. Faced with doing the sequel *Hellboy II: The Golden Army*, Del Toro recycled many of his own motifs, notably multiplying the Cronos device of his debut film into a golden army. Nonetheless, some of Del Toro's Hitchcockian quirks are foregrounded in this Hollywood blockbuster. To begin, his insistence on using the music of Barry Manilow recalls ironically his criticism of Hitchcock's split with Herrmann.

In *Alfred Hitchcock* Del Toro decries the outcome of making *Torn Curtain*, a film which he considers second-rate, a mere compendium of what Hitchcock had done before. He writes: 'The most remarkable aspect of the project was that it led to the final break-up between Bernard Herrmann and Alfred Hitchcock, since the latter became enamoured of the film having a pop score and the former (equally stubborn) refused to compose it' (1990: 453). Hitchcock wanted pop and Herrmann refused to do pop.[26] Consequently they split. Faced with the daunting challenge of trying to make Julie Andrews, the prim Maria of *The Sound of Music* (1965), into a convincing love interest for the method actor Paul Newman in the film, Hitch had his reasons to want accessible melodies. For one, he feared the public would expect her to sing. For another, he wanted a different profile. According to Jack Sullivan in *Hitchcock's Music*, the tension and 'pride' around not repeating oneself is what ultimately caused the Hitchcock/Hermann break-up.

As Del Toro's career evolves and the stakes get higher to repeat earlier triumphs, Del Toro understands and revisits Hitchcock's artistic stances. Reminiscent of Hitch's defence of pop music, on the director's track of *Hellboy II* Del Toro acknowledges that he knew from the beginning that he wanted to use Barry Manilow's music in his film. Hollywood executives balked that it did not fit the tone of a superhero film. Del Toro however held firm. The male-bonding scene in which Hellboy and Abe (Doug Jones) chug cans of Mexican beer while singing love-sick karaoke to 'I Can't Smile Without You' is the most memorable scene of the whole film, often cited in the film's reviews.[27] The sweeping camera movements and the final overhead shot enhance its importance. Moreover the incongruous superimposition of the bourgeois family man's point of view epitomised by Manilow's song on the chaotic world of Big Red

Male bonding to Barry
Manilow: Hellboy and
Abe chug beer and sing 'I
Can't Live Without You.'

begets a positive audience reaction. Del Toro achieves his particular success in *Hellboy II* through the savvy insertion of humour through contrast, a technique learned from Hitchcock.

IX. CONCLUSION

In the Spanish-speaking world, no other film director has written as extensively on Hitchcock as Guillermo del Toro. In 2009 he reissued, without revisions, his early book on Hitchcock, which he now calls 'a kind of "Hitchcock for beginners"' and 'a time capsule' (2009: 13, 15). No other Latin filmmaker is more consciously aware of the full range of Hitchcock's techniques, innovations, narrative structures, motifs and career path than Del Toro. Elements of tone that characterise the Master of Suspense, namely the presence of humour in suspense films, prevail throughout Del Toro's work, as they do in the work of other Latin filmmakers whose work discussed in this book. However, more particular to Del Toro is the moral sensibility of his films and its relationship to the films' underlying tensions. This, too, Del Toro specifically contemplated in his early film criticism. In *Alfred Hitchcock* Del Toro lays out what he perceives as Hitchcock's rules of success, as taken up by other directors. As shown in this chapter, he never wavers from these fundamentals of suspense in, one, solid and interesting characterisation, including that of very ordinary people, and, two, the creation of melodramatic situations with moral and ethical depth (1990: 47). This preoccupation with moral concerns is one of the unifying principles of all of Del Toro's films to date as he adapts Hitchcock's rules to his own filmic universe of horror.

In conclusion, Del Toro is the instance of a self-conscious and self-constructed auteur, very much in the style of Hitchcock as well as Almodóvar, De la Iglesia and Amenábar. Like them, he has worked through popular genres, consciously depleting his film projects from immediate cultural localisms with the aim of appealing to broader international audiences while, ironically, reinscribing other more universal versions of cultural specificity, i.e. the treatment of the Spanish Civil War in two films along broad Manichean lines and blending these with gothic horror and black humour.[28] His career is built around the doubled consciousness of himself and a series of cultural and historical models. These include the Hitchcock shadow in his work and a series of Mexican and Spanish cinematic intertexts: Cuarón, Erice, Almodóvar, among others.

NOTES

1   Del Toro's book appeared in a small press run of 2,000 copies in paperback from the University of Guadalajara Press. The well-worn condition of the spine of the copy owned by the Filmoteca (Spanish Film Archives) in Madrid suggests that the obscure book found some significant readership among film students and scholars even before it was reissued in 2009 without revisions.

2   Del Toro came of age with Alejandro González Iñárritú of *Amores perros* (2000) and Alfonso Cuarón of *Y tu mamá también* (2001), the poster boys for a new Mexican cinema. Their films, which focused on the contemporary moment with fast-paced editing and innovative storytelling, were enormous hits both in Mexico and significantly, globally, as well. Marvin D'Lugo notes not only the stylistic break, which *Amores perros* represents, but probes its cultural significance: 'Precisely because of its clever balance between the cultural speci-ficity of its Mexican subject-matter and what might be termed its transnational texture, *Amores perros* needs to be read not simply as a product of a revived Mexican cinema, but as a pointed interrogation of the position of Latin America's increasingly urbanized culture situated as it is in the slip zone between communities on the margins and mass-mediatised, global culture' (2003: 222). Regarding Del Toro, Deborah Shaw finds 'it more fruitful to seek out the authorial voice, which is large, ambitious, and always transnational, rather than categorising his films as straightforward examples of Mexican, Hollywood, or Spanish filmmaking' (2013: 20). Shaw attributes the creation of Del Toro's authorial style particularly to his sustained collaboration with Guillermo Navarro (2013: 4).

3   The tenth anniversary reissue of *Cronos* includes a scene from *Matilda*.

4   See Shaw on Cuarón's early career (2013: 176–200).

5   See http://www.dicksmithmake-up.com/training-programs/advanced-course.aspx.

6   See Ana Cruz, *Bertha Navarro: Cineasta sin fronteras* (2008). In the prologue Del Toro gives her credit for his start: 'Without a doubt it's her fault that I make movies', and also for keep-ing independent filmmaking alive in Mexico (2008: 5).

7   Jeff Lipsky from October Films, *Cronos*'s American distributor, however, assessed the decidedly mixed success of this multiple strategy: 'Despite our best efforts to reach that segment, the response in L.A. was fairly lackluster. But the (original) film did very well with audiences that go to see cutting-edge, stylized cinema from anywhere in the world' (quoted by Richard Harrington, *Washington Post*, 22 May 1994).

8   James Rose in his study of *The Devil's Backbone* explains: 'During his childhood, del Toro spent a lot of his time with a woman he calls "grandmother". This woman was not his biological grandparent – she had died during childbirth – but his grandmother's sister. A strong and devout Catholic, del Toro's grandmother 'basically' (Romney 2006) raised him. He has commented that she was a very scary woman but someone who loved him deeply' (2009: 11).

9   World film history is littered with examples of directors who flopped with projects they

were forced into, especially at the critical juncture of shifting national industries. One example is Hitchcock's *Jamaica Inn* (1938), his last British film, a costume drama, and a candidate as one of his worst films. He agreed to direct it largely because it was based on a Daphne du Maurier story and he wanted to close the deal with Selznick to move to Hollywood and do *Rebecca*, also based on a Du Maurier text.

10 *Hellboy II* repeats the motif with a green blob that Abe drops down a New York City grate.

11 See Del Toro's interview (2008) 'Guillermo del Toro confesó su temor de ser secuestrado en México' ('Guillermo del Toro confessed his fear of being kidnapped in Mexico') and Gilbert Cruz, *Time* (2011).

12 It is intriguing to find the vestiges of the Mexican script, such as Sor Juana's poetry, in the final product.

13 In his book-length study of *The Devil's Backbone* James Rose elided the connection. Although he quotes Del Toro on the film's construction 'on a rhyme', Rose explains the narrative structure as 'instances of doubling' and 'parallels and connections between certain characters' (2009: 19). He never mentions Hitchcock's duality films, as Del Toro himself does.

14 Del Toro discusses the shocked reaction of Arthur LaBern, the novelist of the work upon which *Frenzy* is based: 'When he saw the film for the first time, Arthur LaBern considered it in "bad taste" and found the script "overwhelming," complaining bitterly of the dialogue. Frankly the film's "bad taste" is precisely what puts it higher up on my personal list of Hitchcock favourites. Thanks to letting himself forget the limits of good taste he gives shape to his most sordid work' (1990: 463).

15 See http://www.reelviews.net/php_review_template.php?identifier=1443

16 See also Deborah Shaw on *Cronos*'s language mix (2013: 24–5).

17 The religious *mise-en-scène* is a common element in some martial arts movies as well. For example, the climactic sequence of John Woo's classic *The Killer* (1989) begins in a church.

18 On Goth history, music and aesthetics see Hodkinson (2002) and Fuentes Rodríguez (2007). A tragic incident gave Goth culture a more sinister association in the US when the perpetrators of the Columbine school massacre (20 April 1999) were initially identified as Goth, white supremacists.

19 *Torrente: el brazo tonto de la ley* (1998) and *Torrente 2: Misión en Marbella* (2001) were some of the highest-grossing films in Spain of all time. Interestingly, Del Toro himself dubbed Segura's voice in English for *Blade II*.

20 See McGilligan 2003: 596–7 for an excellent account of how Hitchcock charmed the censors to keep the shower sequence as he intended.

21 In *The Wrong Man* Hitchcock highlighted that Manny kept his rosary when he was booked.

22 Marvin D'Lugo interprets the film in *Guide to the Cinema of Spain*: 'Though the film is generally seen within the narrow confines of a biting attack on capital punishment, it is also an insightful but bitter look at the discrepancy between the static values of the past in Spanish culture and the intensifying changes of contemporary European culture [which] provides much of the film's scathing black humor' (1997: 108).

23 The presence of a moral tone is evident in the very structure of the fairy tale. Precisely because it is so skeletal or simplified it accepts allegorical political interpretations according to its various exhibition locations. Del Toro himself points out the various 'layers' of his film. Future studies may expose local allegorical interpretations for the film across Latin America. Deborah Shaw is more sanguine about what I have termed the allegorical

potential of the film as she argues that 'a commercial imperative to generate the pleasures of the text had led to the fantasy structure imposing itself on the realist forms, with the resulting falsification of history' (2013: 89). She finds that the film's happy ending might lead viewers to assume that the Nationalists had been defeated far sooner than was the case. Nonetheless for Shaw the film's singularity lies in how Del Toro 'rewrites the female role to allow for the development of a feminist (young) heroine' (ibid.). My reading complements this view by showing how Del Toro's admiration for Hitchcock, and especially *Frenzy*, plays out in Mercedes' revenge.

24   In Spanish film studies Borau's film represents national cinema. Phrases in the *Diccionario del cine español* (Dictionary of Spanish Cinema, 1998), a project for which Borau served as chief editor, such as 'an emblematic title for the history of Spanish cinema' (1998: 380) and 'the key movie of the political effervescence that Spain was living while Francoism was in its final stages and the country was moving toward democracy' (1998: 381) are indicative of its historical importance. *The Poachers* transcends its *mise-en-scène* and generates a political reading or an 'inevitable metaphorical reading of authoritarianism and repression which the country lived under Franco' (1998: 380). *Diccionario del cine español* describes *The Poachers* in the following way: 'Taking its cues from a nucleus of characters who lived trapped in a natural universe marked by violence and by an atmosphere of frustration, within an atavic forest in which the least domesticable instincts appear naked, Borau weaves a parable about family disintegration and the animal nature of the human being' (ibid.). It was precisely because of the ferocity of its metaphorical critique that the dictatorship required numerous cuts before authorising the film's screening. Borau totally opposed any cuts. His resistance to these threats won out which gave even more cultural and political resonance to the film when it was shown nationally and internationally. After winning the Golden Shell at the San Sebastián Film Festival, *The Poachers* received its general exhibition licence and went on to become an enormous commercial hit in Spain.

25   In *Blood Cinema* Marsha Kinder analyses multiple shaving scenes, which she calls 'an icon of masculinity and castration that is ubiquitous in Spanish movies from the silent period to the 1990s' (1993: 118–9).

26   For a more detailed explanation of the break-up see Jack Sullivan, 'The Rip that Wouldn't Mend: *Torn Curtain*', in *Hitchcock's Music* (2006: 276–89). Sullivan argues that the problem was more complex than an issue of the marketability of pop music but was fundamentally a question of their realisation of and abhorrence to mutual dependency. For Sullivan the fact that both Hitchcock and Herrmann were repeating themselves at that stage of their careers exacerbated the situation.

27   The beer appears to be Tecate, the first Mexican beer to move to cans, which are now exported. Emblematic of the reviews, Michael Atkinson observed: 'The film's high point is a beer-drunk idyll shared by Ron Perlman's Red and Doug Jones' amphibian, both of them heartsick and crooning along to Barry Manilow's "Can't Smile without You"'; http://old.bfi.org.uk/sightandsound/review/4453.

28   This aspect has been especially well explored with respect to *The Devil's Backbone*; see Aguilar (2005) and Lázaro-Repoll (2007).

CHAPTER SEVEN

Understanding Osmosis:
Hitchcock in Argentina
Through the Eyes of
Juan José Campanella

I. INTRODUCTION TO 'OSMOSIS'

At the press conference of the 2009 San Sebastián Film Festival for Juan José Campanella's film *El secreto de sus ojos* (*The Secret in Their Eyes*) I asked the Argentinean director whether he was influenced by Hitchcock. His quick answer was '¿Quién no ha sido influenciado por Hitchcock? Por osmosis' ('Who hasn't been influenced by Hitchcock? By osmosis'). He then responded to what had been my lead-in to this question, first a comment that *The Secret in Their Eyes* was an amazing film because of the tension between a particularly Argentinean sense of humour and the thriller genre, which characterises Hitchcock's work, and second a query about at what stage in the filmmaking process this tension between comedy and drama primarily developed. Campanella went on to acknowledge and comment on the importance of what he called the 'balance' between humour and drama in his films. Moreover he described his working process, 'Tiendo a escribir más comedia de lo que se filma' ('I tend to write more comedy than what gets filmed'). This chapter will analyse elements of Campanella's career that make him a Latin Hitchcock, addressing both television and film, and explore the Hitchcockian traces in *The Secret in Their Eyes*. The strategy will not be to suggest direct quotations of Hitchcock's films, although we will develop analogies to specific movies, but rather to show how characteristics of Hitchcock's cinematography pervade Campanella's work and shape it at its most meaningful junctures. To recall, Argentina, Mexico and Cuba have historically had the most developed film industries in Latin America. To consider this process of 'osmosis' in a historical and political context will allow us to appreciate both the unique

José Juan Campanella between Soledad Villamil and Ricardo Darín at the press conference for *The Secret in Their Eyes* at the 2009 San Sebastián Film Festival.

characteristics of the reception of Hitchcock in an important region of Latin America and to address the role of the transnational or crossover in building a career as a filmmaker in Argentina.

If in the course of this book we were to discuss only directors who looked to Hitchcock as an initial model for becoming successful directors, especially through crossover or transnational recognition – that is, to build their careers on Hitchcock's model – then Juan José Campanella (b.1959) might be left out because of his anomalous genre choices. For the past two decades Campanella's reputation has never been as a director particularly associated with Hitchcock. He achieved worldwide recognition with his third film *El hijo de la novia* (*The Son of the Bride*, 2001), an upbeat, even sunny melodrama that was nominated for the Best Foreign Film Academy Award, a huge achievement in Latin America. Yet there is a darker side to Campanella's work in film, and equally importantly in television, that has received much less attention. Indeed 'Joe' Campanella is a successful mainstream Argentinean director who at significant moments modelled his crossover career on Hitchcock's. One turning point happened at the movies when he was in his twenties.

II. EARLY CAREER DIRECTIONS: CROSSING OVER FOR FILM SCHOOL, HAVING THE LAST LAUGH WITH *THE CONTORTIONIST*

Campanella claims that seeing Bob Fosse's film *All That Jazz* (1979) in Buenos Aires, on the very day he was set to enroll in his final year of engineering courses, made him decide to abandon his engineering studies and apply to the Tisch School of the Arts at NYU to study film and become a director. *All That Jazz* could serve as an emblem to Campanella's approach to his work, for although it has an underlying darker tone, it was most often marketed for its more upbeat musical dazzle. Nonetheless, Campanella's fascination with *All That Jazz*, a tale of artistic brilliance and self-destruction, and an ironic statement of directorial ego, did fit the mood of the times in Argentina. Many Argentineans, in particular many artists and intellectuals, were leaving the country for political reasons, as these were the years under military dictatorship called the Proceso (Process of Social Reintegration) or the Dirty War (1976–1983).

Although Campanella moved to the US for film school in 1983, the direction for his break into the international film industry was not immediately clear. The portfolio of projects in Spanish he brought with him to the US reflected Argentinean national political concerns. In 1979 Campanella wrote and filmed a 22-minute short in Spanish called *Prioridad nacional* (*National Priority*). He co-wrote and co-directed his first feature-length film, the Spanish-language docudrama *Victoria 392* (*Victory 392*, 1984), with Fernando Castets. They filmed in Buenos Aires where the film opened in 1984, a year after Raúl Alfonsín's election, which represented Argentina's return to democracy.

Still, in the 1980s Campanella did make the most of his film studies in New York. For one, unlike Amenábar, a generational contemporary, he completed his degree programme. In crossing over to the US Campanella was being trained for a viable global industry while in Spain Amenábar felt he was studying the local habits of a commercial dinosaur. For another, in 1988 Campanella's thesis film *El contorsionista* (*The Contortionist*) won the prize for best science fiction short at NYU. It was based on the comic book *El contorsionista*, written by the prolific Argentinean comic book writer Carlos Trillo and illustrated by Mandrafina.[1] The film's title is deceptive since it has nothing to do with full-body gymnastic contortionism, but rather with philosophical musings on what constitutes pleasure and performance.

The Contortionist tells the story of Bruce Bailey, 'The Contortionist', who is having a crisis over being able to perform on stage. In a nod to the thriller genre, Bailey is being physically pursued to perform. When he gets on the subway, a black man in the carriage puts a knife to his throat to force him to do his act there because the man does not have the money to see it in the theatre. Bailey refuses. In another scene, a streetwalker threatens him with a gun claiming he has a bounty on his head. Bailey overpowers her and she dies in his arms after the gun goes off. Subsequently inside a room he engages in a long conversation with a woman. As she stares out a window through tattered curtains, she recalls the old days when people watched 'Let's Make a Deal' on television. (Implied is that in 2049 there is no television.) Nostalgically she remarks that the show's participants joyfully picked the least practical choice behind the curtain. Bailey

In an expressionistically lit frame in *The Contortionist* a woman stares out a window through tattered curtains and recalls 'the old times' when people watched 'Let's Make a Deal' on TV.

Low-angle shot of Bailey on stage as he contorts himself into a laugh in *The Contortionist*.

High-contrast shot of a woman reacting intensely to Bailey's performance in *The Contortionist*.

finally does go on stage and contorts his expression into a laugh. The film then cuts from a medium shot of Bailey's laugh to multiple reaction shots of spectators contorting with emotion as well. For instance, in an expressionistically lit close-up an intense hypnotic gaze dominates one woman's face as she reacts to Bailey's stage performance. In his dressing room after the show Bailey receives a contract renewal, the last laugh indeed.

Although set in 2049, the black and white retro visual style of *The Contortionist* – emphasising extreme shadows, high contrast and nighttime urban decay – recalls not only Mandrafina's noir comic book illustrations (see for example, a cover from *La Iguana*, written by Trillo and illustrated by Mandrafina)

An example of Mandrafina's noir cover art for the magazine *Iguana*.

but also, as a filmic adaptation, an earlier period of German expressionism. Campanella's aesthetic look for his apprenticeship film uncannily follows Hitchcock's trajectory, for as the 2009 exhibition 'Casting a Shadow: Alfred Hitchcock and His Workshop' at the Deutsche Kinemathek Museum documents, Hitchcock served an important apprenticeship in Berlin with F. W. Murnau in 1924–25.[2] Besides directing some of his first films, *The Pleasure Garden* (1925) and *The Mountain Eagle* (1926), in Germany,[3] Hitchcock worked there as scriptwriter and art director on other silent melodramas and also observed Murnau filming his silent masterwork *Der Letze Mann* (*The Last Laugh*, 1924). This training in filmic technique impacted on Hitchcock's visual style and was the foundation for his yeoman work ethic throughout his career. In choosing to adapt a graphic novel and its noir style, Campanella follows in Hitchcock's German shadows in *The Contortionist*. It is likewise possible that the English title of Murnau's film, *The Last Laugh*, inspired Campanella to begin his own American career with the tale of climactic laughter. Significantly the short's narrative intersects not only with that of Murnau's silent film but also with that of one of Hitchcock's most famous black and white sound films.

Both the expressionist aesthetics and the plot of *The Contortionist* recall the early sequences of *The Thirty-Nine Steps*. Mr. Memory (Wylie Watson), like Bailey, is challenged by the audience to perform and put himself in a trance. The

Low-angle, expressionist shot in *The Thirty-Nine Steps*: Mr. Memory is challenged by the audience to perform.

In *The 39 Steps* the curtains of the flat to which the mysterious woman brings Richard Hannay are filmed with high contrasts of dark and light.

Close-up of a woman in the audience asking Mr. Memory a question in *The 39 Steps*.

nature of their performances and their bond with the audience is subliminal. In Hitchcock, when a gun goes off in the theatre, a mysterious woman accosts the protagonist Richard Hannay and pleads with him to take her home with him. She hides from view by pulling the blinds in his rented room. Throughout the sequence the backlit curtains figure prominently in the *mise-en-scène*. Similarly in *The Contortionist* the scene with the woman by the curtain occurs after a gunshot at the theatre. In both films the theatrical or filmic performance serves as a frame story. In both the editing effectively creates suspense in the narrative of a fugitive. In both multiple reaction shots emphasise audience participation and laughter.

The response to Campanella's short was strong. In 1989 it was selected to compete at the Festival of Clermont-Ferrand, the top international festival for shorts, where it won a special jury prize. This international exposure gave significant impetus to his career.[4] His attention to the classics, particularly to the German expressionist style beloved by Hitchcock, was the underpinning of this success.

III. THE HITCHCOCKIAN PREQUEL *THE BOY WHO CRIED BITCH* AND OTHER *LIFESTORIES* OF ADOLESCENT VIOLENCE

In the early 1990s Campanella's career took on an even more decidedly Hitchcockian turn. After graduating from film school, he stayed on in New York City and was given the opportunity to direct his first film in English, also his solo-directing debut, *The Boy Who Cried Bitch* (1991). Written, perhaps surprisingly, by a woman, Catherine May Levin, and supposedly based on an actual case, the film told the story of the adolescence of a sociopath or psychotic killer. Campanella said he 'wanted to see what Charles Manson, the Hillside strangler, and John Hinckley were like as children'.[5] The shock of the 'b' word in the film's title sets the tone for the film's transgressions.[6] Although the fascination for serial killings and the aggressive tone recall Hitchcock's *Frenzy,* Campanella most importantly begins to explore a paradoxical moral vision, of finding evil close to home, in *The Boy Who Cried Bitch* that is characteristic of Hitchcock's work. In *Shadow of a Doubt* and *Frenzy*, for example, Hitchcock explored the notion that evil, particularly serial killings, could be done by people such as Uncle Charlie who outwardly seem good and wholesome.

The film tells the coming of age story of the 12-year-old Dan Love who is sent to a prep school by his divorced mother who can no longer deal with him. Expelled from the prep school, due to his escapades with a Vietnam vet/maintenance man/child molester there, Dan is sent onto a children's psychiatric hospital. There he falls in love with a young woman, a fellow patient. However he so disrupts the other patients that the hospital seeks to remove him. His mother, unwisely, agrees to let him come home to live with her; he slaughters her. Film critics from radically different perspectives found *The Boy Who Cried Bitch* both disturbing and convincing primarily because it repeats Hitchcock's 'persistent theme' that 'evil might dwell next door in Hitchcock's world, or in one's own household; there is no sanctuary' (McGilligan 2003: 311). Writing for *The Austin Chronicle* (27 March 1992), Marc Savlov called the boy a 'ferocious main character as a sort of teddy bear kid gone awry, for inexplicable reasons' and the film 'dangerously close to reality' (http://www.austinchronicle.com/calendar/film/1992–03–27/the-boy-who-cried-bitch/). Writing for the online site 'Spirituality and Practice' (1991), Frederic and Mary Ann Brussat compared the film to an AMA report on adolescent psychological problems and drew the following lesson: 'Up until its bloody and senseless finale, *The Boy Who Cried Bitch* offers a scary and gripping portrait of a disturbed boy who resists treatment and spreads his destructiveness in ever larger circles. Violence in the home breeds more violence is the message of this troubling film' (https://www.spiritualityandpractice.com/films/films.php?id=6283).

The Boy Who Cried Bitch brought Campanella to the attention of cable television producers interested in filming reality projects about juveniles. Between 1992 and 1996 he directed six episodes of the HBO docudrama series *Lifestories: Families in Crisis* based on real cases of social problems of adolescents. His first episode was 'No Visible Bruises: The Katie Koestner Story' about date rape. As was customary in the series, after the fictionalised re-telling of the case the real person, for this episode Katie Koestner, appeared in a coda to the episode to provide more information and offer support to those who may find themselves in a similar situation, victims of sexual assault. That same year as 'No Visible Bruises', Campanella also directed 'Dead Drunk: The Kevin Tunell Story' about a drunk-driving vehicular homicide in Virginia that sparked the formation of MADD (Mothers Against Drunk Driving), and 'A Child Betrayed: The Calvin Mire Story' about the sexual molestation of a child by a priest. He won a Best Director Emmy for 'A Child Betrayed'. With *Lifestories,* 'serious' television that had extensive impact in high school and college classrooms, Campanella mastered directing gritty material for television and worked with top-notch TV actors, such as Claire Danes who played Heidi Leitner, a lesbian coming out. Like Hitchcock later in his career Campanella developed a strong background in television. It also paid the bills, and kept him in contact with the US industrial network, truths of which Hitchcock was completely aware throughout his career, too. Moreover, just as Hitchcock's television series coincided with the initial global acceptance of the medium, Campanella's television work in the 1990s coincided with the diversification of the broadcast medium and the rise of cable throughout the world. Like Hitchcock, Campanella worked on the transformative edge of the industry. The skills he developed for television at this transformative stage carried over to his film work, too. This knowledge was simultaneously an advantage and a curse.

IV. NOT-NOIR BUT CLOSER TO *NOTORIOUS*: THE GENRE AND TONAL MIX OF *LOVE WALKED IN*

With his next film project, the US/Argentinean co-production *Love Walked In* (1997), Campanella began to explore other transnational opportunities. For his first attempt at writing a script in English for a feature-length narrative film he adapted the novel *Ni el tiro del final* (*Neither the Final Shot*, 1981) by the Argentinean writer José Pablo Feinmann, who received co-script writing credit on the movie. Despite keeping Feinmann's title, which is a well-known tango verse, for the Argentinean release of the film, Campanella erased all Argentinean cultural specificity from the film.[7] Only transnational Latin traces remained, exemplified best by the casting of the Spanish actress Aitana Sánchez-Gijón in the siren role of Vicky Rivas. She represented a generic Latina type, similar to the way another Spaniard, Antonio Banderas, passed as a credible Che Guevara in the film of the musical *Evita* (1996). Only minimal attempts were made to clarify her roots or explain her heavily accented English. Even when she spoke in Spanish to answer a phone call from her mother and insist she wasn't going home yet, how or why the Spanish Vicky ended up in Long Island with Jack, or wanted to stay there, was left unsaid.

The pseudo-noir film *Love Walked In* opened at the 1997 Sundance Film Festival then was released internationally over the next two years. It tells the story of the money-making scheme of Jack Hanaway (Denis Leary), a lounge pianist at a Long Island club and aspiring author of crime novels, and his wife Vicky Rivas, a torch singer at the club. Jack sets Vicky up to tempt Fred Moore (Terence Stamp), the club's owner, into an affair with the collusion of Fred's wealthy wife and a private eye, Eddie Bianco (Michael Badalucco), an old friend of Jack's. Eddie, Vicky and Jack hope to blackmail Fred, but the plan falls through because at least in this first stage Fred will not fall to temptation and risk losing access to his wife's money. This plot about a man who spies on his wife as a willing participant in adultery recalls both *Indecent Proposal* (1993) and, more classically in the Spanish tradition, Cervantes' short novel 'El curiososo impertinente' ('Ill-Advised Curiosity'), which is interpolated in his masterpiece *Don Quijote de la Mancha*.

After the private eye is killed in a car crash, Vicky and Jack decide to make one last attempt to run the scam on their own. Vicky will seduce Fred at a birthday bash at his mansion. Jack brings along a gun as well as a camera. He cannot use either since Vicky closes the curtained balcony doors to the bedroom before she and Fred finally do have sex. Distraught, Jack and the gun fall out of his spying perch in a tree at the feet of Fred's bodyguard and Fred's stepson who beats Jack up, though sparing his hands, for attempting the assault on Fred. Vicky abandons Jack for Fred. She succeeds in moving on with her career, too, to a higher end club.

Reviewers everywhere of *Love Walked In* honed in on Campanella's attempt to mix genres, particularly to disrupt the noir atmosphere and plot with comic elements. In *The Boston Phoenix* Peter Keogh warned viewers anticipating lighter fare from the film's title, 'Any thought that Juan José Campanella's directorial debut might be a blithe romantic comedy vanishes with the opening image: an eviscerated cat' (23 February 1998). The desire to shock as well as to mix humour in drama recalls Hitchcock. Despite Keogh's observation, as we have seen this was not Campanella's debut by a long shot. Still the comment underscores that *Love Walks In* was indeed an important commercial debut. It was his first film with well-known actors and mainstream distribution, by Columbia

TriStar in the US. Where Keogh anticipated comedy but got gore, reviewers for major US publications judged the film according to noir genre standards. Stephen Holden in his *New York Times* review claimed the 'plot cuts against film noir convention with a tenacity that is downright perverse' (20 February 1998). When Roger Ebert panned *Love Walked In*, he extensively analysed the confused genre codes:

> 'Love Walked In' proves something that nobody ever thought to demonstrate before: You can't make a convincing film noir about good people. Noir is about weakness and temptation, and if the characters are going to get soppy and let their better natures prevail, what's left? Has there ever been a thriller about resisting temptation? The movie has two other problems: It requires the female lead to behave in a way that's contrary to everything we know about her. And it intercuts the action with an absurd parallel story, a fantasy the hero is writing. He hopes to become a novelist, but on the basis of this sample, he should stick to playing the piano. Oh, and the filmmakers should have guessed that the big ending, where the hero falls out of a tree, would inspire laughs just when the movie doesn't need any. (20 February 1998)

Ebert faults Campanella not just for the comic ending but also for the awkward and ill-timed insertion of comic dialogue throughout the film. For example, Vicky asks her husband how far she'll have to go in this scheme: 'Make out? How much? Second base? Third? Home run?'

Love Walked In, though definitely a flawed project, foreshadowed Campanella's penchant for counterpoint structure, for interweaving the tale of a writer's drafts with a main story that he later realised in the masterful *The Secret in Their Eyes*. In *Love Walked In*, however, the disjunctive writing scenes have the effect of both isolating and escalating the violence. Nonetheless if one excises the writing scenes from *Love Walked In* as Ebert urges, what is left is an amalgam of allusions to 1940s movie classics, especially to *Casablanca* and Hitchcock's *Notorious*. Through these classic allusions in the genre mix the film aspires to be not just noir but also romance and thriller. To recall, mixing genres was more common in Hitchcock's most successful films, like *Notorious*, *Vertigo* or *North by Northwest*, than generic purity. In *Love Walked In* Jack's demeanour and cynical piano monologues clumsily evoke the persona of Humphrey Bogart in *Casablanca* but without any of the gut-wrenching impact of the wartime compromises of Rick Blaine and Captain Renault. The *mise-en-scène* of The Blue Cat in Westhampton, Long Island, which screams low-budget location, falls too far away from the exotic original. What is decidedly missing

Summoning the shock of *Psycho*'s toilet bowl sequence, *Love Walks In* shows the toilet flush down a ring, as Jack rejects the advances of a 'cougar.'

in Jack's class-resentment monologues, or anti-capitalist drivel, is a backbone of historical events and political references. In this he may have been following Hitchcock who famously ignored recommendations to add specific references to the Spanish Civil War in *Foreign Correspondent*.

One specific allusion to Hitchcock in Jack's monologues is a riff on the code-breaking toilet bowl sequence in *Psycho*. As Jack plays his piano and talks to the crowd as a voiceover, the film shows an extensive toilet sequence in flashback. Jack tells the story how he scorned the opportunity to change his circumstances and literally seize wealth when he resisted the temptations of a 'cougar' or older woman on the prowl for sex with a younger man. She threw her huge diamond ring in the toilet and told Jack to grab it. He flushed the toilet instead.

In *Psycho* Marion flushes the paper with the account of what she stole down the toilet in her hotel room. Hitchcock broke with the Motion Pictures censorship code when he showed a toilet in use for the first time on screen. He was able to hold off the censors because he convinced them that by flushing an object that was intimately connected to the film's theme and moral dilemma, he was not indulging in prurient motives. *Love Walked In* is not only in dialogue with Hitchcock's use of the toilet to describe a moment of moral reckoning, but also with his irreverent tone. The toilet scene becomes a leitmotif in the film. Throughout, both Jack and Vicky refer to it and reconsider if he should have grabbed the ring or not.

Through the emblematic story of the ring, *Love Walked In* presented a world of moral uncertainty. Feinmann's novel had specified a political scenario, the early years of the Dirty War in Argentina, for this conundrum. When Campanella transferred the tale to Long Island, however, he denuded it of historical and political contextualisation. He only began to anchor a tale of moral uncertainty in Argentinean history much later when he adapted another novel for *The Secret in Their Eyes*.

Besides referencing Hitchcock's toilet scene, Campanella borrows the party scene. Guillermo del Toro remarked that a party scene is standard fare for a Hitchcock film and, moreover, that *Notorious*'s visual aesthetics is the gold standard among Hitchcock's party scenes. To recall, in *Notorious*'s most famous crane shot Hitchcock sweeps the camera down a staircase to show the key to the wine cellar in Alicia Huberman's (Ingrid Bergman) hand. Campanella follows this Hitchcockian rule by making a party scene the climax of *Love Walked In*. The beach sequence that precedes the party literally gives a guide to its plot with a map on the sand. The film establishes both the predominance of a visual aesthetic and the importance of camera angles to it as in *Notorious*. Jack maps out the final attempt at seduction and blackmail in drawings on the sand behind their rented beach house. He fights with the private eye, who wants to give up the case, and steals his gun. The final shot of the sequence is a bird's-eye-view

A wash out in *Love Walks In*: bird's-eye-view of the map Jack (Dennis Leary) plots on the sand to show his plan for seduction and blackmail.

Making Mrs. Moore (Marj Dusay) swivel her head, Vicky (Aitana Sánchez-Gijón), wearing a short version of Ingrid Bergman's black ball gown in *Notorious*, walks in on her mission to seduce Fred Moore in *Love Walks In*.

of the map on the sand as the waves begin to obliterate it. It both prefigures the project's failure and the stylistic aesthetic of low and high angles – up and down staircases, and from the tree to the balcony – in the subsequent party scene.

When Vicky makes her entrance at the party in her sparkly black dress, she recalls Ingrid Bergman, another high-cheekboned beauty in black evening attire who spoke in accented English, as Alicia Huberman in *Notorious*. In both cases gazes are riveted on them at a party. Fred's wife almost dislodges her neck vertebrae as she turns to check Vicky out. Both Vicky (Marj Dusay) and Alicia were sent on missions to seduce the owners of the mansion, Fred and Sebastian (Claude Rains) respectively. The cat-and-mouse game to entice Fred up the mansion's staircase in *Love Walked In*, however, pales in comparison to the spy game in the basement of *Notorious*. Simply put, the allusions in the party/seduction scene are not as original as the beach map. Nonetheless, Campanella's study of classic Hollywood, and his attempt at commercial success by eliciting comparison to these films, is in evidence everywhere. In Argentina, where the original novel *Ni el tiro del final* had been well received, and hence where the film had a better chance of positive reception, Campanella's film fell flat. Nonetheless it did elicit indirect comparison to Hitchcock. In a review entitled 'Un policial que falló la puntería' ('A crime film that missed the target') in *La Nación* Adolfo C. Martínez pronounced the film 'regular' (mediocre) with a wordplay that mixes references to a well-known tango lyric and Hitchcock's moniker, 'the master of suspense': 'The final result is a suspense film without any suspense. Something fatal for the genre' (14 January 1999). Trying to be a Latin Hitchcock had not worked out.

V. THE RETURN TO ARGENTINA: CROSSOVER TRIANGULATION AND TRANSNATIONAL SUCCESS WITH A DIFFERENT GENRE

After the decidedly mixed, if not outright bad, reviews for *Love Walks In*, Campanella regrouped and returned to Argentina to make films in Spanish. He reconnected with Fernando Espest with whom he had co-written scripts before leaving for New York. They pulled out an old draft from that period on which to base their first new collaboration. Reassessing his commercial strategy, Campanella calculated he could better connect with his audience through a different popular genre. For his next three films, all of which were collaborations with Espest, he turned away from noir to romantic comedy. This genre change and the return to writing in his native language rekindled his sense of humour and led him to express working-class solidarity. In a sense Jack's downbeat social class monologues from *Love Walked In* were put back into context, making sense as simplified Peronist politics. The resultant trilogy of films in Spanish – *El mismo amor, la misma lluvia* (*Same Love, Same Rain*,

1999), *El hijo de la novia* (*The Son of the Bride*, 2001) and *Luna de Avellaneda* (*Avellaneda's Moon*, 2004) – established Campanella's reputation as primarily a Latin American director and significantly blurred connections to his American apprenticeship and his work in television, through both of which Hitchcock had seeped in through osmosis.

It is a common pattern that directors who begin their careers looking to Hitchcock's model find their own distinctive style or artistic vision mid-career. What is different about Campanella is that not only does he return again to Hitchcockian aesthetics and genre concerns later on but also that when he crossed back to Argentina his new work was repeatedly judged there as a transnational product or, worse, as a Hollywood sell-out. Since issues of national identity and globalisation framed the reception of Campanella's romantic comedy trilogy, an analysis of these films allows us to step back and consider what constitutes critical components of national and transnational cinema, of the local and the global.

As a transnational director Campanella symbolised what Tamara Falicov calls 'The Cinematic Tango', the dual allegiances to Europe and Latin America manoeuvering around Hollywood:

> Argentine cinema might be described as dancing a complicated tango, with the Hollywood film industry on one arm and European cinema on the other. While it is entangled with both partners, one more commercial, one more auteurist, it is a cinema that cannot be separated from its Latin American comrades, who are watching the awkward tango from the periphery of the dance floor. While it has historically aimed to distance itself from its Latin American neighbours by invoking its European immigration origin story, it cannot escape its position in world geopolitics, economic stability or geographic location ... protectionist policy measures (taxes on movie tickets, low-interest film loans, subsidies, co-participation agreements and so on), even within a neoliberal environment, are unique to the Argentine situation, partly due to its position as a 'Europeanised' Latin American country. On the one hand, legislators and film lobbyists envision Argentina as an industrialised country with a strong state-supported culture similar to a social-democratic European country. On the other, proponents of a 'populist' perspective argue that Argentina should be categorised within the Latin American paradigm; it is seen as a subordinate, developing nation in need of industry protection. (2007: 5)

Over the period from 1999 to 2006 Argentina suffered one of the greatest financial crises in its history. Campanella's popular romantic comedies, which reaffirmed family ties and community values as sustenance against the economical collapse, served as escapist fare for the local market.

VI. THE POPULIST TRILOGY, BACK TO THE TANGO

Campanella's first box office success in Argentina and to a lesser extent abroad was *Same Love, Same Rain*, billed as a 'romantic-social comedy'. The title, a verse from the tango 'Por la vuelta' ('A toast to our return') of Enrique Cadícamo, to music by José Tinelli, acknowledged the local Argentine audience.[8] As Campanella observed to Lorena García of *La Nación*, in 'Cine local, como de Hollywood' ('Local cinema, like Hollywood's'), he took a populist perspective through his choice of everyday protagonists who lived on the margins of history:

> It is somewhat the story of those who never were in anything, those who weren't the protagonists of the history. I mean to say: those who were not the disappeared, nor the Malvinas veterans, nor those who went bankrupt with the 1050 decree. But indirectly we have all suffered. (15 September 1999)

The film tells the story of Jorge (Ricardo Darín), a short-story writer who works for a left-leaning weekly, and Laura (Soledad Villamil), a waitress. He falls in love with her when he spots her in the back seat of a taxi cab with the window open craning her neck so the rain can fall on her face. Jorge and Laura fall in and out of love over the course of the two decades beginning in 1980. Meanwhile at the newspaper Jorge's stories are cut down, censored and dropped from regular rotation. When he attends the opening of a film that adapts another one of his stories, he leaves in horror at the lurid perversion of his work. The conflicts in the newsroom reflect the political tensions of the era. When a veteran reporter is let go, the other workers chip in to support him, but he commits suicide. Jorge (Ulises Dumont) eventually loses his job, too, but reuniting with Laura in the rain leaves him optimistic.

Same Love, Same Rain won all the major Silver Condor awards, the Oscars of Argentina, and was a breakthrough vehicle for the romantic starring duo of Villamil and Darín. When Julia Montesoro interviewed Campanella for an article in *La Nación* entitled 'El mismo amor, pero un éxito sin igual' ('The same love, but an unequalled success'), he confessed, 'In the US I feel like I don't have an identity; on the other hand I find it in Argentina' (10 October 1999). Yet some doubted that Campanella could naturally channel an Argentine identity. Guillermo Ravaschino writing for cineismo.com found the film inauthentic, by which he meant Hollywood-like:

Like some auto paint jobs *Same Love, Same Rain* has three layers. The meticulous excess, which is the first layer, favors naturalness. But naturalness has to serve another, very different layer, which is structured by political commonplaces and clichés of romantic cinema from the cradle of Hollywood. This layer is the most opposed to naturalness. And it becomes ever more essential, to the detriment of the other layers. http://www.cineismo.com/criticas/mismo%20amor,%20la%20misma%20lluvia,%20el.htm

Ravaschino criticised Campanella for not staying with the simple story of a youth unconcerned with politics and at the same time for simplifying the story's political background:

Initially one would say that Jorge is just an average kid. But Campanella refused to, didn't know how to, or didn't feel capable of telling a story along these simple lines. Firstly he lets certain echoes of the last military dictatorship enter through the window. Since it all starts off in 1980, and not three or four years earlier, *Same Love, Same Rain* gives itself the luxury of being a 'repudiation' of the most innocuous kind: the disclosure of a raid based on what happened before, which occurs while at a restaurant. (ibid.)

Campanella responded to accusations of making 'a comedy in the Hollywood style' by noting a difference in his use of humour in *Same Love, Same Rain*:

Perhaps people say that it seems like American cinema, because in the movie there are jokes that make one laugh, there are scenes that make one emotional. People point out that it's well made, has good photography and production values. As for content, I connect it more to Italian comedy – where the situations are not funny, but the characters act in an amusing manner – than to Hollywood comedy. Because even though funny situations happen in the comedies that Hollywood makes today, they don't have irony or sarcasm, characteristics which are otherwise typical of Argentinean humor. (Quoted in Montesoro 1999)

Although the humour of *Same Love, Same Rain* was not the same as in, for example, a Julia Roberts movie, it was not that far off from the humour of Hollywood or Italian films of an earlier era. The simplification of political events was a hallmark of these films, too. It served as the stylised backdrop to Campanella's next film, his most successful comedy, *The Son of the Bride*.

In *The Son of the Bride* the workaholic 42-year-old Ramón Belvedere (Ricardo Darín) runs an Italian family restaurant fallen on hard times at the

peak of Argentina's economic implosion. Ramón is divorced and less than attentive to his girlfriend Naty (Natalia Verbeke). His father (Héctor Alterio) wants
to give his mother (Norma Aleandro), who is suffering from Alzheimer's, the
church wedding they never had. Eventually Ramón is forced to sell the restaurant business to investors and let his longtime employees go, but his parents
finally have their wedding ceremony.

Any film that ends with a wedding, as this one does, is pure melodrama.
There are no weddings in Hitchcock. This comedy played well internationally
because of the tender family story and the social consciousness generated by the
timely representation of Alzheimer's. Campanella's own mother was suffering
from the disease at the time he wrote the film's script. *The Son of the Bride* was
Argentina's Academy Award entry and was shortlisted, although it did not win.
Despite the film's popular appeal, Fernando López in his *La Nación* review,
'Expertos en comedias emotivas' ('Experts in emotional comedies'), expressed
discomfort with melodramatic simplification: 'when it plays on the sentimental
chord and gets close to melodrama, the language becomes more direct – at times
it borders on sententious and overwrought – and the film pales' (16 August
2001). Significantly, though, López goes on to praise the film by reclaiming
Campanella as Argentine:[9]

> *The Son of the Bride* is a very Argentine film in several ways: in the recog-
> nisable nature of the characters, in the manner in which one can see them
> seek a balance in the midst of the fight for survival, emotional misfortune
> and others' judgements; in the exercise of a playful, caustic, and many time
> self-directed humour, which acts as a defensive shield to adversity; in the
> resigned familiarity with an abnormal situation that has already become
> routine; and in the diffuse and malleable limit that separates what is legal
> from corruption or immorality. (ibid.)

American reviewers also praised the film for its Argentinean realism, albeit
again a simplification of events. Stephen Holden wrote in the *New York Times*
that it was tempting to view Ramón's 'exhausting' midlife crisis as 'emblematic of Argentina's precarious economic health' (22 March 2002). However, in
Argentina the film was not universally well received.

At the same moment as this populist trilogy identified Campanella as
Argentine, looking from outside of Argentina in, these films alienated some
Argentinean film critics, particularly those writing for *El Amante,* an influential Argentinean film journal, and for *Cineismo,* an Argentinean online cinema
journal. Taking international and especially European art-house cinema for
comparison they disparaged Campanella's films as formulaic. This reaction was

also pronounced for the third film in the trilogy, which was a European co-production.

Avellaneda's Moon, which again starred Ricardo Darín, was an Argentinean/Spanish co-production. In Spain it was nominated for the Goya for Best Hispanoamerican Film. But unlike *The Son of the Bride* it received little US distribution.

The film tells the story of the eponymous social club in provincial Buenos Aires that has fallen on hard times, as have its members. Ramón Maldonado (Ricardo Darín), who was born at the club on carnival night in 1959, loses his job and is separating from his wife Verónica (Silvia Kutika). She and others are looking for love on a tight budget. Their son also loses his job and plans to emigrate to Spain. When the club is fined for not filing reports over the last fifteen years, the members debate disbanding and selling the place to transform it into a casino and to take on jobs working in it. The vote to sell wins. Ramón's son leaves for Spain.

Avellaneda's Moon has one of the funniest, ironic representations of the perils of globalisation in all of Campanella's films. Ramón's wife tells him she wants a separation because their relationship lacks romance. One of the telltale signs, she explains, is that he no longer even wears cologne. Ramón stops off to buy some. Looking at the fancy packages in the store window, he first asks for the Calvin Klein cologne he used to wear, but the price is too high, so the clerk suggests a name brand Argentine cologne on the same shelf. The price is still too high. They go down the possibilities in the store; all are too expensive for Ramón. Without missing a beat in his sales pitch the clerk walks right out of the front door of the store beckoning Ramón to follow him to the 'annex'. The store clerk seamlessly transforms into a street vendor as he stations himself beside a sidewalk display with knock-offs. He repeats the same sales pitch he gave inside, first for the Calvin Klein 'type' cologne, made in Taiwan – too expensive – then for the imitation of the Argentine brand – also too much money. Finally the clerk suggests rows of simple plastic bottles of a natural local 'artisanal' production and launches into a description of the scents. Acknowledging that he found

Framing for anonymity in *Avellaneda's Moon*: The storekeeper guides Ramón to the 'annex' or the street to offer him cheaper cologne.

In *Moon of Avellaneda* the display of cheap imports and 'artisanal' brands on the sidewalk, all that Ramón can afford, shows how far down Argentines have slipped economically.

In a parody of a luxury transaction, the street vendor squats down to package the home-made cologne with an extra gift in *Moon of Avellaneda*.

something with a rock bottom price he can afford, Ramón sighs, 'De paso, co-laboramos' ('At the same time we collaborate') – that is, they support each other and a national industry. Throughout the whole sidewalk sequence medium shots bisect the bodies in order not to show the actors' faces, only their hands. At the end of the sequence the clerk squats down, showing visually how low the country has fallen, and puts the bottle into a cardboard box with shredded paper. Ever keeping up the sales pitch, he explains to Ramón that he has saved money because with these local products he is not paying for any marketing. In an ultimate parody of a luxury transaction the vendor inserts a small cheap soap as an gift extra. In a latter sequence, his wife and friend complain about the bad smell in the room when Ramón uses the cologne. This is situational comedy played at its best. Repetition of a paradigm generates the humour. Likewise it not-so-subtly critiques how globalisation has marginalised the average Argentine, as it depicts the lengths that Argentines had to go to survive the economic crisis.

In all three of Campanella's Argentine romantic comedies there are similar scenes of disillusion such as the cologne sale that express social critique and working-class solidarity. Campanella recuperated a locally inflected sense of humour through this trilogy.

What is less studied than Campanella's internationally successful film trilogy is his television work of the same period. This television work was more global, as was Hitchcock's whose most productive period coincided with the advent of television. To clarify, Hitchcock reached a wider audience through television, for his original series and for the rebroadcasting of his films over the years, than he ever did in movie theatres. Interestingly Campanella alternated between films in Argentina and television projects in the US and Europe – eight episodes for Comedy Central in 2000 of *Strangers with Candy*, which fictionalised the true story of a 46-year-old drug addict who returns to the high school classroom – then in 2002/03, two episodes for NBC of *Law and Order: Criminal Intent* and one of *Dragnet*. In 2006 his crossover career inspired the theme of his television project, seven episodes of a television series *Vientos de agua* (*Winds of Water*), a Spanish/Argentinean coproduction, the first series which Campanella wrote. *Wind of Water* alternated between stories of a Spaniard who emigrates to Argentina in the 1930s because of the Spanish Civil War, and an Argentinean who emigrates to Spain in 2001 because of the financial collapse. Campanella himself became a Spanish citizen in 2006.

VII. A RETURN TO HITCHCOCK AND CLASSIC NARRATIVE FILM: A NEW TRIUMPH WITH *THE SECRET IN THEIR EYES*

In 2009, Campanella launched his most cinematographically ambitious film: *The Secret in Their Eyes*, an Argentinean/Spanish co-production. With this film he revisited the thriller, the generic territory of his early career while reprising the model of the love story from his populist trilogy. He enhanced the romantic connection by reuniting the same actors from *Same Love, Same Rain*. Even among Campanella detractors in Argentina, whose sarcastic critiques we will consider shortly, the universal opinion is that *The Secret in Their Eyes* is Campanella's best film to date. Narcisco Brega opens his article in *El Amante*: 'At this point now no-one, or almost no-one, would dare dispute, at least not too emphatically, that *The Secret in Their Eyes* is Juan José Campanella's best movie, whatever this may mean for the person who makes that statement' (2009: 23). The international acclaim at festivals and in award nominations for the film was loud and strong. In Spain it was nominated for nine Goyas, including the co-production duo of top categories – Best Picture, as well as Best Hispanoamerican Picture. It won the latter. Most significant for its overall international box office success, the film made the short list of five finalists for the Best Foreign Language Film Academy Award, a triumph for Campanella and a source of national pride for Argentinean cinema. Then despite being an underdog to *Das weisse Band: Eine deutsche Kindergeschichte* (*The White Ribbon*, 2009) and *Un profète* (*The Prophet*, 2009) in the competition, the film won the Oscar. Pedro Almodóvar presented the award to Campanella.

Many critics point out that *The Secret in Their Eyes* reflects a return to classic Hollywood filmmaking in its structure and narrative. The film tells the story of Benjamin Espósito (Ricardo Darín, again) who in retirement from his job as a judicial court clerk is writing a book inspired by an old unsolved homicide case. Over the intervening decades Espósito has kept his love intact for Irene Menéndez-Hastings (Soledad Villamil), now a judge, with whom he worked on the case.

A young married woman, Lisa Colotto (Carla Quevedo), was raped and murdered in her own home in 1974. The lack of resolution to the case has long haunted Espósito and obsessed the victim's husband Ricardo Morales (Pablo Rago). In the aftermath of the crime, each day Morales sits in train and bus stations and watches for signs of his wife's killer. Investigations lead not only to the pursuit, arrest and conviction of Colotto's killer Isodoro Gómez (Javier Godino) but also the renewal of an office grudge between Espósito and Romano (Mariano Argento), a supervisor who was reprimanded for his heavy-handed tactics in the original investigation. To settle this old score Romano plots to have Gómez, a common criminal, included in an amnesty release for political prisoners. Furthermore he sets him up as an undercover assassin for the government upon his release. After a meeting in Romano's office Espósito and Menéndez-Hastings are shocked when Gómez gets in the elevator with them and threatens them with a gun. Shortly after, three Triple A paramilitaries (members of the far-right death squad Alianza Anticomunista Argentina) break into Espósito's house, killing Pablo Sandoval (Guillermo Francella), a good friend and co-worker who is sleeping off a drunken binge there. Espósito imagines Sandoval died heroically in his place.

Many years pass. When Espósito visits Morales at his farm he discovers that Morales had kidnapped his wife's killer after Gómez threatened Espósito. Since then Morales has kept Gómez isolated and chained in a cage in a shed. Espósito simply leaves the farm and finishes his manuscript in which he manages to admit his love for Irene. When she reads it, she also declares her affection. They pledge to make their love work.

As suggested in my own questioning of Campanella at the San Sebastián Film Festival, with which this chapter began, one key to this film's success is that it reflects a return to Hitchcock, to what Campanella called Hitchcockian 'osmosis'. Subsequent sections will explore these complex and far-reaching connections through close analysis of *The Secret in Their Eyes* in terms of the following: first, the love story or romance within the thriller; second, the balance between humour and drama especially in the manipulation of suspense; third, the multiple endings and their political, ideological and ethical implications; and fourth, the chase scene and the role of cinematographic ambition or innovation.

VIII. FROM ROMANTIC OBSESSION TO NEW BEGINNINGS: THE TEMPO OF TERROR AND ROMANCE VIA *VERTIGO* AND *NORTH BY NORTHWEST*

The Secret in Their Eyes is based on a novel by Eduardo Sacheri originally entitled *La pregunta de sus ojos*, then reissued with the same title as the film. Campanella and Sacheri collaborated on the script.[10] Significantly, the movie greatly expands the role of Irene from that in the novel. For one, it introduces a romantic relationship between Irene Menéndez-Hastings and Benjamin Espósito. Reprising the romantic duo of the actors Ricardo Darín and Soledad Villamil recalls aspects of romantic comedy from Campanella's earlier films. For another, the film enhances Irene's role in the workplace, in particular making her a more active prosecutor than in the novel. In the film, Irene is a successful judge who apparently has it all – prestigious job, husband and children. Though older than she is and now retired, Benjamin on the other hand never rose higher than a clerk in the judicial office because he lacked a degree. This representation of hierarchical differences and the societal change to a more assertive role for a woman in *The Secret in Their Eyes* also reflects changes made from novel to film. Most of the shift in emphasis from novel to film occurs along gender lines between Irene and Benjamin's co-worker, Pablo Sandoval. Significantly, in the novel Sandoval initiates the successful interrogation of the accused murderer, Isidoro Gómez, by baiting him with insults to his manhood. In the film Irene fills the same role and uses the same dialogue as Sandoval does in the novel. Having Irene nail the sexual predator and murderer by unmasking his insecurities affects gender revenge. Thereby the film presents a more powerful, activist image of women than the novel does. It symbolises the era of Cristina Fernández de Kirchner, President of Argentina (2007–), and that of Brenda Johnson (Kyra Sedgwick), Los Angeles Police Department Deputy Chief in *The Closer* (2005–2012), cable's most widely-viewed scripted show in US television history during its run.[11]

These two major changes in Irene's role, highlighting romance and police procedure or prosecution, moreover represent the genre mix of *The Secret in Their Eyes*. Its complex hybrid structure at times alternates and at other times combines terror and romance through subtleties of tempo and tone. By appreciating this hybrid structure, a departure from Campanella's trilogy of romantic comedies, we can see how Campanella returned to Hitchcock, for Hitchcock achieved a similar balance in his mature period in films such as *Vertigo* and *North by Northwest*. Some critics have seen this balance as one of the most important characteristics of his aesthetics throughout his career. As Truffaut wrote, 'It was impossible not to see that the love scenes were filmed like murder scenes, and the murder scenes like love scenes' (1984: 345).

Extreme close-up of Irene's (Soledad Villamil) eyes in the credit sequence sets a romantic tone to *The Secret in Their Eyes*.

The Secret in Their Eyes opens with close-up shots of eyes, both of Irene and of Benjamin, that both establish a leitmotif and recall *Vertigo*'s credit sequence. Both films tell the story of a man's lifelong obsession with a woman. They are fundamentally love stories. The film's misty eyes set a more romantic tone than did *Vertigo*'s threatening eye that turns red in Saul Bass's vision. A similar change in tone to red, which implies a frightening loss of control, however, occurs in *The Secret in Their Eyes* in an early flashback to the murder scene. The spectator is forced to confront a full-screen image of Liliana Colotto's (Carla Quevedo) nude body, bloody and bruised, sprawled across the floor, limbs out-stretched, eyes wide open. In both films images of eyes as leitmotifs signify alternately romance, then terror.

Nonetheless, Hitchcock's presence in *The Secret in Their Eyes* is less a matter of direct citations, such as we have suggested with regard to the *Vertigo* credit sequence, than a more indirect appreciation of the complexity of classical cinematographic structure and melded genres, in this case one that combines romance and terror, which *Vertigo* epitomises. In short, the classical composition of *The Secret in Their Eyes* owes its cinematic heritage to *Vertigo*. Both are rooted in music. Bernard Herrmann's score for *Vertigo* was profoundly influential. Jack Sullivan in *Hitchcock's Music* characterises it thus: 'More than any cinema music, [*Vertigo*'s score] enacts the despair and stubborn persistence of our attempts to re-create the past' (2006: 234). Likewise in his article 'Pretérito Imperfecto Futuro Perfecto' ('Preterite Imperfect Future Perfect') in *El amante* Gustavo Noriega points to the obsession with memories and their uncertain character in *The Secret in Their Eyes* as a principal strength of the film:

> The memories that appear in the movie, in the form of flashbacks, often turn out to be false (the execution carried out by Morales), exaggerated (the farewell in the train station) or pure suppositions (the final heroic gesture of Sandoval). The anchoring of the movie to the past is neither firm nor indisputable. To this common aspect of all police procedurals – uncertainty regarding what happened with respect to a specific crime – Campanella adds layers of ambiguity that transcend the genre and take on wider implications. (2009: 16)

Given this manipulation of time, Noriega concludes, 'the impact of *The Secret in Their Eyes* is global' (2009: 17). Even without directly comparing the scores of *Vertigo* and *The Secret in their Eyes* and how they specifically enhance the films' structures, we can note the importance and appreciation for classical musical composition in the two directors. Sullivan documents Hitchcock's collaboration with Herrmann and the latter's musical sources of inspiration.[12] To prepare for shooting *The Secret in their Eyes* Campanella studied audiotapes of Beethoven's 'Moonlight Sonata'. He claims the structure of the third movement – 'the tonic and the dominant with modulating bridges' – inspired the film's structure of two themes, based on the love story and the police story:

> I tried to make sure that we wouldn't be changing tempo and theme at the same time. When we switched from one narrative to another, we were still in the same energy. We would only change the energy within one theme. We had to find all these bridges to modulate from one narrative to another easily, to flow in and out of all the themes: starting with theme one, theme two, then back again to theme one, theme two, and then the development of the coda; the end where everything gets mixed up. We worked with that sonata structure in mind. I became obsessed.[13]

This emphasis on music as a source of film structure in order to control changes in tempo and theme between romance and thriller looks back to Hitchcock and forward to new beginnings.

To give one specific example of film structure as a musical composition, or as a study of tone and tempo, it is revealing to compare the endings of *North by Northwest* and *The Secret in their Eyes*. To recall, *North by Northwest* ends with the famous cut to a tunnel sequence to signify the lovemaking. Similarly *The Secret in Their Eyes* ends reimagining the encounter on the train platform between Irene and Benjamin. These two romantic endings signify new beginnings. However, they are also in stark contrast to the resolution of the respective thriller plots. In *North by Northwest* the climactic confrontation happens at the Russians' house; in *The Secret in Their Eyes*, at Morales' farm. Both are isolated locales. Between the climactic scenes there is another that modulates the tension, changes the tempo and tone. In *North by Northwest* the main characters depart from an airport, an emblematically classic transition. In *The Secret in Their Eyes* Benjamin Espósito visits Pablo Sandoval's grave. Campanella discusses how he came upon this bridge in musical terms:

> I didn't want to end everything with question marks, even though I wanted to leave it to the audience to decide whether Espósito tells on Morales or

not. That's actually what audiences in Argentina are going crazy about. They argue, 'Is Campanella supporting vigilante justice?' I knew that was an answer I didn't want to provide in the movie; but, I wanted to provide at least one answer and I wanted to end the last story, the love story, and come back to the home key. When we started writing the script, I knew we couldn't go from the scene with the cage – which, hopefully, if it worked, would be a strong dramatic scene – to the next scene where Espósito professes his love to Irene. I needed a little bit of time for the audience to make the transition and that's when we came up with the idea of Espósito taking flowers to the grave of his friend Sandoval. It was related to the case because Sandoval was killed during the case; but it was also related to the love story. Sandoval is associated with both stories. That scene served as a bridge and perhaps also contributed to the feeling of yet another ending. I can understand the criticism that the film has too many endings, but it was the best of the possibilities I had to work with. (Quoted in Guillen 2009)

Like *North by Northwest*, Hitchcock's great chase movie, *The Secret in Their Eyes* does not end with the solution to the crime, or even with the restitution of justice for the sad 'wrong man', the husband Ricardo Morales. As we have seen in the above quote, Campanella chose to leave these aspects of the plot open-ended. Morales still could be his wife's killer. Espósito may or may not report Morales' kidnapping and incarceration of Gómez. As in *North by Northwest*, the film ends reestablishing the balance between comedy and thriller. Espósito puts a flower on Sandoval's cemetery niche, then the film cuts to Espósito deciphering his midnight note of 'Temo' ('I am afraid'), by adding the missing letter 'a' to make 'Te amo' ('I love you'). In a final make-over, so to speak, since Espósito had not dared to express his love before, a newly confident Espósito strides into Irene's office. When the film cuts to the close-up of her smiling face, as she says 'It'll be complicated', the final balance between thriller and romance is reached. It is as satisfactory a final resolution as the kiss and suggestive tunnel shot at the end of *North by Northwest*.

Richard Allen calls this type of ending in Hitchcock's comic thrillers like *North by Northwest* a 'romantic renewal'. He explains: 'Hitchcock, the godlike narrator, orchestrates a self-evidently fictive universe to yield blessings upon its hero and heroine, come what may, and the anarchic force of human sexuality serves only to fuel rather than to undermine romantic renewal' (2007: 13). This idea of romantic renewal modeled on Hitchcock in *The Secret in Their Eyes* led to allegorical readings, and biting criticisms of the film, which we will consider in a subsequent section.

IX. BANKING ON HUMOUR, MASTERING SUSPENSE

At San Sebastián when Campanella acknowledged the presence of Hitchcockian 'osmosis' in his films he highlighted the balance between humour and drama. In *The Secret in Their Eyes* ironic humour plays against the meshed genres of romance and political thriller. Particularly in sequences with Pablo Sandoval, played by Guillermo Francella, a well-known comic actor in Argentinean television, humour is interjected to balance tension and achieve suspense, the trait most closely associated with Hitchcock.

Early in the film, the crime investigation unfolds through a series of wrong accusations. Romano manufactures trumped-up charges against two immigrant labourers, who are beaten into confessing to the murder in order to close the case. Espósito storms into the jail, unmasks the sham and frees them. Back at headquarters he denounces Romano for the travesty of the false arrests and launches into a public brawl with him in the corridor. In the heat of the moment Romano makes a final verbal threat, 'You don't know who you're dealing with. You don't have the slightest idea.' The sequence cuts leaving the words suspended in the minds of the spectators and giving them greater importance as a premonition. The tension is typical of a political thriller. At this moment the threat is left out there for Espósito who has bettered his rival. The verbal warning likewise invites the audience to watch Espósito's back, so to speak. Romano affects his revenge much later in the film, and much more perversely, when he releases the actual murderer to allow him to be useful as an undercover assassin for the military government during the Dirty War. However, before reaching this political climax and settling of scores, the film plays with an alternation of humour and terror.

After Romano's threat, the film cuts to one of many humourous scenes, deploying as much physical as verbal humour, with Espósito's co-worker, the office clerk Sandoval. Serving as comic relief in *The Secret in Their Eyes*, Sandoval answers the office phone with inventive zingers, such as 'Blood Bank', 'Tactical Revolutionary Command' or 'Sperm Bank, Loan Department'. Almost all of his dialogue, and the repartee he generates in the film reflects a particularly Argentinean tendency to sarcasm and dark humour. In an article entitled 'Poné a Francella' ('Send In Francella') Nazareno Brega applauds the depth of the performance of Guillermo Francella: 'Francella adds mischievousness to his character and takes away the sense of resignation' (2009: 23). To give one example of Sandoval's dark humour, when his new female boss Irene walks into the office in a black dress, Sandoval compliments her: 'A saint has died today. Because an angel's dressed in mourning.' She acknowledges his remark and rejoins: 'It's a method we angels have to lose five pounds.' After Irene closes her office door, Espósito laments that he cannot come up with such quick 'piropos' ('flirtatious compliments') although we have already heard him spew out a half dozen of them to every woman he passed as he entered the building at the beginning of the day. To which Sandoval knowingly replies: 'It's easier for me. I'm not in love.'

Like Hitchcock, Campanella masters suspense in *The Secret in Their Eyes* by alleviating the tension through humorous interjections. In their resurrected investigation Espósito and Sandoval drive out to the provincial city of Chivilcoy to break into the house of the mother of the suspected criminal Isidoro Gómez and find clues to his whereabouts. As the sequence begins, the duo is filmed from behind sitting in the car on the stakeout. Sandoval breaks the tension with comic banter, as he complains he has to pee and that Espósito has seen too much *Perry Mason*. Once in the house the camera follows Espósito from behind as he searches each room, increasing the tension. He finds Gómez's letters in a drawer and sits down to read them. Framed in mid-body only, Sandoval enters the room, approaches Espósito in the foreground from behind and lays his hand on Espósito's shoulder. The gesture, which is repeated in several subsequent scenes, startles him and the viewer, which leads to a funny verbal exchange. Sandoval takes the letters from Espósito to look them over. While the latter sets off to check for envelopes in the trash, Sandoval tucks the pack of letters in his coat rather than returning them to the drawer. Their search in the waste bins is cause for visual humour until they pause to listen for the old woman coming home and then hide from her. A low-angle shot of the woman's dog chasing them out of the house ends the sequence with yet another comic touch.

A subsequent sequence, a flashback that imagines Sandoval's death, represents another example of how Campanella develops a scene visually through a shift in the balance between comedy and thriller. This instance adds depth to the film's message since it derives its force from the political context of the Dirty War. Espósito has rescued Sandoval for the umpteenth time in a drunken stupor and taken him to his own home because his wife refuses to take him in. The scene begins by reprising Sandoval's role as a comic foil to Espósito. The classic situation of a drunken man being taken home plays out in dialogue and physical comedy. However, when Espósito steps out for a moment, three burly men burst into the house. They are backlit by stripes of light from the side, like ////, which William Rothman has identified as a classic Hitchcockian motif.[14] The darkness of the room symbolises the danger.

In a subtle heroic visual gesture, with the intruders at the doorway, Sandoval turns a photograph of Espósito over on the table. It is a tribute to Hitchcock's style that the film respects the audience to interpret a visual clue to understand one of the most frightening realities of 1970s Argentina: the extralegal assaults

Leitmotif of suspense: anonymous as framed in mid-body, Sandoval scares Espósito when he puts his hand on his shoulder from behind in *The Secret in Their Eyes*.

A comic exit in *The Secret in Their Eyes*: Gómez' mother's dog chases Espósito out the door.

of various paramilitary groups during the Dirty War, mostly sanctioned by the military government. In the film, Sandoval's gesture encourages viewers to interpret the visual cues. The photograph would give the secret police an image of what Espósito looks like. Sandoval knows the score: these men have come to 'disappear' Espósito. When men ask 'Are you Espósito?', Sandoval answers 'Yes, I am.' As in classic Hitchcock, the audience is kept in the know. The film cuts. When Espósito returns to his house, he finds the bloody corpse of Sandoval. He knows, and the audience knows, through the repetition of the clue of the overturned photo, that Sandoval allowed himself to be mistaken for Espósito.

The search scene in Chivilcoy is only one of many similar scenes in *The Secret in Their Eyes* that typify a television police procedural, a genre in which Campanella has achieved considerable success in the US. To recall, from 2000 to 2010 he directed seventeen episodes of *Law and Order: Special Victims Unit*, a series that focuses on sexual crimes. Audiences can generally follow police

The //// Hitchcockian motif marks the Triple A paramilitaries who come to assassinate Espósito, but kill Sandoval.

drama scenes without any special understanding of the historical or political context. However, other important scenes in *The Secret in Their Eyes* that also show the influence of Hitchcock's aesthetics, such as the flashback to Sandoval's death, depend on a more local understanding of the political and historical context. These scenes have generated a polemical debate in Argentina about the moral stance of the film.

X. HISTORICAL REVISION WITH A 'FALSE NOTE'?: CAUGHT IN THE ELEVATOR OF *NORTH BY NORTHWEST*

Consider the situation in a thriller of an elevator full of people. First a pair of good guys get on the elevator to escape the pursuit of the bad guys but the bad guys muscle in and catch the same elevator. Tension mounts, but nothing will happen in the elevator itself because there is an unwritten code of polite conduct and public behaviour in such a space. *North by Northwest* plays this situation for comic effect. Accompanied by his ditzy yet domineering mother (Jessie Royce Landis), Roger Thornhill (Cary Grant), who is being mistaken for the spy George Kaplan, tries to escape the bad guys in a hotel. Just when Thornhill and his mother get in an elevator, the goons jump out of another elevator on the floor and join them in the same one. Breaking the tension, mother blurts out: 'You gentleman are not trying to kill my son, are you?' Sequentially everyone in the elevator bursts out laughing. The film cuts to multiple reaction shots of the heavies and the other passengers laughing at mother's irrational suggestion until she laughs along, too. Grant's own visage communicates incredulity. Keeping up the politesse and following upon the good manners of his mother when they reach the lobby Thornhill gallantly proclaims 'Ladies first' and makes the goons wait for the women to exit. He runs out with the women. According to Ernest Lehman, *North by Northwest*'s screenwriter, Cary Grant questioned Hitch's direction in the scene.[15] He did not believe the situation worked, or that the audience would buy into the plausibility of the bad guys playing along with the

In *North by Northwest* mother (Jessie Royce Landis) protects her son (Cary Grant) and challenges the social etiquette of the elevator.

Low angle, big gun: In *The Secret in Their Eyes* Gómez gets in the elevator with Irene and Espósito and shows his power.

public code of conduct. But despite Grant's reservations most viewers enjoy the ride and mother's banter even more so.

The Secret in Their Eyes recalls the thriller situation of *North by Northwest*'s elevator sequence. Irene and Espósito are shocked when the assassin Gómez gets in the same elevator with them. They instantly recognise each other. Packed together, the smartly groomed Gómez openly plays with his gun. The low-angle shot shows how he and his gun loom large in the foreground.

Gómez's brazen gesture shows that he is now in a position to take them out at any moment with impunity. However, unlike in Hitchcock's comic thriller where mother names the threat at hand and breaks the tension, no one speaks in the elevator in *The Secret in Their Eyes*. But like Grant, Campanella had doubts over whether the scene, precisely because of this silence, would work or not:

> The scene that plays powerfully in Argentina is the elevator scene where Gómez has evaded punishment and threatens Irene and Espósito. Thank God it works because – when I was editing it – I was doubtful: 'Does this work?' But it did work because it represents a society that has shut up and shut down; a society that has accepted fear. That's why I chose to set the movie in the pre-dictatorship days rather than during the dictatorship be-cause everyone in those pre-dictatorship days were [sic.] already succumb-ing to fear by refusing to talk about it. I wanted to show that moment where they make the choice of shutting up, looking away, and running away. (Quoted in Guillén 2009)

For most viewers outside of Argentina the elevator scene only plays as thriller, as a dramatic counterpart to Hitchcock's comic situation. The glances emphasise the leitmotif of eyes. However, as we see in the above quote from an interview at the Toronto Film Festival, Campanella intended a political message for his eleva-tor sequence. In a historical revision that opens up the pre-dictatorship years to scrutiny he accuses Argentineans, and especially the Argentinean justice system, as represented by Irene whose eyes are downcast in the elevator, of not speaking up to denounce the rise of the paramilitaries in the early 1970s. Considering how Hitchcock dealt with an elevator sequence in a thriller reveals the significance not just of the visual leitmotif, but more importantly of the aural, of the role of silence.

Although he praises Campanella's reinterpretation of Argentinean history overall, the critic Gustavo Noriega, witing in *El Amante*, faults how the historical revision and Campanella's accusatory writing are woven into the movie's timeline, especially in the scene in Romano's office that precedes the elevator confrontation:

> A scene in the ministry, probable den of the Triple A, gives rise to one of the few false notes of the film. Irene and Espósito go to see an ex-police officer, now a government functionary, to reproach him for having liberated the killer of Morales' wife. In the discussion, which becomes more direct and threatening with each exchange, he answers their shouts by saying: 'You don't know the country that's coming.' In the context of the film it is a false note that only makes sense retrospectively. The reference warning of the Dictatorship stands out and appears as a concession to a commonplace within a movie that is very rigorous about its historical references. (2009: 17)

Noriega calls Romano's warning to Irene and Benjamin an anachronistic error since Romano cannot have known *a priori* that Argentina would become a military dictatorship. This critique is excessively harsh. The comment is a prediction that the film moreover puts into a specific historical context. In the background of the previous three sequences a news programme plays on television that shows Gómez guarding Isabel Perón at a public rally. This media background shows not only that Gómez is a free man but also that he is now a paid assassin for the government. This foreshadows the actions of a dictatorship and reinforces Romano's prediction. The specificity of the newsreel with Isabel Perón (President of Argentina, 1974–1976), whose political role few viewers outside of Argentina would know, makes the scene more than a commonplace view of Argentinean politics.

Gómez (Javier Godino) inserted into TV history next to President Isabel Perón in *The Secret in Their Eyes.*

Shifting the historical and political timeframe of the film to 1974, rather than 1968 as in the novel, made possible an important act of historical and political revision. Campanella unmasked how the societal attitudes that marked the bleak period of the Dictatorship were already forming several years earlier than is generally credited. This historical revision connected the film not only with the local Argentinean context, still processing revelations from the Proceso, but also with the global context that expected Latin American cinema to be social political discourse, particularly about the Dirty War. The success of Luis Puenzo's *La historia oficial* (*The Official Story*, 1985), which won the Best Foreign Language Film Academy Award, set this pattern placing expectations and limitations on subsequent filmmakers to include and exploit the topic of the Dirty War in order to launch their projects internationally. Campanella's *The Secret in Their Eyes* speaks to the model, but also more importantly shifts the discourse to address more nuanced and polemical contemporary concerns.

XI. THE POLEMICS AROUND MULTIPLE ENDINGS: FROM THE HERMETIC WORLD OF *SHADOW OF A DOUBT* TO THE FALSE FLASHBACK OF *STAGE FRIGHT*

Although the interpretation of the elevator and ministry sequences provoked some controversy, it was nothing compared to the hue and cry surrounding the film's multiple endings. To recall in brief, there are four 'endings' that appear in the following order: first, a false flashback to Morales killing Gómez by putting him in the trunk of his car and shooting through the lid; second, a climactic scene where Morales attends to Gómez in a cage and is discovered by Espósito; third, Espósito's visit to Sandoval's grave; and finally Benjamin and Irene's declaration of their romantic commitment to each other. These endings were criticised on aesthetic, political and ethical grounds. The critic Eduardo Rojas in an article 'Espejos del alma' ('Mirrors of the soul') in *El Amante* led the charge by accusing Campanella of being formulaic – 'why use the still unhealed wounds of our recent history as a simple guessing game?' Rojas questioned the film's historical validity and lamented the political effects of aesthetic choices – 'Why do movies insist on vindicating private vengeance to the detriment of the claims of victims and family members? Why invent a story that contradicts the presence of those claims?' To understand Rojas' comments and the major controversy over the film's endings it helps to return to how the film radically changed the book's ending. Then we will explore how Hitchcock's films problematised the interface between aesthetics and moral and ethical issues in ways similar to *The Secret in Their Eyes*: first, in terms of cinematographic closure in *Shadow of a Doubt*, and second, in terms of the false flashback in *Stage Fright*. The debates in Hitchcock criticism suggest an important cinematographic context.

The film substantially alters the book's ending to emphasise the participation of the viewer in constructing the story. In the book, a dying Morales writes a letter to Espósito asking him to carry out final requests in a visit to his farm. When Espósito arrives, he finds Morales already dead from a self-injected overdose. Exploring the farm he discovers the assassin Gómez dead, too, in an isolated building where Morales had jailed him for many years and intuits that Morales lured him out there to cover up the evidence of the kidnapping and murder. Espósito buries Gómez's body and calls the police to report Morales' death. In the film, the climatic ending at Morales' farm is completely different. Espósito discovers Morales' secret jail with Gómez still in it alive. Espósito silently acknowledges the situation and leaves it as it is. The scene is tonally golden and the light is grainy as if dust were floating in the air. The *mise-en-scène* communicates the sense of a period piece, of years having gone by. As the camera pans over the jail cell with its jailer and prisoner from the point of view of Espósito, the film acknowledges and may implicitly sanction Morales' personal sense of justice. At that moment Espósito, and the viewer, are complicit to the crimes. In the novel Espósito hides evidence of the kidnapping and murder of Gómez to preserve Morales' reputation in the provincial town, but he participates in other normal police procedures, even when the police themselves raise suspicions about Morales' odd storage barn. In contrast the film establishes a hermetic system of justice removed from normal police channels.

This manipulation of the narrative to acknowledge a different set of circumstances and an independent or hermetic sense of justice recalls the ending of *Shadow of a Doubt* in the sequence of Uncle Charlie's funeral. Uncle Charlie is being set to rest in a religious ceremony inside the church without ever having been publically unmasked as a killer. Outside of the church his niece Charlie, who has just survived Uncle Charlie's attempt to kill her on the train, says to Jack, Charlie's police detective friend: 'I couldn't have faced it without someone who knew.' The dialogue and the *mise-en-scène* privilege the position of the viewer and give her access to a closed system with its own satisfying sense of justice. *The Secret in Their Eyes* replicates Hitchcock's aesthetics and moral view when Espósito walks away from Morales' house just as the niece Charlie in *Shadow of a Doubt* stays outside of her uncle's funeral in the church. These films represent a closed system in which the viewer has privileged access to a subjective ethical code. The critic Rojas faults Campanella's lack of cinematographic ambition and describes the film's characterisations as ahistorical, Manichean reductionism:

Why stereotype the good and the bad guys outside of their historical context? As to the latter, Romano is a genetically configured bastard; Espósito, the good guy, has a sense of justice that exceeds his will. Where did this atypical Argentinean dude come from? And why does he then betray his own nature by ultimately becoming an accomplice to the private vengeance of Morales? (2009: 21)

To say the least Rojas likes rhetorical questions, which are by nature open-ended and leave their barbs floating in the air. His mocking comments, such as asking where this lone ranger came from, that imply that Campanella does not know the national character, illustrate the almost vindictive nature of some criticism of Campanella in *El Amante*. Although Rojas concludes that Espósito acquiesces to the justice of Morales' private vengeance, Campanella intended to leave the audience not knowing if Espósito ever reveals what he knows about Morales as Gómez's jailer. Visiting Sandoval's grave, another one of the endings, is in musical terms, the bridge between the two themes. The multiple endings do have the effect of leaving the public resolution of Morales' case unresolved. In this Campanella follows Hitchcock's model in *Shadow of a Doubt*, *Suspicion* and *Rebecca*.

It is important now to consider a different cinematographic 'error', the false flashback, that Hitchcock and Campanella both exploited with some regrets because it breaks the film's continuity, an unwritten bond of trust with the audience. The false flashback that is only corrected in the ending made *Stage Fright* one of Hitchcock's most controversial films especially among French critics. Even when he spoke with Truffaut, Hitchcock doubted the wisdom of having duped the audience. Hitchcock remarks, 'I did one thing in that picture that I never should have done; I put in a flashback that was a lie' (Truffaut 1984: 189). To recall, at the beginning of *Stage Fright* Jonathan Cooper (Richard Todd) unburdens himself of the story of the murder of the husband of Charlotte Inwood, a famous actress (played by Marlene Dietrich), to Eve Gill (Jane Wyman), who is in love with Jonathan, as she speeds their car along a highway. The whole scenario, in which he implicates Charlotte for the murder and frames himself only as participating in a cover-up, is presented as a flashback from Jonathan's point of view. The false flashback begins with a dissolve that takes us to the realm of Jonathan's memory. The error of the flashback is only revealed through the secret of the protagonists' eyes at the end of *Stage Fright*. Eve and Jonathan are cowering together in the theatre's basement to avoid the police. As he retells the story of the murder of Charlotte's husband, and admits to the crime, Jonathan literally transforms his face into that of a killer before her loving eyes. Jonathan then speculates

The dissolve in *Stage Fright* from the point of view of Jonathan (Richard Todd) that begins the false flashback/car scene to reveal he was only an accomplice to the murder of Charlotte's husband (Marlene Dietrich).

The story in the eyes: in the basement under the stage Eve (Jane Wyman) now sees Jonathan as a murderer and reacts with horror in *Stage Fright*.

Reverse shot: Jonathan's (Richard Todd expressionistically lit eyes capture his madness as he contemplates killing again in *Stage Fright*.

that if he kills her, too, he will go free since 'It'll be a clear case of insanity.' The sequence shows this transformation in a shot/reverse-shot in which only their eyes are lit against extreme shadows.

Campanella likewise employs the technique of a false flashback in the dénouement of *The Secret in Their Eyes*. Espósito visits Ricardo Morales' farm in the country; Morales tells Espósito that he kidnapped and killed Gómez. The film cuts to show Morales shoot through the lid of a car trunk, where we assume Gómez lies. Espósito leaves the house but then returns again to discover that Morales is keeping Gómez alive in a cage in the farm's shed. The viewer is left with a sense of moral justice achieved outside of the usual channels. Espósito will keep the secret and not go to the police. The narrative construction as a closed system that privileges the spectator recalls many Hitchcock films – *Rebecca, Suspicion* and *Shadow of a Doubt*, among others.

In the one ending of *The Secret in Their Eyes* concerning Gómez's incarceration Campanella respects the spectator and obeys Hitchcock's major cinematographic law: always think about the audience. Nonetheless another of the endings of the film is a false flashback. This technique violates that dictum.

Like Hitchcock, Campanella had some doubts about his own choice of a false flashback. Although he recognises it as 'a lousy end', he defends his choice by referring not to *Stage Fright* but to manipulating the language, or the music, of suspense:

> The dramatic climax is the scene with the cage. I had two challenges there. In order for the scene with the cage to be surprising, for it to totally work, it had to be based on Morales and his stated assertion that he did not believe in the death penalty. When he tells Espósito the story about how he killed Gómez in the trunk of the car, that had to play as the climax of the movie. If it wasn't played as the climax with the swelling music and the whole thing, then as an audience you would have an inner feeling that something was missing, like there's one more beat, and you're going to start looking for that beat. So that scene *has* to play like it's the end of the movie. A lousy end, a very obvious end, but I don't mind for a second that you think that it's a bad ending; it *has* to feel like the ending. So that comes at the price of already having one ending that is not the real ending, you know? But I feel that was an appropriate price to pay for the surprise of the dramatic ending of the scene with the cage. (Quoted in Guillen 2009)

In *The Secret in Their Eyes* Campanella reduces the length of time that the audience is left deceived in comparison to the prolonged or 'indirect' continuance of the lie in *Stage Fright*. Truffaut even tries to get Hitchcock to agree that Jonathan lied three times. Hitchcock replies bluntly, 'I agree the whole thing was very indirect' (Truffaut 1984: 190). Their self-reflexive critiques show how deeply they thought about their audience at every stage of filmmaking.

XII. CUT TO THE CHASE, OR SOME FINAL REMARKS ON COMMERCIAL SUCCESS AND MOTHER'S MACGUFFIN

Campanella won the 2010 Academy Award for Best Foreign Language Film over Germany's heavily favoured *The White Ribbon* and France's *The Prophet*. This second Oscar nomination was the charm for Campanella. For the first time the field included two 'thankful to be nominated' South American films, *The Secret in Their Eyes* and Peru's *La teta asustada* (*Milk of Sorrow*). Campanella interpreted his win as 'shattering preconceptions' about South American films for this category, which European films have dominated. Like Fernando Trueba thanking his 'God' Billy Wilder when he accepted his Academy Award for *Belle Epoque* in 1994, Campanella managed one good joke in his speech: 'I want to thank the Academy for not considering Na'vi a foreign language.' Both Trueba and Campanella acknowledged the significance of Hollywood in their minute of fame, but Campanella, in his ironic wink to *Avatar* (2009), underscored Hollywood's commercial and ideological dominance. What commercial success means to Campanella, and for the interpretation of his films, has been controversial for a long time, as it was for Hitchcock.

'The chase,' Hitchcock explained in a 1951 *New York Times* interview, 'makes up about 60 per cent of the construction of all movie plots – even *Hamlet*' (quoted in McGilligan 2003: 311). Showing a Hitchcockian appreciation of visual innovation and plot construction, the chase scene at the Huracán soccer stadium is fittingly the *piece de resistance* of *The Secret in Their Eyes*. Campanella's scene gives the impression of being one continuous shot as Espósito and Sandoval run after the assassin Gómez. The editing, done by Campanella himself, masterfully hides the multitudinous cuts from swooping helicopter shots, crowd pans, and point-of-view chase shots.

The relationship with mother is what brought soccer into the film. To recall, Pablo Sandoval breaks the code of Gómez's letters to his mother, which they stole from her house in Chivilcoy, when he realises that all the names mentioned in them are soccer players. Sandoval calls on the help of his bar buddy, alias the Notary, who spews out soccer history like a computer, to tell Espósito what each of the players mentioned in the letters are famous for. This *tour de force* at the bar supports Sandoval's observation that the one thing a guy can't change in his life is his passion. (Sandoval's passion is hanging out at the bar and getting drunk with friends; Espósito's passion is to secretly love Irene.) Sandoval convinces Espósito that Gómez will have altered his travel routine and workplace to evade them, but because he can't change his 'passion' the one place where they can find Gómez is at a soccer game. Hence Sandoval and Espósito set off to chase him down at the Huracán soccer stadium.

Hitchock enters into the discussion of Gómez's letters to mother, too, for it is through a comparison to Hitchcock that Eduardo Rojas, writing in *El Amante*, criticises Campanella's control of narrative. Rojas blasts Campanella's representation of mother, specifically in comparison to Hitchcock's in *Psycho*, as ridiculously forced and academic, neither sufficiently intimate nor sufficiently political:

> Incidentally, the whole soccer subplot that serves to lead into the famous scene is bogus in its very conception: a textbook psychopath (ask Castagna: perhaps, unavoidably at this moment due to their long suffering, every Racing fan is a psychopathic individual) communicating with his mother, the sweet little old woman, in soccer code. Do you imagine Norman Bates conversing lovingly with his mother over baseball? I don't. (2009)

For Rojas, for whom Hitchcock is a constant referent, Campanella uses soccer, 'the opium of the masses', to reach a commercial common denominator. Rojas forgets that the letters to mother function as a MacGuffin. They have neither intrinsic value nor deeper psychological interpretation. They serve to advance the plot, to get to the chase.

Nowadays in the Spanish-speaking world Campanella is called 'industrial' – that is, a commercial director, as opposed to either an independent director or art-house director.[16] He achieved this status by treading in Hitchcock's footsteps – crossing the boundary of sexual violence in *The Boy Who Cried Bitch*, learning television filming techniques in cable series, alternating work in his home country and the US, finding the right leading man for his aesthetics in Ricardo Darín, and most importantly achieving a balance of humour and thriller/drama, a sophisticated mix of genres, that is portrayed with techniques found in Hitchcock's films, with *The Secret in Their Eyes*. Perhaps not surprisingly Campanella's status as an auteur continues to provoke controversy in Argentina as seen in the discussion of the September 2009 issue of the Argentinean film magazine *Amante de cine*. The discussion continues to play out in extensive blog exchanges. Diego Batlle, a frequent critic for *La Nación*, decried the editorial policy of *El Amante* as frankly anti-Campanella. In general *La Nación*'s coverage of *The Secret in Their Eyes*' international success has been universally positive. Adolfo C. Martínez's review 'Juego de mentiras, verdades y secretos' ('Play of lies, truths and secrets') in *La Nación* predicted the controversy described in this chapter: '*The Secret in Their Eyes* is a film which doubtless will give us a lot of good things to talk about, a work that overall makes national cinema proud' (13 August 2009). Campanella's career continues to be reassessed.

XIII. EPILOGUE AND A REPRISE OF A NATIONAL IDENTITY IN *METEGOL*

'No puede cambiar de pasión.' ('He can't change his passion.')

– Pablo Sandoval

Campanella truly never let go of the MacGuffin from *The Secret in Their Eyes*, the obsession for soccer. In 2013 working again with the writer Eduardo Sacheri, Campanella adapted the short story 'Memorias de un wing derecho' ('Memories of a right wing') by Roberto Fontanarrosa (1944–2007), an Argentinean icon for his cartoons, graphic novels and short fiction, for an animated movie *Metegol* (*Underdogs*), called *Futbolín* in Spain. Like *Toy Story* (1995) or *The Lego Movie* (2014), *Underdogs* brings to life the figures of a foosball table in a town's bar to help a young boy, Amadeo, who has loved them obsessively. Amadeo's hometown is being taken over and modernised by Grosso, a soccer media star. The grown-up Amadeo takes control of his loyal foosball team, a group of underdogs, to play a revenge soccer match against Grosso and his team, the professionals. The foosball figures are lead by Capi, the right winger of Fontarrosa's story.

With a budget of over $20 million, *Underdogs* was in 2013 the most expensive animated movie ever made either in Argentina or in Spain, the two countries of the co-production.[17] The film, whose opening was well timed to coincide with the lead-up to the 2014 World Cup in Brazil, was a huge box office and critical success worldwide, although its opening in the US has been delayed until 2015. In 2014 *Underdogs* won the Goya for best animated film, the Motion Picture Association of Argentina Awards for best adapted screenplay, sound and original score, and the Platino (Ibero-American awards begun in 2014 in Panama) for best animated film and original score.

The initial success of *Underdogs* positioned Campanella as a commercial or popular auteur whose global filmic circuit is constructed outside of the US, and especially in Spanish-speaking countries. Many reviews carried subheadings such as that of Pablo Scholz in *El Clarín*, 'El film no tiene nada que envidiarle a Hollywood' ('The film has nothing to envy Hollywood for') that invite a David and Goliath comparison.

When Diego Batlle, frequent critic for *La Nación*, reviewed the movie for Otroscines.com, he pointed out not only that Campanella's author's 'spirit' comes across clearly in *Underdogs*, but also that this nostalgic 'spirit' continues to be problematic in Argentina:

If *Avellaneda's Moon* – the most debated film of Campanella's filmography – that divided opinion into fans and detractors – is the closest model for

Underdogs, it's probable (and it's already happened in the first reactions on Twitter) that a fierce debate will again arise. I thought that within the realm of an animated movie of mass consumption that this tension, that irritation that the Campanellian spirit provokes in many (through that nostalgic streak, that vindication of 'foundational' values) was going to dissipate, but for better or worse, we are faced with a Campanella in all his artistic and ideological dimensions. (http://www.otroscines.com/criticas_detalle.php?idnota=7605)

Batlle goes on to say that *Underdogs* portrays 'argentinidad a palo', roughly 'a strict Argentineness'. Despite his global status as the most successful Argentinean director of the twenty-first century, not everyone respects his work or views his films as reflecting current national cinematic trends. Ironically Campanella's detractors, those associated with *El Amante de cine* and many others on blogs, criticise him for being old fashioned, especially in his narrative choices, and yet he took on a project to revolutionise the Latin American movie industry through 3D animation. What this achievement might prove is that he is at heart a popular auteur, and a top-rate commercial director for TV, as was Hitchcock in his day.[18]

NOTES

1   See http://www.tebeosfera.com/1/Autor/Guionista/Trillo/Carlos.htm, and on the same site, Alberto D. Kloster, 'Carlos Trillo, Sinónimo de éxito, permanencia y persistencia' ('Carlos Trillo, synonym of success, permanence and persistence'); http://www.tebeosfera.com/1/Documento/Articulo/Guionistas/Carlos/Trillo.htm.
     An author of many graphic novels, most with contemporary Argentine settings, as well as several books on this artistic tradition, Trillo's work had a wide impact in Argentina and in Europe. His comic strip *El loco Chávez* appeared regularly in the newspaper *El Clarín* from 1975 to 1985 and was adapted for television, but was censored and withdrawn.

2   See William Cook, 'The Master and Murnau', *The Guardian*, 27 February 2009.

3   Michael Balcon, the producer of these films for Gainsborough Pictures, observed that he had to have them made in Germany because in England there was resistance, especially from distributors, at giving new directors a chance; see Sloan 1993: 3.

4   In 2003 Campanella returned to Buenos Aires to teach a class on scriptwriting for 400 public school students. He used *The Contortionist* as a principal source for the class and argued against excessive explications in cinema: 'One has to avoid those distancing effects that cool or dilute the spectator's connection to the story. It's better to make the audience live the story, besides telling it to them' (quoted in Lorena García, 'El "professor" Campanella', *La Nación*, 20 June 2003).

5   Quoted in Marc Savlov, 'The Boy Who Cried Bitch', *The Austin Chronicle*, 27 March 1992.

6   When first released in Spain as *El niño que gritó puta*, newspaper reviews censored the title and abbreviated 'p_'.

7   The tango is 'Desencuentro' ('Missed Encounter') by Aníbal Troilo (music) and Cátulo

Castillo (lyrics). The tango ends 'Por eso en tu total/ fracaso de vivir,/ Ni el tiro del final/ te va a salir' ('For this in your utter failure at living, not even the final shot is going to come out right'); http://www.todotango.com/320/Desencuentro.

8 See Pablo Piedras, 'Nuestra propia historia de amor' ('Our own love story'); http://www.cinenacional.com/critica/nuestra-propia-historia-de-amor. The tango tells the story of two lovers who separate but who meet again, to toast each other with a glass of champagne: 'La historia vuelve a repetirse/mi muñequita dulce y rubia/ el mismo amor/ la misma lluvia.../el mismo, el mismo loco afán' ('The story repeats again, my sweet, blond doll, the same love, the same rain, the very same, crazy desire'); http://www.hlmtango.com/letras-de-tango/p/1/por-la-vuelta/.

9 See also María Laura Paz, '"El hijo de la novia" de vez en cuando la vida', in Mónica Satarain, Ed., *Plano secuencia: 20 películas argentinas para reafirmar la democracia*, 2004: 208–11.

10 At the 2009 San Sebastián Film Festival press conference Campanella confessed that it was difficult to settle on an English title for the film, since the Spanish 'sus ojos' can mean 'their eyes', 'your eyes', 'his eyes' and 'her eyes'. The latter choice, which was in the running, would have emphasised the romantic story.

11 See Gloria Goodale, '"The Closer" opened doors for women – and basic cable', *The Christian Science Monitor*, 12 July 2010.

12 See Sullivan 2007: 222–34.

13 Michael Guillen, 'Evening Class with Juan José Campanella', 27 September 2009, at the Toronto Film Festival; http://micropsia.blogspot.com/2009/09/evening-class-interview-with-juan-jose.html.

14 See Rothman on *North by Northwest* (2014: 180–4). The motif is self-reflexive, 'associated with the movie screen' (2014: 234).

15 See commentary track of the 2009 remastered DVD of *North by Northwest*.

16 Another Argentinean filmmaker who deserves this recognition is the late Fabián Bielinsky, who also studied Hitchcock as a model for his caper film *Nueve reinas* (*Nine Queens*, 2000), as well as his psychological thriller *El aura* (*The Aura*, 2005).

17 Although all movies are team endeavours, animated movies expand the size of the team to extremes. According to Gregorio Belinchón in *El País* around 300 animators worked in the Belgrano, Argentina studios on *Metegol* under the direction of Campanella and Gastón Gorali, head animator and creative director of Catamandú Studios, and another group worked in the Madrid SPA Studios under the direction of Sergio Pablos, who had worked on *The Hunchback of Notre Dame* (1996), *Hercules* (1997) and *Rio* (2011), among other movies.

18 Campanella has consolidated his status as a top-rate director for TV, both in the US, for Fox's *House* (2007–2010) and AMC's *Halt and Catch Fire* (2014) and in Argentina, for *Recordando el show de Alejandro Molina* (Remembering the Alejandro Molina Show, 2011) and *El hombre de sus sueños* (The Man of Your Dreams, 2011–2012). In general his US TV work tends to mystery or crime genres, whereas his Argentinean TV work is in comedy and romance. Reviews of his Argentinean TV series episodes in Argentina seldom fail to mention his work in the US as a sign of high production values and prestige.

They Became Notorious

This study demonstrates the crucial importance of Hitchcock to the development of cinema in Spain and Latin America far beyond what has been acknowledged before. Five of the most successful filmmakers in the Spanish-speaking world, as defined by awards and box office returns, modelled their transnational careers on Hitchcock's and mined the aesthetics of his films in their own. Several themes are also apparent in what Hitchcock distinctively represented in Spain and Latin America.

First, as his films premiered and also as the five filmmakers studied here reinterpreted them in recent decades, Hitchcock meant technical and artistic innovation, synonymous with modernity and progress. His successful crossover from a more marginal national European cinema to Hollywood supremely illustrates this model. In Spain an important liberal sector celebrated *Rebecca* both as technical innovation and as a resistance to a repressive moral code. Even the hegemonic critics of *ABC* and *Film Ideal*, though they abhorred Hitchcock's 'vulgarity', or sexual freedom, could not avoid recognising his artistic talent. In Mexico on the other hand, *Mr. and Mrs. Smith*, rather than the period piece *Rebecca*, was hailed as Hitchcock's crossover and the apogee of modernity. Both films furthermore celebrated couples in more open relationships. *Mr. and Mrs. Smith* reflected a new Mexico of capitalist aspirations. The ability of brand new Mexican theatres to screen Hitchcock's film, as the latest in cinematographic art, and to showcase the stars of Hollywood due to direct flights into the country spoke of progress and to national pride.

Second, in Spain and Latin America Hitchcock's films were not just appreciated as suspense or thrillers, but for a much broader generic mix, and furthermore for their glamour and glitz and sexual innuendos. Emblematic of this reception, *Notorious* was launched and continues to be known with the more melodramatic titles of *Tuyo es mi corazón* (*My Heart is Yours*) or *Encadenados* (*Coupled*). In Spain *North by Northwest*'s Eva Marie Saint left the public star struck by her erotic attraction. In Mexico Ingrid Bergman's suits in *Cuéntame tu vida* (*Spellbound*) were sold as the latest fashion, the new 'chic'.

Third, although licentious elements in his films were celebrated, in Spain and Latin America Hitchcock, who was educated by Jesuits, was recognised as a Catholic director. In Spain he spoke of the exact number of churches in his films and *The Wrong Man* inaugurated the Week of Religious Cinema in Valladolid. Subsequently major Latin filmmakers also explored religious iconography and moral issues from their own Catholic upbringing and tradition while alluding to Hitchcock's aesthetics. Close analysis shows vivid examples in Almodóvar's *Bad Education*, De la Iglesia's *Day of the Beast* and Amenábar's *Open Your Eyes*, as well as almost all of Del Toro's films.

Fourth, the combination of comedy and drama epitomised the view of Hitchcock's work in Spain and Latin America. Humour was essential both in his initial reception as well as in his later impact on the five major filmmakers. Reviews of Hitchcock's films celebrated his humour. Significantly, as seen in close analysis, the early career building films of the five Latin Hitchcocks – *Labyrinth of Passions*, *Women on the Verge of a Nervous Breakdown*, *Day of the Beast*, *Thesis*, *Cronos* and *Love Walked In* – evidenced strong comic elements. Comparing John Orr's analysis in *Hitchcock and Twentieth-Century Cinema* of American Hitchcock, of US filmmakers who were Hitchcock disciples (David Lynch and Christopher Nolan) or French Hitchcock (Eric Rohmer and Claude Chabrol) to our director studies shows that humour plays a far greater role in Latin Hitchcock.

Fifth, the study and imitation of Hitchcock began in the earlier stages of filmmakers' careers and were a major factor in their respective success. The key films for each constituted as follows: for Almodóvar, it was initially *Spellbound*, but later *Rear Window* and *Dial M for Murder*, *The Trouble with Harry*, *Topaz* and *Vertigo*; for De la Iglesia, *Vertigo* and *Saboteur*, *Dial M for Murder*, *The Trouble with Harry* and *Strangers on a Train*, *North by Northwest* and *The Man Who Knew Too Much*; for Amenábar, *Psycho* and *Vertigo*; for Del Toro, *Psycho* and *Notorious*; for Campanella, *The Thirty-Nine Steps* and *North by Northwest*.

Not surprisingly these five directors seldom looked to what I have termed Hitchcock's crossover moment in Spain or Latin America, but rather studied and drew on the films that marked Hitchcock's acknowledged Hollywood success. Only Amenábar looked directly to Hitchcock's crossover film, *Rebecca*, as inspiration for his first English-language film, *The Others*. For his early film *Labyrinth of Passions*, Almodóvar turned to *Spellbound*, a film still profoundly associated with Spanish cultural history. In his breakout film *Day of the Beast*, De la Iglesia turned to *Vertigo,* a film also embedded in the same Spanish cultural imaginary, and *Saboteur*. However, what these five filmmakers selected from Hitchcock often reflected an appreciation of how Hitchcock made 'magic', as Spanish critics termed his work, with limited resources. For instance in their debut films, Del Toro with *Cronos* and Amenábar with *Thesis* looked to *Psycho*, which Hitchcock made with less costly TV filming techniques. Like Hitchcock, most came to directing from a field of artistic design.

Finally, critics have rarely acknowledged these connections, i.e. the debt to Hitchcock, or more significantly neither have the filmmakers themselves. In fact they often hid or underplayed it. When the huge Almodóvar exhibition was staged in Paris at the French Cinematheque in 2006, on which he collaborated, the room dedicated to filmic influences did not include any allusions to or mention of Hitchcock. Although it is still only available in Spanish, Almodóvar's commentary on *The Skin I Live In* and *Vertigo* marks a change in this pattern. Amenábar simply dismisses Hitchcock as overvalued. De la Iglesia has given the most direct responses in recent years claiming to have adapted Hitchcock's *Weltanschauung*, though he, too, says that he 'stole' from Hitchcock, implying that he surpasses the master. Del Toro turns academic in his director's tracks; he talks and publishes about Hitchcock. Campanella underplays the idea of influence by calling it 'osmosis'.

Conventionally we can speak of Harold Bloom's *Anxiety of Influence*, but Michel Foucault's *Archaeology of Knowledge* (1995) and *Discipline and Punish* (2002) are more productive as a critical approach to understand 'osmosis' or influence in a globalised landscape. For Foucault, first, the author (here a director or filmmaker) as subject only exists within the discursive practice – that is, in a globalised landscape of commercial and cultural reception. Just as the interpretation of the film text is produced cross-culturally, so too are the filmmaker's image and connection to the text generated in the cultural discourse. Second, according to Foucault the relationships of power that are generated at this historical juncture are now self-policing strategies. Hence, for example, the aesthetic heritage of a film as product is elided to sustain its marketability, or to recall Walter Benjamin, its 'aura' as a 'unique' entity. As García Canclini observed to his later regret, Hitchcock in Latin America was long dismissed as a commercial quantity. He was disparaged as the 'master of sensationalism'. Likewise similar negative critiques dismissed the work and public image of the directors we have studied here. Campanella's *The Secret in Their Eyes* was called 'middle brow'. Yet the artistic and the commercial came together in Hitchcock. This combination strongly defines his followers.

All five Latin directors studied in this book became notorious. They not only made it in the Spanish-speaking world, but they also made it to Hollywood. Although some eschew the opportunity, they all can and have done interviews and director's commentary tracks in English. Three of them – Almodóvar (*All About My Mother*), Amenábar (*The Sea Inside*) and Campanella (*The Secret in*

Their Eyes) – won Academy Awards for Best Foreign Language Film. Del Toro's *Pan's Labyrinth* (2006) was nominated for that category, but won in three others in the overall competition – art direction, cinematography and make-up – an equal or more impressive showing. Almodóvar also won another Academy Award in 2002 for Best Original Screenplay for *Talk To Her*. De la Iglesia is the underachiever of this group, having never been nominated for an Academy Award. His most significant awards were the 1996 Goya for Best Director for *Day of the Beast*, the 2010 Silver Lion for Best Director for *The Last Circus* (called *A Sad Trumpet Ballad* at the Venice Film Festival) and the 2009 Spanish National Film Prize, a lifetime achievement award. His career most parallels that of Hitchcock, who also never won an Academy Award.[1] Hitchcock received an honorary award from the Academy in 1968, and then in his decline was feted with the lifetime American Film Institute award in 1979. These recognitions mean a place in the canon, longevity in the profession and more support for subsequent projects.

These five filmmakers are connected in ways that go beyond their own films, mostly in terms of their roles as producers. Like Hitchcock as their careers progressed they made new investments. The production companies they established have enabled them to function independently, mostly without state-sponsored protectionism. For Almodóvar, producing his own films has given him the unique freedom, or luxury, to shoot his films linearly, that is, to follow sequentially the written script. Almodóvar gave De la Iglesia his first break by producing *Mutant Action* for El Deseo.[2] He also produced Del Toro's *The Devil's Backbone*. El Deseo's twenty-first-century productions represent a wide generic range that spans melodrama, drama and comedy: Isabel Coixet, *My Life Without Me* (2003) and *The Secret Life of Words* (2005); Lucretia Martel, *La niña santa* (*The Holy Girl*, 2004) and *La mujer sin cabeza* (*The Headless Woman*, 2008); and Damián Szifrón, *Relatos Salvajes* (*Wild Tales*, 2014).[3]

Del Toro (sometimes, but not always with his friends and fellow filmmakers Cuarón and González Iñarritu)[4] has actively produced and promoted new talent for some time. Notably Del Toro produced Sebastián Cordero's debut *Crónicas* (*Chronicles*, 2004) and *Rabia* (*Rage*, 2009), both thrillers for Tequila Gang, his own production company, as well as J. A. Bayona's extremely successful first film, *El orfanato* (*The Orphanage*, 2007), a mystery thriller reminiscent of *Pan's Labyrinth*. Although I limited my selection for this book, the Ecuadorean filmmaker Cordero deserves to be in this company, for he is a Latin Hitchcock for a new generation.[5] Likewise Amenábar has moved on to produce films besides his own in backing Oskar Santos' *El mal ajeno* (*For the Good of Others*, 2010), a sci-fi thriller derivative of *Open Your Eyes*.[6] Besides producing some of his own films and the sci-fi television series, *Plutón B. R. B Nero* (2009), De la Iglesia has begun to produce the work of young Spanish talent with Esteban Roel and Juan Fernando Andrés' *Musarañas* (*Shrew's Nest*, 2014), a psychological and claustrophobic thriller. To launch this initiative to produce fantasy, suspense and thriller movies, De la Iglesia founded a new company, Pokeepsie Films, with Carolina Bang, who starred in several of his films. Even more than De la Iglesia with *Plutón B. R. B. Nero*, Campanella is known for producing many television series, both in Argentina and in the US. His collaboration, as producer of Daniel di Fellipo and Gustavo Giannini's animated feature film, *Plumíferos* (*Free Birds*, 2010), the first 3D movie made with open source ware, marked new generic and artistic directions for Campanella that culminated in the box office hit *Underdogs*, his directorial debut in animation. The work of these five directors as producers, which is both a supportive and gate-keeping role, is how the influence of, and their take on, Hitchcock will continue into another generation. Future studies will undoubtedly explore how and to what extent the director/producer impacts the artistic direction, distribution and exhibition, as well as the reception of the films produced under the brand of a 'popular auteur' (Buse, Triana Toribio and Willis 2013: 4).

A few comments are perhaps due rearding these filmmakers as people and how they may have imitated Hitchcock's distinctive presence and perhaps his physique, too. Almodóvar, for the photographer Juan Gatti, assumed well-known poses of Hitchcock in his own publicity photos. The struggles of Almodóvar, De la Iglesia and Del Toro with excessive weight over the years have also been well documented. Hitchcock and Orson Welles, who is enjoying a renaissance, too, with new films about him in Spain and Latin America, were known as overweight men.[7] Someone else may want to explore if these are feminised men who found in Hitchcock's soft body and overactive mind a kindred body type and a way to self-esteem. As a woman, who moreover began this project confronting a new trend toward the stereotypically 'masculine' thriller genre, I will point out the obvious – that these major imitators of Hitchcock are all men. In my research I did not find any case of a major woman filmmaker in Spain or Latin America who built her transnational career looking to Hitchcock. More recently, Isabel Coixet in *Mapa de los sonidos de Tokio* (*Map of the Sounds of Tokyo*, 2009) and Lucrecia Martel in *The Headless Woman* have delved into genres and moral dilemmas that could be considered Hitchcockian, and have worked in a transnational context. Their films come, however, at a mature stage of their careers, which have also been built more through art-house than commercial productions. Many other individual films from across Latin America and Spain allude to Hitchcock's films in a myriad of ways. I will only name a few examples here, merely to reconfirm the breadth of his influence over the time period studied in this book: Gustavo Graef-Marino's *Johnny Cien Pesos*

(*Johnny One Hundred Pesos*, Chile, 1994), Luis Ospina's *Soplo de vida* (*Breath of Life*, Colombia, 1999), Fabián Belinsky's *Nueve reinas* (*Nine Queens*) and *El aura* (*The Aura*), Rodrigo Plá's *La zona* (*The Zone*, Mexico, 2007), José Luis Guerín's *En la ciudad de Sylvia* (*In the City of Sylvia*, Spain, 2007), and Juan Carlos Maneglia and Tana Schembori's *Siete cajas* (*Seven Boxes*, Uruguay, 2012). I hope that this study will give future critics and filmgoers reason to pause to evaluate seriously the local and transnational adaptations of commercial cinema, and to discover and interpret other connections to the Hitchcockian canon in the Spanish-speaking world. At the very least I have tried to begin to draw attention to these areas of research. Hitchcock seldom disappoints. As a coda to this study, let me add a brief anecdote about such an unlikely experience.

When I have told friends that according to the newspapers, *Champagne* was Hitchcock's first movie to open in both Spain and Mexico, they have given me a blank stare, followed by the befuddled comment, 'Hitchcock made a movie called *Champagne*?' It truly was an inauspicious beginning in international distribution. Yet in studying the trajectory of how Hitchcock's films were first received in Spain and Mexico and how five major Spanish and Latin American directors began their transnational careers studying Hitchcock we have seen that the early stages, although not necessarily the first film advertised, were the most significant. As these five directors consolidate their impact on a younger generation of filmmakers, I suspect and hope that Hitchcock's presence will continue to be felt as an extension of our humanity, not as a shadow of a forgotten original but as the creation of a new work, in another language. By celebrating how films nurture each other across borders this book salutes these six masters.

NOTES

1 *Rebecca*'s Best Picture Academy Award went to the producer David O. Selznick.

2 See Marina Díaz López, 'El Deseo's "Itinerary": Almodóvar and the Spanish Film Industry', in D'Lugo, 2013: 107–28.

3 In her categorisation of different aspects of the transnational, Deborah Shaw argues that since Almodóvar and Martel make their films within a specific national/local context but circulate them through transnational distribution and exhibition networks, they differ from other Hispanic filmmakers, such as Del Toro and Amenábar, whom she calls 'transnational directors' because the latter exploit funding possibilities outside of their national contexts and employ 'transnational modes of narration' to reach global audiences (2013: 11). Specifically because of the Hitchcockian imprint on Almodóvar and Martel (in *The Headless Woman*), which is primarily a 'transnational mode of narration', I would not set Almodóvar and Martel apart from the main directors discussed in this book, but would term them all 'transnational directors'.

4 On their joint company, Cha Cha Cha, see Shaw (2013: 2–3).

5 Cordero, as the next iteration, followed not Hitchcock's but Del Toro's path into English-language film with his sci-fi thriller *Europa Report* (2013). The film underperformed and

was overshadowed by Cuarón's *Gravity* (2013).

6   See Jordi Revert (2010) '"El mal ajeno": El dolor de la impostura' ('"The Good of Others":
     The Pain of Imposture'); http://www.labutaca.net/criticas/el-mal-ajeno-el-dolor-de-la-
     impostura/.

7   See Benamou (2007). Del Toro considered Orson Welles the model for the main charac-
     ter of the 2014 TV series *The Strain*, which adapted his novel; Chris Hayer (2014) '"The
     Strain": Corey Stoll used Orson Welles as inspiration for Ephraim Goodweather'; http://
     www.zap2it.com/blogs/the_strain_corey_stoll_orson_welles_ephraim_goodweather (ac-
     cessed 14 July 2014).

Bibliography

Acevedo-Muñoz, Enrique (2006) 'Melo-Thriller: Hitchcock, Genre, and Nationalism in Pedro
Almodóvar's Women on the Verge of a Nervous Breakdown' in David Boyd and R. Barton
Palmer (eds) After Hitchcock: Influence, Imitation, and Intertextuality. Austin, TX: University
of Texas Press, 173-194.
____(2009) Pedro Almodóvar. London: British Film Institute.
Ades, Dawn (2000) Dalí's Optical Illusions. New Haven, CT: Wadsworth Atheneum Museum of
Art/Yale University Press.
Aguilar, Carlos (ed.) (2005) Cine fantástico y de terror español 1984–2004. Donostia-San
Sebastián: Semana de Cine Fantástico y de Terror de San Sebastián-Donostia Kultura.
Alcalá, Manuel, Norberto Alcover Ibánez and Equipo Reseña (1977) La cultura española durante
el franquismo. Bilbao: Ediciones Mensajero.
Allen, Richard (2007) Hitchcock's Romantic Irony. New York: Columbia University Press.
Allison, Mark (2001) A Spanish Labyrinth: The Films of Pedro Almodóvar. London: IB Tauris.
____(2009) 'Mimesis and Diegesis: Almodóvar and the Limits of Melodrama', All About
Almodóvar: A Passion for Cinema. Minneapolis: University of Minnesota Press, 141-165.
Almodóvar, Pedro (2002) 'Hable con ella' Fotografías de Pedro Almodóvar. Madrid: FNAC España
y El Deseo.
____(2004) La mala educación: Guión cinematográfica. Madrid: Ocho y Medio.
____(2012) La piel que habito. Barcelona: Editorial Anagrama.
Almodóvar, Pedro, Juan Gatti, Catherine Millet, Matthieu Orléan, Frédéric Strauss, Antonio
Tabucchi and Sergio Toblana (2006) ¡Almodóvar: Exhibition! Catalogue of the Exhibition, 5
April-31 July. Paris: Editions du Panama, La Cinémathèque Française.
Amador, María L. and Jorge Ayala Blanco (1980) Cartelera cinematográfica, 1930–1939. México
DF: Universidad Nacional Autónoma de México.
____(1982) Cartelera cinematográfica, 1940–1949. México DF: Universidad Nacional Autónoma
de México.
____(1985) Cartelera cinematográfica, 1950–59. México DF: Universidad Nacional Autónoma de
México.
Anderson, Benedict (1991) Imagined Communities: Reflections on the Origins and Spread of
Nationalism, rev. ed. London: Verso.
Angulo, Jesús and Antonio Santamarina (2012) Álex de la Iglesia. La pasión de rodar. Donostia/
San Sebastián: Euskadiko Filmategia/Filmoteca Vasca.
Anon. (1951–1974) Cine asesor. Madrid.
____(1981) Fernando de Fuentes. Cuatro películas mudas mexicanas. Cartelera cinematográfica,
1960–1969. México: Centro de Capacitación Cinematográfica.
____(1997) 'El cine en España,' Dirigido 258, June, 74.
____(2004) 'Alejandro Amenábar: "No me importa reconocer que soy gay"', Cooperativa, 31
August. http://www.cooperativa.cl/p4_noticias/site/artic/20040831/pags/20040
831125516.html (accessed 10 June 2014).
Appadurai, Arjun (1996) Modernity at Large: Cultural Dimensions of Globalization. Minneapolis:
University of Minnesota Press.
Atkinson, Michael (2008) 'Hellboy II: The Golden Army', Sight and Sound; http://old.British Film
Institute.org.uk/sightandsound/review/4453 (accessed 24 June 2014).
Aulier, Dan (1998) Vertigo: The Making of a Hitchcock Classic. New York: St. Martin's Press.
Aviña, Rafael (2004) Una mirada insólita: Temas y géneros del cine mexicano. Mexico City:
Cineteca Nacional and Editorial Océano de México.
Ballesteros, Isolina (2013) 'Women on the Verge of a Nervous Breakdown: From Madrid (1988)
to New York (2010)', in Marvin D'Lugo and Kathleen M. Vernon (eds) A Companion to Pedro
Almodóvar. Chichester: Wiley-Blackwell, 367-386.

Barroso, Miguel Angel and Fernando Gil-Delgado (2002) *Cine español en Cien películas*. Madrid: Jaguar.

Basterra, Francisco G. (1989) 'Pedro Almodóvar pierde el Oscar y rompe con Carmen Maura en Hollywood', *El País*, 31 March; http://elpais.com/diario/1989/03/31/cultura/607298411_850215.html (accessed 15 March 2014).

Batlle, Diego (2013) 'Metegol, de José Juan Campanella', 18 July; http://www.otroscines.com/criticas_detalle.php?idnota=7605 (accessed 27 June 2014).

Belinchón, Gregorio (2013) 'El último gol de Campanella', *El País*, 28 December; http://elpais.com/elpais/2013/12/26/eps/1388084713_003491.html (accessed 30 June 2014).

Beltrán, Mary (2005) 'The New Hollywood Racelessness: Only the Fast, Furious (and Multiracial) Will Survive', *Cinema Journal*, 44, 2, 50–67.

Benamou, Catherine (2007) *It's All True: Orson Welles's Pan-American Odyssey*. Berkeley, CA: University of California Press.

Benjamin, Walter (1969) *Illuminations*. Ed. by Hannah Arendt, Trans. by Harry Zohn. New York: Schocken Books.

Bernardinelli, James (1997) '*Mimic*'; http://www.imdb.com/reviews/84/8497.html (accessed 20 June 2014).

____(2002) '*Blade II*' http://www.reelviews.net/php_review_template.php?identifier =1443

____(2004) '*Bad Education*' http://www.reelviews.net/php_review_template.php?identifier=1971

Bloom, Harold (1997) *The Anxiety of Influence: A Theory of Poetry*. 2nd edition. Oxford: Oxford University Press.

Bogdanovich, Peter (1963) *The Cinema of Alfred Hitchcock*. New York: The Museum of Modern Art.

Bolín, Guillermo (1958) '*Vertigo*', *Blanco y negro*, 2414, 9 August, 63–5.

Borau, José Luis (ed.) (1998) *Diccionario del cine español*. Madrid: Alianza.

Boyd, David (ed.) (1985) *Perspectives on Hitchcock*. New York: Prentice Hall.

Boyero, Carlos (2008) 'Matemática brillante y fría', *El País*, 18 January.

____(2009) 'Tan respectable como fría,' *El País*, 9 October.

____(2010) 'Álex de la Iglesia arriesga y gana,' *El País*, 8 September.

Boyd, David and R. Barton Palmer (eds) (2006) *After Hitchcock: Influence, Imitation, and Intertextuality*. Austin: University of Texas Press.

Brega, Narciso (2009) 'Poné a Francella', *El amante*, 208, 23 September.

Brody, Richard (2014) '"Film Noir": The Elusive Genre,' *The New Yorker*, 23 July; http://www.newyorker.com/culture/richard-brody/film-noir-elusive-genre-2 (accessed 2 September 2014).

Brussat, Frederic and Maryann Brussat (1991) '*The Boy Who Cried Bitch*', *Spirituality and Practice*, September; https://www.spiritualityandpractice.com/films/films.php?id=6283 (accessed 25 June 2014).

Brutvan, Cheryl (2008) *Antonio López García*. Boston: Museum of Fine Arts.

Bryne, Barry (2008) 'The Oxford Murders', *Screen International*, 1637, 21 March.

Buse, Peter, Núria Triana Toribio and Andy Willis (2007) *The Cinema of Álex de la Iglesia*. Manchester: Manchester University Press.

Camí-Vela, María (2001) *Mujeres detrás de la cámara. Entrevistas con cineastas españolas de la década de los 90*. Madrid: Ocho y Medio.

Caparrós Lera, and José María Caparrós (1999) *Historia crítica del cine español (Desde 1987 hasta hoy)*. Madrid: Ariel.

Casas, Quim (2004) 'Guillermo del Toro (II): Itinerario del relato gótico', *Dirigido*, 338, 46–59.

Castro de la Paz, José Luis (1999) *El surgimiento del telefilme: Los años cincuenta y la crisis de Hollywood: Alfred Hitchcock y la televisión*. Barcelona: Paidós.

____(2000) *Alfred Hitchcock*. Madrid: Cátedra.

Cervantes Saavedra, Miguel de (1977) 'Donde se cuenta la novela del Curioso impertinente' (XXXIII), 'Donde se prosigue la novela del curioso impertinente' (XXXIV), 'Donde se da fin a la novela del Curioso impertinente,' *Don Quijote de la Mancha I* (ed) John Jay Allen. Madrid, Cátedra, 383–426.

Chavez, Kellvin (2004) 'Interview with Guillermo del Toro'; http://latinoreview.com/films_2004/ sonypictures/hellboy/guillermo.html (accessed July 2008).

Cochran, Sara (2007) *'Spellbound', Dalí and Film. Catalog to the Exhibition at the Tate, MoMA, and Fundación Dalí.* New York: Museum of Modern Art.

Codell, Julie F. (ed.) (2006) *Genre, Gender, Race and World Cinema.* Chichester and Malden, MA: Wiley-Blackwell.

Comas, Angel (2002) *De entre los muertos/Vértigo. Chinatown.* Barcelona: Dirigido.

Compitello, Malcolm (1999) 'From Planning to Design: The Culture of Flexible Accumulation in Post-Cambio Madrid', *AJHCS,* 3, 199–219.

Cook, William (2009) 'The Master and Murnau', *The Guardian,* 27 February. http://www. theguardian.com/film/2009/feb/27/alfred-hitchcock-berlin (accessed 25 June 2014)

Correa Ulloa, Juan David (2005) *Pedro Almodóvar: Alguien del montón.* Bogotá: Panamericana Editorial.

Costa, Jordi (2008) 'En contra: 'Los crímenes de Oxford', *Fotogramas,* January; http://www. fotogramas.es/Peliculas/Los-crimenes-de-Oxford/Critica (accessed 4 June 2014).

Cox, Alex (2008) 'I gave my right arm to be in this film', *The Guardian,* 17 April.

Cozarinksy, Edgardo (1974) *Borges y el cine.* Buenos Aires: Sur.

Cruz, Ana (2008) *Bertha Navarro: Cineasta sin fronteras.* Guadalajara: Universidad de Guadalajara.

Cruz, Gilbert (2011) '10 Questions for Guillermo del Toro', *Time,* 5 September; http://content. time.com/time/magazine/article/0,9171,2090370,00.html (accessed 21 June 2014).

De la Iglesia, Alex (2011) 'Discurso íntegro de Álex de la Iglesia, Gala, 25 Premios Goya', *El Mundo,* 14 February; http://www.elmundo.es/elmundo/2011/02/14/cultura/1297639056. html accessed 4 June 2014).

De la Iglesia, Alex and Jorge Guerrichaechevarría (2008) *Los crímenes de Oxford, guión cinematográfica.* Madrid: Ocho y Medio.

Del Toro, Guillermo (1990) *Alfred Hitchcock.* Guadalajara: Universidad de Guadalajara.

____(2006) *El laberinto del fauno. Guión cinematográfico de Guillermo del Toro.* Madrid: Ocho y Medio.

____(2008) 'Entrevista: Guillermo del Toro confesó su temor de ser secuestrado en México', 11 December. http://www.informador.com.mx/entretenimiento/2008/61796/6/guillermo-del-toro-confeso-su-temor-de-ser-secuestrado-en-mexico.htm.

____(2009) *Hitchcock por Guillermo del Toro.* Madrid: Espasa.

Del Toro, Guillermo and Chuck Hogan (2009) *The Strain.* New York: HarperCollins.

____(2010) *The Fall.* New York: HarperCollins.

De Prada, Juan Manuel (1997) '"El Día de la Bestia": De Madrid al Apocalípsis', *Madrid en el cine, Nickel Odeon,* 7, 196–8.

Deutelbaum, Marshall and Leland Poague (eds) (2009) *A Hitchcock Reader.* Chichester: Wiley-Blackwell.

Deveny, Thomas (2010) 'Alejandro Amenábar, composer', *Bulletin of Spanish Studies,* 87, 2, 195–224.

Diéguez, Antonio (2014) 'Amenábar ficha a Emma Watson para su próxima película', *El Mundo,* 14 February; http://www.elmundo.es/loc/2014/02/14/52fcf040ca474177318b457c.html (accessed 7 September 2014).

D'Lugo, Marvin (1997) *Guide to the Cinema of Spain.* Westport, CT: Greenwood Press.

____(2006) *Pedro Almodóvar.* Urbana, IL: University of Illinois Press.

D'Lugo, Marvin and Kathleen M. Vernon (eds) (2013) *A Companion to Pedro Almodóvar.* Chichester: Wiley-Blackwell.

Ebert, Roger (1994) *'Cronos',* 6 May; http://www.rogerebert.com/reviews/cronos-1994.

____(1998) *'Love Walked In',* 20 February; http://www.rogerebert.com/reviews/love-walked-in-1998.

____(2004) *'Bad Education',* 21 December; http://www.rogerebert.com/reviews/bad-education-2004.

____(2005) 'El Crimen Perfecto: An Imperfect Crime Comedy', *Chicago Sun Times,* 2 September; http://www.rogerebert.com/reviews/el-crimen-perfecto-2005.

____(2009) 'Broken Embraces', 16 December; http://www.rogerebert.com/reviews/broken-embraces-2009.

Elena, Alberto and Marina Díaz López (eds) (2003) The Cinema of Latin America. London and New York: Wallflower Press.

Epps, Brad and Despina Kakoudaki (eds) (2009) All About Almodóvar: A Passion for Cinema. Minneapolis: Minneapolis, MN: University of Minnesota Press.

Epstein, Daniel Robert (2003) 'Guillermo del Toro', 3 November; https://suicidegirls.com/girls/anderswolleck/blog/2678868/guillermo-del-toro/ (accessed 20 June 2014).

Estivill, Josep (2009) 'El espíritu del caos: Irregularidades en la censura cinematográfica durante la inmediata postguerra' ('The Spirit of Chaos: Irregularities in Cinematographic Censorship during the Immediate Post War Period') in Laura Gómez Vaquero and Daniel Sánchez Salas (eds) El espíritu del caos: Representación y recepción de las imágenes durante el Franquismo. Madrid: Ocho y Medio, 63–84.

Estrada, Marién (2007) '"¡Corte!...¡corte!...¡y más corte!": La censura en el cine mexicano' ('"Cut!... Cut!.. and More Cuts!": Censorship in Mexican Cinema'), Fundación Manuel Buendía; http://mexicanadecominicacion.com.mx/fmb/foromex/censura.htm (accessed May 2010).

Evans, Peter William (1996) Women on the Verge of a Nervous Breakdown. London: British Film Institute.

____(1999) Spanish Cinema: The Auteurist Tradition. Oxford: Oxford University Press.

____(2005) 'Las citas fílmicas en las películas de Almodóvar', Almodóvar: el cine como pasión. Cuenca: Ediciones de la Universidad Castilla-La Mancha, 155–160.

Falicov, Tamara (2007) The Cinematic Tango: Contemporary Argentine Film. London and New York: Wallflower Press.

Fein, Seth (2001) 'Myths of Cultural Imperialism and Nationalism in Golden Age Mexican Cinema', in Gilbert M. Joseph, Anne Rubenstein and Eric Zolov (eds) Fragments of a Golden Age: The Politics of Culture in Mexico Since 1940. Chapel Hill, NC: Duke University Press, 159–98.

Feinman, José Pablo (1981) Ni el tiro del final. Buenos Aires: Editorial Pomaire.

Fernández, Fausto (2008) 'A favor: "Los crímenes de Oxford"', Fotogramas, January; http://www.fotogramas.es/Peliculas/Los-crimenes-de-Oxford/Critica (accessed 4 June 2014).

Fernández Cuenca, Carlos (1972) La Guerra de España y el cine. Madrid: Editora Nacional.

____(1974) El cine británico de Alfred Hitchcock. Madrid: Editorial Nacional.

Fernández-Santos, Elsa (2002) '"Me gustan los perdedores felices": Álex de la Iglesia estrena "800 balas" un "western" que retoma su idea de la épica de lo ridículo', El País, 18 October.

Fernández Valenti, Tomás (2004) 'El hombre y el demonio', Dirigido, 337, 26–8.

Feuer, Alan (2009) 'The Trauma Surgeon of Wall Street', New York Times, 13 November, MB1.

Floristán (1947) 'Alfredo Hitchcock y Wagner,' 'Rapsodia de la Quincena', Fotogramas II, 7, 15 February, n.p.

Fontanarrosa, Roberto (n.d.) 'Memorias de un wing derecho; http://www.rosario.gov.ar/mr/multimedia/repositorio/semana-de-la-lectura/memorias-de-un-wing-derecho (accessed 27 June 2014).

Foucault, Michel (1995) Discipline and Punish: The Birth of the Prison. Trans. Alan Sheridan Smith. New York: Vintage.

____(2002) Archaeology of Knowledge. Trans. Alan Sheridan Smith. New York: Routledge.

Francis, James, Jr. (2013) Remaking Horror: Hollywood's New Reliance on Scares of Old. Jefferson, NC: McFarland.

Freixas, Ramon (2002) '"800 balas": Los restos del naufragio', Dirigido, 317, 13.

Fuentes, Victor (1995) 'Almodóvar's Postmodern Cinema: A Work in Progress', Post-Franco, Postmodern: The Films of Pedro Almodóvar. Westport, CT: Greenwood P, 155–170.

Fuentes Rodríguez, César (2007) Mundo gótico. Barcelona: Quarentena Ediciones.

Gale, Matthew (ed.) (2007) Dalí and Film. New York: Museum of Modern Art.

Garci, José Luis (2013) Noir. Madrid: Notorious Ediciones.

García, Lorena (1999) 'Cine local, como de Hollywood', La Nación, 15 September.

____(2003) 'El "professor" Campanella', *La Nación*, 20 June; http://www.lanacion.com. ar/505004-el-profesor-campanella (accessed 25 June 2014).

García Canclini, Nestor (2004) *Diferentes, desiguales y desconectados: mapas de la interculturidad*. Barcelona: Gedisa.

García Escudero, José María (1961) 'Cultura y televisión', *Film Ideal*, 74, 18–19.

García Riera, Emilio (1998) *Breve historia del cine mexicano*, Primer Siglo (1897–1997). México, D.F. and Zapopan, Jalisco: Instituto Méxicano de Cinematografía and Ediciones MAPA.

Gil, Alberto (2009) *La censura cinematográfico en España*. Barcelona: S. A. Ediciones.

González González, Luis Mariano (2009) (eds) *Fascismo, 'kitsch' y cine histórico español (1939–1953)*. Cuenca: Ediciones de la Universidad Castilla-La Mancha.

Gómez Vaquero, Laura and Daniel Sánchez Salas (2009) in Laura Gómez Vaquero and Daniel Sánchez Salas (eds) *El espíritu del caos: Representación y recepción de las imágenes durante el Franquismo*. Madrid: Ocho y Medio.

González-Sinde, Ángeles (2010) '12263 Orden CUL/2073/2010, de 14 de julio, por la que se concede el Premio Nacional de Cinematografía correspondiente a 2010', *Boletín de Estado* 184, Sec. III, 66465.

Goodale, Gloria (2010) '"The Closer" opened roles for women – and for basic cable', *The Christian Science Monitor*, 12 July; http://www.csmonitor.com/USA/2010/0712/The-Closer-opened-doors-for-women-and-for-basic-cable (accessed 28 June 2014).

Goscinny, René and Albert Uderzo (1974) *Les Lauriers de César*. Paris: Hachette.

Gottlieb, Sydney (1995) *Hitchcock on Hitchcock: Selected Writings and Interviews*. Berkeley, CA: University of California Press.

Graham, Helen and Jo Labanyi (1995) *Spanish Cultural Studies: An Introduction*. London: Oxford University Press.

Greydanus, Stephen D. (2010) 'A History of Violence: *Agora*, Hypatia and Enlightenment Mythology', *Decent Film Guide*; http://www.decentfilms.com/articles/agora (accessed 13 June 2014).

Grimes, William (2009) 'Robin Wood, Critic and Hitchcock Fan, Dies at 78', *New York Times*, 23 December, B15.

Gubern, Román (2005) *Historia del cine español*. Madrid: Cátedra.

Güell, María (2008) 'Cuanto mejor es un actor, más fácil resulta trabajar con él', *ABC- Sevilla*, 18 January, 76.

Guillen, Michael (2009) 'Evening Class with Juan José Campanella', *Micropsia*, 27 September; http://micropsia.blogspot.com/2009/09/evening-class-interview-with-juan-jose.html (accessed 28 June 2014).

Guimón, Pablo (2007) 'De las malas calles a Freixenet', *El País*, 27 November.

Guthman, Edward (2000) 'Sexy, Violent "Perdita" Finally Arrives in U.S. / Tiny unauthorized "Vera Cruz" clip held up release', *San Francisco Chronicle*, 16 January; http://articles.sfgate.com/2000–01–16/entertainment/17634715_1_perdita-durango-arnold-schwarzenegger-film-directed.

Halbfinger, David and Sharon Waxman (2007) '*The Departed* Wins Best Picture, Scorsese Best Director', *New York Times*, 26 February.

Harrington, Richard (1994) '*Cronos*', *Washington Post*, 22 May; http://www.washingtonpost.com/wpsrv/style/longterm/movies/videos/cronosnrharrington_a0abc7.htm (accessed 20 June 2014).

Hayer, Chris (2014) '"The Strain": Corey Stoll used Orson Welles as inspiration for Ephraim Goodweather', 10 July. http://www.zap2it.com/blogs/the_strain_corey_stoll_orson_welles_ephraim_goodweather-2014–07 (Accessed 18 July 2014)

Hergé (George Prosper Remi) (1974) King Ottokar's Sceptre (The Adventures of Tintin). Boston: Little, Brown and Company.

____(1975) Tintin in Tibet *(The Adventures of Tintin)*. Boston: Little, Brown and Company.

____(1976) The Calculus Affair *(The Adventures of Tintin)*. Boston: Little, Brown and Company.

____(1979) Tintin in America *(The Adventures of Tintin)*. Boston: Little, Brown and Company.

____(2009) *The Adventures of Tintin, vol. 7: The Castafiore Emerald/Flight714/Tintin and the Picaros*. New York: Little, Brown Books for Young Readers, Hachette Book Group.

Heredero, Carlos F. (1994) *El lenguaje de la luz: Entrevistas con directores de fotografía del cine español*. Alcalá de Henares: Festival de cine de Alcalá de Henares.

____(1997) '*Carne trémula*: "Thriller" pasional y carencias emocionales', *Dirigido*, 261 (October), 22–3.

____(1997) *Espejo de miradas: Entrevistas con nuevos directores del cine español de los años noventa*. Alcalá de Henares: Gráficos Ballesteros, Festival de Cine de Alcalá de Henares, Fundación Colegio del Rey, Comunidad de Madrid, Caja de Asturias, Fundación Autor, Filmoteca de Generalitat Valenciana.

____(1999) *20 nuevos directores del cine español*. Madrid: Alianza.

Hernández, Omar and Emile McAnany (2001) 'Cultural Industries in the Free Trade Age: A Look at Mexican Television', in Gilbert M. Joseph, Anne Rubenstein and Eric Zolov (eds) *Fragments of a Golden Age: The Politics of Culture in Mexico Since 1940*. Chapel Hill, NC: Duke University Press, 389–414.

Higginbotham, Virginia (1998) *Spanish Film Under Franco*. Austin: University of Texas Press.

Hirschberg, Lynn (2004) 'The Redeemer', *New York Times Magazine* (5 September), n.p.; http://www.nytimes.com/2004/09/05/magazine/05ALMODOVAR.html?_r=0 (accessed 5 March 2014).

Hodkinson, Paul E. (2002) *Goth: Identity, Style and Subculture*. Oxford: Berg.

Holcomb, Mark (2002) 'Monsters, Inc.', *Village Voice*, 26 March; http://www.villagevoice.com/2002–03–26/film/monsters-inc/ (accessed 21 June 2014).

Holden, Stephen (1998) '"*Love Walked In*": Torch Songs and a Suspicious Wife,' *New York Times*, 20 February; http://www.nytimes.com/library/film/022098walked-film-review.html (accessed 26 June 2014).

____(2001) 'Plastic Surgery Takes a Science Fiction Twist', *New York Times*, 14 December.

____(2002) '*Son of the Bride*', *New York Times*, 22 March; http://www.nytimes.com/movie/review?res=980DE4DD1F38F931A15750C0A9649C8B63 (accessed 27 June 2014).

____(2004) 'Lured by Stories and an Ambiguous Femme Fatale', *New York Times* (9 October), n.p.; http://www.nytimes.com/2004/10/09/movies/09bad.html (accessed 11 March 2014).

Holland, Jonathan (2008) 'Review: "The Oxford Murders"', *Variety*, 29 January; http://variety.com/2008/film/reviews/the-oxford-murders-1200548576/ (accessed 4 June 2014).

Hopewell, John (1986) *The Spaniards: A Portrait of the New Spain*. New York: Viking.

____(1989) *El cine español después de Franco*. Madrid: El Arquero.

____(2014) 'Telefónica Studios Boards Alejandro Amenábar's "Regresión"', *Variety*, 10 June; http://variety.com/2014/film/news/telefonica-studios-boards-alejandro-amenabars-regression-1201217318/ (accessed 14 June 2014).

Izaguirre, Boris (2005) *El armario secreto de Hitchcock*. Madrid: Espasa.

Ivachow, Lilian Laura (2009) 'Pesos (de) ley', *El amante*, 208, 18.

Jackson, Kevin (2008) 'Behind the scene at the museum', *Sight and Sound*, 18, May, 10.

Jonquet, Thierry (2002) *Mygale*, trans. Donald Nicholson-Smith. San Francisco: City Lights.

Jordan, Barry (2012) *Alejandro Amenábar*. Manchester: Manchester University Press.

Jordan, Barry and Rikki Morgan-Tamosunas (1988) *Contemporary Spanish Cinema*. Manchester: Manchester University Press.

Karstulovich, Federico (2009) 'Principiantes', *El amante* 208, 19.

Keane, Marion (1999) '*39 Steps*', Liner notes, Criterion Collection, Janus Films.

Kehr, David (2010) 'It Leaps (Gasp!) Off the Screen', *New York Times*, 10 August, C1.

Kercher, Dona (2002a) 'Hitting the Mark from Television to Film: Violence, Timing and the Comedy Team in Álex de la Iglesia's *Muertos de risa* (1999)', *Post Script: Essays in Film and the Humanities*, Special Issue on Spanish Cinema, 21, 2, 50–63.

____(2002b) 'Looking for Don Quijote's Own Shadow: An Interview with Manuel Gutiérrez Aragón about His Film *El caballero Don Quijote* (2002)', *Arizona Journal of Hispanic Cultural Studies*, 6, 129–40.

____(2005) 'Violence, Timing and the Comedy Team in Álex de la Iglesia's *Muertos de risa*', in Xavier Mendik and Ernest Mathjis (eds) *Alternative Europe: Eurotrash and Exploitation Cinema Since 1945*. London and New York: Wallflower Press, 53–63.

____(2013) 'Almodóvar and Hitchcock: A Sorcerer's Apprentice' in Marvin D'Lugo and Kathleen
M. Vernon (eds) *A Companion to Pedro Almodóvar*. Chichester: Wiley-Blackwell, 59-87.

Keogh, Peter (1998) '*Love Walked In*', *The Boston Phoenix*, 23 February; http://www.filmvault.
com/filmvault/boston/l/lovewalkedin1.html (accessed 26 June 2014).

Keyser, Les and Barbara Keyser (1984) *Hollywood and the Catholic Church: The Image of Roman
Catholicism in American Movies*. Chicago: Loyola University Press.

Kinder, Marsha (1987) 'Pleasure and the New Spanish Mentality: A Conversation with Pedro
Almodóvar,' *Film Quarterly* 41.1, 33–44.

____(1993) *Blood Cinema: The Reconstruction of National Identity in Spain*. Berkeley: University
of California Press.

____(2004) 'Reinventing the Motherland: Almodóvar's Brain-Dead Trilogy', *Film Quarterly* 58.2,
9–25.

____(2005) 'Reinventar la patria: la trilogía de Almodóvar sobre la muerte cerebral', *Almodóvar: el
cine como pasión*. Cuenca: Ediciones de la Universidad de Castilla-La Mancha, 257–268.

Kinder, Marsha (ed.) (1997) *Refiguring Spain: Cinema, Media and Representation*. Chapel Hill,
NC: Duke University Press.

King, John (2000) *Magical Reels: A History of Cinema in Latin America*. London: Verso.

Kloster, Alberto D. (2003) 'Carlos Trillo. Sinónimo de éxito, permanencia y persistencia',
Tebeosfera, 031019; http://www.tebeosfera.com/1/Documento/Articulo/Guionistas/Carlos/
Trillo.htm (accessed 25 June 2014).

Koemer, Joseph Leo (2009) *Caspar David Friedrich and the Subject of Landscape*. London:
Reaktion.

Kolker, Robert (ed.) (2004) *Alfred Hitchcock's 'Psycho': A Casebook*. New York: Oxford University
Press.

Lázaro-Repoll, Antonio (2007) 'The Transnational Reception of "El espinazo del diablo"
(Guillermo del Toro 2001)', *Hispanic Research Journal*, 8, 1, 39–51.

Leff, Leonard (1999) *Hitchcock and Selznick: The Rich and Strange Collaboration of Alfred
Hitchcock and David O. Selznick in Hollywood*. Berkeley, CA: University of California Press.

Lerman, Gabriel (1997) 'Entrevista: Guillermo del Toro', *Dirigido*, 261, 51–3.

____(2004) 'Guillermo del Toro', *Dirigido*, 337, 29–31.

Lev, Leora (2000) 'Tesis, Review of the Film', *Film Quarterly*, 54, 1, 34–8.

Lewis, David (2010) 'Review: "The Oxford Murders," a boring whodoneit', *The San Francisco
Chronicle*, 13 August; http://www.sfgate.com/movies/article/Review-Oxford-Murders-a-
boring-whodunit-3256157.php (accessed 4 June 2014).

López, Antonio (1993) *Antonio López García: Exposición antológica. Pintura. Escultura. Dibujo.
Madrid, May-July*. Madrid: Museo Nacional Centro de Arte Reina Sofía.

López, Fernando (2001) 'Expertos en comedias emotivas', *La Nación*, 16 August.; http://www.
lanacion.com.ar/327864-expertos-en-comedias-emotivas (accessed 27 June 2014).

Losilla, Carlos (1998) 'Hitchcock a la sombra del cine negro', *Dirigido*, 269, 60–3.

____(2005) '*El pisito* y *El cochecito* de Marco Ferreri', *Dirigido*, 346, June, 70–7.

Manuel, Don Juan (1969) *El conde Lucanor o Libro de los enxiemplos del Conde Lucanor e de
Patronio*. Ed. José Manuel Blecua. Madrid: Editorial Castalia.

Marsh, Steven and Parvati Nair (2004) *Gender and Spanish Cinema*. Oxford: Berg.

Martin-Márquez, Susan (1999) *Feminist Discourse and Spanish Cinema*. Oxford: Oxford
University Press.

Martialay, Félix (1964) 'Alienación: Verdad y aparencia', *Film Ideal*, 158, 15 December, 827–30.

Martín-Barbero, Jesús (1987) *De los medios a las mediaciones: Comunicación, cultura y
hegemonía*. Mexico: Ediciones G. Gili.

Martínez, Adolfo C. (1991) 'Un policial que falló la puntería', *La Nación*, 14 January; http://www.
lanacion.com.ar/124544-un-policial-que-fallo-la-punteria (accessed 26 June 2014).

____(2009) 'Juego de mentiras, verdades y secretos', *La Nación*, 13 August; http://www.
lanacion.com.ar/1161592-juego-de-mentiras-verdades-y-secretos (accessed 30 June 2014).

Maslin, Janet (1997) '"Mimic": The 6-ft. Cockroach, Waiting for the Train', *New York Times*, 22 August;
http://www.nytimes.com/movie/review?res=9E07EED6143EF931A1575BC0A961958260.

Martínez, Guillermo (2004) *Los crímenes de Oxford*. Barcelona: Destino.

Mazdon, Lucy (2000) *Encore Hollywood: Remaking French Cinema*. London: British Film Institute.

McDonald, Paul and Janet Wasko (eds) (2008) *The Contemporary Hollywood Film Industry*. Chichester: Wiley-Blackwell.

McDevitt, Jim and Eric San Juan (2009) *A Year of Hitchcock: 52 Weeks with the Master of Suspense*. Lanham, MD: Scarecrow Press.

McFarland, James Francis, Jr. (2013) *Remaking Horror: Hollywood's New Reliance on Scares of Old*. Jefferson, NC: McFarland.

McGilligan, Patrick (2003) *Alfred Hitchcock: A Life in Darkness and Light*. New York: Regan Books.

McLuhan, Marshall (1994) *Understanding Media: The Extensions of Man*. Cambridge, MA: MIT Press.

McVey Gill, Mary, Deana Smalley and María-Paz Haro (2006) *Cinema for Spanish Conversation*, 2nd edition. Newburyport, MA: Focus.

Méjean, Jean-Max (2007) *Pedro Almodóvar*. Barcelona: Ediciones Robinbook.

Miller, Henry K. (2008) 'The Oxford Murders', *Sight and Sound*, 18, 7, 69.

Mira, Alberto, (ed.) (2005) *The Cinema of Spain and Portugal*. London and New York: Wallflower Press.

Modleski, Tania (2005) *The Women Who Knew Too Much: Hitchcock and Feminist Theory*, 2nd edition. New York: Routledge.

Moldes, Diego (2004) *La huella de 'Vertigo'*. Madrid: Ediciones JC.

Monsiváis, Carlos (1995) 'Mythologies', in Paulo Antonio Paranaguá (ed.) *Mexican Cinema*, trans. Ana M. López. London: British Film Institute and IMCINE, 117–27.

Monterde, José Enrique (2000) 'Los "quiméricos inquilinos" de Álex de la Iglesia', *Dirigido*, 294, 32–3.

Montesoro, Julia (1999) 'El mismo amor, pero un éxito sin igual', *La Nación*, 10 October; http://www.lanacion.com.ar/156750-el-mismo-amor-pero-un-exito-sin-igual (accessed 27 June 2014).

Moral, Tony Lee (2005) *Hitchcock and the Making of 'Marnie'*. Lanham, MA: Scarecrow Press.

Mulvey, Laura (1989) *Visual and Other Pleasures*. Bloomington, IN: Indiana University Press.

Mussachio, Humberto (2007) *Historia del periodismo cultural en México*. Mexico City: Consejo Nacional para la Cultura y las Artes.

Noriega, Chon A., (ed.) (2000) *Visible Nations: Latin American Cinema and Video*. Minneapolis: University of Minnesota Press.

Noriega, Gustavo (2009) 'A favor: Pretérito Imperfecto Futuro Perfecto', *El amante*, 208, September, 16–17.

Nowell-Smith, Geoffrey, (ed.) (1996) *The Oxford History of World Cinema*. Oxford: Oxford University Press.

Nuñez Gorritti, Violeta (2006) *Cartelera cinematográfica peruana, 1940–1949*. Lima: Ediciones Muchacha.

Ordoñez Divi, Marcos (1997) *La bestia anda suelta: ¡Álex de la Iglesia lo cuenta todo!* Madrid: Ediciones Glenat España.

Orr, John (2005) *Hitchcock and Twentieth Century Cinema*. London and New York: Wallflower Press.

Paglia, Camille (1998) *The Birds*. London: British Film Institute.

Papamichael, Stella (2008) 'Review: "The Oxford Murders"', *BBC*. 16 April. http://www.bbc.co.uk/films/2008/04/21/the_oxford_murders_2008_review.shtml (accessed 4 June 2014).

Paranaguá, Paulo Antonio (ed.) (1995) *Mexican Cinema*. London: British Film Institute.

____(2003) *Tradición y modernidad en el cine de América Latina*. México: Fondo de Cultura Económica.

Paz, María Laura (2004) '"El hijo de la novia" de vez en cuando la vida', in *Plano secuencia: 20 películas argentinas para reafirmar la democracia* (ed) Mónica Satarain. Buenos Aires: La Crujía Editores.

Pérez-Reverte, Arturo (1988) *El maestro de esgrima*. Madrid: Alfaguara.

___(1990) *La tabla de Flandes*. Madrid: Alfaguara.

___(1993) *El Club Dumas*. Madrid: Alfaguara.

___(1994) *Territorio Comanche*. Madrid: Alfaguara.

___(1996) *El capitán Alatriste*. Madrid: Alfaguara.

Perriam, Chris (2003) *Stars and Masculinities in Spanish Cinema: From Banderas to Bardem*. Oxford: Oxford University Press.

Piedras, Pablo (2001) 'Nuestra propia historia (de amor)', 11 July. http://www.cinenacional.com/critica/nuestra-propia-historia-de-amor (accessed 27 June 2014).

Pomerance, Murray (2004) *An Eye for Hitchcock*. Brunswick, NJ: Rutgers University Press.

Porta Fouz, Javier (2009) 'Perseguidos por el pasado', *El amante*, 208, 21–2.

Pramaggiore, Marie and Tom Wallis (2008) *Film: A Critical Introduction*. Boston: Pearson.

Prince, Stephen (ed.) (2004) *The Horror Film*. New Brunswick, NJ: Rutgers Univesity Press.

Quevedo, Francisco de (1990) *El Buscón*, ed. Pablo Jauralde Pou. Madrid: Castalia.

Ravaschino, Guillermo (1999) http://www.cineismo.com/criticas/mismo%20amor,%20la%20misma%20lluvia,%20el.htm (accessed 27 June 2014).

Rendell, Ruth (1986) *Live Flesh*. New York: Random House.

Revert, Jordi (2010) '"El mal ajeno": El dolor de la impostura', 23 March. http://www.labutaca.net/criticas/el-mal-ajeno-el-dolor-de-la-impostura/ (accessed 18 July 2014).

Reviriego, Carlos (2006) 'Frenesí', in Guillermo Balmori (ed.) *El universo de Alfred Hitchcock*. Madrid: Notorious Ediciones, 198–201.

Rey, Florián (1946) 'Florián Rey, enemigo del doblaje, por Del Arco', *Fotogramas*, 3, 15 December, n.p.

Robles, Jesús (ed.) (2001) *Nicole Kidman, 'Los Otros', una película de Alejandro Amenábar*. Madrid: Ocho y Medio.

Rodríguez Marchante, E. (1997) '"Perdita" no, "Perditísima"', *ABC*, 26 September, 130.

Rodríquez Marchante, Oti (2002) *Amenábar, voluntad de intriga*. Madrid: Páginas de Espuma.

Rodríguez, Hilario J. (2001) 'Los vivos y los muertos', *Dirigido*, 304, September, 38–41.

Rojas, Eduardo (2009) 'En contra: Espejos del alma', *El amante*, 208, 20–1.

Rodríguez, Jesús (2004) *Almodóvar y el melodrama de Hollywood: Historia de una pasión*. Valladolid: Editorial Maxtor.

Rohter, Larry (2010) 'Footage Restored to "Metropolis"', *New York Times*, 4 May, C1.

Rojas, Eduardo (2009) 'Espejos del alma', *El amante*, 208, September.

Rooney, David (1997) 'Review: "Perdita Durango"', *Variety*, 6 October.

Rose, James (2009) *Studying 'The Devil's Backbone'*. Leighton Buzzard: Auteur.

Rothman, William (2014) *Must We Kill the Thing We Love?: Emersonian Perfectionism and the Films of Alfred Hitchcock*. New York: Columbia University Press.

Ryall, Tom (1986) *Alfred Hitchcock and the British Cinema*. London: Croom Helm.

Sacheri, Eduardo (2005) *La pregunta de sus ojos*. Buenos Aires: Galerna.

___(2009) *El secreto de sus ojos*. Madrid: Alfaguara.

Sánchez Aguilar, Francisco (1978) *Todo Buñuel*. Mexico: Cineteca Nacional.

___(2000) *Siglo Buñuel*. Mexico: Casa Juan Pablos and Cineteca Nacional.

___(2004) *Cinefilia es locura*. Mexico: Casa Juan Pablos.

Sánchez-Biosca, Vicente (1995) 'El elixir aromático de la postmodernidad o la comedia según Pedro Almodóvar', in José A. Hurtado and Franciso M. Picó (eds) *Escritos sobre el cine español 1973–1987*. Valencia: Ediciones Textos Filmoteca, 111–23.

Sánchez Fernández, David Miguel (2012) *Cines de Madrid*. Madrid: Ediciones La Librería.

Sánchez Martínez, Alfonso (1973) *Iniciación al cine moderno*. Madrid: Magisterio Español.

Sánchez Noriega, José Luis (2002) *Historia del cine: Teoría y géneros cinematográficos, fotografía y televisión*. Madrid: Alianza.

Santamarina, Antonio (2001) 'Un sugerente melodrama gótico: "El espinazo del diablo"', *Dirigido*, 300, 22–4.

Santos Fontela, Carlos (1999) '"La soga", más allá del alarde técnico', *Blanco y negro*, 1 August, 41.

Saragoza, Alex (2001) 'The Selling of Mexico: Tourism and the State, 1929–1952', in Gilbert M. Joseph, Anne Rubenstein and Eric Zolov (eds) *Fragments of a Golden Age: The Politics of Culture in Mexico Since 1940*. Chapel Hill, NC: Duke University Press, 91–115.

Satarain, Mónica (2004) *Plano Secuencia: 20 películas para reafirmar la democracia*. Buenos Aires: La Crujía Editores.

Savlov, Mark (1992) 'The Boy Who Cried Bitch', *The Austin Chronicle*, 27 March. http://www.austinchronicle.com/calendar/film/1992-03-27/the-boy-who-cried-bitch/ (accessed 25 June 2014).

Scholz, Pablo (2013) 'En busca de la hazaña', *Clarín*, 18 July. http://www.clarin.com/espectaculos/busca-hazana_0_958104326.html (accessed 3 July 2014).

Scott, A. O. (2010) 'Recasting the Cold War as the Hitchcock Years', *New York Times*, 2 June: C6.

Seguin, Jean-Claude (2013) 'Is there a French Almodóvar?' *A Companion to Pedro Almodóvar*. Chichester: Wiley-Blackwell, 432–52.

Shaw, Deborah (2013) *The Three Amigos: The Transnational Filmmaking of Guillermo del Toro, Alejandro González Iñárritu and Alfonso Cuarón*. Manchester: Manchester University Press.

Silbergeld, Jerome (2004) *Hitchcock with a Chinese Face: Cinematic Doubles, Oedipal Triangles, and China's Moral Voice*. Seattle: University of Washington Press.

Sloan, Jane E. (1993) *Alfred Hitchcock: A Definitive Filmography and a Biography*. Berkeley, CA: University of California Press.

Smith, Dick (2014) 'Dick Smith's Advanced Professional Make-up Course', http://www.dicksmithmake-up.com/training-programs/advanced-course.aspx (accessed 20 June 2014).

Smith, Paul Julian (1994) *Desire Unlimited: The Cinema of Pedro Almodóvar*. London: Verso.

____(2003) *Contemporary Spanish Culture: TV, Fashion, Art and Film*. Cambridge: Polity Press.

Solis, Fidel (1935) 'La pantalla y sus artistas', *El Universal*, 17 November, Sect. 1, 5.

Spoto, Donald (1999) *The Dark Side of Genius: The Life of Alfred Hitchcock*. New York: Da Capo Press.

Stevens, Brad (2000) '"Perdita Durango": A Case Study', *Senses of Cinema*, 5; http://sensesofcinema.com/2000/feature-articles/perdita.

Stevens, Dan (2005) 'A Murder in a Store, Then Blackmail on the Installment Plan', *New York Times*, 19 August, B8.

Stack, Peter (1999) 'Thriller Goes From Eye-Opening to Eye-Glazing: Absurd plot sinks promising story', *San Francisco Chronicle*, 30 April.

Strauss, Frédéric (1995) *Pedro Almodóvar, Un cine visceral: Conversaciones con Frédéric Strauss*. Madrid: El País, Aguilar.

____(ed.) (2006) *Almodódar on Almodóvar*. Revised ed. Trans. Yves Baigneres. London: Faber and Faber.

Sullivan, Jack (2006) *Hitchcock's Music*. New Haven, CT: Yale University Press.

Thomson, David (2009) *The Moment of Psycho: How Alfred Hitchcock Taught America to Love Murder*. New York: Basic Books.

Tinelli, José and Enrique Cadícamo (n.d.) 'Por la vuelta' http://www.hlmtango.com/letras-de-tango/p/1/por-la-vuelta/ (accessed 27 June 2014).

Tresnlowski, Alex (2001) 'Hearts Wide Shut', *People*, v.55, n.7 (19 February) http://www.people.com/people/archive/article/0,,20133675,00.html

Troilo, Aníbal and Cátulo Castillo (1962) 'Desencuentro', *Todo Tango*. http://www.todotango.com/320/Desencuentro (accessed 26 June 2014).

Truffaut, François (1984) *Hitchcock/Truffaut: The Definitive Study by François Truffaut*, rev. ed. New York: Simon and Schuster.

Vera, Cecilia, Silvia Badariotti and Débora Castro (2002a) *Cómo hacer cine 1: 'Tesis' de Alejandro Amenábar*. Madrid: Editorial Fundamentos.

____(2002b) *Cómo hacer cine 2: 'El día de la bestia' de Álex de la Iglesia*. Madrid: Editorial Fundamentos.

Vernon, Kathleen M. (2009) 'Queer Sound: Musical Otherness in Three Films by Almodóvar', *All About Almodóvar: A Passion for Cinema*. Minneapolis: University of Minnesota Press, 51–70.

____(2013) 'Almodóvar's Global Marketplace,' *A Companion to Pedro Almodóvar*, Malden, MA: Wiley-Blackwell, 387–411.

Vernon, Kathleen M. and Barbara Morris (eds) (1995) *Post-Franco, Postmodern: The Films of Pedro Almodóvar*. Westport, CT: Greenwood Press.

Vidal, Nuria (1988) *El cine de Pedro Almodóvar*. Barcelona: Ediciones Destino.

____(2004) *Escenarios del crimen*. Barcelona: Ediciones Océano.

Williams, Linda (2004) 'Discipline and Fun: Psycho and Postmodern Cinema' in Robert Kolker (ed.) *Alfred Hitchcock's Psycho: A Casebook*. New York: Oxford University Press, 164–204.

Wood, Robin (2002) *Hitchcock's Films Revisited*, Revised Ed. New York: Columbia University Press.

Yacowar, Maurice (2010) *Hitchcock's British Films*, Second Ed. Detroit: Wayne State University Press.

Žižek, Slavoj (1993) *Looking Awry: An Introduction to Jacques Lacan through Popular Culture.* Cambridge, MA: MIT Press.

____(2003–4) '*Vertigo*: The Drama of a Deceived Platonist', *Hitchcock Annual*, 12, 67–82.

Zurián, Francisco A. (2013) '*La piel que habito*: A Story of Imposed Gender and the Struggle for Identity', *A Companion to Pedro Almodóvar*, Malden, MA: Wiley-Blackwell, 262–278.

Zurián, Francisco A. and Carmen Vázquez Varela (eds) (2005) *Almodóvar: el cine como pasión. Actas del Congreso Internacional 'Pedro Almodóvar'*, Cuenca, 26–29 November 2003. Cuenca: Ediciones de la Universidad Castilla-La Mancha.

INDEX